JAZZ AND JUSTICE

Jazz and JUSTICE

Racism and the Political Economy of the Music

GERALD HORNE

MONTHLY REVIEW PRESS
New York

Library of Congress Cataloging-in-Publication Data
Names: Horne, Gerald, author.
Title: Jazz and justice : racism and the political economy of the music /
  Gerald Horne.
Description: New York : Monthly Review Press, 2019. | Includes
  bibliographical references and index. |
Identifiers: LCCN 2019017464 (print) | LCCN 2019017611 (ebook) | ISBN
  9781583677872 (trade) | ISBN 9781583677889 (institutional) | ISBN
  9781583677858 (pbk.) | ISBN 9781583677865 (hardcover)
Subjects: LCSH: Jazz — Social aspects — United States — History. |
  Jazz--Political aspects — United States — History. | Music and race — United
  States — History. | Jazz musicians — United States — Social conditions. |
  Jazz musicians — United States — Economic conditions.
Classification: LCC ML3918.J39 (ebook) | LCC ML3918.J39 H67 2019 (print) |
  DDC 306.4/84250973 —dc23
LC record available at https://lccn.loc.gov/2019017464

Typeset in Minion Pro and Bliss

MONTHLY REVIEW PRESS, NEW YORK
monthlyreview.org

5 4 3 2

Contents

Introduction

BUCK CLAYTON WAS READY TO RUMBLE.

It was about 1934 and this Negro trumpeter found himself in Shanghai, a city on the cusp of being bombarded by marauding Japanese troops. But that was not his concern. Instead, what he thought he had escaped when he began performing in China had followed him across the Pacific Ocean. "White guys [were] saying," he wrote decades later, "there they are. Niggers, niggers, niggers!" These incendiary epithets lit the fuse and "soon fists were flying" and "when it was all over the Chinese onlookers treated us like we had done something that they had always wanted to do and followed us all the way home cheering us like a winning football team."[1]

He may not have recognized it at the time of the fracas, but Clayton's Asian encounter illustrated several themes that had ensnared Negro musicians, especially practitioners of the new art form called "jazz." Often, they had to flee abroad, where they found more respect and an embrace of their talent. And often the sustenance found there allowed them to develop their art and sustain their loved ones. Overseas they were capable of fortifying the global trends that in the long run proved decisive in destroying slavery and eroding the Jim Crow that followed in its wake.[2] The pianist Eubie Blake, born in 1883, referring to Canada and Europe, was moved to argue—extravagantly and emphatically, though understandably given the United States was his reference point—that "color don't make any difference to *them* people and I can understand why a lot of Negroes stayed over there to live."[3] Back home they were forced to fight to repel racist marauders, some of whom had hired them to perform.

Furthermore, the presence of these exiled artists of African ancestry undergirded existent hostility to U.S. imperialism, shoring up the generally faltering position of African Americans back home. Thus, one study of the music in Paris concludes that jazz served to sustain "anti-Americanism" and this artistic bent also meant "solidarity with African Americans in opposition to white Americans." A French book on the music had an "astonishing" 150 editions, indicating why, during the Cold War, says critic Andy Fry, Washington "represented a greater threat to Europe than Communism."[4] This point inferentially raises the related matter of the new music seen as an analogue to democracy in the interaction between and among musicians on the bandstand and the ineffable reality that the bulk of the artists were of African descent, leading Washington to sponsor concerts abroad of the music. Ironically, analogizing jazz to democracy, a frequent Cold War trope, belied the fact that the music was embraced by Italian fascists, among other anti-democratic miscreants.[5]

A glimpse of this phenomenon was exposed when the Negro composer and musician Benny Carter arrived in Copenhagen as Clayton was being pummeled in Shanghai. When he exited the train, he was recognized as a celebrity. "I was literally lifted onto the shoulders of people," he said decades later, "and they carried me out of the station to a waiting automobile and I was taken to my hotel with this crowd behind. And I was really never so thrilled." He was stunned to ascertain that Europe was less racist toward those like himself in comparison to his homeland; in Europe he found "acceptance of you just on the basis of you as a human being."[6]

This is a book about the travails and triumphs of these talented musicians as they sought to make a living, at home and abroad, through dint of organizing—and fighting. I approach this subject with a certain humility, well aware, as someone once said, that "writing about music is like dancing about architecture," that is, "using one artistic vocabulary to portray another" is inherently perilous.[7] This task is made all the more complex when writing about this form of music, where the historical record is studded with various and often contrasting versions of the same episode. The co-author of the informative memoir of a well-known pianist asserted that "Dr. [Billy]

Taylor has told more than [one] version of the same story. He noted the fallibility of memory and had a healthy sense of humor about the inconsistencies that can result."[8] The problem is that the historian thereby runs the risk of circulating misinformation, a prospect I will seek to evade in the pages that follow.

WHAT IS THIS MUSIC CALLED JAZZ? Why does it carry this name and where did it develop?

"Jazz," according to the late Euro-American pianist, Dave Brubeck, speaking in 1950, was "born in New Orleans about 1880" consisting of "an improvised musical expression based on European harmony and African rhythms."[9] (The critic Leonard Feather is among those who question the "Big Easy" birth, despite its seductively powerful appeal,[10] while saxophonist Von Freeman said that "jazz is not that old," the bandleader Sun Ra "said it began billions of years ago.")[11] Brubeck could have added that this music presupposes mastery of musical instruments, particularly—though not exclusively—piano, strings (bass fiddle, guitar, etc.), horns (saxophone, trumpet, clarinet, trombone, etc.), and yes, percussion (especially drums). Brubeck was informed by critic Marshall Stearns, who said in 1954 that the new music is "improvised Afro-American music with strong European influences," the instruments wielded not least.[12] In accord with Brubeck was the late saxophonist Eddie Barefield, who in 1977 defined the music in which he excelled as "something with a beat" that involves "improvisation."[13] The musician Joe Rene said in 1960 that the art form in which he was distinguished was nothing but filling in a melody, a task he ascribed to the trumpet[14] a musical instrument whose importance stretches back generations.[15]

The subversive impact of this new form has been said to "subvert racial segregation, musically enacting . . . [an] assault on white purity," and the music was said to have "encouraged racial boundary crossings by creating racially mixed spaces and racially impure music, both of which altered the racial identities of musicians and listeners."[16]

Alert readers may have noticed that I have introduced the term "jazz" with a bodyguard of quotation marks. This is meant to signify the contested employment of this term. Thus the master percussionist

Max Roach did not embrace this word: "I prefer to say," he announced in 1972, "that the music is the culture of African people who have been dispersed throughout North America."[17] Elaborating, Roach argued—in a nod to the difficult working conditions that accompanied a music associated with bordellos and Negroes—that the very term "jazz" meant "the worst kind of working conditions, the worst in cultural prejudice . . . small dingy places, the worst kind of salaries and conditions that one can imagine . . . the abuse and exploitation of black musicians."[18] Artie Shaw, the late reedman, said in 1992 that the "word 'jazz' is a ridiculous word."[19] Randy Weston, the celebrated pianist, also has disparaged the word "jazz."[20] Revealingly, because of the negative connotations of the term, the musical group now known as The Crusaders went to court to remove "Jazz" from their name and, said one source, became "far more successful financially."[21] On the other hand, saxophonist Dexter Gordon, according to his biographer, "understood the debate about the word 'jazz' but he stood proud of the word."[22]

This music is said to have its roots in the Slave South—New Orleans more specifically. But even this, like the presence of Clayton in Shanghai, is contested. One analyst argues for a kind of "candelabra" theory of the origins of this music, arising simultaneously in various sites for similar reasons. Thus, like New Orleans, the San Francisco Bay Area had ties to a wider global community, meaning the influence of diverse musical trends and instruments, particularly opera and its Italian traditions, not to mention a bordello culture that provided opportunities to play. One of the many theories about the term "jazz" is that it originated in the early twentieth century among Negro musicians in the hilly fog-bound California metropolis.[23] The drummer Zutty Singleton, born in 1898, has argued that, long before New Orleans, St. Louis had been a center of ragtime, one of the musical tributaries of "jazz," and, as a result, musicians in the Missouri city were more technically adept and sophisticated than their Louisiana counterparts.[24]

Given that both St. Louis and New Orleans hugged the Mississippi River, where riverboats overflowing with performing musicians plied the muddy waters, it is possible that this new music developed simultaneously in both cities. In that regard, it would be a mistake to ignore that other Mississippi port city—Memphis.[25] "Outside of New York City and Detroit," according to one analyst, this Tennessee town "probably has given the world more outstanding jazz artists than any other city."[26] The well-informed Dempsey Travis has argued passionately that "if jazz was not born in the nightclubs and speakeasies on the South Side of Chicago, then it was certainly incubated in them."[27]

This music is also an offshoot of the music known as "the blues," a product of those of African origin in Dixie, which expressed their hopes and pains: hence, one scholar has characterized the blues as a veritable epistemology.[28] Given that "jazz is an offspring of the blues" and both Memphis and New Orleans are neighbors of the state of Mississippi, the crucible of the blues, there is reason to consider the Magnolia State as a "father of jazz." This general region also propelled W. C. Handy, the "Father of the Blues," to fame. Both facts serve to provide reason to take Memphis into account when assessing the roots of jazz. (Contributing to the varied roots of "Negro music" is Handy's contention that the tango—of Afro-Argentine origin— strongly influenced his own interpretation of the blues.)[29] Like New Orleans, Memphis too was a den of iniquity, as suggested by William Faulkner.[30]

Adding to a version of the "candelabra" theory of the origins of the music are the words of the legendary journalist J. A. Rogers, who argued that the roots of the music could be found "in the Indian war dance, the highland fling, the Irish jig, the Cossack dance, the Spanish fandango, the Brazilian maxixie, the dance of the whirling dervish, the hula hula of the South Seas"—and the "ragtime of the Negro."[31]

Still, New Orleans' claim as the seedbed of this music is bulwarked by the fact that the aftermath of the U.S. Civil War (1861–1865) and the onset of the War with Spain in 1898 with troops embarking and disembarking from the mouth of the Mississippi River, led to various musical instruments being snapped up by Africans, as military and naval bands dissolved. Moreover, by 1850 New Orleans was by some measures the bordello capital of the new Republic, leading to more cabarets, nightclubs—meaning more music—at a time when San Francisco was hardly an adolescent city.[32] Reportedly, distressed soldiers dumped their instruments in pawn shops in New Orleans and Negroes then bought these battered tools of music cheaply.[33]

On the other hand, one analyst claimed that "Cuban natives"—and not the New Orleans keyboardist Jelly Roll Morton who claimed parentage—"started jazz in 1712."[34] Interestingly, when enslaved Africans in Barbados in 1675 were launching a revolt, the signal for launching was to be sent by trumpet.[35] By 1688, authorities on this Caribbean island had declared illegal the "using or keeping of drums, horns or other loud instruments which may call together or give sign or notice to one another, for their wicked designs and purposes."[36]

Whatever the case, it appears that the first authenticated appearance of the word "jazz" in print was, perhaps tellingly, in the *San Francisco Call*, on 6 March 1913.[37] (Another analyst suggests the word "jass" first appeared in the *Chicago Defender* on 30 September 1916.) The clarinetist Emile Barnes, born in 1892, recalled such tunes as "Jazz Me Blues" and observed that the term used to describe this art form was associated with copulation (not seen as a plus) and thus was seen as negative, such as a woman saying "such and such . . . wanted to jazz me."[38] Others have linked the word "jazz" etymologically to various West African languages or to the French—"jaser"—or to Jezabelle or Jasmine perfume or even to baseball (references there can be found as early as 1912).[39]

In turn, the Negro composer Will Marion Cook is of the opinion that ragtime with its syncopated and "ragged" rhythm, which developed at the end of the nineteenth century, as U.S. imperialism began to extend its overseas reach, was shaped by the trips of Negro sojourners to ports in North Africa and western Asia dominated by the then Ottoman Empire.[40]

Of course, the various forms of music developed by enslaved Africans in North America and their descendants were rooted in the continent of their origin, Africa itself, particularly West Africa, stretching from what is now Dakar southward to Luanda. The now discredited notion that Africans were "natural musicians," which facilitated the popularity of "Blind Tom, the Slave Pianist" and his rival "Blind Boone" of St. Louis,[41] should also be considered in contemplating the rise of this new music.

New art forms are often pilloried, not least because they are misunderstood, but jazz carries the added burden of being billed as one of the few art forms developed in North America and done so primarily by African Americans, who had been pilloried because of their earlier slave status and adamant refusal to accept supinely a slaveholders' republic.[42] This contributed to an "anti-jazz" movement, preceded by "anti-ragtime" fervor. This hostility made it easier to rationalize the gross exploitation of these musicians, since, as it was said, they were seen as "mere" Negroes, playing "Negro music."[43] In 1927 Pope Pius XI spoke of the "discordant cacophony, arrhythmic howls and wild cries" of the new music. (It is likely he was not speaking ex cathedra.)[44] Dialectically, however, the difficult conditions under which this innovative music was produced helped to create conditions for the improvisation that was part of its essence. In a 1999 interview, the famed trumpeter Clark Terry recalled that because of the "derogatory things that would happen to you, the negative things, the pitfalls . . . you'd go crazy" absent improvisation. So the musicians would play games and engage in pranks. "I'd practice left-handed," he said. "I'd practice upside down" and "if there's something that seems to be synonymous with jazz," he continued, "it's good comedy," which also involved improvising. He experimented with different tonguing and buzzing with his horn, with this dedicated experimentation undergirding the high art thereby created.[45] In similar fashion, the versatile instrumentalist Eric Dolphy started experimenting with the bass clarinet in order to distinguish himself from musicians he saw as less talented but receiving more opportunities than himself, so he wanted to do something different.[46] "Do something different" is another definition of the music called jazz.

Generally concurring, in a 2007 interview, the critic Nat Hentoff argued that these musicians he lionized "took risks all the time. That's what improvisation is all about. If they were black, they took risks whenever they traveled down South"[47]—or, as in the case of Buck Clayton, perambulated in Shanghai. This well prepared them for taking musical risks, enhancing their art.

Unfortunately, some of these musicians were taking risks without traveling southward. In 1981, the trombonist Vic Dickenson, born in Xenia, Ohio, in 1906, recalled that "across the street from our house was a [forest] and the Ku Klux Klan used to meet there. They'd stand in a circle in their robes in that wood and burn their crosses and that upset me all during my childhood."[48] The bassist Milt Hinton had a similar experience. Born in 1910 in the heart of darkness that was Vicksburg, Mississippi, his grandmother, he recalled, was a "slave" of "Jefferson Davis's father," speaking of the leader of the so-called Confederate States of America that rebelled in 1861 in order to perpetuate enslavement of Africans.[49] It is difficult to imagine a more horrid racist pedigree, a point ratified in 1988 when Hinton recalled chillingly, "One of the clearest memories of my childhood in Vicksburg is the lynching I saw when I was seven or eight. . . . There was a bonfire and fifty or sixty men were drinking out of whiskey jugs, dancing, cursing and looking up towards a tree over their heads. And in this big tree I saw a figure shaped like a person hanging from a long wire cable attached to a branch . . . he was covered with blood." Yet the murderers "kept shooting their guns up at the dangling body" as a "couple of men [were] dragging over a gasoline drum and putting it under the hanging body. Then someone else threw a torch at the can and the place lit up like it was daytime. . . . I'll never forget that blaze," he said morosely, "and watching that body shrivel up like a piece of bacon while the crowd cheered."[50] The question for our purposes is: to what extent did such experiences shape the passion and bathos of the music?

In sum, an unwelcome accompanist of this music as it was birthed was the kind of violence—and threats thereof—that Dickenson and Hinton witnessed in their youth. It was in 1900 in New Orleans that, in light of racial unrest, a local editor called boldly for the "FINAL SOLUTION" of the Negro Question, adding ominously, "Race war means extermination."[51] Assuredly, this outrage impelled exile abroad where this music could flourish, just as it impelled an adroit improvisation necessary for survival in such adverse conditions.

For the musician Billy Harper, born in 1943, this state of affairs was unsurprising. Speaking in 1971, he said, "'Since most people [*sic*] have been taught to hate and fear the black man and in this country this music represents one of the strongest parts of his culture,'"[52] it was hardly shocking that these Negro artists became frequent targets of delirious bile. Yet, as Ellis Marsalis, born in 1934, observed in 1971, the fact that these artists created a unique cultural form did not save them from bigotry, but it may have enhanced it. This pianist and patriarch of what has been seen as the First Family of the music, said then that "the only advantage the black musician has is that music being first a talent and then a craft, the establishment is forced to deal with him in a manner that they are not forced to deal with him when they are hiring garbage men,"[53] which was simply infuriating to adversaries of the Negro.

Inexorably, this pattern of iniquity created an ecosystem that influenced those who might have thought they were on the side of the angels. According to the well-regarded historian and critic Lewis Porter, "The racism in our society makes it all too easy for white authors to take a condescending attitude to the jazz they write about."[54] In this vein, the historian and musician Ingrid Monson has referred contemptuously to "what I term the 'white resentment narrative,'" for example, those who feel that melanin-deficient musicians and writers have not received their due, because of "Crow Jim"—i.e. a "Jim Crow" visited upon Euro-Americans, i.e. a kind of inverted oppression allegedly perpetrated by African Americans.[55]

Thus, because of the ingrained racism of the society in which the music was born, allied with the objective exploitation of musicians generating wealth, all this combined to create a culture inimical to the health and well-being of the artists. An early pioneer of the music was James Reese Europe, born in 1880, whom Eubie Blake, pianist extraordinaire, purportedly called the real "'King of Jazz'" and not the aptly named pretender, Paul Whiteman.[56] Tragically, Europe was stabbed to death by a drummer during the First World War, this after being gassed and hospitalized on the battlefields of Europe.[57] A few years later, horn player Leo "Snub" Mosley, born in 1905, was slated to perform in Texas. As he recalled, "They advertised us on the front page of the newspaper: 'FAMOUS NIGGER BAND HERE TONIGHT,'" which was a prelude to another occasion when the notorious terrorists, the Ku Klux Klan, planned to tar and feather him and his bandmates, "just because we were playing for the white people." This planned act of terror may have been inspired by white competitors, since "there was some white opposition too from the biggest white band around there, the Jimmy Joy band that played hotels in Dallas and the Muehlebach Hotel in Kansas City."[58]

During the Second World War, the drummer Philly Joe Jones was hired as a trolley operator, one of eight Negro men given such a position in Philadelphia (one of the themes of this book is how so many of these musicians found it difficult to make a living pursuing their art and often had to find other means of support). Reporting for work the first day, he found that white strikers had shut down the entire intercity transport system in protest of this desegregated hiring. The racism was so intense that an armed military guard was placed on every streetcar so that Blacks would not attack white operators travelling through Black neighborhoods and vice versa. "I remember this hateful chapter of my teenage years," said the musician, Benny Golson. "It was terrible."[59]

Again, the question to consider is, inter alia, what was the impact of such horror on musicians? Did it give their artistry a certain fury and anger? Did it impel them to protest, for example, unionizing and protesting generally?

It was also during the war, whose bloodiness may have inspired the like-minded on both sides of the Atlantic, that the saxophonist Charlie Parker, born in 1920, and his fellow musician Oscar Pettiford, born in 1922, were attacked by a soldier in a New York City subway, with the latter stripped naked. Then in Pine Bluff, Arkansas, Parker was bashed in the head with a bottle after he refused to play a requested tune from a white man in the audience. [60]

Understandably, brutalization led to organization by the intended victims. The aforementioned James Reese Europe, helped to organize the "Clef Club" in Harlem about a century ago, a combination gathering space for musicians, labor exchange, performance space, and a way to circumvent malign influence on the music. In coming decades similarly oriented musicians formed the Jazz Composers' Guild, Collective Black Artists, the Los Angeles–based Union of God's Musicians and Artists' Ascension, and Chicago's Association for the Advancement of Creative Musicians.[61]

Nevertheless, one of the most influential reactions to the kind of normalized exploitation to which musicians were routinely subjected was spearheaded by the bassist and bandleader Charles Mingus,[62] born in 1922: he sought to form a company to distribute his recorded compositions. But it was then that Morris Levy, who operated the iconic Manhattan club known as Birdland and who looked and talked like a Hollywood thug besides, warned the corpulent composer about gangsters, that is, those like himself: "These people, they'll kill your wife, they'll kill your mother, they'll kill your babies."[63] Mingus's partner, Max Roach, recalled later that "we would have to take pistols to Boston, to collect" since "they'd hold on to the records." His interviewer, Amiri Baraka, responded that the stiff opposition to this initiative was because the powers that be "didn't want that concept of musicians trying to run their own affairs"—and "the Black thing made it worse."[64] Thus, by 1955 the predictable had occurred: "There is a great deal of interest in Debut Records," the joint Mingus-Roach enterprise, said the message from Rochester, New York. "The only catch is, of course, there is no place to buy them."[65]

A pioneer in seeking to take control of the music was the saxophonist, flutist, and clarinetist Gigi Gryce. His attempt to establish a publishing company and record label was aided by a lawyer better known for assisting radical causes, William Kunstler. Bruce Wright, yet another activist Manhattan lawyer, also served him. His comrade, the similarly engaged bassist Reggie Workman, recollected that Gryce was "pressured by somebody in the publishing field." That is, they "threatened him in some way that he became paranoid," compelling Workman to "leave him. . . . He'd be so nervous . . . this twitching nervousness that got worse and worse." Gryce was forced out of the business by powerful interests, "possibly with underworld connections," according to one analyst. "He and his family were harassed, threatened and intimidated," leaving Gryce "clearly terrified," engendering the reaction that drove Workman from his side.[66]

Levy was not unique. Sam Giancana, a leading mobster, like many of his comrades, invested heavily in Las Vegas, which after 1945 became a major site for hiring musicians. His lover, Judith Exner, observed that he was poisoned with racism and fought the Black

Power upsurge of the 1960s that sought to encroach on these gang-sters' sinecure in the entertainment industry; thus, he announced regularly that "he hated all niggers."[67]

Hence, as a result of the pestilence to which they were subjected routinely, musicians were compelled to engage in various kinds of self-help as a simple matter of survival. Trumpeter Roy Eldridge, born in 1911, was among those who carried a gun—this was in the 1940s; his comrade Artie Shaw recalled that Eldridge "saw himself as travel-ing through a hostile land and he was right."[68] Clark Terry was of like mind. "All the cats from St. Louis," he said, "carried a shank . . . a knife. So did I." This was in the early 1950s. [69]

In case a weapon was not nearby, some musicians also developed a taste for boxing. Percussionist Stan Levey, who played alongside lumi-naries like Charlie Parker, was a boxer of some skill. The point made in his biography is that "Fighting and drumming are both all about hit-ting and timing," though this hardly explains the boxing skill of Wallace Roney, the Philadelphia-born trumpeter, born in 1960, nor does it shed light on Levey's recollection of pianist Red Garland born in Dallas in 1923 sparring combatively with perhaps the greatest boxer of them all: "Sugar" Ray Robinson.[70] The pugilistic acumen of trumpeter Miles Davis is well-known.[71] Davis's musical tribute to the late heavyweight boxing champion, Jack Johnson, has been emulated by the recent musical salute to Muhammad Ali by trombonist Craig Harris.[72] The masculinist environment of the music business shaped this combative response, but, as well, musicians (especially drummers and trumpeters) often had quick hands and supple fingers, along with sharp reflexes, all of which made for often forceful encounters with foes.

There was also collective enterprise. Early on, Negro-owned recording companies included Sunshine Record Company formed by Johnny and Reb Spikes in 1921; Leroy Hurte's Bronze Records in 1940; and Leon and Otis Rene's Excelsior, then called Exclusive, in Los Angeles.[73] In 1961, the musician Harold Battiste formed a record label, inspired by the Nation of Islam and their self-help philosophy. The fact that he received a mere $125 for playing saxophone on the blockbuster hit by Sonny and Cher "I've Got You Babe" impelled him further: "That's all," he said disgustedly.[74]

The writer Ishmael Reed has argued that the Nation of Islam was a "competitor" of the traditional Italian and Jewish-American branches of organized crime.[75] It is well known that the First World War–era movement led by Jamaican-born Marcus Garvey served as predicate to the rise of the NOI in the 1930s, and that earlier Pan-African movement was not unknown to musicians. "Garveyites were prevalent," says the saxophonist Sonny Rollins, born in 1930, when he was growing up in Harlem.[76] Drummer Panama Francis, born in 1918 in Miami, said, "I played my first gig—it was on the Fourth of July at the UNIA Hall in 1931," the initials signifying the Universal Negro Improvement Association, Garvey's vehicle.[77] Trombonist Roy Palmer in the early 1920s led a 35-piece band of the UNIA in Chicago.[78] Paul Barbarin, the drummer born more than a century ago in New Orleans, said that the Onward Brass Band of which his uncle was a member were adorned with plumed hats akin to those worn by Garveyites.[79]

The hegemonic influence of mobsters in the music business combined with weak unions to deflect class consciousness and accentuate the normative white supremacy. Inevitably, musicians, agents, club owners, and the like from this Euro-Americans community became involved with the new music that was developing. Nick LaRocca, a cornetist and trumpeter born in New Orleans in 1889 and of Italian ancestry, claims to have made the first recording in the jazz idiom in 1917 and, besides, has argued that the music is not indebted to African American culture. (Of course, Italians—especially Sicilians who were represented heavily in New Orleans—had close cultural ties to North Africa and did not leave this behind upon landing in Louisiana.) By 1936, discordantly he had begun to refer to the style of music known as "Dixieland" as "strictly a white man's music."[80] He also takes partial credit for popularizing of the very term "jazz."[81]

By 1937, LaRocca was cited for the proposition that "white man's music started jazz," emphasizing the "tremendous importance the white man played in originating swing."[82] By 1958, he was singing the same tune, downplaying Negro contributions to the music and claiming that "we're . . . the pioneers." He stoutly argued, "I'm [not] prejudiced against the Negro," while adding, "I don't believe in giving

the Negro credit for something he didn't do." As his native New
Orleans was being buffeted by hurricane force anti–Jim Crow winds,
he castigated "mixing . . . if God meant him to be white, or meant
any other people to be different, he would have made us all one color.
. . . this is plain common sense." For if "these niggers" or—correct-
ing himself—"Negroes came to New York . . . they would have been
thrown [out] on their ears, not shoved out the door, but thrown out
bodily . . . that's how ignorant the Negroes were. . . . The Negro has
never invented anything new," he claimed, particularly a form of music
that has swept the planet. "Take [Louis] Armstrong away from 'em
and they'll go back to Africa," he included in an incoherent flourish.[83]
That same year, 1958, his fellow Italian-American musician Johnny
Lala, trumpeter and pianist who had played alongside Al Jolson—he
of "blackface" infamy—adopted what might be considered the Dixie
moderate viewpoint in conceding that, yes, the Negroes may have
made the music but "whites improved on it—you understand."[84] By
1961, he was still banging on in the same vein, reportedly "angered"
with the idea that the music whose creation he claimed had "Negro
(even African) roots."[85]

This racist discourse was shaped by the reality that it was difficult
for some to accept that a fecund artistic form that has attracted global
attention was birthed by those of African descent. LaRocca is worthy of
attention not because his meritless claims are worthy of contemplation
but simply because he reflects a deep strain in the music, present at the
creation, that reasserted itself continuously in succeeding decades.

SINCE MOBSTERS WERE OFTEN OF ITALIAN or Jewish extrac-
tion, this often contributed to ethnic or ethno-religious attacks upon
them, not least by musicians. The pianist "Jelly Roll" Morton, who
said that the new music was his invention, was acerbic in declaring
that "there is a new system being used to put every one out of the
music business but Jews. Since the Jews are in a dominating position at this time, they are in control of the union, radio stations,
publishers, booking agents & etc. . . . The union officials that's now
in office was considered Communist before they entered office &
believe me they have to put most everyone out of business but the

Jews or Communists . . . using Fifth Column activities in this field."[86] Experience, as the saying goes, is a harsh teacher and such was the case for these musicians subjected to brutalizing exploitation in a context of weakened working-class organization. The raconteur Al Rose said of the Negro pianist and journalist Dan Burley that "when I first met him, [he] was as racist as a black can get [sic]. He endorsed the utopian ideals of Marcus Garvey. . . . And he was sure that whites were sadistic, untrustworthy, savage, greedy . . . and most of all, stupid." Burley's experience—he was born in 1907 in Kentucky—led him to these conclusions.[87]

Most of the figures in the pages that follow are men—especially men of African descent—and, to a degree, this is a reflection of the fact that the music they pioneered had roots in Africa. However, this geographical arc does not explain the gender imbalance. Black women faced severe obstacles in seeking to make their mark musically. Vi Redd, born in 1928, a gifted saxophonist and vocalist, moonlighted as a teacher. Yes, Philly Joe Jones was among the male artists who often had to work in other jobs to support their art, but Redd faced an added burden, being passed up for jobs because of bias against women, men walking off the bandstand as soon as she arrived—and worse. She was forced to endure a ceaseless flow of sexual banter uttered by bandmates and fans alike. The critic Whitney Balliet, who had the ability to make—and break—careers wrote infamously that "most women lack the physical equipment to say nothing of the poise for blowing trumpets and trombones, slapping bass fiddles or beating drums." Still, the rise of the anti–Jim Crow movement that also served to propel feminism began to change this odious scene, though echoes of the past continued to persist.[88]

Inevitably, as organized crime figures ascended in the music that from its inception was shaped by a bordello culture, African American counterparts arose to challenge them. And the bordello culture was not conducive to gender parity among musicians. By the 1960s, according to one observer, John McClain "owned L.A.'s baddest jazz club, the It Club [and] was also one of the city's biggest drug dealers. Some say he was 'the Black Godfather.'" This notoriety meant that he spent years in jail, but not before mentoring Dick Griffey of Solar

Records, who in turn helped the twenty-first-century mogul Marion "Suge" Knight assemble Death Row Records. Reportedly, Griffey was of the opinion that "everything Suge ever thought about doing I've done . . . ten times."[89]

Los Angeles, within hailing distance of Nevada, which became a headquarters for organized crime, provided a model for McClain to emulate. In the early 1940s, the musician Buddy Collette was performing in a club in L.A. when in walked an angry Mickey Cohen, a known mobster. "When he saw that the band wasn't playing yet," Collette recalled, "he pulled a gun. 'I'll give you three minutes to get on the stand!'" Suddenly, "two or three of Mickey's guys were hitting the waiters in the head with chairs. Mickey just locked the door and told the band to play while all the fighting was going on."[90]

However, as the rise of McClain suggested, African American initiative in this business—beyond performing—accelerated in the 1960s and thereafter with the ascendancy of the anti-Jim Crow and concomitant Black Power movement. By 1967, a Jazz Musicians Association was formed and by late 1969 they had opened a record store in Manhattan, at Avenue A and 14th Street, with pianist Horace Silver, saxophonist Jackie McLean, and pianist turned television commentator Gil Noble in attendance.[91] A few months later, musicians described as "expatriate jazzmen" had started a nightclub in the Canary Islands, yet another attempt to escape the murderous likes of those like Cohen.[92] A few months after that, Black musicians in Los Angeles assailed movie studio policies and organized a picket line engineered by 100 members of the Black Musicians Association and the National Association for the Advancement of Colored People (NAACP). They demanded a 25 percent quota in hiring, which in itself was a rebuff of the merger between the previously racially divided local affiliates of the union, the American Federation of Musicians, which included 1,100 African Americans out of a membership of 14,000.[93] By October 1970, a group of more than sixty fiery musicians led by Rahsaan Roland Kirk and Lee Morgan interrupted a taping of the *Merv Griffin Show* on CBS in Manhattan, demanding more jazz and other black musical expressions. This took place at the studio on Sixth Avenue and 47th Street. The "Jazz and Peoples Movement," as they were called, entered brusquely to accusatory shouts: "In Russia, they would have put you in jail five minutes ago."[94]

Attempts byBlack artists and Black people generally to assume more control of the art form they created were not greeted with equanimity. In recounting the history of the new music, the story is told—not altogether accurately—that after Storyville, the red-light district in New Orleans, was restricted severely, musicians headed northward to Kansas City, though the serpentine Mississippi River, the water highway, would have taken them much more easily to Memphis or St. Louis. In any case, there was an efflorescence of organized crime in Kansas City that was tied to a political machine that ultimately produced a U.S. senator and president: Harry S. Truman. Into this maelstrom stepped the Negro entrepreneur with roots in Texas— Felix Payne. He began as a barber, then moved into nightclubs, where he became a partner of "Piney" Brown, a blues belter (immortalized in song by singer Big Joe Turner). Apparently, Payne was tied to a faction of organized crime in his ventures and another faction took umbrage, which led to his being kidnapped and stripped naked in January 1929 and forced to walk in sub-freezing temperatures. Payne, an amateur tennis player and NAACP donor, was also a newspaper publisher and in his newspaper glowing tributes were printed about Johnny Lazia, a crime boss ultimately slain by mob competitors in 1934. Payne was also caught up in the epochal transition of Negro voters from the party of Abraham Lincoln—the Republicans—to the Democrats, whom they continue to support overwhelmingly. Payne, during this tumultuous time, highlighted the racial segregation that was a feature of Democratic Party conventions during this era.[95]

As the example of Payne suggested, Negroes involved in the business of music felt the need to have powerful patrons, a variation (if not inversion) of the theme of "self-help." The vibraphonist Lionel Hampton had an uncle in Chicago who worked for the gangster Al Capone, which helped to propel both his initial popularity and his ultimate success as a bandleader.[96] He became a prominent supporter of U.S. presidents Ronald Reagan and George H.W. Bush[97] and, perhaps not accidentally, an abysmal exploiter of the musicians in his band.[98] "I admired Lionel," said the trumpeter Joe Wilder, who was employed in his band, "but I didn't like the conditions that he created for the band. The band was treated like we were [in] shackles," that is, "virtually in slavery." Predictably, "you were always being reminded that if you complained about something. . . . We travel maybe two or three hundred miles and get to the town where we were going to play and instead of just checking into the hotel, he'd call a rehearsal" though "we're tired as we can be . . . at the end of the job, he might play another 40 minutes or so overtime, for which none of us are going to be compensated. If you said anything about it, he was quick to remind you that 'where else can you play?' Don't forget. There's no place else for black musicians to play. 'If you don't like it here, I've got 500 other [musicians] who are waiting in line to play in this band.' So you had that sort of a sword hanging over your head all the time." Hampton studiously sought to "avoid paying the men what the job was worth . . . I very often made a statement that if slavery were coming back, I'm sure he'd be one of the first idiots to vote for it." Wilder was with the band for six months, up to entering the Marines in 1943, which may have seemed like a respite in comparison.[99]

Naturally, crass labor exploitation led to the creation of unions of musicians to bargain collectively for improved wages and working conditions. Virtually from the inception of the new music, artists sought to organize unions, though Jim Crow often foiled their best efforts. Johnny De Droit, bandleader, born in 1892 in New Orleans, was a staunch union man since with their adequate protection "[you] know how long you're going to play and how much you're going to get. Before the union was organized," he said, musicians "had to wait thirty to sixty days before they got their money." His father organized the union as a result. Absence of a strong union led artists into problematic situations, such as recording under various names to escape adhesion contracts with record companies. [100] During the First World War era, the union sought to shape the sound of the new music by mandating that one of every five instruments had to be a string instrument, since it was thought that those who played same were thought to be not getting enough work.[101]

Union organizing was taking place in the era of Jim Crow, which meant unions organized on racial lines. It was in late 1943 that Walter

White of the National Association for the Advancement of Colored People contacted James Petrillo, the leader of the American Federation of Musicians. There were 673 locals or branches, he said, in the United States and Hawaii, and thirty-one in Canada (also part of the 673 total). Of these, thirty-two were designated as "so-called 'colored'" and of the remaining 641, eight had subsidiary locals thereby admitting Negroes to a limited second-class membership. At that juncture, only two branches—those in New York City and Detroit—admitted Negroes to full membership. This inequity, White lamented, delivered "great economic loss" to African Americans and, perhaps not coincidentally, "caused competition between colored musicians and white musicians tending to lower scales for both."[102] The authorities went to great lengths to enforce Jim Crow rigidity. In 1944 in Gadsden, Alabama, unionized musicians in the band of Fletcher Henderson—a prominent African American musician—refused to allow three musicians defined as "white" to play alongside him unless they blackened their faces with burnt cork.[103]

But then as the anti–Jim Crow movement took flight, an impetus was created to merge these separate bodies of segregated unions of musicians. However, this often meant Black musicians relinquishing their treasuries and headquarters and being swallowed whole by often insensitive larger unions composed of Euro-Americans, often meaning a net loss for African Americans and souring many on the very notion of "racial integration." This, in turn, benefited the Nation of Islam, which, in any case, was often a lonely voice opposed to what became a disastrous experiment in desegregation.[104]

The debilitating of the organized left did not leave musicians unaffected. The trumpeter Bunk Johnson, born in New Orleans in 1879, migrated to San Francisco, where he found that the "white" union barred him and other Negro musicians from playing at numerous sites. But then Harry Bridges, left-wing leader of a stevedores' union, who was accused of being a Communist and was threatened more than once with deportation to his native Australia, offered Johnson assistance and told the union that if they did not change course he would seek to organize a competing union. Admittedly, however, Bridges's démarche was unusual.[105]

The weakening of unions and the stubborn persistence of white supremacy was a theme, at any rate, of the historical trajectory of the music. Reinforcing these pestilent trends was the profit that inhered— for some—in this process. By 1973, the producer and impresario John Hammond was seeking to convince CBS Records, an industry giant, to reissue a two-record album of the music of Teddy Wilson. This progressive pianist, once known as the "Marxist Mozart," because of his political predilections, made these recordings in the 1930s and, said Hammond, "was paid a hopelessly inadequate flat fee for recording without artist royalties. . . . We have, of course, made a fortune on many of the Teddy Wilson reissues featuring Billie Holiday without paying Wilson anything whatsoever."[106]

Thus, those who hired these musicians often did quite well for themselves, and this list includes Ahmet Ertegun, the man of Turkish origin, who became captivated with the music of Duke Ellington at London's Palladium in the early 1930s and went on to found Atlantic Records, recording such stalwarts as Dizzy Gillespie, the Modern Jazz Quartet, Charles Mingus, and John Coltrane. By 1989, he was on a first-name basis with the uber-banker David Rockefeller, whom he entertained at his lovely estate in Bodrum, Turkey, along the picturesque Aegean Sea. Numerous U.S. politicos also partook of his gracious hospitality there.[107]

It has been said of chess grandmasters that to reach that exalted status presupposes ineptitude in everything else, not least because of the time commitment required to excel. Assuredly, to gain mastery on their instruments required a like manner of time by musicians, which left little time for labor organizing or even attending to the "business" of "show business." According to trombonist J. J. Johnson, the saxophonist John Coltrane was a "practice-aholic," a man utterly devoted to mastering his horn. And this descriptor could be applied to those not as famous as the Philadelphian.[108] His fellow saxophonist, Charlie "Bird" Parker, was said to practice almost fifteen hours daily.[109] The bassist Ron Carter admitted to practicing eight hours a day.[110]

THE SECOND WORLD WAR, as we shall see, brought enormous changes to the enormous music industry, not least the shellac restrictions that limited production of recorded music on discs. This placed a premium on the value of live performances, but in 1943 Walter White of the NAACP complained to Mayor Fiorello La Guardia of New York City about the revocation of the license of the Savoy, a club where innovative music was being concocted by (mostly) African American artists. This was "unwise," said White as he scoffed at the purported justification for the revocation: U.S. soldiers were contracting sexually transmitted diseases there. This could have happened at the Waldorf, he countered, referring to a posh Midtown hotel. He objected to the companion idea that "white people cannot patronize the Savoy," which was actually a brazen attempt to enforce racist segregation since the authorities also objected to the notion that "colored and white people dance together" at the Savoy: this objection hindered dancing and contributed to the companion idea that the music played should be for listening.[111] On the other hand, White, a cultural commissar of sorts, earlier had welcomed the "inducement to Negroes to study music as art rather than as entertainment which can be commercialized," endorsing the turn toward jazz as a concert art rather than music for dancing.[112]

Still, Charles Buchanan of the Savoy was in high dudgeon about the prospect of shuttering what he termed the "world's finest ballroom" situated at 140th Street and Lenox Avenue in Harlem.[113] Complicating matters was a "confidential" report from the FBI warning that the U.S. Communist Party, in the process of electing the African American leader Ben Davis to the New York City Council, was "very much concerned about the closing of the Savoy" and were "taking up the cudgels."[114]

DESPITE THE FREQUENT AND REPETITIVE announcements of the demise of the music we call jazz, it has persisted. In 1980 the musician and entrepreneur Dr. Billy Taylor ascertained that a "well-produced hard bop record or a reissue by a respected artist earns back production costs with U.S. sales of 5,000 to 10, 000 within one year." Considering that the vocalist and guitarist George Benson was then selling "over a million units" gave a hint of the profits to be made when it was thought the music was withering. Grover Washington, Jr., the saxophonist, routinely sold a half million units, while the group Weather Report fluctuated between these two figures. Dexter Gordon, McCoy Tyner, Woody Shaw, and Bobby Hutcherson were then reaching 50,000 to 100,000 units. A few decades earlier Theolonius Monk, Bill Evans, and John Coltrane were capable of selling 100,000 records in the United States alone. Though his music was often scorned, Atlantic Records was pleased with the sales of Ornette Coleman, as was Blue Note subsequently. Their music was derided at times as well, though Anthony Braxton and Cecil Taylor sold albums marketed by Arista that approached 20,000 in sales in the United States alone. It was not unknown for Keith Jarrett to sell 400, 000 records, with each unit selling for $16. Success in the area of 40,000 to 60,000 had been attained by Gary Burton and Jack De Johnnette. Fantasy Records survived for years on the music of Dave Brubeck, then backed Credence Clearwater Revival, a kind of rock group, which registered millions in record sales, then financed the blockbuster movie *One Flew Over the Cuckoo's Nest*, which grossed more than $100 million. Fantasy was financed by a group of investors who realized a hundredfold return on their investment. Thus Fantasy was able, at least for a good while, to circumvent the single greatest problem of an independent label: getting paid by distributors.[115]

Clive Davis of Columbia Records well knew the dynamics of the industry in which he played a major role. "Profits more than doubled in 1968, doubled again the following year and rose dramatically again in 1970," he chortled. Simultaneously "black radio was also becoming increasingly militant; black Program Directors were refusing to *see* white promotion men," forcing the hiring of more African Americans. One of his stars, trumpeter Miles Davis, released an album, *Bitches Brew*, that sold 400, 000 units.[116]

This bright picture notwithstanding, by 1990 executive Ahmet Ertegun said that "most current jazz recordings, which are made for the contemporary market, sell under 10,000 copies."[117] By 1991, Ertegun was distraught, lamenting that "due to the recession there is a general job freeze in the music industry and it's even difficult for people who have had years of experience." [118]

The contrast between the upbeat words of Davis and the lament

of Ertegun continues, as the music continues to sway. There is little
doubt that as this century proceeds, digitalization will challenge the
ability of musicians to make a decent living,[119] though Deutsche Bank
is among those predicting a continued expansion of streaming revenue, i.e. music distributed online.[120] The global recorded music market
has decreased significantly in recent years, reflecting the change from
an analog to a digital market.[121] Still, it would be a mistake to locate
this crisis exclusively within the bounds of either the music industry
generally or the subset that is "jazz" more particularly. The culture
industry generally—including movies, museums, theater—all face
unique challenges today.[122]

This ineffable point should remind us all that there are terribly destructive forces—racism, organized criminality, brutal labor
exploitation, battery, debauchery, gambling—from which grew an
intensely beautiful art form, today denoted as "jazz." It is the classic
instance of the lovely lotus arising from the malevolent mud. A good
deal of this book concerns the mud, but in order to digest this malodorous substance as I was writing these pages, I often found myself
listening to the pulchritudinous tunes of the musicians who continue
to prevail against difficult odds. I recommend that readers emulate
this writer. [123]

1. Original Jelly Roll Blues

NEW ORLEANS HAS A JUSTIFIABLE CLAIM to being the birth-place of the music known as jazz. The African roots of Black New Orleans reach deeply into Senegal and Guinea, regions with rich and extensive musical traditions,[1] particularly with regard to stringed instruments and percussion, the heart of rhythm sections that distinguished the new music. However, this music was often played with instruments of European origin, for example, the horn devised by Belgium's Adolphe Sax in the early 1840s, and the European influence was strong at the mouth of the Mississippi River.

Nevertheless, the wider point is that these European instruments (and those of African derivation, too, for example the banjo and drums) were infused with the unique culture that arose in New Orleans' Congo Square, one that reflected a potpourri of West African and North American influences.[2] Interviewed by the pacesetting Jazz Studies initiative of Tulane University in 1958, Alice Zeno—the mother of clarinetist George Lewis and born in 1864—spoke of her grandmother, born in 1810 and passing away in 1910. This elder spoke to her granddaughter in Wolof; the younger also spoke French, the language she spoke more than English in the first years of her life—before learning German and Spanish. Zeno in some ways resembles the new music that arose in the late nineteenth century, a mélange of African, European, and North American influences.[3]

Still, Africa was at the root: U.S. Negro missionaries in the Congo in the late nineteenth century were stunned to hear melodies reminiscent of "Swing Low, Sweet Chariot," then a musical staple back home.[4]

The bassist Gene Ramey, born in Austin, Texas, in 1913, said that his grandmother "remembers coming from Madagascar, yeah, at the age of four or five. . . ."[5] Yet another bassist, George "Red" Callender, has spoken of his "Ashanti," a West African ethnic group, ancestry.[6]

New Orleans may have been the opera capital of the United States during the antebellum era.[7] Reportedly, New Orleans was the only U.S. city to maintain an opera company continuously in the nineteenth century, the Civil War years (1861–1865) excepted. It also has a rich history of Free Negro culture, which included a militia with drum companies. Some Free Negro musicians were educated abroad, circumventing the U.S. preoccupation: depriving Negroes of education of all sorts.[8] After the Civil War, a number of musicians in bands with the vanquished so-called Confederate States of America dumped their instruments in pawnshops in New Orleans, and Negroes happily bought some of these battered instruments, tools that jump-started the creation of a new musical art form.[9] Moreover, the banjoist known as Creole George Guesnon, born in New Orleans in 1907, argued passionately that "I don't believe there is any other city on the face of the earth as rich in Negro folklore and unwritten legends as New Orleans," a phenomenon that fed imagination and creativity, contributing to the blossoming of a new music.[10]

There were other peculiar tendencies shaping the emerging new music. John Wiggs, a bandleader born in 1899 in New Orleans, spoke movingly of those he called "bottlemen," who collected glass vessels and accompanied their task by blowing on horns—often three feet long—rendering beautiful blues songs that could be heard blocks away. Later he noticed the same trills and flourishes of these men replicated by trumpeters, particularly the "bending of notes." They also used cowbells. Children were drawn to these men as they exchanged dolls for bottles.[11] Some of the earliest performances of the new music that took place were heard along Franklin Street inside such places as the Twenty-Eight Club and the Pig Ankle Cabaret; these "spasm bands" used homemade instruments and often honed their art on street corners. Some white and "Creole-of-color" residents dismissed it as "bawdyhouse music."[12]

Invention and innovation were the watchwords of this new music and were represented by the father of Joseph Thomas. The younger was a clarinetist and vocalist born in 1902; the elder played a broom, drawn across the thumb, that sounded like a violin.[13] Mary Lucy Hamill O'Kelly, born in Vicksburg in 1876, recalled in 1958, "I can't remember when I first knew jazz as being jazz. I just thought it was sort of embroidery that the Negroes put on tunes that they played." She observed, "They'd add little extra notes and quivers and trills and runs and syncopation and make the thing sound entirely different," a fair estimate of the new music.[14] There were other influences on the music. The talented trumpeter Clark Terry, born in St. Louis in 1920, attributed his distinctive style to emulating "mariachi [Mexican] players who are forced to master their mouthpieces before they're given the horns."[15]

The opera brought by European migrants also delivered a panoply of musical influences surrounding Negroes. By 1910, New Orleans also happened to have more Italian Americans than any other U.S. city, which further contributed to the rich stew of musical influences.[16]

THE MUSICIAN PAUL BARBARIN SAYS that growing up he could hear bands playing even if they were almost two miles away. Fewer buildings, he says, meant sound traveled with more facility, allowing exposure to diverse forms of music. Singers with booming voices could also be heard, even if they were speaking in a language other than English. He grew up with the sound of French since his mother spoke the language—she "speaks good French . . . she always talk in French . . . we understood it."[17] One witness claims that the scintillating cornet playing of the legendary Buddy Bolden "was so powerful they could dance to his music 10 miles away."[18]

Charles Elgar, born in 1879 in New Orleans, studied violin with a French teacher, who was an assistant conductor with the French Opera.[19] The first trumpet teacher of Johnny De Droit, born in 1892, was from the Republican Guard in France and was also first trumpet in their band.[20] His parents spoke French.[21] The mother of Albert Burbank, born in 1902, spoke to him in French (he would answer in English); this clarinetist often sang in French.[22] According to Buddie Burton, trumpeter Natty Dominique also spoke French.[23]

Bassist George "Pops" Foster was born in 1892 to a father who spoke French.[24] His mother was said to speak about seven languages.[25] Paul Beaulieu, born in 1888 in New Orleans, studied cello with a French artist who was in the city working with a local opera company. He recalled that Alphonse and Ulysses Picou spoke as much or more "Creole French" as they did English.[26] Bella Cornish, once known as Isabella Davenport, was wed to Buddy Bolden's sideman, William "Willie" Cornish. Born in Biloxi, her father was "a Frenchman," she said. [27] Danny Barker, born in New Orleans in 1909, was a guitarist who also was part of this lineage. "My grandmother spoke French. My grandfather spoke French. They also spoke Creole, that is, a broken French."[28] Ferrand Clementin, born in 1894 and perhaps best known as a comrade of the trombonist Kid Ory, recalled that French was spoken in his family and French songs were sung.[29] The trumpeter known as Don Albert, born in New Orleans in 1908, spoke French, too.[30]

Then there were those like Israel Gorman, a clarinetist born in 1895, who served in France for a year or so during the First World War, a venture in which he was not alone in participating.[31] Thus Joseph "Fan" Borgeau, born in 1891 and best known as a banjoist, served in Germany during the war, though he was a French interpreter in France.[32]

A role model for many of these musicians was Victor Eugene Macarty, with roots in nineteenth century New Orleans, who received a music education in Paris, then became active in the Republican Party. In the aftermath of the U.S. Civil War, he launched a boycott that shuttered the local opera house because of its Jim Crow seating policies.[33]

As Macarty's example illustrated, the Gallic influence further impelled the movement of musicians to France where they could at once escape penurious Jim Crow and—by their very presence—influence the Old Continent against their homeland. The knowledge of French also opened musicians to diverse influences, musically and otherwise. New Orleans was remarkable in another respect. So many of the Negro musicians coming to maturity as this new music was emerging were familiar with other languages besides English, which

exposed them to various musical genres and opened doors to pursuing their artistic visions abroad.

There was also the German population of New Orleans, which
displayed a fondness for music and song, including its own choruses,
string quartets, a conservatory, and orchestra. By the 1890s, as the
new music was taking flight, this group was enthusiastic about their
singing societies and preserving German songs. German bands often
offered entertainment to the masses as they paraded on many festive
occasions and gave concerts in numerous places throughout the city.[34]

African Americans extended their experience when some wound
up in Cuba and the Philippines after the United States declared war
on Spain in 1898. Noah Cook, born in 1879 in Livingston Parish,
Louisiana, trained as a jockey before decamping to the Philippines by
1900. It was there that he familiarized himself with a song often sung
in Cuba by the troops that became a standard: "There'll Be Hot Time
in the Old Town Tonight."[35] William "Willie" Cornish, born in 1875,
also fought in this transoceanic conflict.[36]

Another influence came from Mexico. Charles Elgar studied
clarinet with Luis Tio, who hailed from there. A number of famed
clarinetists, including Barney Bigard and Jimmy Noone, did so too. In
1885 a contingent of Mexican musicians arrived in New Orleans for
the Cotton Exposition, familiarizing themselves with a city where several of these sojourners chose to reside. Tio and his brother Lorenzo
spoke Spanish, of course, but, said Elgar, "developed the English and
French . . . You'd never know that they weren't original New Orleans
fellows." Elgar too was struck by the presence of opera companies featuring "fifty men in the pit," a real "monster thing." Speaking of this
orchestra, he said, "You could go in the gallery for thirty-five cents."
Both of his parents were opera devotees and a couple of times a week
took him to the opera: "The more I heard it, the more I fell in love
with it," he said. It was a constant presence in the city until it burned
down in 1919.[37]

But it was not just high-minded opera that shaped the cultural
consciousness of some musicians: bordellos arose in New Orleans
simultaneously with the arrival of the new music. As early as 1850, New
Orleans was deemed to be the "red light capital" of the Republic.[38]

Minimally, these sites provided a venue for musicians to play and contributed to a nightlife. One analyst claims that in fin-de-siècle New Orleans, prostitution "has never before or since had in America a heyday such as it had in ragtime New Orleans . . . In 1899 the New Orleans police admitted to the existence of 230 bordellos, 30 houses of assignations, and about 2,000 prostitutes." Assuredly, a color bar then existed, but by 1899 the press was reporting a proliferation of assignations between Negro men and women defined as "white" (the press was not as concerned about Negro women and men of differing ancestry).[39] Piano playing with various trills was a component of these sites, and musicians improvised, setting the stage for the new music. Bolstering the "candelabra" thesis about the multiple origins of the new music is the report that the pianist Eubie Blake, born in Baltimore in 1887, began playing at a local bordello at the tender age of fifteen.

It would be an error to imagine that the origins of the new music were separate and apart from the wider U.S. society or even how African Americans were maltreated. The following pages will suggest a brand of male supremacy that was hardly unique to practitioners of the new music but certainly characterized some of them. Purportedly, Blake's father, who was enslaved on a large Virginia plantation, was used as a "stud," fathering twenty-seven children "of which he knew." After the Civil War, he married and fathered ten more offspring, one of whom was the renowned pianist.[40] Even the precursor music known as "ragtime," which catapulted Eubie Blake into prominence, was similarly linked to sexuality, brothels, and dens of vice.[41]

"Every whorehouse had piano players," said "Pops" Foster, but "Lulu White's had the most,"[42] a reference to the most notorious Negro proprietor. A turning point arrived during the First World War era when the authorities moved to circumscribe her busy business.[43] There is some question as to whether the crackdown on brothels ignited a scattering of musicians that had made a living in Storyville, the red-light district of New Orleans.[44] The percussionist Paul Barbarin, born in 1899, recalled that "Jelly Roll" Morton, one of the early giants of the new music, toiled on "Basin Street, at Lulu White's house" and had to find other options when her business was hampered. As for

Barbarin, he moved to Chicago in 1917 and wound up working in the stockyards.[45]

"Fan" Borgeau was also familiar with this bordello, recalling that a pianist there—Ed Mercier—also worked as a pimp. As for Borgeau, he claims to have visited the red-light district at the age of nine, since his uncle lived there. He also recalls that Manuel Manetta, the multi-instrumentalist born in New Orleans in 1889 and an early influence on the city's musicians, played at White's. This entrepreneurial madame, he says, employed blondes, brunettes—all kinds of women—in her twenty-six-room house.[46] She was a "great big sort of dark-skinned woman," he said, unlike those she employed (though others described her as being a "mulatta"). He says that he knew her sufficiently well to once hold her blonde wig.[47] White's presence notwithstanding, Negro men generally were barred from brothels in Storyville—"Even the black crib prostitutes were available to whites only," according to one historian.[48] One analyst observes that during the second decade of the twentieth century New Orleans was "densely crowded with music . . . not just in the brothels but also in the many cabarets, honky tonks and dance halls," meaning "two dozen bands played . . . every night" in the town.[49]

Of the giants of New Orleans music, Kid Ory, the trombonist born in Louisiana in 1896, also was said to play at Lulu White's bordello—along with playing at sex shows.[50] The versatile instrumentalist Manuel Manetta, born in New Orleans in 1889, knew White, recalling that she hailed from White Castle, Louisiana. At her place of business, champagne was sold for $25 per bottle. Hours for musicians were nine till three in the morning without exception.[51] Johnny Sala, of Sicilian ancestry and born in New Orleans in 1894, called White an "octoroon" and said she "didn't have no white woman in there," speaking of her brothel. "But she had Negroes but you couldn't tell they were colored all right. All [were] beautiful . . . and nothin' but white men went in there."[52]

"Yes," concurred clarinetist Barney Bigard, born in 1906 in New Orleans; Morton worked for White and besides, "was a gambler, a pimp and everything."[53] Agreeing was Eubie Blake, who said that Morton "knew all the pimps."[54] Actually, said Johnny St. Cyr, the banjoist and guitarist born in New Orleans in 1890, analysts have not properly accessed the chain of causation, in that instead of pianists being influenced by playing in brothels, these musicians all happened to be "halfway pimps anyway," with Morton being an example.[55] Manuel Manetta recalled that Morton's lover ran a brothel—"She had a lot of stalls in there; in fact, they had white and colored stalls"—and Morton performed there.[56]

The presence of Morton returns us to the complicated question about the new music's origins. Hayes Alvis, bassist and tubist, born in Chicago in 1907, felt "there was something to that claim on his [Morton's] business card that he created jazz," though he did not connect this to the point that he "had tendencies toward voodoo.."[57] Morton's sister, Frances Mouton Oliver, sees her brother as emblematic of New Orleans in that he spoke French as a child—their grandmother could not speak English—and the language of Voltaire was the language of their home, too: "He created jazz in 1901," she concluded modestly.[58] Ferdinand Joseph LaMenthe (or LaMothe), born in 1890 and known widely as Jelly Roll Morton, apparently worked as a pimp, making further complex the origins of the new music.[59]

Morton's accompanist, Volly de Faut, concedes that the pianist "was one of the first to have a real jazz style," an indication that Morton's creation bravado was not altogether misplaced.[60] Whether the creative Morton could claim parentage for the music has been questioned but it is evident that, like Charlie "Bird" Parker years later, he exhibited traits that did not necessarily enhance his longevity, cultivated in his early performance venues. Paul Barbarin said that Morton was "mostly a gambler . . . He'd lose maybe four or five hundred dollars" and that proved to be his "downfall—easy come, easy go."[61] Danny Barker said that Morton "took on the lifestyle of the notorious night people of the underworld," including being an expert marksman with a pistol.[62] Earl "Fatha" Hines, the pianist born in Duquesne, a town near Pittsburgh, in 1903, arrived in Chicago in the 1920s where he found "you had to *act* bad whether you were bad or not," meaning aggressively tough. "Jelly Roll Morton had found that out long before I did," he conceded, "and that's why he carried a gun and talked loud."[63]

Moreover, the crassly exploitative nature of the music business often left artists in a foul mood. Morton claimed that he had been "robbed of three million dollars" during his career by agents, club owners, and other vultures, not to mention those he accused of copying his music and style.[64] Actually, said Creole George Guesnon, Morton "always carried him a big old ivory pistol" and "always talked [about] shooting somebody."[65]

Jim Crow notwithstanding, as early as 1889 press reports were referring contemptuously to "this thing of white girls becoming enamored of Negroes becoming rather too common," a trend that obligatorily inflamed ire—not leaving those like Morton unaffected—and was destined to foment a crackdown.[66]

Of course, these questionable performance venues bred traits that would bedevil Morton and musicians for generations to come, helping to spur an attempt by many of these same musicians to gain more control over their places of work.

But it was not simply the unique environs of the brothel that led Morton down this road of pistol packing. According to the reedman Volly de Faut, born in Little Rock in 1904, Morton was also a "pool shark," which was another reason for him to "carry a .38 pistol right in his belt," but this decision was driven by the reality that these "were hoodlum times, I mean bootleggin' times" with men of ill temper presiding. There was, besides, a "tendency in those days . . . for white managers to exploit Negro talent" and given the absence or weakness of unions, self-help was often the only option available—a phrase and a trait that was to blossom decades later with the simultaneous rise of the Nation of Islam and the decline of worker organization. De Faut lamented the all too typical fate of the performers "Buck and Bubbles," brilliant dancers both: "A manager signed them to a ten year contract when they were little kids and paid them just chicken feed.." Back then, he lamented, a "colored man . . . had a pretty rough time making a buck," and Morton was no exception. He adapted to his environment, that is, "he put on a big front," including carrying a flashy pistol.[67]

Morton also happened to be of a lighter hue, which was not a minor quality in a color-obsessed society. In 1938, the researcher William

Russell sought to find Bill Johnson, billed then as the "oldest living jazz musician" (he was older than Buddy Bolden and had worked with Lil Armstrong in Milwaukee and Chicago). Years later, he returned to the Midwest in search of Johnson and found that he had moved to San Antonio and that he had crossed the color line, had chosen to "pass," an option open to him because of his lighter skin color.[68]

The climate in which this music was forged at times was unhealthy, making the beautiful art created therein all the more remarkable. The trumpeter Clark Terry said of bandleader Fate Marable that he "never was able to settle down until he primed himself with a couple of slugs of whiskey. It used to be so strange" in that he would "wake up . . . get up and hurriedly before he brushed his teeth . . . sometimes in his pajamas, run around the bar and get a drink, and then he would start his day." That musicians often performed in venues where imbibing alcohol was encouraged—if not being the raison d'être of the venue—hardly discouraged alcoholism,[69] which could allow unscrupulous proprietors to cloud the thinking of musicians by plying them with various brews. (Club owners were not the only employers who sought to manipulate workers by dispensing intoxicants; apparently there were those who felt that Negro servants worked harder under the influence of cocaine.)[70]

There was a "long association of jazz with alcohol," according to one scholar, meaning "many musicians suffered from alcoholism." Musicians often ran up a tab as they grabbed drinks from the bar—or were plied with same—that could consume their paycheck. The unusual late-night working hours sapped energy, disrupting circadian rhythms, and often led to unusual musical rhythms. Unscrupulous club owners were not averse to "paying" musicians with alcohol. They were also not above closing their establishment every thirty days, issuing a new lease to a dummy lessee, and reopening under a new name, thereby cheating the artists and, perhaps, driving them to drown their sorrows in drink.[71]

Louis Armstrong once told Buck Clayton "how many people he knew had been killed in little clubs while listening to jazz by somebody that was either jealous or drunk. Louie once told me that even he had once been cut."[72] In some ways, this renowned trumpeter and vocalist can be viewed as the shining embodiment of the new music. After all, the erudite scholar, Dr. Allison Davis, was said to have remarked that this musician's rendition of "'West End Blues' may be the greatest thing American civilization has ever produced," a statement that is hardly exaggerated and thus casts into bold relief his own hardscrabble existence in Louisiana.[73] For Armstrong's own experience in New Orleans provides a glimpse of the atmosphere in which the new music was incubated. As a youngster, he was playing in the streets "when all of a sudden a guy on the opposite side of the street pulled out a little old six shooter pistol and fired it.." Without hesitating, the budding trumpeter "pulled out my stepfather's revolver from my bosom and raised my arm into the air and let her go.." In a transformative episode, he was arrested and jailed. "I was scared," he confessed, "more scared than I was the day Jack Johnson knocked out Jim Jeffries," a reference to the tumultuous day when the ebony heavyweight champion defeated his white challenger, leading to racist pogroms nationally. Armstrong was sent to the "Colored Waifs' Home" for boys, which fortunately did not derail his career.[74]

Alcohol at times loosened the tongues of those in the audience, often not in a good way. Danny Barker has said that "in the Negro joints we played relaxed, at home; but in the white joints were all eyes and ears, and anything could happen . . . there were descriptive slurs," he said, including "niggers, darkies, Zulus, piccaninnies . . . monkeys, gorillas, Ubangis . . . tar babies, ink spots." At times, these musicians crossed an actual—and metaphorical—border: "Mississippi. Just the mention of the word . . . amongst a group of New Orleans people would cause complete silence and attention. The word was so very powerful that it carried the impact of catastrophes, destruction, hell, earthquakes, cyclones, murder, hangings, lynchings, all sorts of slaughter. . . ." But it was not just the Magnolia State since tales of "Alabama, Florida, Texas and Georgia were equally fearsome." [75]

The climate in which this music was forged was also unhealthy in terms of the violence often inflicted upon denizens. African Americans were a frequent target but indicative of the hostile climate that spilled over to ensnare others, Italian Americans, too, were targeted at times. It was in 1891 that this latter group was subjected to what has been described as the "largest lynching in American history," referring to almost a dozen men who were murdered in one fell swoop in response to allegations concerning their presumed attack on local law enforcement. As noted, these Italian Americans were primarily of Sicilian origin, "some 70 percent" of the total according to one estimate, and, it was said, they were "unconsciously . . . tolerant" of Negroes, "even friendly with them," displaying an "indifference to American racism," a blatant violation of dominant norms that was bound to spark retaliation. The "White League," known to torment African Americans, was also accused of "waging war against Italians." Reputedly "50 percent of the major American papers in every section of the country . . . approved" of the lynching. Theodore Roosevelt called it "a rather good thing." Opinions began to shift when it was reported that a substantial Italian fleet was making its way across the Atlantic with the aim of attacking U.S. coastal cities. The fact that African Americans had no such patron to intervene on their behalf helped to spur a "Pan African" Congress to cure this defect with the aim of strengthening the ancestral continent. Also, Negro musicians began at this juncture to migrate abroad where they were in a position to lobby on behalf of those left behind.[76]

Retrospectively, the attack on Sicilians and Sicilian Americans and Italians and Italian Americans seems to have been designed to drive a wedge between them and their African-American neighbors and co-workers, at a time when one contemporary scholar has spoken of a "General Strike" in the Crescent City in 1892, "the first inter-racial strike in the country."[77]

As noted, anti-Italian pogroms were an extension of what was befalling Africans. New Orleans had one of the largest concentrations of Negroes in North America, which impelled the rowdiest of their antagonists to seek to bludgeon them.[78] At the time of the most significant anti-Negro explosions of this era, in New Orleans in 1900, "Big Eye" Louis Nelson Delisle, a multi-instrumentalist, was playing bass at a club, accompanying Buddy Bolden, when his father was killed and himself nearly so. He was prompted to make the strategic decision to give up on the cumbersome bass and focus on the clarinet; as one analyst put it, this smaller instrument "would be easier to run with if another mob was chasing him"—yet another example of how racism and the political economy shaped the music. Whatever the case, Bolden's cornet was smashed during the riot, sending a contrary message. Likewise, a staggered Lorenzo Tio left the city altogether.[79]

The crucible in which this new music emerged was often rife with dangers of various sorts—cheating employers not least—which in turn shaped the art form. Taking risks and improvisation nestled near the heart of the music.

Ineluctably, an increasingly popular music identified with African American men was designed to incur wrath in a racist society. At the same time, the perhaps not coincidental arrival of jazz with the rise of U.S. imperialism at the turn of the twentieth century contributed to seeing this new music, as one astringent critic put it, as the "natural accompaniment to the death march of Western civilization as a whole."[80] It was an unwelcome trend in the United States, exacerbating the preexisting Negrophobia.

On the other hand, there was the proliferation of electricity, feeding the popularity of the phonograph and recorded music. Thomas Edison's device marked the onset of the modern music industry and allowed musicians to reach into the most obscure corners of the planet.[81] The critic Leonard Feather argued that Kid Ory's "Sunshine Blues" and his "Creole Trombone" were the first genuine recordings of "black jazz," recorded, interestingly enough, in Los Angeles rather than New Orleans.[82] Ironically, recorded music simultaneously opened an income stream and yet another opportunity for exploitation. Electricity also facilitated the popularity of certain musical instruments—for example, the electric guitar—which transformed the music. The rise of electricity also dovetailed with the rise of radio, yet another device that propelled the new music.[83] But these technological advances also buoyed the increasingly strident critics alarmed by the popularity of music produced mostly by Negro men.

The critic identified as Mrs. Marx E. Oberndofer of the General Federation of Women's Clubs asked plaintively, "Does jazz put the sin in syncopation?" The answer was an emphatic yes. This music, it was said accusingly, was that "expression of protest against law and order, that Bolshevik element of license, striving for expression in music."

Concurring, Fenton T. Bott found that "jazz is the very foundation and essence of salacious dancing." This alarmism grew as the sales of phonographs surged to 158 million by 1919, allowing for further dissemination of the music. One poster blared ominously, "STOP HELP SAVE THE YOUTH OF AMERICA DON'T BUY NEGRO RECORDS." "If you don't want to serve Negroes in your place of business," it was advised, then "do not have Negro records on your juke box or listen to Negro records on the radio." A radio station in Chicago was scorned for playing this music by Negroes.[84]

This new music was compelled to assume an "outlaw" mantle, forcing musicians to constantly peer over their shoulders for angry antagonists. An improvisatory spirit stuck with the music even as it migrated northward to Chicago and New York and Kansas City.

At any rate, in southern Louisiana, there was the difficulty of dealing with a police force that seemed to prey on Negro men; it was rare for a jazzman not to have spent at least one night sitting in a precinct lockup after a gig that somehow had gotten out of hand. One night in 1915 Sidney Bechet and "King" Oliver were enjoying a drink in a local tavern when a customer was shot dead right in front of their eyes, a riveting experience not designed to inspire confidence. Another time, an Oliver-Ory band was raided by the police, and band members who could not come up with what today seems like a pittance in bail money had to spend a night in jail. A disenthralled Oliver fled to Chicago, which created an opening for Louis Armstrong, who soon joined him there, this after working as a bellboy, carpenter, coal cart driver, and stevedore.[85]

One hypothesis suggests that as Storyville began to close during the late stages of the First World War (1914-1918), a "Jazz Diaspora" was incited, though there is evidence to suggest that musicians were departing the Crescent City even earlier. (Edmond "Doc" Souchon, guitarist and writer, born in 1897, claims that less than 5 to 10 percent of the musicians played in Storyville.)[86] Then there came the impact of the Great War. This titanic conflict that saw numerous Africans in arms, often led to many being compelled to fight in Europe. Willie "The Lion" Smith earned his nickname in France during the war after manning what were called "Big French 75 guns" for forty-nine days straight.[87]

St. Louis, just up the river and already a capital of sorts of rag-time, benefited from this scattering from New Orleans. Trumpeter Clark Terry, an early influence on Miles Davis, recalled the showboats plying the Mississippi River, while pointing out that "a lot of the cats got off there," meaning the Missouri city, especially since this town "was always known for beautiful, fine ladies." Besides, not unlike New Orleans, in St. Louis "any days of the month, you'd have three or four parades" in which musicians could display their talents.[88]

There were other disincentives that argued against Negro musi-cians remaining in New Orleans. By 1902, Local 174 of the American Federation of Musicians was chartered and was strictly reserved for musicians defined as "white."[89] Dancing to this beat, bandleader "Papa Jack" Laine, born in New Orleans in 1873, said of one musi-cian, "When I found out he was a nigger, that's when I stopped hiring him. . . . I saw his daddy and that was enough." As for the trombonist Dave Perkins, he did not realize he was a Negro since he was "fair as a lily" with blue eyes, the implication being that he too would be passed over for a job. Laine was not poor; his father was a contractor, undermining the argument that bigotry was purely a product of the Euro-American dispossessed, frightened by labor competition from across the color line.[90]

Perforce, union protections in Dixie—meaning New Orleans—were weak, where they needed to be strong, given the prevailing atmo-sphere. Pianist and guitarist, Frank Amacker, born in the Crescent City in 1890, recalled that often club owners would not notify bands they were fired, and band members would only ascertain this upon arriving to play and finding a new band in their place.[91]

Despite the wealth they created for club owners, recording com-panies, and the like, these musicians often performed in adverse conditions, one factor among many in creating or worsening health problems.[92] Cornetist and bandleader Joseph "King" Oliver also developed dental problems, "pyorrhea of the gums," according to his spouse, and was blind in one eye. He felt compelled to grant loans to his sidemen, who often did not repay him. Oliver became depressed, though unlike others similarly situated, he steered clear of alcohol, but that only harmed relations with his bandmates, who were not so inclined.[93] Evidently, the pyorrhea was an impediment to Oliver's horn playing, making it difficult for him to play certain notes.[94] Saxophonist George "Big Nick" Nicholas, born in 1922, asserted, "Saxophone player, trumpet player, they always have this problem with their teeth so I had some work done on my lower mouth and it cost me twelve hundred," followed by a "partial bridge put up in my upper part of my mouth. That cost thirty-one hundred. . . . Through the years your mouth, your gums and your bone structure" are affected by the stress of playing with a device attached to your lips: "All that pressure through the years, you know, it wears away and the bone structure wears away and then your gums recede. So I had six caps put in in 1950 and my gums started receding." Fellow horn man Maynard Ferguson "has all of his teeth capped . . . Sonny Rollins has got a lot of work . . . Coltrane had a lot of work done in his mouth."[95] The contemporary of Louis Armstrong, Norman Brownlee, recalled that the trumpeter roughened his mouthpiece by rubbing it on the curb and this roughness apparently combined with a lot of pressure, causing his lips to deteriorate.[96] Reputedly, Sidney Bechet played a saxophone since the mouthpiece was easier on his teeth, compared to a clarinet.[97] Such was the occupational hazard of the horn man, following in the footsteps of Oliver.

Sadly enough, it was not just teeth. Trumpeter Herman Autrey, born in 1904, said late in life, "I have glaucoma and cataracts and all that junk." This meant a "cornea transplant," adding, "I was blind once upon a time . . . two or three months, I guess." He seemed to connect this malady to "bad whiskey" and did not mention the occupational hazard of playing often in smoky cellars. His spouse had a job, keeping them both afloat. There was no pension or support otherwise from the union. "From the union," he spat out, "they wish you would drop dead soon, because they don't want to pay that thousand," speaking metaphorically. "That's the worst union in the world," he maintained furiously. "I told them that, too, and they know it . . . they don't give a damn about nobody or help nobody," certainly not this Alabaman. "They're the worst bunch of bastards—I told them! They know me!" With gathering outrage, he proclaimed that if you "go in there 10:00, 11:00 o'clock [even] 2:30 they go home. The place is closed at 3:00." With gathering outrage, he insisted, "I'll starve to death before I go in there."[98]

Pianist Oscar Peterson, born in 1925, was afflicted by the malady that often beset those who pounded the ivory keys for a living: arthritis in his hands. "It just hurts to play," he said, just as it hurt his many fans to be deprived of his consummate artistry.[99] Fellow keyboardist Horace Silver struggled with scoliosis: is it possible that the problem he suffered from, the curvature of his spine, emanated from—or was worsened by—long nights bending over the piano while playing?[100]

The cornetist Harrison Barnes, born in 1889, had dental problems too, an occupational hazard for those in his field (he played trombone, too). The seedy environments he performed in may shed light on why he contracted syphilis and how he was afflicted with a tumor—"big as a baseball," he said. And yet, despite his skill as a musician, he was forced to work almost two decades as a flue welder, simply to pay the bills.[101] Born in 1891, Joseph "Fan" Borgeau, whose nickname stemmed from his Chinese appearance, worked as a lottery vendor for thirty-six years, despite his ability as a pianist; one job was typical: the piano keys were so sharp that his hands could be left bloodied.[102]

Suggestive of the discomfiting reality that horrendous conditions endured by skilled musicians have yet to disappear is that Herbie Hancock, one of today's leading keyboardists and now an elder statesman, recalled his early days when he was "playing music into the wee hours every night and then trying to deliver mail all day. . . ." He was a "complete wreck," he confessed, and "actually fell asleep standing up. . . ." Unsurprisingly, he "got sick too."[103]

There was also the occupational hazard of getting from one gig to another. Saxophonist Arnett Cobb, born in 1918, suffered from pleurisy and tuberculosis, but in 1956 he endured "a nearly fatal car accident [that] necessitated spinal surgeries and the use of crutches he'd require" until he died in 1989.[104]

Drummer Freddie Moore, born in 1900, endured an experience that was hardly atypical. He was playing in Duncan, Oklahoma, for a group of Euro-American customers, when one among this group—a "cracker," in his words—pulled a blackjack and began to club him in the head. "King" Oliver grabbed the assaulter's wrist while shouting

"Don't do that, don't kill my drummer. That's the only drummer I've got here." The police were summoned but more than a dozen of the assaulter's comrades declared they intended to lynch Moore. The shaken percussionist abandoned his drum set, clambered down a fire escape, and caught a freight train to Tulsa, the band's next stop. He dared not register at the hotel where the band was slated to stay for fear of being found. Instead, he resided with an unnamed "landlady." Three weeks later, he returned to Duncan with his face blackened and his hair longer, which foiled detection. But this adventure was not the end of his travails, for Oliver called him "skunk foot" since his feet perspired so much when drumming , which contributed to sore feet, at times hampering the removal of his shoes (not to mention generating a striking aroma).[105] The superb drummer Max Roach once observed that "most of the good drummers have bad feet. Because you do a lot of exercising. You work. Sometimes I see somebody . . . walking strangely. I say, it's got to be a drummer."[106] It was not just drummers. Reportedly, saxophonist Zoot Sims, born in 1925, had trouble with his feet because of having to stand and play on so many different engagements.[107]

It was not simply the arduousness of performing, it was also that artists often had to perform when they might have been better off in a hospital bed, quarantined. Pianist Horace Silver confessed, "I once played in San Francisco with a 104-degree temperature,"[108] a product of "the show must go on" mentality, as well as the inadequate bargaining power by artists that was a by-product of this mantra.

Scholar Frederick J. Spencer is not far wrong in concluding recently that "it has become an accepted fact that jazz musicians tend to be more liable than other professionals to die early deaths . . . from drink, drugs, women [sic] or overwork." The venues for their performance—speakeasies, clubs—encouraged drinking and often were controlled by unsavory characters not opposed to using violence to attain goals. According to Spencer, a few jazz businessmen even preferred to hire addicts: "Some record companies and club owners would only hire junkies. With them they could be sure they wouldn't insist on their rights."[109] In addition, according to scholar Ronald L. Morris, "Most leading jazz entertainers after 1880 were closely allied with racketeers," and the impresario and producer John Hammond "believed no fewer than three in every four jazz clubs and cabarets of this distant period were either fronted, backed or in some way managed by Jewish and Sicilian mobsters," though those of Irish origin were also prominent.[110]

The new music, in short, got off to a rocky start, navigating—and influenced by—war, pogroms, racism, and adverse working conditions. Yet these formidable barriers could not restrain the rise of a music that proved to be sufficiently potent to overcome.

2. What Did I Do to Be So Black and Blue?

"PROHIBITION," THE ERA LASTING ROUGHLY from 1920 to 1933, sought to restrict the manufacture, sale, and transportation of alcoholic beverages. It happened to coincide with the proliferation of electricity, the advent of radios as a virtual home appliance, and the rise of phonograph records. All had a dynamic impact upon the enhanced popularity of the new music. As is now well-known, the attempt to ban alcoholic beverages provided a boost for illicit sales, thereby empowering mobsters, who, in any case, already had a toehold in the nation's political economy. The music migrated into the emerging "speakeasies" and as much as the supposed clampdown on New Orleans' Storyville, which was said to disperse musicians to Kansas City (hundreds of miles west, by the way, of the serpentine Mississippi River highway northward), the new trends delivered a jolt of adrenalin, contributing mightily to the enhanced popularity of the new music. Though Prohibition and its demise has been seen as being transformative of the music, musician Milt Hinton thought it was the decline of silent movies that was critical, meaning a decline of pit orchestras, meaning fewer jobs—particularly for violinists—just as the Great Depression crept closer.[1] Lionel Hampton, bandleader and conservative, agreed with Hinton, and he mentioned in passing that it caused Hinton to switch from violin to a more supportive bass, since the opportunities for the former for a man like himself were not frequent.[2]

Saxophonist Russell Procope, born in New York City in 1908, was stunned by the discordance delivered by Prohibition. It meant frequent raids—"Even the Musicians' club they used to raid," he said, "on any trumped-up excuse because they used to have gambling in the back room and all that," that is, poker tables and blackjack tables. The "standing joke," he said, "was you could [go] in almost any apartment house and knock on almost any door and get something to drink," meaning more opportunities for raids.[3]

Prohibition may have contributed to a preexisting climate of repression. It was not the proximate cause of what Eddie Barefield endured in the 1920s. "Some rich man" hired him and his fellow musicians to play but "the cops caught them and beat them up and beat the guy that was giving the party. Some of the guys were crippled for the rest of their life and some of them died from it and [the cops] broke up all their instruments." Another time he was in Benny Moten's band in Beaumont, Texas, and "Jimmy Rushing was sitting on the bandstand with white socks on a guy walked up there and pulled out his gun and said, 'Nigger, take those white socks off.'"[4]

The musical genius Art Tatum had similar experiences in his native Toledo, where he was born in 1909. Pool halls and gambling joints were owned mostly by a Detroit mobster who had ties to the criminal "Purple Gang," which terrorized northern Ohio from the earliest days of Prohibition. Tatum honed his marvelous piano skills at Charlie's Chicken Shack, a nightspot in a Negro neighborhood owned by Johnnie Crocket, a place where mobsters were often found. Tatum at times played other gigs out of fear as a result of the pervasive influence of racketeers. Prohibition meant that these newer speakeasies were desperate for performers, a vacuum filled by the likes of Tatum.[5]

As in Toledo, so it was in Harlem, in that Prohibition brought more nightspots to the neighborhood. One estimate details that there were an astounding "twenty-two thousand speakeasies . . . in Manhattan alone" then, with a goodly number found uptown.[6] Beginning in 1923 and continuing for a decade, Harlem was characterized as the Port Said of the eastern seaboard of North America. Shortly after this fateful decade commenced, Owney Madden, the British-born jackanapes and racketeer, had compelled many African American club owners to sell their enterprises.[7] In further empowering mobsters, Prohibition brought more fear to musicians. Singled out in New York City were pianist Teddy Wilson and trumpeter Roy Eldridge. These two men were picked out to be examples in dissuading other musicians from moving downtown for a wage bonanza. Hyman "Feets" Edson was a manager of the film star George Raft, and both were in turn close friends of Owney Madden. Later, Edson managed Erskine Hawkins's band. This unsavory character began threatening to shoot off these musicians' fingers if they moved downtown. Unsurprisingly, Eldridge carried a weapon; as bandleader Artie Shaw put it, "he saw himself as traveling through a hostile land and he was right."[8]

Neither Toledo nor Harlem were sui generis. In St. Louis in the 1920s, as the popularity of the new music continued to spread, members of the segregated local of the American Federation of Musicians began a campaign to stop "white" establishments from hiring Negro musicians. This campaign took the form of picket lines in front of these enterprises. The problem for the picketers was that often these clubs were owned by racketeers who were hardly about to be intimidated by nonviolent protest.[9] In a sense, this protest boomeranged and provided an incentive for gangsters to solidify ties with Negro artists.

In some ways, what unfolded in the Mound City was a battle between the influential and virulently anti-Negro Ku Klux Klan and mobsters, embodied in the so-called Charlie Birger gang, named after the man born as Shachna Itzak Birger, of Lithuanian Jewish origin. Wielding their machine guns expertly, the Birger gang battled the KKK, and by the end of 1926 these terrorists, who also harbored anti-Semitism, were functionally inactive.[10] This did not happen through friendly persuasion. A typical incident occurred in September 1925 as a modest crowd was listening to a band, when without warning three men barged inside and opened fire with automatic weapons.[11] Before then a fracas erupted at a popular cabaret called Jazzland located at Grand and Easton not far from the Mississippi River. On one side was the Russo gang, composed of Italian American bootleggers. Their opponents included Klansmen known for holding mass rallies featuring thousands; at one gathering 1,000 men and 700 women were sworn in underneath two huge flaming crosses while Klan-friendly lawmen stood guard. Nonplussed after one confrontation, the gangsters sought to use dynamite against the KKK, also known to harbor anti-Catholic and anti-Italian forces.[12]

Miles Davis was born in this region and he well knew of the "bad gangs"—"real bad ones," he stressed that proliferated in his homeland. Davis also knew of the infamous massacre of Negroes in East St. Louis in 1917 that featured organized criminal efforts by Euro-Americans. "Black people there who survived used to talk about it. When I was coming up," said the trumpeter, "black people I knew never forgot what sick white people had done to them back in 1917."[13]

Roughly, Prohibition provided Negro artists with a difficult choice, symptomatic of the harsh options encountered by Africans since their arrival on these shores: ally with racketeers to foil Klansmen.

"What Prohibition did," says bandleader, Cab Calloway, "was place liquor under the control of the underworld gangs. And as long as the underworld controlled liquor, they controlled a number of clubs in Harlem as well," not to mention nationally, speaking of the sites where the new music was performed. "There was booze all over the country in those days," he said knowingly, "but there was more of it in Harlem." The profits were so handsome that bloody competition ensued, gang wars, with musicians often caught in the crossfire. Calloway recalled an attack in the 1920s on the aptly named Plantation Club in Harlem: "All the windows of the club had been broken and pieces of half the tables and chairs were on the sidewalk and in the street," leaving this performance venue in a "shambles," and the "mirrors on the walls . . . smashed to smithereens. Somebody had taken an axe to the tables and chairs. The hanging chandeliers had been pulled down and smashed," apparently at the behest of a competitor, the owners of the Cotton Club. In response, a few weeks later, Harry Block, a comrade of Owney Madden, suspected of sponsoring the assault, was found dead, his lifeless body riddled with bullets in the elevator of his apartment building. This violent atmosphere did not leave musicians unaffected, inexorably influencing their performances. Calloway recalled playing at the Crazy Cat at 48th and Broadway in Manhattan. "Four guys were sitting there with their coats and hats . . . from the mob. Wide-brimmed hats, long cloth coats, one of them had on shades. They were all white guys. I tried to be cool but inside I was scared to death." These men were exemplars of "pure muscle," for "'the mob didn't play games. They were for real." The performance setting was meant to transmit a not so subtle message. Thus, at the Cotton Club, said Calloway, "the bandstand was a replica of a southern mansion" from the slavery era; "even the name Cotton Club was supposed to convey the southern feeling. I suppose," he mused. "The idea was to make whites who came to the club feel like they were being catered to and entertained by black slaves." But it was not just Harlem that was unsettling; Calloway recalled a performance in St. Petersburg, Florida, where a racist patron tossed a bottle that bounced off the head of his drummer, Lester Maxey, leaving the dazed man, "bleeding like a stuck pig." Then in Texas he found a white man could hit a Negro in the mouth if he wanted to but had to pay a $300 fine as a token; his bandmate Benny Payne was thus assaulted but fought back, with a riot ensuing at the club.[14]

Interviewed by pianist Dr. Billy Taylor the bassist Milt Hinton corroborated the story about racists paying $300 for the opportunity to punch a Negro in the face. "They hit Cab Calloway . . . This is the God's honest truth," he added to calm the doubters. "We had to get off the bandstand and go down underneath . . . and that began Cab Calloway not wanting to do a lotta travelin' down there," meaning Dixie. "For a black group to come down with all this sophistication, they didn't like it too very much" there. As Calloway himself put it, "You comin' down here all sharp" like "New York slickers" and you had to "watch yourself" as a result. Since, said Hinton, "they didn't like us comin' down with all those beautiful shows. . . ."[15] Hinton added that seeking succor in Negro neighborhoods brought no necessary surcease. Usually traveling musicians "got overcharged by the local hotel owners and the people who ran the rooming houses. All of them were black," he said, "but that didn't matter. They knew we couldn't stay in the bigger places." Ruefully, Hinton observed, "We all resented this kind of treatment." Hinton thought that in turn "whites in these towns would try to turn local blacks against us," contributing to a circle of distrust.[16]

The Cotton Club, while barring Negroes as customers, hired Negro women as dancers and the like, though they had to be of lighter skin,

worsening a rift among African Americans, making them more susceptible to exploitation.[17] The influence of racketeers also facilitated
horrendous conditions for labor. Lena Horne recalls that when she
tried to quit working there, bosses "made it clear" this was unacceptable, instructing that "nobody had any right to quit a Cotton Club
job," a kind of neo-slavery apparently. They punctuated their objection
when "they got nasty. They beat him up," speaking of her agent—they
"dunked his head in the toilet bowl and threw him out."[18] The former
Cotton Club dancer Howard Johnson recalled that Horne's stepfather
was "beaten unmercifully" by thugs because he "once took issue when
the mobsters refused to raise Lena's pay."[19]

Organized crime was not a force for racial equality, in other words;
mobsters enforced a system that undergirded Jim Crow, rudely
imposing noxious effects on Negroes. Black people visited Smalls
Paradise in Harlem, though musician Danny Barker suggests there
was a trickle-down aspect of Jim Crow in that "black Cubans" visited
yet another club, while Barbadians went to another, and "people from
Virginia" to another and so on.[20]

Dempsey J. Travis, the Chicago-based writer, also spoke disparagingly of this conflicted era—the 1920s—when Owney Madden
controlled the East Coast's booze and beer distribution; Al Capone
reigned over Chicago and its environs; Johnny Lazia controlled the
police, liquor, and gambling in Kansas City, Missouri, and the Purple
Gang dominated Detroit's subculture—all sites where the new music
began to flourish. "These cities," says Travis, "were controlled by the
'Jazz Slave Masters' and some of the very best Black musicians were
their serfs. Talented jazz musicians were chained to bands and spe-
cific nightclubs and saloons in the same manner as the antebellum
Negroes were shackled to plantations." They were "inmates behind
the 'Cotton Curtain,'" an apt metaphor since control from the top was
so pervasive that many musicians found it difficult to perform at a site
not of a boss's choosing. This was all racially and ethnically coded, he
said, since "the keepers of the cash box were usually Jewish or Italian
and occasionally, they were mob-connected Blacks."[21]

His recollection was substantiated by the jazz singer Ada "Bricktop"
Smith, born in West Virginia in 1894, who ultimately chose voluntary

exile in Mexico after a lengthy stay as a club owner in France: "No one in the saloon business can avoid gangsters, hoods, petty crooks and other types of criminals," she conceded; this was a "built in nuisance." In 1924 she opened her Parisian nightspot and, she confessed, by then "the French underworld was beginning to take some cues from American gangsters. They got them from American gangster movies," pointing to these cinematic tributes as a primer in that it led these Parisians into "organizing protection rackets," indicating the global reach of U.S. piratical tactics. For these men could quickly "get nasty" and "those who protested found themselves at the wrong end of a bullet or a switchblade." As in the United States, these Gallic imitators also pushed prostitution—and "each time they were more threatening"—and then various illegal drugs. She began to arm herself as a result, mimicking those back home, the difference being that a Black woman in North America most likely would have had difficulty opening a club in the first instance.[22]

Horn man Benny Carter, born in 1907, in the early 1930s became acquainted with George Rich—"he was a great fan of mine," he conceded—who was a "sporting gentleman," a euphemism for gangster. When the Club Harlem was being liquidated, then in a losing rivalry with the Cotton Club, Rich intervened. When Carter visited him, "he started raising cushions . . . getting up cash from this chair, upholstered chair and from this sofa, and I never saw so much money, just being dug up right in front of me . . . and the next day he became the owner of the Club Harlem." His motivation? "You've got to have a place for your band," he told Carter, who, staggered, pointed out, "His only purpose for buying the club was to keep my band together." After a messy split with his spouse, Carter was "pretty broke and George loaned me $150 . . . to pay my fare back to Paris." Thus arose Benny Carter and "The Club Harlem Orchestra."[23] Not coincidentally, this beau geste also obligated the composer, arranger, and bandleader to this questionable patron.

This is no trifling matter since, according to critic Leonard Feather, Carter was a trailblazer because as a bandleader he was "the first genuine full-scale integrator," even though Benny Goodman is often given credit for this feat. But, says Feather, the bespectacled clarinetist hesitated to hire Coleman Hawkins at the behest of John Hammond, the producer. The emphasis on Goodman's purported trailblazing has hindered the necessity of focusing on others. For example, Feather stresses the pathbreaking efforts of Rex Stewart, perhaps the music's reigning intellectual, who was crossing the color line in hiring as early as 1934 in Harlem.[24]

As ever, those at the top of the pyramid of capitalism were the beneficiaries in the first instance. This list included Arnold Rothstein, termed by his biographer as "King of the Jews," who helped to fund the groundbreaking Negro musical *Shuffle Along*, which propelled the career of pianist Eubie Blake. Rothstein's personal aide, Thomas A. Farley, born in Virginia in 1875, was a "gentleman of color" who had his tuition to Columbia University paid by his benefactor. Rothstein was also accused of being one of the earliest of the drug dealers, reportedly importing 1,250 pounds of heroin and allying with opium dealers.[25] Pianist Fats Waller was friendly with Rothstein, though understandably wary of him.[26] Rothstein was not singular, for New York City also featured the presence of mobster Casper A. Holstein, whose roots were in the former Danish West Indies, recently purloined by Washington from Copenhagen.[27] By the 1920s he was running the Saratoga Club in Harlem.[28]

One of Holstein's comrades was another personality of Caribbean heritage, Stephanie St. Clair, born in Guadeloupe. Like others, she was concerned when he was kidnapped at gunpoint shortly after betting more than $30, 000 at Belmont Park; at the time he was sporting jewelry worth a like amount and thus a $50,000 ransom was demanded. Ultimately, he was released at 140th Street and Amsterdam in Harlem after frenetic negotiations. Shortly thereafter, Rothstein was shot in a New York hotel; this attack on the man viewed as the "kingpin" of Jewish organized crime was also viewed with grave concern by his comrades, as a small fortune tied up in gambling and speakeasies was at stake. But the problem for his Negro competitors was their lack of influence at City Hall, which meant they were to suffer greatly from police harassment, which proved to be undermining.[29]

The pervasiveness of Jim Crow continued to hamper the ability of Negroes to gain a foothold in the nightclub business and other venues where the new music was beginning to flourish. On the other hand, the "Great Migration," or the mass movement north from Dixie and the Caribbean to urban centers, also delivered the right to vote from those fleeing the Deep South and enhanced political power that could be leveraged for economic gain. Chicago was an example of this trend. What was called "policy" or "playing the numbers" was an ostensibly illegal lottery of sorts that was termed "the biggest black-owned business in the world with combined annual sales, sometimes reaching the $100 million mark and employing tens of thousands." Negroes profiting from this enterprise at times dabbled in the arts, bringing opportunities for musicians. These entrepreneurs under-wrote a thriving urban culture of theaters, dance halls, and the like. Those profiting included Jesse Binga, Eudora Johnson Binga, Fenton Johnson, and John "Mushmouth" Johnson. But as so often happened, the authorities viewed Negro wealth, particularly if produced by questionable means, with a more jaundiced eye than that generated by others similarly situated, particularly since their Euro-American competitors were often connected politically and able to wield such power on behalf of their cronies. Mr. Binga, banker, was arrested, convicted, and imprisoned and eventually became a janitor. Still, it was undeniable that a dazzling excitement emerged from this combi-nation of Negro gambling syndicates, Negro entertainment, and the related desire to forge Black Politics in order to elude the crushing of the two.[30]

Near the center of these trends was the famed pugilist Jack Johnson, a bass fiddler of note in his own right, who opened a popular club in Chicago as early as 1912.[31] Despite the problems faced by Negro musicians in places like Chicago, it was undeniable that compared to Dixie, including New Orleans,[32] migration northward had a lib-erating impact. This liberation was enjoyed noticeably by the pimps, card sharks, pool hustlers, and drug dealers who came to populate "Bronzeville" and the clubs there too.[33] Musician Milt Hinton found it unsurprising that Chicago emerged as a polestar of the new music, particularly compared to New York City, since the Illinois town had "three times as many blacks" as the eastern city, meaning "three times as many theaters and nightclubs as New York."[34]

Chicago was an unpropitious site for the ascension of this music. Prior to the influx of Negroes during the First World War era, Chicago already was known as a place where mobsters had deep influence over politics and judges. Labor racketeering was detected there as early as the 1890s, and criminally inclined comrades virtually controlled nearby Cicero, Stone Park, Calumet, and Chicago Heights.[35]

It took a while for Black political power to bloom in Chicago, and in the interregnum a gang war erupted in the 1920s with Al Capone emerging triumphant. The firebombing of clubs was not uncommon, with musicians caught in the crossfire. Similar warfare was detonated in Harlem with a Negro-owned club falling victim, contributing to the rise in this Manhattan neighborhood of Capone's colleagues and imitators. This led to violent attacks on musicians, giving rise to a desire for protection which took the form of self-help, that is, carrying of weapons and banding together in unions, or allying with one gangster faction to foil another. This latter factor influenced certain musicians to tout the wares of their protectors, which could mean more references to controlled substances in their music and lyrics.[36] The Italian mobster was viewed as one of the most important impresarios of the new music, hiring musicians to entertain at his enterprises.[37] Indeed, Capone has been called the "patron saint" of the new music; it was in Chicago that the saxophone was popularized and rapidly became the paradigmatic instrument of jazz.[38] The blaring of these horns could hardly drown out the cacophony of gunshots, for in 1926–27 most notably, there was an unbelievable skein of violence and carnage.[39]

Louis Armstrong arrived in Chicago during this tense moment, and mobsters helped him to get his first job in New York City after he arrived there from the Midwest in 1924.[40] Armstrong was subjected to extortion by plug-uglies early on. His life was threatened unless he forked over a sizeable portion of the money he received from performing. Still, it was whispered that these threats were propelled by musical competitors—defined as "white"— who resented his popularity.[41]

The ties Armstrong forged in Chicago shaped his career trajectory. Joe Glaser, who helped to shape his career as a manager and agent, was seen as a front for Capone via running one of the mobster's brothels; his venality was exposed when he was indicted for rape. In a sense, Armstrong chose one set of thugs to protect him against another; such was the sorry plight of musicians then. Glaser's mob connections meant that Armstrong was at times slated to appear in mob-tied joints, such as Ciro's in Philadelphia. These shark-infested waters also contributed to Armstrong accusing his then spouse—the protean pianist, composer and arranger Lil Hardin, who helped to shape his repertoire and early popularity—of "running around with one of the Chicago pimps while I was at work." Thus, a rift developed between the trumpeter and the woman who masterminded his early career.[42]

Andy Kirk, the bandleader, tubist, and saxophonist born in 1898, said that Glaser "acted like a crook." The fact that he almost did hard time in prison based on credible accusations of raping teenage girls added credence to this perception. "Nobody likes a little nigger pussy better than Joe Glaser" was his profane response. By 1928, he had received a ten-year sentence for attacking a fourteen-year-old girl. Still, a grateful Satchmo argued that Glaser "saved me from the gangsters." Besides music and boxing, the well-connected Glaser introduced the future movie mogul Jules Stein to mob mouthpiece Sidney Korshak: "Everyone knew that Stein worked for Al Capone in Chicago," remarked actor Robert Mitchum, indicating the reach of organized racketeering.[43] Like Kirk, bassist Milt Hinton was no fan of Glaser either. He was "the guy we all disliked because he was a terror . . . I knew him, I knew his . . . mother" he said of a man he dismissed as a mere "pimp."[44]

Glaser was born in 1897 and raised in Chicago and admits to running a "booking agency" at 127 North Dearborn by the early 1920s as musicians began descending upon the town.[45] He also owned and operated the Sunset Café, which later became the Grand Terrace, both hotspots for the new music. He claims that he boosted Armstrong's career when he hired him for "Carroll Dickenson's band," where he played "1st trumpet."[46] Glaser, the son of a physician, intended on following in his father's footsteps before he discovered an aversion to the sight of blood. He then left medical school. Often accused of running a "plantation," he also managed boxers, including such titans as Sugar Ray Robinson, Sonny Liston, and the man then known as Cassius Clay; he also dabbled in dog breeding and baseball. The wealth accrued allowed him to tool around town in a Rolls-Royce.[47] Prohibition's end, in other words, did not end opportunities for corrupt profiteering; it simply allowed exploiters to move their ill-gotten gains into other businesses or deepen their penetration of the music business.[48] The blustering Glaser, backed up by mobsters, had a grating voice and a low boiling point that terrified those forced to endure his unbridled wrath. [49] Profane curses and brutal imprecations were directed at those who displeased him, including clients responsible for his wealth, not to mention those seeking to hire his clients.[50] The tough voice and evil temperament terrified anyone confronted for the first time by his wrath.

The *Chicago Defender*, a lodestar of the Negro press, reported in 1928 that Glaser was a "firm member of the Al Capone organization"[51] and was said to have administered an "opium pad." The mob connected lawyer Sidney Korshak was Glaser's attorney, helping to make sure he did not wind up behind bars. The comedian and actor Bob Hope, who was to become fabulously wealthy, was also a Glaser client. Still, Armstrong was a prized client, as suggested by Glaser's impecuniousness when he first met the trumpeter. Soon he was raking in tens of thousands of dollars per week, with Armstrong a major reason why. In return, Glaser gifted a Star of David with rubies on a gold chain that adorned Armstrong's neck for the rest of his life. The cynicism of this arrangement was exposed when Glaser purportedly said of those like Armstrong, "these shines are all alike. They're so lazy." But the artist had few options. In the early 1930s he was confronted by cutthroats who demanded money and offered to "protect" him for a fee, inducing Armstrong to flee to Europe,[52] where he spent a year nursing a lip worn by overwork.[53]

This was a wise exit on his part since these mobsters had demanded $6,000 and threatened to murder him if he did not comply.[54] Safely abroad, Armstrong then unburdened himself, telling a journalist about the anxiety he felt when these miscreants invaded his dressing room in Chicago. "I stood up to them," he said from the safety of Europe, though quickly he "called for help. Thereafter I had a bodyguard of six men and one night the gangsters shot at me through the window of my motor car. . . . That really was the start of the campaign," he said with anger, adding boldly, "I had the opportunity to defy them." [55]

Glaser made no secret of his ties to Capone, apparently feeling that it could be intimidating. "Shine" was not the only disparaging term he heaped on his Negro clients; he added "schwarzes," a like insult. The critic Nat Hentoff once saw a painting of the antebellum South on the wall of his office, featuring "happy darkies playing banjo and singing."[56] Glaser was asked once how he became involved in show business. "On account of the whorehouses," was his prompt reply, implying that enterprise's tie to the performing arts. Digging into the bottom drawer of his desk, he extracted a photo of two old brownstones. The picture revealed two men standing by a used car lot with a large sign reading "Joe Glaser's Used Car Symposium": one man was Glaser, the other was Roger Touhy, one of his salesmen, an apprenticeship before he became a leading racketeer and a supplier for Glaser's brothels.[57]

Jimmy McPartland, a former spouse of the more celebrated Marian, a pianist, confirms that "everybody worked for the mob in Chicago. Al Capone used to come into one place where I was . . . he'd send one of his torpedoes over with a fifty or a hundred. One night one of 'em shot a hole in Jim Lanigan's bass and then asked him how much a new one would cost," a maneuver that doubtlessly was attention grabbing.[58]

Earl "Fatha" Hines the pianist, born in 1903, knew well the racketeer-influenced Grand Terrace in Chicago where he often performed. "They always had four or five men there—floating [near] me" and "pistol play" was recurrent. "I was heading for the kitchen one night and this guy went pounding past and another guy came up behind me and told me to stand still and rested a pistol on my shoulder and aimed at the first guy and would have fired if the kitchen door hadn't swung shut in time. Some of the waiters even had pistols." Unabashedly, he confessed, "Racketeers owned me too," but fortunately, as the progressive movement gained momentum, Hines said he "bought my way out of the Grand Terrace in 1940 after I finally learned about all the money I was making and wasn't seeing."[59] Hines worked routinely from 10:30 in the evening until 4:30 in the morning, seven nights per week. Despite the violent madness swirling all around, he and his bandmates were "like three monkeys: see no evil, hear no evil, speak no evil. Otherwise you might be found dead in Jackson Park someplace."[60] The critic Stanley Dance commented about the pianist, "There is scarcely anything he hates more than writing letters"[61]—unsurprisingly, and to the detriment of history, but perhaps a reflection of nervousness about committing innermost thoughts to paper for fear of where they might end up.

Seeking to protect the value of this performer, Capone provided Hines with a bodyguard. Unlike other artists, Hines said he did not pack a pistol though he had an astonishing "40 or 50 bodyguards" alongside him. He may have needed every one when he arrived in Valdosta, Georgia: "Some hecklers in the crowd turned off the light and exploded a bomb under the bandstand. Sometimes when we came into a town, the driver of our chartered bus would tell us to move to the back of the bus to make it look all right and not get anyone riled up." The problem? Those soaked in the brine of Jim Crow "never expected to see the Negroes dressed like we were, have the intelligence and self-assurance that we had." "We were the first freedom riders," said a weary Hines later, speaking of his travails then: "It was brutal in those days." As for mobsters, he said, "I knew Al Capone like I'm talking to you . . . he used to come to the Grand Terrace two or three times a week and he would say, 'I don't like your handkerchief. And fix the handkerchief and there was a fifty dollar [bill] in it.'"[62]

"Pittsburgh was no heaven," said Hines, speaking of his former city of residence, "but when I got to Chicago, I thought it was the worst town in the world. I found some of the most dangerous people in the country on 35th Street when I started working there. I knew how to duck and dodge but somebody was always getting hurt. Everybody carried a gun and you had to act as though you were at least a bit bad."[63]

Hines was a stern critic of the evolving economic underpinning of the music business. A "good part of the blame for the doldrums that has many top-rate musicians toting bags in railroad stations belongs with the handful of booking agents who are strangling jazz with their monopoly hold," he said. This was a "hangover from the days when gangsters muscled in on the entertainment world and used nightclubs as a front for their rackets. I know because I indirectly worked for the mob. . . . There's not a single big name of the show world . . . Duke Ellington . . . Cab Calloway, Louis Armstrong—who haven't at one time or another had contact with the syndicates," meaning mobsters.[64]

The aforementioned pianist, composer, and bandleader Duke Ellington, born in 1899 in Washington, D.C., had a similar experience near the same time. While performing in Chicago, mobsters sought to extort him. They presented their demand to Sam Fleischnick, who was then the Washingtonian's road manager. "All our boys carry guns," he replied, adding with gusto, "If you want to shoot it out, we'll shoot it out." The suave Ellington considered fleeing when he heard of this contretemps, but then he telephoned the influential owner of a Manhattan club and this man arranged for the Ellington band to survive without overt molestation in Chicago.[65] But mimicking Armstrong, he forged an alliance with Irving Mills, born in Russia in 1894, who somehow became the publisher of some of the pianist's most famous compositions, including "It Don't Mean a Thing If It Ain't Got That Swing," "Sophisticated Lady," and "Mood Indigo," which enriched this manipulator and his descendants.[66] Mills also was an agent for Cab Calloway. Mills succeeded Moe Gale after, said the bandleader, "the mob and Herman Stark" intervened.[67]

John Hammond, who worked for Mills, was moved to remark "how tremendously Duke was being exploited" by Mills. A consensus has emerged that Mills's lengthy and fabulously successful career was underwritten by his lion's share of Ellington's copyrighted tunes.[68] It was not just Ellington, however. Evidently, Fats Waller, on July 17, 1929, for a pittance, assigned all rights, title, and interest in such iconic tunes as "Ain't Misbehavin'" and, ironically, "What Did I Do to Be So Black and Blue" and other leading compositions to Mills.[69] Thus, by December 1944, Waller's widow was advised solemnly that she visit the "collector of Internal Revenue and advise him that you have received no income from your husband's estate."[70]

The restrained Leonard Feather termed "questionable" the practice of Mills of putting his name on Ellington's compositions: "I don't
think he wrote a note of music in his life," he said of Mills. Mills, said
Feather, even placed his name on a composition, "Mighty Like the
Blues," that the critic wrote. In response to Mills, Ellington formed
Tempo Music, one of the first Negro-owned publishing companies, a
move soon emulated by Jimmy Lunceford. W. C. Handy was among
the very first Negro composers to become a publisher, said Feather,
while adding accurately that it remained "very difficult for anybody
black to make much headway because of the tremendous amount of
racism that was prevalent" in the United States.[71]

Ellington well knew that the modus operandi of these unscrupulous thugs included dropping in on targeted clubs, shutting the
doors, and ordering the entire staff—band, chorus "girls," and singing and dancing waiters—to put on a show, with failure to comply
inviting brutal retaliation. Ellington probably knew of likewise situated nightspots in his own town of Washington, while in Chicago he
spoke directly of the unfortunate tuba player Mack Shaw: "The police,
gangsters, or somebody had caught Mack out in Chicago, beaten his
face in and broken up all the bones. This cat would be blowing his
tuba and blow out a loose bone. He had a whole lot of loose bones
in his face and he'd just put them together again and continue blowing." Ellington was an habitué of the Cotton Club in Manhattan and
knew that this enterprise was connected in turn to mobsters both in
the Empire State and Philadelphia; little "Brotherly Love" was exuded
when gangsters in the latter town were seeking to induce a club owner
there to allow Ellington to escape a gig there so that his band could
perform in Manhattan. A few well-chosen words proved to be convincing, and Ellington and his band headed hurriedly northward.[72]
Ellington, who was the subject of a 1931 kidnapping plot, came to
carry a pistol, along with his "entire band," he confided.[73]

Sited at 142nd Street and Lenox Avenue in Harlem, the Cotton
Club generally barred Negroes from entering, even when they arrived
alongside others not so designated. As was the case generally, the local
police sternly warned that racially mixed couples should be barred. It
had been owned by Bernard Levy, well known as a bootlegger and

numbers banker,[74] before the notorious racketeer Owney Madden seized control.[75]

Madden was quite the character, according to Ellington drummer Sonny Greer. "He was over Dutch Schulz, Al Capone and all of them." Madden was a "little, tiny guy. Talked like a girl" with an accent that betrayed his British origins, but he also owned a casino in Hot Springs, Arkansas, and thus was familiar with the worst Jim Crow had to offer. Yet, said Greer, he "loved Duke because him and Duke used to sit up and play 'Grits' and all that, 'Coon Can' all night long. . . . He loved Duke and he loved me." Mercer Ellington, the bandleader's son, realized that Madden appreciated the profit generated by these artists, allowing for money laundering so that cash from his illicit enterprises could be sanitized: "It was a way to turn over a good front." Barney Bigard, another bandmate, sensed a split between Madden and Capone, leaving Ellington to lean toward the former: "This guy was Duke's bodyguard. He'd go get Duke from the theatre with his machine gun between his legs, and they had bullet-proof glass. You see there were two factions. . . . They had to protect their men from each other."[76] Like many mobsters, Madden had varied political ties, including to the still potent Tammany Hall in New York City.[77]

Ellington was not the only musician who had to confront the malignant influence of organized crime. "My Uncle Richard and Al Capone had a good business relationship," said vibraphonist Lionel Hampton. "Capone called my uncle every day." Hampton, who became a key fundraiser for the Republican Party, saw the mobster as a kind of latter-day Medici, responsible for the rise of the new music. "History has proved that Al Capone was the savior of the black musicians in those days. His nightclubs alone employed hundreds."[78] Hampton, born in 1908, received his first vibraphone from a wealthy uncle who had been the leading bootlegger on Chicago's South Side and also served as manager for songstress Bessie Smith.[79]

Musician Mezz Mezzrow, born in 1899, who "learned to play the sax in Pontiac Reformatory," knew that Capone "owned a piece of the Arrowhead," a favorite haunt of clubbers, "as well as the whole town, including the suburbs." The club was sited in neighboring Indiana. As a result of this ownership tie, the music itself was downgraded,

termed contemptuously "'nigger music'" and "'whorehouse music,'"
with those plying their trade in this musical form "looked down on."
As for Burnham, Indiana, the site of these escapades, it was basically
a Capone subsidiary, ensuring degradation. "There never was a town
sewed up as tight as Burnham," said Mezzrow of a town that "was
under the syndicate. The chief of police was our bartender and all the
waiters were aldermen."[80] Agreeing, trumpeter and bandleader Max
Kaminsky argued that during the 1920s "almost everyone in Chicago
in those days was sooner or later, in one way or another—mostly
another—involved with racketeers and gangsters."[81]

Playing before often drunken audiences, replete with racists with
pistols, Armstrong and other artists were vulnerable, as they focused
on their performances and not necessarily the dangers that lurked.
Then there was the basic issue: would one be paid after working?
Danny Barker saluted Bert Hall, a trombonist, politician, and gambler
who left Chicago for New York City and attracted adherents when he
helped to introduce reforms into the musicians' union local that were
welcomed by Negro members who had been victimized more than
most by employers who refused to pay performers, serving further to
explain Armstrong's tie-up with Glaser. Barker also recalled that "Jelly
Roll" Morton was among the artists who was "forever beefing" about
being cheated by the American Society of Composers, Authors and
Publishers (ASCAP) and the mangling of his copyright protection
and how he was induced to sign "his songs over to some publishers
and they became wealthy but Jelly received no royalties as the composer." Then those like Morton were cheated further when "a whole
lot of black music . . . wasn't played on radio stations, theaters and
Hollywood movies. This was done purposely through racism." In a
metaphorical ending for the man who was said to have invented the
new music, Barker recalled that "an old underworld acquaintance of
Jelly's, a dope fiend and a notorious thief, sneaked into the undertak-
ing parlor during the night and with a chisel and a hammer, removed
the four-carat diamond from Jelly's front tooth"[82] and then departed.

Being cheated was part of the job of being a Negro musician then.
"We were stranded all over the United States," said saxophonist, Eddie
Barefield, born in 1909. Why? At times, the promoter would not pay

them or "sometimes the guys would run off with the money after the intermission and leave us."[83] One could not necessarily trust the bandleader or his favored mates. Once he told a band he was with that he was departing for Cab Calloway's group, and a "free-for-all on the bandstand" ensued and "everybody jumped on me but . . . Roy Eldridge" and one other. "I was just throwing guys all over the bandstand. We fought all the way down to the hotel" for "ten or fifteen blocks," followed by "fighting in the cars." Yet "they didn't pay me anyway and I ended up with a black eye."[84]

CLUBS THAT FEATURED PERFORMANCES of the new music had appeared in Manhattan in the 1920s. The Village Vanguard, which became the premier venue for star artists, started as an all-purpose entertainment joint in 1934 but quickly turned to jazz. It is likely that it is the oldest club where this music is played in the world, or outside of New Orleans, at least. By 1936, Nick Rongetti, a lawyer and aficionado of the music, opened an eponymous club, Nick's, at the corner of Seventh Avenue and 10th Street, which highlighted so-called traditional jazz. By 1945, as the music reached a critical turning point, Eddie Condon opened a club carrying his surname, with gangster backing, indicating that this force remained resonant.[85]

This "traditional" form of the music was exemplified by the appropriately named Paul Whiteman, who somehow gained the moniker "King of Jazz." Like LaRocca, his being surrounded by African American musicians did not seem to impact him positively but instead seemed to engender the opposite reaction, as when he bet on the size of the penis of Negro musician Wilbur Daniels. Of course, this was during a time when these descendants of the enslaved were routinely and insultingly referred to as "jigaboos."[86] This was during a time, says pianist Dr. Billy Taylor, "when white artists took most of the credit for jazz."[87]

This was also during a time when the music was seen as a vector of degradation—propelled by the degraded—particularly in the degradation of women defined as "white."[88] What this hysterical reaction reflected was that African American artists were talented and, at times, had celebrity and income, making them attractive to some

Euro-American women, a confluence of circumstances that at times had generated violence and lynching. The clubs where the music was performed were often the site of what was termed euphemistically as "race mixing," seen as a foretaste of the collapse of the color line generally, meaning stiffer competition for resources (and sex).[89]

This injurious influence had an impact on artists. At a time when much music degraded Negroes as "prancing, dancing and fighting," the eminent composer and violinist Will Marion Cook, born in 1869, was said to carry a weapon, but worse, he took his anti–New Deal propaganda to outspoken heights.[90] It was Cook who controversially demanded a boycott of Louis Armstrong given his management ties since "the Jews of Hollywood, the stage [etc.] exploit only the worst and basest of my race. Let's stop it now." This would have been bad enough if he had chosen to stop there but, instead, he punctuated his inflamed remarks with "Heil Hitler!" He had studied music in Berlin[91] and was an example of Negroes whose outlook had been so warped by the United States that they turned to outright fascism.

As Prohibition was lurching to a close, coincidentally the Great Depression began to bite, inducing a further outflow of musicians from New Orleans. The mostly Euro-American musicians who came to characterize the music known as Dixieland also included musicians who reflected the dominant culture of Jim Crow, hampering the ability of interracial combos, further limiting opportunities for Black musicians.[92] Danny Barker was among the artists forced to flee northward, in his case, to New York City. Pushing them out was the prospect of "more money. Make more money. [Being] treated better" than in Dixie, though some "stayed there," meaning Louisiana, "because their wives didn't want them to go." Yet, Barker continued, "the Depression set and there was no work" since this wave of misery "hit the South earlier than it hit other parts of the country." After arriving in New York he found more suffering musicians, "dying of grief," including those with "great talent. They became alcoholics. They became dope addicts . . . bums on the street begging for nickels . . . they'd be downtown with their hands out, begging . . ." Taking pity, his spouse "fed more musicians than the Salvation Army" to the point where Barker "had to put iron bars by the doors to keep them from [kicking down]] my kitchen" door. As for New York, he said with bitter experience, "It'll make a man out of you or kill you . . . all that goes with the music."[93]

3. One O'Clock Jump

IT WAS NOT JUST CHICAGO AND HARLEM and Paris that benefited from the mass flight from Dixie. Roy Wilkins, who was to become a leader of the National Association for the Advancement of Colored People, was residing in Kansas City during this era. This midwestern metropolis on the Missouri-Kansas border was a hotbed of organized crime—and Jim Crow, too. The difference with Dixie was the ability of many more to cast a vote, and that modicum of political power was hardly minor and certainly was perceived as such by those fleeing Arkansas and Mississippi for this town. Still, Wilkins recalled then that "in those days, even good manners could be a crime for a black man," and apartheid was prevalent "right down to [the] bootstraps" in that "neighborhoods, schools, churches, hospitals, theaters and just about everything else were as thoroughly segregated as anything in Memphis." There was a "large black ghetto," said Wilkins that proved to be a hothouse for the flourishing of emerging musical trends. "Most Negroes in town," he said, "were jammed into the Central East Side," while on the "North Side," there were "Italians and Negroes [who] lived easily side by side," though this was in a sense illusory since "there didn't seem to be any limit to what the white people would do to keep blacks from moving up," including violence. The *Kansas City Star*, the major mainstream newspaper, did not report on the bombings designed to keep Negroes from moving into apartheid neighborhoods and "refused to print even a photograph of a Negro." This miasma of intimidation meant, he said, that "almost all entertaining was done in the home, because the Jim Crow laws barred black people from most public watering holes, theaters and the like." This presupposed that those willing to violate this brutal edict were sufficiently hardened to be unafraid of confrontation. Wilkins, a journalist for the Negro press, was told by the authorities that he was a "marked man" because of his willingness to expose illegal activity, a salient factor that ultimately contributed to his departure for Manhattan.[1]

Others were not as lucky in escaping and had to deal with the far-reaching political machine of Tom Pendergast, who was sufficiently powerful to propel one of his underlings, Harry S. Truman, into the White House. As in Chicago, there were "Negro jazz raids," this time aided by the city's police chief, John Miles. At that point, "KCMO" had more murders per capita than Chicago, but the authorities seemed preoccupied with rousting Negro musicians and club owners. The pressure placed on both, which induced frazzled harriedness, may have played a role in the impromptu performances now known as "jam sessions."[2]

Brothels and gambling joints flourished under Pendergast's dominion, as he invested heavily in construction materials, liquor, taxicabs, hotels, and race tracks, all of which were facilitated by his political tentacles stretching from the suites to the streets.[3] *Time* magazine, then arbiter of middlebrow opinion, announced with wonder in 1934 that Pendergast's machine was responsible for "nominating and electing" a mere "county judge, Harry S. Truman, to the U.S. Senate."[4] As early as 1931, Truman gushed, "I am obligated to the Big Boss," speaking of Pendergast, who, he claimed curiously, was "all man."[5]

Pendergast was ruthless, with a quick and at times violent temper, made more menacing by his coarse, gravelly voice. Thousands worked for him, including those who tended to his horses. He was a hopelessly addicted gambler on horses, and during the depths of the Great Depression he bet millions of dollars monthly, sometimes losing a hundred thousand dollars in a single day, a loss facilitated by the immense profits he garnered from payoffs, kickbacks, bribes, and other bounties of graft. Because of his mismanagement, Kansas City had the greatest per capita deficit ever accumulated by a U.S. municipality. He routinely deployed thugs at electoral polls to guarantee results. His crew included plug-uglies, ruffians, and ex-convicts who would beat senseless any who complained. He thus had a unique tie to the underworld, yet Senator Truman assailed his prosecutors from the floor of Congress.[6]

This rationalization occurred, although threats, violence, and bombings accompanied Negro attempts to escape neighborhoods where they were consigned. Red-light districts favorable to brothels were sited routinely in Negro neighborhoods too, and then grew exponentially during the Pendergast reign since his machine skimmed a percentage of their profits. Pendergast and his comrade Johnny Lazia installed other forms of vice in Negro vicinities. Naturally police were far more draconian in confronting Negro-operated vice, as opposed to other varieties. There was a harbinger of the post-1932 shift of the Negro vote nationally from the Republicans to the Democrats: in brief, this shift was evident as early as 1925 in Kansas City. Ellis Burton and Felix Payne, Negro gamblers and nightclub owners, were in the vanguard of this epochal transition. However, this didn't bar the 1929 kidnapping of Payne by his alleged "'business partners" with the order to produce $20,000 cash. The unseemly Burton was accused of hiring a thug to assault an organizer for the predominantly Negro union, the Brotherhood of Sleeping Car Porters. Bandleader Benny Moten, according to instrumentalist "Hot Lips" Page, was tied directly to Pendergast.[7] Pendergast formed an alliance with Felix Payne, local Negro powerbroker, who was co-owner of the Kansas City Giants, a Negro baseball team. He also initiated a Negro newspaper and, like Pendergast, was close to Moten. However, when Pendergast fell, so did this periodical, along with clubs that employed the likes of Moten.[8]

But Moten and other Negro musicians did not have many choices. Not only did the local philharmonic orchestra refuse adamantly to hire these artists but also barred them from attending concerts. However, at Western University, the "Tuskegee Institute of the Midwest," across the river in Kansas City, Kansas, Negro artists found a niche and were educated in the intricacies of music, and this trickled down to public elementary and high schools and into the wider community. As early as the 1920s, Negro elementary school teachers introduced into the curriculum of their schools the history of African Americans in music.[9]

Even after being placed on probation in the aftermath of a criminal conviction. Pendergast violated the terms of this status by aiding Senator Truman's political campaigns. In fact, his nephew, Jimmy Pendergast, directed the successful attempt to win the Democratic nod for the future president.[10] It was not just Truman who sought Pendergast's favors, according to officialdom. Despite being described as a "political boss" by the authorities, governors, judges, and the like were "craving" an "audience and favors" from him. His influence over the "ready mixed concrete" market provided him with further reach in this boomtown. "Vote fraud investigations and prosecutions" dogged him.[11]

But as powerful as Pendergast was, in some ways he played second fiddle and deferred to Johnny Lazia, the top mobster in Kansas City. Born in 1897, he was jailed in 1916 on charges of highway robbery, but then received an early release from a Pendergast-connected lieutenant governor. One of his early ventures was forcing stores to carry his soft drinks. He claimed to control 7,500 votes of fellow Italian Americans.[12] These voters, it was thought, were not necessarily progressive. As African Americans moved into neighborhoods favored by these relatively recent immigrants, they were said to have "turned with fury" on the newcomers, as "homes of Negroes were dynamited."[13]

Lazia was part of a wider influx from Sicily that arrived in the Midwest in the late nineteenth century. Many had arrived in New Orleans, then fled north for various reasons, one factor being the lynching of the 1890s (suggesting that the lack of a direct river tie between the two cities did not bar connection). Many worked in the packing houses and rail yards of the Midwest. Many fell under the influence of "Brother John"—Lazia—and his burly bodyguard, Charles Carrollo. They effectuated an entente with their Irish and Irish-American competitors, on the higher altar of "whiteness."[14] In other words, by the beginning of the new century, many of the clubs in New Orleans were owned by Sicilian immigrants and tied to organized crime, but rampant bias drove many away to more favorable climes in Missouri and Illinois.[15]

Pendergast was receiving tens of thousands of dollars regularly from dog races, a good deal of which was poured into his incessant gambling, particularly on horseracing. Testifying against him, New Orleans' Arthur Slavin, a nightclub owner in Kansas City with ties to the Cuban Gardens, spoke almost enviously about one of Lazia's clubs: it "had a dance floor and dining room one side and a casino on the other side for gambling. Dice games, card games"—and more. Local banks were among Lazia's boosters, he said; they were eager to handle his cashier's checks. At one point, Lazia had an accident crossing a bridge and the result was that his eyes were affected, causing furious blinking and twitching. His spouse, Marie Lazia, says her husband "nearly lost his eye; he was ill for a long time" too, leading to "three operations." By 1929, "he was not up at all," virtually recumbent. He had developed glaucoma. Cuban Gardens opened on September 15, 1929, but Lazia was not in the mood to enjoy the festivities: "I had to wear a bandage on my right eye all through the year 1929," he told the court and "it made me nervous" since "my eye was inflamed. . . ." It was "terrible, torture, terrible pain," he said, speaking in early 1934. Lazia's bodyguard Carrollo, a felon but president of North Side Finance Company, was also an investor in Cuban Gardens. His alias was "Charlie the Wop" and along with Lazia he too was indicted for violating laws on prohibition of alcohol.[16]

In the courtroom, Lazia's jaws and teeth rhythmically chomped on a wad of gum while he kept blinking, his weak eyes barely glimpsed through his thick spectacles. Previously it had been observed that Lazia was frequently in and out of the office of Eugene C. Reppert, the local police chief.[17] It was Pendergast who appealed to White House honcho James Farley for assistance in settling the income tax charges faced by Lazia.[18]

In early July 1934, shortly before dawn, Lazia, a power in the Democratic Party political machine, was struck with a hail of machine gun bullets. Before expiring, he said breathlessly, "If anything happens," call Pendergast, "my best friend, and tell him I love him." Presumably, Lazia's attempt to elbow his way into the beer business contributed to his demise. Lazia and his fellow corrupt politicos had been receiving payoffs from increasingly restive owners of beer parlors and night club proprietors. The funeral procession for Lazia extended for several miles, an indication of the overwhelming majorities at the polls he helped to deliver to Pendergast.[19]

At the zenith, there were about 250 clubs performing the new music in Kansas City. After Lazia's murder, scrutiny of these enterprises intensified, to their detriment. Musicians were not oblivious to or protected from this gunplay. After Lazia's death, Jesse Price and his bandmates were ordered into a large automobile by armed gangsters and driven to a lonely spot on Cliff Drive overlooking the city. There the mobsters impressed upon them the naked power wielded by nightclub operators, hammering home the utter seriousness of their anti-union policies, meaning, of course, that musicians better not complain about poor pay levels.[20]

AS SO FREQUENTLY HAPPENS AMONG the U.S. right wing in their perpetual quest to dilute the potency of Negro-phobia, a myth developed suggesting that Irish Americans too faced rampant bias, not unlike that which ensnared Negroes, up to and including signs stating, "No Irish Need Apply"; as an attempt to dilute the poisonousness of white supremacy, this was an urban myth of victimization in that, as one analyst put it, "the names of local politicians read like the roster of a unit in the Irish Republican Army." The Scotch-Irish Truman was among those favored, as suggested by his moniker: the "Senator from Pendergast." Appropriately, the outlaw Frank James, brother of the more renowned Jesse, ended his life as a bouncer and floorwalker in the Pendergast-controlled Jefferson Hotel. The Pendergast machine was heavily larded with saloonkeepers and gamblers, the constituency often found when the new music was being exhibited. The machine routinely raided clubs whose owners did not pay tribute, meaning that Pendergast was making a great deal of money by the 1930s. The machine was close to the Catholic Church and parochial schools, providing Pendergast with ever more far-reaching tentacles.[21]

Saxophonist Buddy Tate, who wound up in Kansas City, hailed from Sherman, Texas, a Jim Crow bastion. In 1926, at the age of thirteen, he began playing professionally. And by the age of fourteen, he was performing before segregated audiences, recalling that "you had to kind of stick more to dance music when you played for the white crowd. . . . Playing with the black crowd you could swing all night," raising by implication the matter of what impact segregation had on the music's evolution. His mother wanted him to be a physician, but his father died, and he wound up in Kansas City playing with Andy Kirk's band. As for Pendergast, he concluded, "Everybody dug him," since "he let you make money."[22]

"I knew old Thomas personally," said musician Eddie Durham, born in 1906 in San Marcos, Texas, speaking of Pendergast. Thus Durham well knew why "liquor stores stayed open 24 hours a day" and how and why the machine "would protect . . . gangsters." Negroes worked for Johnny Lazia and vicariously thought "they were big shots because they worked for this big gangster." Often they were armed, just like the leader of the musicians' union and Durham himself: "Everybody in Benny Moten's band had guns." This was necessary for Moten since he would promote dances himself, foiling traditional promoters: "He would rent the auditorium himself" and the "band [served as] the bouncers . . . the reed section all had automatics and the voice section all had revolvers . . . I had a .45." Once Durham went to church and was chagrined when his pistol "fell out" with a clang.[23]

"Everybody carried a gun," mused bandleader Count Basie, born in Red Bank, New Jersey, in 1904, speaking of Kansas City, including "machine guns"; this also meant that "bulletproof vests" were de rigueur. In the ubiquitous clubs, patrons would "shoot at each other, and if you played a song they didn't like, they'd shoot you" too.[24]

The pianist Mary Lou Williams, born in 1910, recalled that in Kansas City "'most of the nightspots were run by politicians and hoodlums and the town was wide open for drinking, gambling and pretty much every form of vice." Bandleader Abie Price carried a pistol—then accidentally destroyed several of his toes with this ill-placed weapon.[25]

Williams, one of the few women to be found on the bandstand, also was aware of the casual corruption that routinely defrauded musicians. Joe Glaser, whose main client was Armstrong, also represented Missourians and was known to maintain double books, that is, as an agent he booked bands at a certain fee, then paid artists at a lower rate, pocketing the difference, plus his percentage of what was taken in at the "door." Andy Kirk, bandleader, told her as much, stressing that "a lot of these promoters stole from the black acts at that time. . . . We were making enough, more than the average black anyway. They [were] skimming off the top, but we knew it." Yet how could they respond effectively given the class and racist biases encoded in society? "'Besides Andy," Williams continued, "Glaser stole from Louis and all the black acts he had, like Lionel Hampton." However, since there was reason to believe that Kirk too kept two sets of books, his victimization seemed less dire. Glaser also swindled Williams.[26]

"See, it's a gangster town," concluded guitarist Eddie Durham, speaking of Kansas City. "I met Pretty Boy Floyd there and I saw Baby Face Nelson," referring to two of the more bloodthirsty mobsters. "These guys paid you double for anything you ever done in Kansas City. They never owed a musician a nickel," unlike other patrons.[27] Buster Smith, a saxophonist who served as a mentor for the better-known Charlie "Bird" Parker,[28] knew that in Kansas City "'big clubs were [run by] . . . big gangsters and they were the musician's best friend," at least paying them after performing. But this patronage came at a high price, as musicians were subjected to a cesspool of gambling, live sex shows, and the like. Waitresses at times picked up their tips with their labia. The Chesterfield Club featured four categories of naked waitresses, two "white," two "black" with pubic hair shaved to represent a heart, spade, diamond, and club. Said Durham, understatedly, "The clubs were very risqué." Bassist Gene Ramey, born in 1913, recalled that as late as 1934, "nude women [were] working there every night," referring to certain clubs where the new music was played. There were "'teenaged boys" sneaking peeks through unguarded windows, though he did not reflect upon the impact of social mores or gender conceptions more generally of such displays. However, he did say that as Prohibition was coming to a close, "the mob began to shift into narcotics sales," with even more impact on the wider community.[29] (In this context, the escapades of Eubie Blake should be noted. His relations with women reflected the degradation of women that flowed from mob-controlled performance venues, as did the relations of others in this environment. Several of his lovers committed suicide as a direct result of their interactions with him, and others were beaten by their spouses, while Blake deplored same-sex coupling. According to an observer, "He hated for show business men, even straight ones, to hug him or kiss him.")[30]

According to a biographer of Charlie Parker, Kansas City clubs featured "men in dresses . . . performing oral sex on other men. . . . Women had sex with other women. Some puffed cigars with their vaginas, others had sex with animals."[31]

This gangster-dominated climate not only shaped patriarchy and degradation. Gene Ramey recalled an era when bandleaders left the musicians they had hired stranded and then bolted with their wages or gambled these dollars away. Or, when the time came to pay musicians, they would receive the equivalent of 50 cents, rather than the $1.50 promised. But even a bandleader like Basie could be cheated by a club owner, as evidenced by a time when he had patches in his pants and holes in his pockets, as he walked the "streets, trying to be a dignified beggar." One time, Ramey and his fellow musicians had been stranded and were all jammed into one room.

But why did Kansas City, of all places, become a beacon for the new music? Gene Ramey arrived there on August 18, 1932, via the "hobo" route, that is, hitching rides undetected on trains, many of which were headed to this center of stockyards. He also played semi-pro basketball, and the sport was developed—if not invented in essence—in nearby Lawrence, Kansas. It quickly became popular among Negro men who saw this college town as a place to know. Another diversion was the fact, said Ramey, that marijuana grew wild along the highway headed to Omaha.[32]

Basie may have been bilked by club owners, but the musician Buster Smith asserts that the bandleader was not wholly innocent. He told the rotund pianist, "I don't think you done me fair about that 'One O'Clock Jump,'" the signature tune of his band as Basie pleaded, "Don't sue me." This was a turnabout in what Smith had thought was a mutually fruitful relationship. "He loved gin and I did too," said Smith. "We were sipping on gin and I'm griping." Undeterred, Smith also mentored Kansas City's own Charlie Parker when the saxophonist turned up in New York City. "He hoboed it there," said Smith. "He came up and slept in the bed in the daytime and my wife and I slept in the bed at night."[33]

IT WAS NOT JUST KANSAS CITY that presented a danger to life and limb. Playing before Euro-American audiences in southern states such as Texas was bound to engender friction too. Once in the 1930s, bandleader Woody Herman was onstage in Texas when he was handed a note demanding that he "stop playing those nigger blues," a crudity that underscored how bluntly Black artists were barred from profiting from their compositions.[34] In the 1930s when the band of King Oliver arrived to play in Texas, one of the musicians recalled that "everyone rushed to see the boys get out of the bus," but "when the driver put the lights on they were struck dumb because we were colored. We unpacked and went into the hall and started to play but no one came in, so the man giving the dance went out and asked [why] they didn't come in, they remarked that they didn't dance to colored music. We were then told to pack up and leave immediately and there were many cars which followed us out of town."[35] Presumably the musicians had not been in violation of a related social norm, that is, it was verboten to be driven by a man defined as "white."[36]

Juan Tizol, a Puerto Rican trombonist born in 1900 who played with Ellington, had similar difficult experiences in the Southwest, which cried out for the development of a countervailing force. Once in Dallas, he recalled, "we were getting ready to play and there were a lot of people there and people started looking at me," probably because he was of a lighter hue than his bandmates. Then he was asked rudely, "'What are you doing playing with those niggers?" At other times, he would be able to fetch food for the band from sites where darker-skinned musicians were banned. "I'd get some food and take it to them," he said. "I used to do that all the time down South."[37]

Further north, bassist turned agent and manager John Levy was performing in Cicero, Illinois, in 1937 when "ten gangsters with their women arrive[d]," and when he sought to depart one of these unsavory characters tapped him with a pistol and said no, he could not leave. Since Levy had become enmeshed in the numbers racket at the tender age of eighteen, he knew it would be unwise to disagree.[38] This illicit business was a kind of lottery that generated substantial profits and thereby attracted the ravenous attention of better connected— mostly Italian-American—mobsters.

This mobster influence was particularly resonant near the Canadian border. Before Prohibition was repealed in 1933, gangsters accumulated great wealth by dint of organizing distilleries, manufacturing and selling lightning and corn whiskey. In Detroit, this was the province of the "Purple Gang." However, in Paradise Valley, where Negroes were proliferating, powerful Black challengers were also flourishing. Formidable barriers prevailed, however, as these entrepreneurs often were ensnared by loan sharks at best and denied capital altogether at worst. It was not unknown for sharks to charge interest rates of 50 percent. One of these challengers, Sunnie Wilson, exhibited the potential of his socioeconomic stratum when he established a school for the Black poor so they could learn how to read and write. His friendships with boxer Joe Louis and Duke Ellington bolstered both to the advantage of their wider community.[39]

Wilson's benevolence could not obscure the pervasive gangster influence that afflicted artists. Pianist Duke Anderson forgot to play at a gig for a gangster in Newark. "Right then and there," he recalled, "I got the worst whippin' I ever got in my life. They broke my jaw and wrist. Eventually, I went back to playin' but from then on, I was scared stiff of anyone who looked like a gangster."[40] Anderson may have been "scared stiff" for quite a while since for a fifteen-year period beginning in the late 1920s there was a sprawling neighborhood known as Newark's "Barbary Coast," featuring what one scholar termed "high-class pimps, prostitutes, gamblers, numbers bankers and hustlers." It was anchored by the "Kinney Club at Arlington and Augusta Streets," Newark's "version of New York's infamous Cotton Club" and "one of Newark's first black nightclubs"—though "three quarters of the customers at the Kinney Club were whites," many of those being racketeers.

One of the key figures of that dissolute era was Herman Lubinsky, a man despised by Negro musicians since his unscrupulousness rivaled, and perhaps exceeded, that of Glaser and Irving Mills, notorious for bilking Duke Ellington and others. "It spoils my whole day to

mention Herman Lubinsky" was the considered comment of musician
Al Henderson. He was the "'worst thief in the world. He made millions
on us [black musicians] and he wouldn't pay you nothin." He was a
"wily, unethical shark," according to scholar Barbara Kukla, driven by
a passionate "desire to steal their songs and talents for a pittance. . . .
Some musicians contend Lubinsky got them drunk"—later hooked
on hard drugs—"then had them sign a contract for a few bucks." Nate
Brown argued with similar passion that "Lubinsky [put] me out of
business. . . . He wanted me to sing the blues but said I didn't sound
Negroid enough." Thus, one journalist is not far wrong in concluding
that "there is no doubt everybody hated Herman Lubinsky." Lubinsky
capitalized on technology as he was a prime mover in installing
jukeboxes at local clubs and taverns, which meant huge profits for
gangsters like himself who owned and controlled these devices; thus,
as Kukla put it, "mobsters either owned the taverns or the owners
were so in debt to them they had to take the jukeboxes whether they
wanted to or not."[41] It was inevitable that at a certain juncture African
Americans would seek to develop their own organized crime factions,
and it was virtually inexorable that they would be crushed by their
competitors often employing the organs of the state.[42]

Further south in the "Garden State," Abe Manley, who also had a
hand in the numbers racket and, reputedly, took his poker seriously,
administered his far-flung business interests from his nightclub in
Camden, across the river from Philadelphia, which was graced by
an elegant piano that cost $8,000. In early April 1931, armed men
invaded his club, followed by the bombing of the site, as other
racketeers sought to oust him. A chastened Manley then moved to
Harlem, where Negro political power was growing, as evidenced by
the rise of Adam Clayton Powell to the U.S. Congress shortly thereafter, with his City Council seat won by the Black Communist Ben
Davis, Jr. Abe's spouse, Effa Manley, also was involved in his varied
enterprises and in 1937 sponsored a concert in Newark featuring
Chick Webb and Ella Fitzgerald. At this juncture, the Manleys had
wealth of an estimated $1 million, quite unusual for a U.S. family
generally and a Negro family particularly.[43] Just as Glaser invested in
boxers, the Manleys invested in the Negro baseball league. A fellow

baseball owner, Gus Greenlee, was invested in the numbers, but like Manley he too was squeezed by Italian and Jewish racketeers, who shifted into numbers as the business of illicit alcohol dried up with the end of Prohibition.[44]

Possibly the Manleys arrived in Harlem unaware of the disturbing case of Barron D. Wilkins. This Negro entrepreneur had come to Upper Manhattan in the early 1900s and by the 1920s was a powerful club owner and a collaborator with boxing champion and musician Jack Johnson, but, said musician Sam Wooding, "Italians," meaning competitors and mobsters, "got hold of Yellow Charleston," a petty Negro gambler with debts and "they told him, 'Look, if you want to get dope [drugs] and all the dope you want, you've got to shoot old man Barron.'" And promptly, that is what the compromised Charleston (also known as William Miller) did. This crime took place "right in front of his place," meaning Wilkins's club, that is, "right there at Seventh Avenue and 134th Street," and then the "white gangsters had him for a while," meaning Charleston, until the furor ebbed.[45]

Unfortunately, travails were not the sole province of the Southwest and Northeast. Jabbo Smith, the trumpeter and rival of Louis Armstrong, born in Georgia in 1908, found it necessary to quit the band of Claude Hopkins because it was "too dangerous" not to do so. "While we were playing," he recalled, "the drivers were supposed to be resting up to drive us. But instead they were out lollygagging, messing around. We'd get through playing, get in the cars and then we'd find out that the drivers were drunk. We'd be so scared riding on those mountain roads, we'd hang on to each other. We couldn't sleep during the rides so we'd be real tired when we got to the jobs," with resultant impact on performances.[46]

Thus, propelled by threats and intimidation, what might be considered a "Jazz Diaspora" kept moving westward, not only to Asia but making an intermediate stop in California before decamping to Honolulu or Shanghai. Elihu "Black Dot" McGee, an important figure on Los Angeles's culturally rich Central Avenue, arrived in the City of Angels from El Paso, Texas, in 1926. Rather quickly he came to own and operate "The Flame," "The Casablanca," "The Congo Room," along with the "Turf Barber Shop," where many patrons gathered not just for a trim but to share bonhomie. A dapper dresser and considered a "a very hip cat," he and his comrades controlled a good deal of the bookmaking business and numbers. Early on, records were sold by McGee and his colleagues, alongside other wares, for example, marijuana and heroin Inevitably, musicians were touched by this business, at times as avid customers of the drugs that permeated their environment.[47]

As the Second World War erupted and Japanese Americans were interned, the African American population of what was to become a major metropolis grew exponentially as Los Angeles became a major battleground politically and culturally.[48]

GIVEN SUCH DIFFICULTIES AT HOME, African American musicians were fleeing abroad, as the "Diaspora" extended westward and eastward alike. Edmund Thornton Jenkins was not a devotee of the new music, but he was a composer born in Charleston, South Carolina, in 1894, as lynching was becoming customary. Still, by 1921 this Negro musician was exiled in Europe where he became involved with the W. E. B. Du Bois–sponsored Pan African Congress.[49]

The growing list of those leaving included New Orleans' Sidney Bechet. He arrived in Liverpool from New York City on 4 June 1919. By 1922 a police file on him in London described his complexion as "swarthy," and the accusation was that he had committed an "assault" on a "female,"[50] a British subject, Ruby Gordon. Bechet had been employed by a club on Tottenham Court Road in London; this "man of colour," as he was described, was listed as 5'3" tall with a "stout build" and a "valid American passport."[51] By 1926, he was playing in Moscow and when asked subsequently where he would choose to settle down permanently to play his music, he replied instantly, "Russia," because he was treated so well. Shortly thereafter, he was in Paris where he was jailed because of a club shooting. He was not necessarily stunned by this turn of events, since, according to his biographer, the saxophonist "regarded mayhem as one of the hazards of a musician's working life. . . . For much of his life he was fascinated by gangsters and hoodlums," not unusual given the clubs he performed in back home.[52]

The pianist Glover Compton, born in Kentucky in 1884, recalled the 1928 incident in Paris. Bechet and Mike McKendrick, banjoist, became embroiled in a fracas, leading to an exchange of gunshots, wounding the stunned Compton in the leg and two women in the shoulder and neck respectively. Neither duelist was hurt. Compton, a pivotal figure, wound up staying in Paris for almost fifteen years, having fled gangster-run clubs in Chicago near 22nd and State Street that had a clientele that was overwhelmingly "white." It was Compton who introduced Earl Hines around Chicago, and it was Hines who replaced Compton in Jimmy Noone's band when the Kentuckian departed for greener pastures in France.[53]

Speaking of his European miseries, Bechet recalled of one of his victims, "I didn't slap her hard," speaking of a woman he was accused of raping. "They knew she was a whore," he claimed. He was deported, nonetheless. As for Paris, he carried a pistol—but was jailed anyway. He wound up running a tailor shop in Harlem, though later he was lionized in Europe for his expert artistry and riveting performances[54]

Embracing Moscow like Bechet did was Darnell Howard, born in Chicago in 1895, who attended school alongside Capone's little brother, "Itchy." By 1925, this clarinetist and violinist was in the Soviet Union with the Singing Syncopators, before heading further eastward to Shanghai.[55]

Though Europe may have been more welcoming to these musicians than their homeland, it would be an error to assume that they were garlanded automatically with roses upon docking at local ports. It was in 1925 that a London periodical referred with contempt to the "Coloured Problem," that is, the recent "attempt to introduce a nigger cabaret to London failed. At the Empire, a room was beautifully decorated by an American artist, with cotton fields in the distance and a nice cookhouse in which a real coal black mammy was to make hot waffles which were to be served while Negroes danced and sang." A man interviewed was unequivocal: "I strongly object to coloured artists being employed where food is served to white people," said one calloused observer. "So nervous am I about coloured shows generally," he said, that "after Jack Johnson the famed pugilist and bassist—had been engaged at a high salary for four weeks by one of my assistants, I wouldn't let him show."[56] Still, the contemporaneous warm reception accorded Paul Robeson in London indicated that there was no unanimous hostility to visiting Negro artists.[57]

Nonetheless, there were objective constraints limiting the arrival of U.S. artists, ancestry set aside. A kind of "protectionism" in Britain sought to bar foreign musicians in favor of the homegrown variety.[58] By 1929, Margaret Bonfield, parliamentarian, was told that "unemployment being created through the advent of Talking Pictures"—that is, the decline in pit orchestras in theatres that had been accompanying silent movies—had "already thrown out of employment some 400 musicians throughout the country, the number of which is increasing weekly and will probably affect thousands more."[59] By 1930, British musicians were complaining bitterly about foreign competition, including challenges to that traditional sinecure: military bands.[60] Still, there seemed to be less resistance in London to granting visas to the Euro-American bandleader Paul Whiteman and his orchestra.[61]

African Americans long had toured Britain's variety circuit with minstrel shows, various revues, and ragtime bands. The date of the arrival of the new music called "jazz" in Britain is usually set in 1919 with the arrival of an original Dixieland jazz band composed of Euro-Americans. However, although Britain may have been more advanced than the United States on matters racial, the hostile propaganda about the new music crossed the Atlantic, leaving some in London to see this art form, propelled mostly by men of African descent, as threatening.[62]

But the musicians kept heading eastward because conditions in the United States were often violently hostile. When asked why Britain was so welcoming to the new music despite the complications delivered, English-born trumpeter Ken Colyer replied that in his nation "we really lost most of our own folk culture and jazz has got an international appeal. . . . That's why we took to it. Because we've got no strong folk tradition anymore, of our own, and [jazz] took the place of it."[63] He could have noted the unavoidable links between the United States and the former "mother country." Keyboardist Roy Carew, born in 1883 in Michigan, had parents from Nova Scotia and grandparents from Britain, an inheritance that facilitated the crossing of musical borders.[64]

Then there were those like cornetist Johnny De Droit, born in New Orleans in 1892, who at one time garnered a then hefty $86 weekly salary but had difficulty grappling with Jim Crow since his spouse was of English and German descent and a blonde besides. He left New York because of difficulty in pursuing his golf game since he would be inevitably grouped with a "'Chinaman, Indian and Nigger," and many of those he encountered wanted him to speak like a "coon" besides. Class conscious—he termed himself a "dyed-in-the-wool union man"—he led his union for years, making his presence in the United States even more problematic. He could not forget that per- former Cliff Curry sang "'Save Your Confederate Money, the South Will Rise Again"—this was through the 1950s—which was hardly reassuring. (By contrast, when he played "China, We Owe a Lot to You," it brought down the house and became a feature of his perfor- mances.)[65] De Droit's experience was hardly unusual, meaning that those like him were prime candidates for expatriation.

Also spending considerable time in Europe was violinist Eddie South, born in 1902, who happened to speak fluent French. However, in touring the United States with the band of Paul Whiteman, recalls pianist Dr. Billy Taylor, it happened that "because he was an African American . . . a curtain was placed in front of him, so that he'd be invisible to the studio audience." Increasingly, he began to spend more and more time in Europe.[66]

Sam Wooding, bandleader, pianist, and arranger, born in Philadelphia in 1895, toured the Soviet Union and Germany in the 1920s. Asked if he followed events back home, the cautiously acerbic musician replied, "No, I was glad to forget it. . . . We were happy to say we were out of it." Wooding was reportedly the first person to bring a jazz band to Russia and the first U.S. band of this type or U.S. band of any sort to record outside of the United States, namely, his Berlin sessions in 1925. Wooding also ventured to South America.[67]

Pops Foster, the self-described "New Orleans Jazzman" born in 1892, played aboard a ship to Belize in 1914. By the 1920s, he observed, "a lot of guys would get jobs on boats from the West Coast and when they got to China they'd jump the boat and get a job play- ing." Some then went south to Australia, which Foster termed the "worst Jim Crow country in the world and the musicians over there didn't want them to play."[68]

Willie Foster, older brother of Pops Foster, was born in McCall, Louisiana in 1888; he had worked in carpentry and painting, but was better known as a violinist. He made ten trips on a United Fruit Company vessel to South America.[69] He was not unique in venturing to Latin America: Jazz man, Lawrence Douglas Harris did well in Mexico playing with carnival bands.[70]

In sum, musicians were fleeing in all directions from their home country, propelled by the new music and the skill to perform it in a way that enticed audiences. As noted, Armstrong fled to Europe and was playing there generally from 1932 to 1935. Fats Waller was in Europe for a good deal of the 1930s. Benny Carter was there from about 1935 to 1938 and Coleman Hawkins from 1934 to 1939. The first Norwegian club that specialized in the new music made sojourning in Europe all the more feasible. Serving to pave the way for successful performances was the rise of recorded music during this same era. Records of "King" Oliver, to cite one example, were released not only in the United States but also in Canada, Argentina, France, Britain, Germany, Switzerland, Czechoslovakia, Sweden, Denmark, Italy, Netherlands, Australia, and Japan. Then there was the overarching factor of these mostly Black artists receiving a more respectful reception abroad. Thus, in 1932 when the mid-level bandleader Rudy Vallee was drawing U.S. audiences of 2,800, Duke Ellington, arguably a more talented musician, was attracting 25 percent of this total. The now forgotten Ben Bernie was drawing 2,000 when Armstrong was attracting 350.[71]

France was to be a favored outpost for fleeing musicians, Bechet's problems aside. Paris may have been neither Utopia nor Nirvana, but it may have seemed that way to those more accustomed to the peculiar folkways of Dixie. As Bechet was being jailed, Jack Hylton, a Euro-American conductor, found himself in trouble with the "French Association for the Protection of the Black Race." According to an observant Negro journalist, somehow he had forgotten that he was "not in the southern part of the United States and let his race prejudice get the better of his good judgment." Hylton had met "Nabib

Gonglia," a Black artist who was performing alongside him. When
Hylton was informed of this fact, he refused to go on stage, but, unlike
in Dixie, it was he who was reproached severely.[72] The following year,
the Negro press reported that even on the French Riviera, "a Negro
may enter, not only with equality but with a preference. All, save
Americans, want to know him," it was said wondrously.[73]

Teddy Weatherford, born in 1903, had been a bandmate of
Armstrong in 1920s Chicago before abandoning North America
for Asia, Shanghai, and then Calcutta. By 1926, he was performing in China and only returned to the United States once in coming
decades.[74] Born in Bluefield, West Virginia, he wound up playing
in Calcutta, Bombay, Ceylon, sites where he was joined at times by
trumpeter Cricket Smith, born in 1881.[75] Buck Clayton, who, as we
have seen, also made his way to China, said that Weatherford was a
"king over there" and "would play four clubs a night." Shanghai was
their favored site; there could be found "two or three gambling casinos inside the place" with "two or three dance floors. . . . Madame
Chiang kai-Shek used to come in there all the time," referring to
the spouse of the man who led the forces defeated by the Chinese
Communist Party in 1949. There was a sizeable exile community, and
Clayton "was learning Russian" since "there [were] a lot of Russians"
and he was picking up the language "pretty well."[76]

An indication as to why so many musicians chose exile from their
homeland, was indicated by Milt Hinton, who became a regular in
pre-revolutionary Cuba. "What amazed me," he said, "is that until
that time, I'd never stayed at a place that served black and white
guests. And everyone was treated equally."[77] Benny Carter, composer and bandleader, thought similarly about Europe. In Harlem,
he recalled, "many white musicians used to come in and listen to the
black musicians and not only listen but sit in with them. Quite often.
But we couldn't go downtown and sit in with them," placing him and
those like him at a disadvantage while privileging those not in this
persecuted category, meaning, "of course," that the latter would learn
lessons to enhance their careers. Whereas Europe was different, he
said, in that there was "acceptance of you just on the basis of you as a
human being."[78]

The development of the phonograph and recorded music helped to create a market abroad for practitioners of the new music, allowing them to seek what often amounted to a sinecure overseas. The critic Leonard Feather argued that Ellington was appreciated more in Europe and Britain particularly than in the United States, notably during the 1930s, which incentivized the bandleader to spend a considerable amount of time abroad.[79] In the ultimate commentary, the grandson of Booker T. Washington, the horn man Booker Pittman, left the United States around 1931 for Europe and did not return home until the early 1960s.[80]

Negro musicians were so prevalent in Europe that during the pre-1975 wars in the former Portuguese colonies in Africa, at one juncture political activists from there were able to reach their homelands without valid papers from European ports by simply dressing them up as " 'Negro musicians' . . . along with a European guide who did have a proper passport." Then, according to the radical intellectual and activist Samir Amin, "At the Luxembourg frontier, which was supposed to be the one with the loosest controls, our musicians gave a good imitation of collective drunkenness," confirming the stereotype, and they flew from there to Africa.[81]

WAR ERUPTED IN ASIA AND EUROPE in the 1930s, and these years were transformative for the new music, establishing patterns that continue to resonate, not unlike what had occurred previously in terms of the mass diffusion of phonographs and radios and the arrival of mass electrification, facilitating the popularity of the electric guitar. That is not all. In the midst of war, the major musicians' union engineered a strike over royalty payments, which bandleader Charlie Barnet termed "one of the biggest nails in the coffin of the big band era, for it brought vocalists very much to the fore. Musical backgrounds were being recorded for them in foreign countries and a lot of records were even made with voices substituting for instruments. Before the strike was over, bands had received a lethal blow."[82]

Simultaneously, the monopoly enjoyed by ASCAP in terms of music royalties and publishing was challenged increasingly by BMI (Broadcast Music Inc.), and, said pianist Dr. Billy Taylor, this "created important opportunities for many African American artists." Dr. Taylor added that since vocalists "belonged to a different union," the musicians' strike opened doors for these songbirds. Moreover, a shellac shortage, due to Tokyo's forces seizing the Malay Peninsula, created opportunities for smaller record companies.[83]

In addition, the eruption of war made exile abroad less attractive, increasing competition for work in the United States. "All jazz is dead in Europe!" it was announced tremulously in mid-1942: "In Switzerland now there are only two Negro musicians"; elsewhere on the continent Negroes were to be found in "concentration camp[s]."[84] Trumpeter Arthur Briggs, born in 1899, spent four years in a Nazi internment camp after starring in Paris. With family in Long Island and California, this Negro artist once played with Noble Sissle. At the camp, he formed a six-piece orchestra, then another with twenty-five pieces that moved easily from "swing" to "classical." He drew upon the talents of 2,000 internees to do so. He also formed a trio that sang Negro spirituals, which was bolstered by the fact that there were "50 colored boys in the camp," according to journalist Rudolph Dunbar.[85]

In Manila one musician, Whitney Smith, wound up in a Japanese-administered internment camp, while another, Bob Fockler, wound up broadcasting for a so-called "Nazi radio station,"[86] while pianist and arranger Sam Wooding, in contrast, said "the Nazi Party didn't want any American music and especially the ragtime or jazz played by blacks. They didn't honor blacks at all. So, they refused, they barred the contract, they discredited the contract."[87]

In Shanghai, the new music was in shambles, with artists fleeing in all directions. After the band of Butch Larkin dared to play "God Bless America" in Japanese-occupied Shanghai in early 1943, he was jailed. Many "white" musicians there were replaced by Filipinos, accelerating an ongoing trend regionally. Bandleader James Albert Spears was found dead, an apparent suicide, and in the Philippines Bill Hegamin—described as a "veteran colored leader and ace pianist"—was, reportedly, "doing okay teaching music and voice and has a large studio," while Ray Reynolds was "now dancing nightly" and doing well for himself.[88] A favoritism toward Negroes was part of Tokyo's wartime policy.[89]

As opportunities abroad dried up because of the exigencies of war, this lucrative outlet for Negro musicians was blocked, generating more intense competition for remaining jobs. This was occurring as the number of jobs for Negro musicians in, for example, Jim Crow Chicago declined by about 30 percent because of the disappearance of Negro-owned clubs in the years leading up to 1940, a process driven by the ravages of the Great Depression, the decline of Negro-owned clubs as a result, the demise of "swing" music, and the perennial: continuing racism.[90]

Consolidation within the industry was also a factor. The Club De Lisa in Chicago "wasn't like any other club in the world," wrote analyst Dempsey Travis. "You could buy anything you wanted within the De Lisa compound in the 5500 block on South State Street. The De Lisa brothers owned the hotel, the gambling operation, the liquor stores and dainty-looking girls who worked the bar stools inside the club." Thus Count Basie, Fletcher Henderson, and the other musicians who performed there were subjected to a kind of monopoly pricing power that could force down fees, as the club tended to drive competitors out of business, which was garnished by Jim Crow that placed these artists in a disadvantaged bargaining position.[91]

The ripples of instability extended southward, too. Arriving on these shores were a number of talented Cuban musicians who contributed to the richness of the music. Machito, the percussionist born Frank Grillo in 1908, had his first rehearsal in Harlem at 122nd Street and Seventh Avenue, the headquarters of the Negro evangelist Father Divine. "They charged us fifty cents an hour for the rehearsal," he recalled. Yet despite his base in Harlem, when his orchestra played in Miami, a Jim Crow haven, they were advertised as hailing "from Cuba," and although his band was "black and white," they evaded local apartheid because they were Cuban. "We even have a bodyguard to take care of us," said the bemused dark-skinned artist, "and they transport[ed] us to Miami Beach. I used to live in a white hotel. I never had [a] problem, we used to eat in Miami City [sic] in those white restaurants, as a matter of fact." His band included an African American, but the wily bandleader sought to keep him from speaking with his betraying accent and that "made the difference," as they

were treated "very good. . . . There was no problem because we were
from Cuba and they consider the Cubans . . . are not black," meaning not descendants of enslaved mainland Africans, the perpetual
antagonist of North American republicans. Yet when the band played
at the Savoy in Harlem "95%" of the audience was black and they
were "crazy" about the music. After all, he said, "We [were] playing
for black and it was black music. . . . You didn't have to make no explanation to a black person about rhythm because . . . they come from
where the rhythm come from." Machito was no stranger to the Savoy:
"I used to go practically every day, every night, to the Savoy because
[drummer] Chick Webb was there [and] Ella Fitzgerald [vocalist]"
too and fellow Cuban Mario Bauza "was in charge of rehearsing the
orchestra."[92]

Machito had arrived on the mainland in 1938, while Bauza was
already there, paving the way, having arrived more than a decade
earlier. (He was to marry the percussionist's sister.) It was on the mainland that Bauza heard the new music, and, he recalled, "I went back
to Cuba and became a saxophone player. I came to New York to live
in 1930 and I joined Noble Sissle's band." The trumpeter then joined
Webb's band, Webb telling him that, "if you can get the American
Negro accent in your music you're going to be great, because you've
got the other side of the coin—the finesse, the technique." He became
Webb's "musical director," then it was on to Cab Calloway's band.[93]
It was Bauza who was partially responsible for the discovery of Ella
Fitzgerald. He also had short stints with the band of Don Redman and
Fletcher Henderson. It was Bauza who was also partially responsible
for the breakthrough that led Calloway to hire Dizzy Gillespie, where
they made music together side-by-side. As world war was erupting,
Bauza joined Machito's band, but the influence he left on the music,
as exemplified by Gillespie, was significant.[94]

The overall environment provided fertile soil for yet another rise of
a phenomenon not unknown to the new music: a vast bubble of tiny
enterprises run by what one commentator termed "dreamers, sharp
operators, would-be tycoons and ambitious fans," many more than
willing to take advantage of a climate that facilitated rough exploitation of African American performers. For Lester Young, already

familiar with Kansas City's unscrupulousness, this development made it harder for him to trust people, especially Euro-Americans he didn't know well, which had an ineluctable impact on his personality and ultimately his music.[95]

Young also accompanied Count Basie, which illuminates what bandleader Charlie Barnet observed. He encountered the touring band of Basie in New York City in the 1930s: "I never forgot the pitiful instruments some of his guys were playing when they first came into Roseland," a local nightspot. "They were held together by rubber bands and I just could not believe it, although instruments like that were not uncommon in other black bands across the country." This decrepitude influenced the music in that "when they got new instruments, they had grown accustomed to a horn that is out of whack" and "it is hard to get used to one on which everything is good." [96] On the one hand, this was outrageous; on the other, this deficiency in instrumentation could force more creativity in making lovely sounds.

Barnet had reason to know. A scion of wealth (the American Sugar Refining Company and the New York Central Railroad), he had relationships with various elites far surpassing those of his peers. Besides, he was married eleven times, providing him with entrees to even more relationships. To his credit, he was among the first Euro-American bandleaders who hired musicians of a different ancestry, and he has been credited with helping catapult Lena Horne, the songstress, to stardom.[97]

Trombonist "Trummy" Young saluted Barnet—"He would fight, man," he enthused, speaking of battling Jim Crow and "so would Boyd Raeburn," bandleader born in 1913. This contrasted with Benny Goodman, born in 1909, who "would [not] go too far for anybody. Not only us but nobody else." Given the conditions musicians faced, few eyebrows were raised when Duke Ellington, according to an interviewer, "used to say that the only basis for racial prejudice is economic," and sideman "Trummy" Young replied, "oh, he's true," both opinions placing them alongside the left and distant from those who saw this pestilence as an individualized psychological delusion.[98] (Despite Young's rosy memories, Barnet confessed that his band had "never played" the Palladium in Southern California "because of their policy of showing no black or mixed bands. So mine became a lily-white band in order that I might finally play the Palladium.")[99]

AS THE 1930S WERE LURCHING to a close, practitioners of the new music had survived the continuation of Jim Crow, and the rise of the phonograph and radio: related opportunities abroad, assisted by the general growth of unions driven by the ravages of the Great Depression, seemed to augur better days coming. The rise of fascism generated a counter-reaction—anti-fascism—which bid fair to open further opportunities for talented musicians. Alongside the ascension of unions was the growing strength of ASCAP, which, inter alia, collected royalties that became more important with the advent of radio and the phonograph. ASCAP in some ways represented the Janus-faced opportunity—and oppression—of Negroes in that it contained the potential to aid the growing raft of African American composers, though it found it difficult to do so while adhering to a Jim Crow diktat. Jelly Roll Morton, for example, did not earn any royalties until 1939, when ASCAP finally allowed him to become a member. He had applied five years earlier but had been rejected. But indicative of the continuing pull of white supremacy, he was placed in the lowest category of membership, where he received a mere $120 annually. Oscar Hammerstein III said that those in the top category—for example, Cole Porter and Irving Berlin—received an average of $15,000 annually,[100] yet another indication of the inflamed conjuncture where racism encountered economics.

4. Hothouse

OVERSHADOWING PERHAPS OTHER FACTORS impacting the music was the change in the music itself, that is, the arrival of the still fecund music known as "bebop,"[1] a form that created rifts among musicians and audiences alike. It featured a fast tempo, complex chord progressions, syncopation, intricate melodies, and rapid changes. Still, this musical turn was not greeted with unanimous approval. When Dizzy Gillespie, born in 1917, and Charlie Parker played in Los Angeles in the early 1940s, they were treated like lepers, and even worse: "Communist lepers" according to critic Leonard Feather during a visit to the old "Billy Berg's Club" on Vine Street. Their music was either laughed at or violently attacked, and one radio station officially banned it.[2]

Thus, in Los Angeles within the ranks of the Negro newspapers, the left-leaning *California Eagle* was supportive of this turn in the music, while the less progressive *Sentinel* was not.[3] Tellingly, the latter has survived, and the former went out of business decades ago.

The forces that helped to ignite the decline of big bands then facilitated the rise of smaller combos suitable for the new turn in the new music. As will be seen, attacks on dancing also facilitated the bebop turn toward listening. The desire to escape the heavy hand of white supremacy as it purloined the work of Negro musicians in turn facilitated the ascension of bebop, which was more difficult to copy by pale imitators, for example, the appropriately named Paul Whiteman.

In any case, conditions had matured for a new musical paradigm to emerge in that according to producer John Hammond the recording industry was "absolutely broke" in the 1930s. Columbia Records, for example, was plunged into bankruptcy and "there was no money for jazz at all," creating a wide opening for experimentation.[4]

The bard of Harlem, Langston Hughes, who had reason to know, says the evocative descriptor *bebop* stemmed from the 1943 rebellion in Harlem, symbolizing in onomatopoeia the sound made by police clubs on Negro heads. This assertion also underscores the revolt of this music, buoyed by contemporaneous events in Harlem.[5] The dislocation delivered in the early 1940s by war not only served to generate bebop but emboldened U.S. Negroes to become more steadfast in confronting white supremacy in its various permutations. During the previous decade, a hallmark was the control of musicians exhibited by mob figures. A counterreaction was signaled in 1939 when the musician Shadow Wilson, born in 1919, was among those appearing in the Negro gangster musical *Paradise in Harlem*.[6]

That is, what emerged was symbolized by how Negro baseball league mogul William Augustus "Gus" Greenlee, an imperial force in Pittsburgh because of holdings in the numbers, boxing, and nightclubs, not to mention hijacking of beer trucks, came to play an increasing role in the music, including connecting Duke Ellington's muse, Billy Strayhorn, to the bandleader and composer. Strayhorn, born in 1914, had similar ties, having played at a Pittsburgh club with whispered mob connections. He was also a Francophile, which facilitated the foreign ventures of Ellington's band (Ellington said that Strayhorn spoke French "very well"). He was politically aware, backing the New Deal and later becoming close to Dr. Martin Luther King Jr. He was fond of alcoholic beverages, making him (unfortunately) typical.[7] According to pianist Cedar Walton he was also victimized by homophobic attitudes because of his sexual orientation.[8]

Though a focus on harder drugs understandably has marked most comment on the new music in the 1940s, alcohol continued to plague, and Strayhorn was not singular. Fats Waller, just before he passed away in 1943, was told by an associate, "Last night I came away from Philadelphia with a heavy heart. I had seen you in such terrible condition from drink that your performance suffered frightfully—you announced to your audience that you knew you were drunk—and your memory was so bad you had to be reminded that you had drawn money earlier in the evening. . . . Your drinking is undermining your health, your artistry and giving you a reputation which will interfere with your bookings and earning capacity."[9] Weeks later, Waller was found dead on a train heading east from California, discovered (ironically) in Kansas City.[10]

Strayhorn was not alone in his fondness for President Franklin D. Roosevelt. On the evening the president died in April 1945, Ben Webster—saxophonist born in Kansas City in 1909—singlehandedly closed down West 52nd Street in Manhattan, where bebop ascended. "Get off the stand," he growled, "nobody's gonna play tonight. Roosevelt's dead."[11]

In brief, the progressive atmosphere symbolized by FDR, reflected in his still remarkable perorations in 1944[12] combined with the continuing dissoluteness of the conditions in which artists were forced to toil, created a symbiosis contributing to a new departure in a music that ever involved a search for creativity and truth.

Neither Strayhorn nor Webster were atypical in terms of political predilections. There was much reason for discontent, including the simple point alleged by yet another writer, Claude McKay, who contended that "even the most famous jazz bands such as Duke Ellington's, Claude Hopkins', Fats Waller's, Count Basie's, Lucky Millinder's, Cab Calloway's, Jimmy Lunceford's, and Louis Armstrong's receive a remuneration on a lower scale than white jazz bands."[13] Then there were the other rich income streams that Black artists often were denied. "The payola game was hot and heavy," according to bandleader Charlie Barnet. "Either by direct payment for playing a tune on the air or by payment for a special arrangement of the tune": this "had begun long before with vaudeville," he said, but with the advent of radio in particular, "the money flew in all directions"[14]—except to some of the more creative bands devoid of the complexions and connections to guarantee otherwise.

THE RISE OF BEBOP ALSO OCCURRED as another new trend was emerging in the 1940s: the transition from dancing to the music to listening. This was hardly accidental, spurred in part by Jim Crow, which frowned upon heterosexual dancing across the color line, which was becoming normative north of the Mason-Dixon Line and was inflaming sentiments nationally. The pianist Randy Weston observed that during the war the "government put a 20 percent tax on dancehalls, which had the effect of killing off a lot of great dancehalls like the Savoy Ballroom in Harlem, the Brooklyn Palace and the Sonia Ballroom. They all closed down."[15] This inflicted significant impact on the music. As club owner and producer George Wein argued, "Dancing is a very big thing. . . . It's a social music" that accompanied it. "When it ceased to be a social music, that's when it ceased to draw blacks," he asserted.[16]

Also related to Jim Crow was the desire of Negro musicians to delve more deeply into the complexities of the music, driven in part by the imperative to flummox non-Negro copycats. Horn man Buddy De Franco, born in Camden, New Jersey, in 1923, said that pianist Bud Powell, "really resented George Shearing," a peer. "Bud would play some line or something and the next set . . . George would play that line. And he would get furious"; "Poor George" may have been "intimidated," but insufficiently to change.[17] There was "so much thievery going on," cried drummer Chico Hamilton, referring to the pilfering of his musical ideas. "I got a friend of mine to be my manager," in response, he said, but that backfired when he "took a whole year of tax money of mine and never paid it and when the government came out, they were going to take my house," yet another steep price being paid for being creative.[18]

According to pianist Mary Lou Williams, her fellow keyboardist Thelonius Monk formed a band "to challenge the practice of downtown musicians coming uptown and 'stealing' the music." Said Monk, "We are going to get a band started. We're going to create something that they can't steal because they can't play it." Nonetheless, a Columbia University student during this time taped live performances of the brilliant pianist that were then released without obtaining his permission, a not infrequent occurrence.[19]

The critic Ralph Gleason of San Francisco recalled that even in this supposed "cosmopolitan" town, the "color line" was drawn "strictly," separating musicians of various ancestries, often forcing them to develop on separate tracks. Then again, said Gleason, he noticed that "white" musicians "literally copied King Oliver's numbers and issued them as their own." This grand theft would not be as easy with bebop, which presupposed an exalted technical mastery of the instrument, difficult to emulate without much practice.[20]

Thus, when Charlie Parker reputedly said that there were "no bop roots in jazz,"[21] he was announcing the birth of a pristine new form, far distant from the grimily exploitative practices of the recent past. Parker's comrade, Max Roach, complained that some of the music of George Gershwin—for example, "Rhapsody in Blue"—was "lifted, the introduction is lifted, and the theme is lifted from Eubie Blake . . . . The introduction to 'Memories of You' is what this guy lifted for his 'Rhapsody in Blue' and used that theme and made a symphony out of it." As for "Benny Goodman's music—that's Fletcher Henderson's."[22]

The critic Nat Hentoff wrote that New Orleans trumpeter Freddie Keppard rejected a 1916 invitation to make the first of all phonograph records for this new form called jazz because he was afraid that his music would then be easier to steal if it were ubiquitously available. Hence, the overwhelmingly Euro-American Original Dixieland Jazz Band is today seen as "the first . . . group to record" in this genre.[23] Tellingly, by 1941, as the bebop trend was being hatched, a visitor to, New Orleans, Charles Rossi, found that the city given credit as the birthplace of the new music "today boasts a quality of *white* jazz as good as you'd find anywhere. I say white because with one exception, I found no colored jazz being played during my short stay."[24]

Quick to capitalize were two men: Ralph Watkins who was then jobless but was a onetime owner of Kelly Stables on West 52nd Street in Manhattan and other clubs, and Morris Levy, a man of questionable ethics, which no doubt made him qualified to control a nightspot. As partners, they took over the floundering Topsy's Chicken Coop on Broadway, in the heart of New York City. Their marketing included catering to younger patrons—prone to adopt rebellious practices in music distinguishing them from their elders—willing to place orders for ice cream, dairy dishes, and milk drinks. At the newly christened Royal Roost there arose what was called the first soda fountain in nightclub history, which reportedly grossed far more profit nightly than the strong drink counterpart. It was here that bebop was honed—some say born. A basement strip joint up the street called The Clique was renamed Birdland and quickly became yet another birthplace for the latest trends in the music. Not coincidentally, the partners owned a music publishing company, allowing for added exploitation of beleaguered musicians.[25]

Levy was not held in high regard by musician and businessman John Levy (no relation nor common ancestry), recounting that he began by running hatcheck and bathroom concessions at nightclubs and was part of the cabal that "coerced" artists "into giving away their publishing rights." Yes, he administered Birdland, but it was "really gangster dominated. You could always see these guys sitting around."[26] "'Publishing is where it's at,'" said Morris Levy. "All I want is to own 20, 000 copyrights that pay two dollars a quarter from record sales— that's $160, 000 a year," that is, an "incredible business." Eventually, the wealthy Morris Levy came to befriend the rising musician and entrepreneur Quincy Jones, who at times stayed with Levy during his Manhattan sojourns.[27]

Morris Levy, who served as Chairman Emeritus of the United Jewish Appeal, according to U.S authorities, came to be under the "control" of Vincent Gigante, a leading racketeer. Ultimately, it was said, Gigante "developed a stranglehold on Morris Levy's recording industry enterprise, in effect turning Levy into a source of ready cash for the [Vito] Genovese LCN [La Cosa Nostra] family and its leaders." In contrast, Levy described himself as an "entrepreneur" with a net worth of "in excess of a million and under a billion," with holdings that included more than ninety companies employing 900 people. Reportedly, Levy's tie to Genovese began when he owned Birdland. Levy's brother was mistakenly killed at the club by mobsters who were attempting to murder Levy himself, who fled hurriedly to Israel for several years.[28]

Of course, Levy's reputed involvement in the heroin trade proved to be quite useful in "hooking" musicians, inducing them to work for less.[29] Coincidentally, Basie borrowed substantial sums from Levy and ended up working many weeks at Birdland for peanuts.[30] Music pioneer Jerry Lieber called Levy "the most mobbed-up guy in the music biz," hardly an exaggeration. Among his specialties was that he "bootlegged 78s and shipped 'cutouts' from the back doors of pressing plants. He shook down songwriters who were easy prey, forcing his name on song credits," a practice mastered by Irving Mills. His own wife was once rushed to a hospital after he beat her senseless in a telephone booth.[31] "He looked and talked like a Hollywood thug," says critic Gene Santoro, which was unsurprising since "most jazz clubs in New York dealt with the Mafia. They had to."[32]

Santoro may have had bandleader Charlie Barnet in mind. "We knew a lot of racket people," he said, "like Charlie 'Lucky' Luciano. When I came home one day, there was a guy who I'll call 'Joe' in the apartment with a gunshot wound in his leg. He had just stuck up a factory payroll and there had been a shoot-out. He had the money with him and he said he'd give some if I needed it. I thanked him and declined the offer," just another day in the life of a musician familiar with "racket people."[33]

IN SHORT, THIS MUSIC, BEBOP, symbolized by the innovations of Kansas City's Charlie Parker, was propelled by various forces. Thus, it was in 1944 in San Francisco that the musicians' union refused to allow the manager of a Sunday session of artists to hire "white" performers to play alongside a noted Negro trumpeter, Willie Gary "Bunk" Johnson, who then was compelled, said an observer, to hire a "small colored combo." The compromised Johnson then felt obligated to make ends meet by doing longshoreman's work,[34] facilitated by the anti-racist International Longshore and Warehousemen's Union, led by presumed Communist Harry Bridges.[35]

Bridges, said producer John Hammond, was a devotee of the new music.[36] and anti-racist to the point that he once called James Petrillo, leader of the morally compromised musicians' union, and threatened to organize a competitor union if no speedy reform was forthcoming.[37] In sum, despite the best efforts of those like Bridges and Johnson, Negro musicians were being driven together by Jim Crow, meaning the most creative and competent artists were forced into a hothouse of innovation, leading to a new turn in the new music.

Fortunately, it was not just Bridges and his powerful union that objected to Jim Crow in the music business. In 1942 Walter White of the NAACP issued a "vigorous protest," reprimanding James Petrillo, the union boss, reproving "the practice of Chicago and other places . . . requiring radio stations to sign contracts to use only white musicians."[38] Petrillo denied the allegation and replied unconvincingly that "the situation is entirely satisfactory to the colored membership."[39] White would have been wise not to take the union boss's words too seriously since it was well known that Petrillo was a comrade of Sidney Korshak, a key fixer for racketeers; Petrillo's rise to union leadership was littered with stories of clubs that were firebombed and stink-bombed for using musicians not represented by Petrillo. His first job was as a union muscleman, and with the backing of mobsters, this man, known, insensitively, as Little Caesar and the Mussolini of Music, was able to lead the often fractious American Federation of Musicians local in Chicago for four decades and the entire union for another eighteen years, with its 250,000 members.[40]

THE BIAS THAT LED TO BRIDGES' protest in San Francisco and White's objection to goings-on in Chicago were hardly sui generis. Lester Young discovered during this time that prestigious hotels in midtown Manhattan were reluctant to hire Black bands, for fear of upsetting racist customers, or at least that was the argument offered.[41] The club owner Max Gordon, who initiated the prominent Village Vanguard in Manhattan, not only had to deal with police officers hassling him about a liquor license, but, he said, "in 1943 you had to think twice before bringing a black woman to the smart Upper East Side of Manhattan."[42]

Walter White of the NAACP, who happened to be quite light-skinned, could have added chapter and verse. In early 1943, in the midst of complaining to Mayor Fiorello La Guardia, he reminded the portly politico that "there are a great many colored people who look . . . white" and thus could—theoretically—be barred from various clubs on spurious grounds. It is "possible," he insisted, "that Mrs. White and I while patronizing the Savoy, as we have done on many occasions could be thought by some policemen" that a "white man and colored woman were dancing," inducing harassment. Police thought that if the Savoy closed, "it would keep white people from coming to Harlem," which he thought was a noxious policy goal. "Some five hundred thousand people were patrons of the Savoy during 1942," he said, and it was the "favorite dancing place of many defense workers." Yet these workers often were harassed by police who chose "to follow each patron after they leave." If the Savoy were closed, the "alternative would be for the colored patrons of the Savoy to dance in downtown places," which was also unacceptable. Those under eighteen years of age were also being barred.[43]

The age bar helped to generate vibrant youthful protest and consciousness, while the dancing bar contributed to a trend of the new music's shift from dancing to listening. Interestingly, the Savoy was owned by Moses and Charles Galewski, of Polish Jewish ancestry, who changed their name to Gale. It had opened in 1926 and was "fronted" by Charlie Buchanan, Negro.[44]

The bunching of Negro musicians uptown was hardly happenstance. Beating one slave can keep the entire plantation in line.[45] Nonetheless, this putrid prejudice was not merely a Gotham matter; in Los Angeles there was a similar attempt to ban "mixed dancing," with "white girl hostesses" choosing to "refuse to dance with Negro servicemen" at a local canteen.[46] The crackdown facilitated the rise in listening, laying the groundwork for the new music known as bebop.

However, there was gnawing sentiment hostile to White's ideas. An otherwise unidentified "white woman" told him bluntly that it was "about time this cesspool for miscegenation between degenerate white prostitutes and Negroes was shut down. . . . I know that your race feels that sharp sense of sweet revenge," she proclaimed, "whenever you see a Negro breaking down the white blood race by having a Negro intermarry with a white woman."[47] The Savoy was instructed that "if the management refused to admit white people, it could remain open." Thus, it was stated, Harlem would be akin to the "Jewish quarters in Germany." Of late, "some 75% of the dancers seemed to be boys and girls ranging from 12 to 16 years of age," an age range that fueled outrage.[48] Joining the fray was Local 802 of the American Federation of Musicians—"on behalf of its twenty-one thousand members."[49]

Across the continent in Los Angeles, a film studio objected to the presence of the youthful guitarist Barney Kessel, born in 1923, a "white musician in an otherwise black cast,"[50] as it was put by an observer. Dimly recognized at the time was that such barriers were hampering the development of these "white" musicians, isolating them not only from those with talent but those on the cusp of developing new musical forms that would prove to be dominant for some time to come. Billie Holiday asserted that once in Detroit she was told she was too light-skinned to play with Basie since "somebody might think I was white if the light didn't hit me just right. So they got special dark grease paint and told me to put it on."[51] Apartheid barriers ironically helped to create a greenhouse of creativity among exceedingly talented Negro musicians.

Drummer Roy Porter, born in Colorado in 1923, was in Los Angeles then and told of "the man who ran the Say When," a popular club, "a racist called Dutch. He'd hire you, man, make it clear what he thought of you"—not much. "Billie Holliday worked for Dutch once during this time. He treated her like she was a dog," no doubt hastening her precipitous decline and premature death. Porter, who described himself as a "mixture of black, Mongolian and English," was a regular visitor to Central Avenue in Los Angeles in the 1940s and noticed that the cops there tended to "harass black musicians and the black pimps that had white whores or any black men with white women." Beyond this venue, there was a "club named Diane's on 8th or 9th Street near Alvarado in the Westlake District . . . supposedly owned by [mobster] Bugsy Siegel and was operated by the Virginia Hill" routinely referred to as a "gun moll." There he worked alongside Benny Carter.[52] The massive influx of African Americans during the war, joining a preexisting progressive movement,[53] allowed some musicians to undermine the rancid bias foisted upon them.[54]

Still, the fact remained that Negroes were barred from certain clubs, even if Negro musicians were performing there.[55] This was notably the case in Los Angeles, thought to be immune from such pestilences, as when during the war a Negro fan was denied entrance to a club where Benny Carter was performing, and Jimmy Lunceford abandoned a gig because of likeminded bias.[56]

Carter felt that because he had neither a Glaser nor a Mills behind him (an exploiter with the heft to enhance a musician's popularity), his historical impact was lessened. By 1943, he found "no blacks in the studio orchestras" in Hollywood, "other than Lee Young," drummer and singer born in 1914. By 1944, he sought to move to a neighborhood where restrictive covenants barred those of his ancestry: "We decided to fight . . . we won it," he said triumphantly. "There were many blacks who didn't want . . . desegregation" of the union locals, a battle he took on nonetheless, delivering mixed results.[57]

Musician Buster Smith, whose alto style influenced Charlie Parker,[58] contends that Hollywood was not unusual in seeking to erect firm Jim Crow barriers. In Dixie, where this Texan frequently performed, "90 percent" of the audiences were "white" and there they did not play the new music: "No, not too much of it. The only time we played much of that jazz was around the colored places." The question then becomes: To what extent did this bifurcated system and the fact that those like Smith played often before non-Negro audiences retard the music's evolution? Bassist Milt Hinton once told him of a gig and "there was this little room underneath the bandstand. And they got locked in there. And they heard all these guys outside who were talking about setting fire to the building."[59]

Smith, born in Texas in 1904, was not just a mentor to Parker, perhaps Kansas City's chief musical contributor, but he also endured experiences emblematic of what Negro artists endured. He confirms that he and others played differently among "white" audiences. "The only time we played much of that jazz," he said subsequently, "was around the colored places." Thus, "in some of the western town[s], way out in West Texas out there, some cowboys would come in there and they didn't want to let us quit playing. You got to play til they say 'stop.'" Since they were packing pistols, their words were even more convincing. Another time in Oklahoma, part of the circuit traversed by Kansas City performers, yet another boisterous Euro-American—he "looked like a big prizefighter" when "he pulled off his shirt," followed quickly by drunkenness, said, "I'm going whup every one of you when you come out, one by one." Then a fellow musician grabbed a music stand, built with steel, then "folded it up" and "rolled that

thing and batted that guy right in the back of the neck . . . batted him
clean down the steps with that thing, right down into the street," then
"we all got in the car and flew!" Another time, in Palestine, Texas, a
sheriff with "two big pistols on wouldn't let nobody dance but himself!" Besides, he "didn't want nothing but 'Turkey in the Straw'" to
be performed—"all the time. And we had to play it," if they wanted to
escape unscathed. This dangerous farce "went on for the whole night."
On another occasion, "cowboys came into the place and shot all the
lights out," and then the stunned musicians "one by one 12 or 13 guys
slip[ped] out, leaving [the] piano player last," at which point he suddenly stopped and ran and jumped in the waiting vehicle too, as they
sped away.[60]

These chilling confrontations unavoidably shaped the musicians.
Early in his career in the 1940s, the trumpeter Miles Davis, born in
1926, was playing with the band of Billy Eckstine in Boston. "All of a
sudden," says his son, Gregory Davis, "a white woman sitting at one
of the front tables, yells out at him, 'Sing it, Blackie. I love that 'Ol'
Man River' voice. Sing your song, chocolate drop." The insulted singer
stopped singing and confronted the woman—and "all the white folks
went crazy. It was like a KKK convention . . . fists flew," and since the
band "had with them every kind of innovative street weapon available
. . . switchblades, brass knuckles, picks, blackjacks—you name it," they
gave as good as they got.[61]

It was also Hinton who recalled that there were those who "came
and paid their money just to heckle the Negro bands, like some people
like to tease an animal and we had no recourse."[62] This was particularly grating for Hinton, a man of multiple talents of whom, it was
announced in 1954, that "if a poll were to be taken among jazzmen of
all styles to determine the most versatile musician," the winner would
be this creative bassist.[63]

There was a related problem. "There was a whole [lot] of black
music," said Danny Barker, the musician, "that wasn't played on white
jukeboxes, radio stations" and "Hollywood movies. This was done
purposely through racism—prejudice." Thus, there were "millions
of jukeboxes around the country," and "many did not spin black artists." There was also the companion unsavory practice of abasement

of these often proud artists: "You had to sing a river song," Barker said angrily, "the 'Robert E. Lee' or 'Swanee'—or you didn't sing at all. That was the racist custom down South," up North, too. Some indignities were comparably harsher. "All black show people having emergencies" of a urological nature were often "hitting the bushes on the highways and byways, because the segregation laws did not allow black backsides to sit on the same toilet as white backsides," leading to "much trouble with many bands and troupes getting into hassles about using toilets that had signs above saying" blaringly, "FOR WHITES ONLY."[64]

Once in 1944, the Ellington band had to appear on stage famished since they couldn't find a place that would serve them in St. Louis.[65] Presumably, and tauntingly ironic, there were toilets available for them to use.

Marshall Royal, born in Oklahoma in 1912, best known for his horn virtuosity with Basie, lamented that "some of the things that a black musician had to experience when I was out on the road . . . was pretty rough to stomach. You would have to get off a bus when you come into town, three o'clock in the morning, and go around and start knocking on people's doors trying to find a place to stay because you couldn't stay in a white hotel and there wasn't any black hotels in the towns." Like others so persecuted, he spoke longingly of exile: "You had to go into another country to even be able to be treated like a man if you were in a black band," since "jazz in every country except the United States is put on a pedestal."[66]

The vicissitudes of travel were a constant complaint among black musicians.[67] It was in July 1942 that Cab Calloway and NAACP leader Walter White sought to improve the parlous travel options. "Because of Jim Crow rulings it was reported, train service is not available to . . . colored bands south of the Mason and Dixon line." This was no minor matter since the "average colored band spends at least eight months of the year on the road."[68] Calloway had good reason to investigate transport options since he often had occasion to flee. Such was the case in Memphis when he and his band performed before a packed house, but, as one writer put it, he and his cohorts "drew more feminine attention than white southern male egos thought proper." A fight ensued, and Calloway and his band were ordered out of town. After this incident, Black bands playing for Euro-American audiences were discouraged by City Hall from playing in public places.[69]

By August 1942, bus travel was eliminated because of fuel rationing, leading to the opinion that the "situation for colored bands is nothing short of desperate." Many did not have vehicles of any type and were hampered by Jim Crow train travel. Even "white bands" found the situation to be "tough."[70] Assuredly, what one journal denoted as the "race segregation problem" hampered Negro bands, forcing them into layoffs, despite their apparent popularity.[71]

Trombonist "Trummy" Young moaned that buses "used to break down all the time," leaving passengers stranded and upset. Baritone saxophonist Harry Carney, born in Boston in 1912, "would drive 12 hours and then go on stage and play," inexorably impacting his performances. "You play a job and you're riding and you're tired," which was "very dangerous." Hence, "several guys got killed, like Chu Berry," the saxophonist, born in 1908 and perishing in 1941. It was after work and the driver-trumpeter, Charlie Shavers, as he recalled, was tired.

Travel difficulties influenced the music. Young said, "I left [Jimmy] Lunceford [and his band] because he did too many one nighters . . . it would kill you almost"—and being paid $10 nightly. He signed on with the affluent Charlie Barnet, who also happened to be Euro-American. Barnet did "pay . . . well," said Young. "He didn't have a lot of hit records or anything but I made more money" there than "[I] ever made with Lunceford . . . perhaps $50 a week" or "more." Then there was the problem that the haggardness of excessive travel could cause horn men in particular to strain unnecessarily, meaning one "blew too hard," that is, "overblew," and destroyed their lips.[72] (The unique Barnet contrasts with a fellow bandleader, of whom Leonard Feather said: "The first man I ever heard using the word 'nigger' was Glenn Miller.")[73] Even "Hot Lips" Page, trumpeter, known for his vigorous playing, "used to complain about his lip getting sore," according to Buster Smith, giving his nickname renewed meaning.[74]

Bassist "Red" Callender had a different problem. "When you play the bass with a big band," he said, "you maybe have to change shirts or undershirts a couple of times a night. So this is how [Jimmy] Blanton first contracted TB," combined with "improper care." He continued,

"You're wringing wet and you go hang out with somebody . . . all night and then you get wiped out." This could be damaging for one like Blanton, who "was very frail" in any case.

Trumpeter Herman Autrey, born in the heart of darkness that was Alabama in 1904, averred that the spouse of Fats Waller once told him, "I wish I knew my husband as well as you do," a forced association forged by incessant travel. The "rough" treatment accorded the travelers often drove musicians closer together and compelled a solidarity and familiarity that could be translated into sterling performances. With the Claude Hopkins band in Dixie, "We had to go knock on doors and say, 'Pardon me, Madam . . . do you happen to have a room'." Exacerbating an already parlous experience was the hassle of seeking fair payment for work done: he once had to threaten to "lower the boom" on Hopkins after his fee was shorted. Instead, he just grabbed him and lifted him skyward. Unfortunately, the rise of bebop harmed his career: "Yes it did. It did," he insisted. It "affected everybody" when the music turned as even "your children say" with a Bronx cheer, "Pop, that's old . . . they don't play that anymore," and "you can't tell them that they're wrong." Fortunately, he was still appreciated in Europe, and, as so often happened, that helped him closer to home. "Toronto," he insisted, reigned as "the greatest jazz town in North America. The people there really go for jazz and they really enjoy it." But Autrey, like others overtaken by the advent of bebop, was resentful, which even hurt when he was forced by the traditional bandleader Lester Lanin to audition, which this veteran found insulting. "I walked the hell out . . . I cursed him out" before acceding, then storming out again yelling "to hell with you."[75]

THERE WERE OTHER SIGNS OF DISSATISFACTION among Negro artists, which primed the pump for an artistic breakthrough. Jelly Roll Morton, a putative inventor of the new music, died in 1941 as this new era of bebop was hatching. But a few years later an interview with him was published that captured the zeitgeist. He was "bitter" about his experience in New York City. "He hadn't been successful there," and "he blamed the gangs. He said the gangs ran the bands in New York. He had no . . . connection with the gangs

there so he had never made any money or gained any prominence."
This lack of connection also meant "his tunes had been stolen from
him and sold in Tin Pan Alley." Thus "Grandpa's Spells" had become
"Glad Rag Doll," meaning he had been cheated of a fortune—or so
he thought.[76] Circumventing racketeers was a preoccupation of musicians. Ironically, wrote instrumentalist Rex Stewart, "King" Oliver
spent a lot time playing in Capone's Chicago, avoiding New York City
because of the influence of the "syndicate."[77]

Danny Barker has asserted that Morton was "forever beefing about
and against ASCAP," since "he signed his songs over to some publishers and they became wealthy, but Jelly received no royalties as the
composer."[78]

Also effectively blocking African American musicians from opportunity was the "white" union. Art Farmer, trumpeter, recalled that
during the war a "lot of guys were in the army and big bands could
still get jobs," which theoretically meant more jobs for those like himself. When bandleader Horace Henderson came to his high school
to recruit, Farmer was ready: "I remember going to school hungry a
lot of times," he recalled. So, then, in Arizona, "we went over there to
the headquarters of the musicians' union in Phoenix but they had no
black members. We said we want to join the union and they said no.
Then we wrote letters back to the headquarters of the union and to
the president saying we want to join the union and they're telling us
we can't join." He moved on to Los Angeles then being transformed
by a simultaneous internment of Japanese-Americans and arrival of
African Americans. There, he recounted, "the black local was 767, the
white local was 47," with the former sited on Central Avenue and 17th
Street: "The house next door was the house of [the] Young family.
Lester's house." The saxophonist had relocated from Kansas City.
"Downstairs was where the offices were, upstairs was just for rehears-
als." But like San Francisco to the north, Los Angeles, he said, was
a "very restrictive town as far as police were concerned. They really
bothered us. . . . They used to stop us . . . just for one joint you could
get 90 days." But the Negro local of musicians proved helpful, further bonding these artists with spillover effects on the music. "It was
unheard of to be a musician and not to be a member of the union,"

said Farmer, speaking in 1995, "like it is now." This earlier situation was due in no small part to the solidarity musicians desired in the face of Jim Crow, which in turn fostered fruitful musical exchanges.[79]

Yet Barney Bigard, who had been thought to be otherwise, was said in late 1943 to be "not a Negro" and was now seeking to join Local 47; musicians of Mexican and Filipino ancestry who had attempted to join Local 767 were forced to join 47 instead, even though some preferred to belong to the Negro local. At this point, only two locals of the American Federation of Musicians—in New York City and Detroit— were said to admit Negroes to full membership; of the 673 locals in the American Federation of Musicians, 631 were limited to those defined as "white" and a few dozen or so were limited to Negroes.[80]

This attempt to bar other minorities from joining the Negroes was not just an attempt to forestall a "colored" alliance against white supremacy; it was also an indication of the ongoing attempt to isolate and persecute African Americans as a result of fighting against the slaveholders' republic and a Jim Crow regime and allying with U.S. antagonists in doing so.[81] By early 1944, it was reported that Bigard was "rejected for membership in [the] white union."[82] Yet by May 1945, it was reported that "though Barney gained his rep with the Duke [Ellington], his new orchestra consists of white musicians."[83]

The rigidly enforced Jim Crow drove artists together and often shielded others from sharing effectively in the resultant musical bounty. "Trummy" Young resided in Harlem at 555 Edgecombe Avenue, #9H, then turned the apartment over to Johnny Hodges, yet another masterly musician. His peer, Don Redman, was next door. Boxer Joe Louis was on the first floor, close by Erskine Hawkins, trumpeter. Unavoidably there was a sharing of ideas, musical and otherwise, with mutual benefit.[84]

Jim Crow perversely and maniacally reinforced musical trends and norms among African Americans to the detriment of those denied access. Thus, the bassist George "Red" Callender, born in Virginia in 1916 but a longtime resident of Los Angeles, recalled when he was tasked to perform at a "Black and White Revue" in New York City, "They needed a bass player," but he did not recognize that the descriptor of the sessions "means just what it says. There was a black part of the show and a white part . . . we'd go on separately. The same band played for both parts but the white part of the show would go on first and the black part would go on second." To his immense benefit, it was there, said Callender, "when I first met Art Tatum," the pianist whose keyboard mastery was seen as almost mystical. Then he met Roy Eldridge, another giant.[85]

Marshal Royal, clarinetist and saxophonist, was in Southern California in the early 1940s. "Italian gangsters, the Rizzoto brothers," as he recalled, "had enough influence with the police downtown that they could run an after-hour joint upstairs" and "they always hired a piano player," luminaries "like Fats Waller." Indeed, "I used to go up there quite often with Fats Waller." It was in such venues, sites of misery and musical exhilaration combined, that new musical trends were developed. "Blues singing," he declared, "came from despair and things that were wrong in people's lives, where people were tearing their hearts out. . . . The same thing [holds] with jazz music . . . new ideas come from jazz guys out of frustration and pride . . . a lot of the things that have come out of jazz are just out of frustration . . . to just try to do something that nobody else can do"—and be "inventive" in doing so.[86]

Drummer Foreststorn "Chico" Hamilton—that's an "Apache name," he said referring to his given moniker, who was in the military from 1941 to 1945, had chilling experiences then: "I was at a lynching and didn't even know it," he said, referring elliptically to being "down in Mississippi."[87] Similarly, the vocalist Jon Hendricks was with U.S. forces in Europe during the war: "We had race riots all the way— constant fights with American white soldiers," not least "because in England or Scotland or Wales there was a shortage of black women," and Hendricks and those like him were embraced across the hetero- sexual color line: "To the southern whites and the northern American whites that was something that we were not supposed to do." Hence, said Hendricks, "they would just attack us in full force and with weap- ons. It caused a lot of—it caused some deaths and a lot of woundings. A lot of blood was shed over this, because this went on all the time. So we took to carrying guns in our waist bands," something not unknown to Negro musicians in the United States in any case.[88]

Whether to join the military was not an easy choice to make for African Americans; that is, why make the ultimate sacrifice for a government and a nation that treated you so shabbily? The drummer Elvin Jones recalled that during the First World War his father received a draft notice. Furious, "he walked from Vicksburg to Jackson. That's 60 miles," he estimated roughly, and "went to the Draft Board, handed them the letter back and said, 'I ain't going' and he walked back to Vicksburg. He didn't give a damn. He said, 'I ain't going nowhere. I ain't going.' That sort of sums it up for me."[89]

By the time the United States entered the Second World War, such anger had not dissipated, particularly since an opponent—Tokyo— had assiduously cultivated African Americans over the years.[90] On the other hand, there was a sense that an anti-fascist war would also mean pushback against Nazism's close cousin, Jim Crow, and this was not far wrong.[91]

The seeds for this later progressive flowering had been planted in the previous decade, with the rise of left-led unions and global anti-racist organizing, as exemplified by the case of the Scottsboro 9, Negroes arrested and on the fast track to execution until the intervention of Communist-backed movements.[92] A prominent producer of the new music, John Hammond, organized a benefit for these defendants in the early 1930s, alongside Duke Ellington and Benny Carter, an event he termed a "great success." Hammond's father, at the urging of Black Communist William Patterson, provided a large donation to the defendants' legal fund. The progressive Hammond began writing for *Downbeat*, but, typically, was forbidden to write of racism or "malpractices" skewering musicians; still, he joined the board of the NAACP in 1935 and continued exposing what he termed the "shocking exploitation of recording artists." He had a firsthand acquaintance with this since his "own favorite hangout" was a small club called the Black Cat, a mob-owned joint in Greenwich Village.[93]

As a producer, Hammond was unusual in his stated concern for exploitation of Negro performers, though, indicative of the pervasiveness of abuse, even he has been accused of profiteering from the miseries of Billie Holiday.[94] The pervasiveness was so severe that Mayo Williams, one of the few Negro producers at Decca, a leading recording company, described by Danny Barker as "in charge of the whole black artists' department," was accused by the guitarist as yet one more executive who cheated him.[95] "You never met. . . . the president of the company," he said, speaking of Decca. "Didn't pay you no respect. You had to deal with Mayo Williams, who was a bandit." Thus, after Barker wrote a hit tune, he was told by fellow musician, James P. Johnson to "bring your vaseline, I said, 'Bring my vaseline for what?'" The reply: "Because you're going to get screwed."[96]

The cruel antics of Joe Glaser were still profiting in the 1940s. "Trummy" Young may have had him in mind when he argued that "the relationship between black performers and their managers was not an honest one. The managers robbed them blind and this happened with practically all the best ones." It was the unrefined Glaser who spoke condescendingly and despicably of "my schwarzers," a tellingly Yiddish term affixed to Negroes.[97] The musician John Levy, who migrated to the business side of the music in part because of disgust with Glaser, observed that this mob-influenced man would not lend a hand to those with aspirations like himself. There were "no blacks in the agency business at that time," he complained, "it just wasn't done."[98]

Another exploiter who continued to thrive during the 1940s was Herman Lubinsky, once described as a "human hemorrhoid and close personal friend of the Devil," and described by another as "a horror story, a wanna-be big shot, a cigar-chomping cartoon character—five feet four, bald, myopic, with a Napoleonic complex and a heart of stone." Though he was a known cheat, his roster of clients included Errol Garner, Billy Eckstine, Dexter Gordon, Fats Navarro, Leo Parker, Miles Davis, Stan Getz, Milt Jackson, and Charlie Parker. Born in Connecticut in 1896, the ultimate commentary about him arose when his son and namesake ran away from home as a teenager.[99]

Lubinsky launched Savoy Records in November 1942 and managed to circumvent the barriers in a way deemed to be legal by acquiring a batch of jazz master recordings from Eli Oberstein, an owner of several record companies, augmented by his own 1939 recordings, mostly made in Newark. Of course, he was not averse to recording acts under pseudonyms to avoid union—and peer—detection and capitalized handsomely on the new music being developed by Charlie Parker, Dexter Gordon, and older hands like Coleman Hawkins and Ben Webster.[100]

The vocalist Jimmy Scott, who left Lionel Hampton's band to toil in a drugstore in Cleveland, also worked with Lubinsky. "He throws in your mind [that] he owns you [with] the contract he's got on you." Though, "I had no legal contract," nor could Scott find any to challenge him. "They knew him so well. Lawyers and everything knew him so well, they didn't want to be bothered."[101] Drummer Roy Porter called him "Herman the Vermin" and added with sorrow, "In his dealings with me I foolishly gave up the rights to my material." Lubinsky, he said, was also a source of the misery inflicted voluminously on Charlie Parker.[102] But as more African Americans became attorneys and accountants in coming years, this frightful situation began to change.

James "Trummy" Young was well aware of being cheated. He heard many guitarists in the "turpentine [timber] fields," and "they'd make their own blues," which influenced his own musical ventures. So trained, he wrote music for a tune to which the fabled Johnny Mercer contributed lyrics, but "my name wasn't on it," he carped. "So I got so angry about it because all the guys knew it was my tune," and "I missed all the royalties." Then there was "Margie," a recording which, he said, "sold in the millions" and "all I got," he said acerbically "was the $33 for making it."[103] Buster Smith, recalls a different kind of theft. He was performing with the renowned "Blue Devils" in St. Louis and was told "just put all you your instruments and your music" in a nearby bag. Naively, he complied. But then someone "just went in the bag," he lamented, "and stole the music," which, for all he knew, was then played by competitors.[104] His mentee, Charlie Parker, performed in Augusta, Georgia, in 1942 but was left unpaid when the sponsor of the event departed with all the funds; something similar occurred in Martinsville, Virginia.[105] According to bassist "Red" Callender, it was Barney Bigard who wrote "Mood Indigo," though it took "twenty years before [he] got his name on it," since "Irving Mills' name was on it."

Though Negro artists received the significant share of exploitation, they were not alone. According to Callender, the guitarist Les Paul, born in 1915 as Lester Polsfuss, changed his name again to Paul Leslie in order to escape what he considered to be an unfavorable contract. Such experiences led Callender to start an eponymous publishing company, and then, with horn man Buddy Collette, a record company named Legend. But it became, he said, "bogged down with the unsavory character we had handling business"; then he learned that "musicians in particular have to be able to watch their own business," a lesson still being ingested. Thus, they started another label—RBG, standing for "Red," "Buddy," and "Grover"Mitchell, a Basie trombonist born in 1930 in Alabama. Then there was simply "Red Records," his own creation.[106]

WHAT WAS HAPPENING IN PART was the favorable climate delivered by a bloody anti-fascist war that placed Jim Crow on the defensive. John Hammond, a music producer and NAACP leader, in May 1942 informed that group's national leader, Walter White, that the National Broadcasting Company and its affiliates "have no Negroes working [there] except as porters," an absence that may have been sparked by the fact that the company's leaders hailed "from the Deep South." One NBC boss "volunteered the information that he was from Florida, that he had been reared by a Nigra mammy," while acknowledging unctuously to establish his purported liberal credentials, "some of his best friends are Jews.'"[107] Nonetheless, NBC had "500 staff musicians," said White—and "no Negroes"—which took some doing, said White, given "the prominence of the Negro in the field of music and general recognition that the best dance bands were those made up wholly or in part by Negro musicians."[108] Thus, young Negro musicians were urged to apply to Leopold Stokowski's "All American Youth" orchestra.[109]

Pianist Billy Taylor limned the formidable barriers that were strewn in the path of those who might want to apply. At Howard University, the historically Negro school that he knew well, "They were so much in the European tradition and they looked down on anything that came from the jazz tradition," but "racial prejudice was such that even if you became as good a violinist as Eddie South," a virtuoso on the instrument, "you were not going to get a job with the Chicago Symphony at that time."[110]

Critic Nat Hentoff cited Howard's Sterling Brown for the proposition that at the hilltop campus "he was never allowed to teach jazz or blues as such, because in some of the black colleges . . . they didn't want jazz mentioned, because jazz had come out of those places, these brothels and gin mills."[111] This glaring omission was not Howard's alone. An expert in the new music, Marshall Stearns, was forced out of Indiana University in 1946 by what was described as an "anti-Negro faction," though he was not part of this proscribed ancestral group.[112]

Despite this encouragement, it was also in 1940, after war had erupted in Europe, that the prominent musician and composer William Grant Still, writing from Los Angeles, informed Walter White about "one colored boy who struck me as being unusually intelligent and talented," who "told me of the opposition he is encountering at home from parents who feel that the only work for colored people" was menial "and who are insisting that he relinquish his dreams of attending a musical conservatory in favor of going to work at once. Their viewpoint is that there are no opportunities for highly developed colored musicians. . . . This boy, unless he has the strength to oppose his parents as well as the world at large, will end up becoming a menial when he might do great things. It made me heartsick."[113]

Thus, the promise of anti-fascist war notwithstanding, Sidney Bechet announced disconsolately in 1941 that "the trouble nowadays is that there are too many musicians. If there weren't too many there would still be good jobs left for colored boys after the white boys got through imitating them and taking away all the best jobs." By 1943, one of the most skilled musicians of his generation was toiling ignominiously in a shipyard.[114] It was during this same conflicted era that his fellow jazzman from New Orleans, George Lewis, was working as a full-time stevedore.[115]

In sum, as the 1940s unfolded musicians faced an enervating climate of Jim Crow, labor exploitation, almost casual racism, and worse. The Pendergast machine of Kansas City by then had been weakened but left a spreading legacy, as symbolized by the presence in Manhattan of the prized export that was Charlie Parker. But

Kansas City was not unique in the Midwest. Clark Terry recalled that in the 1940s, "I heard that Peoria was even more lucrative and if you could get lucky enough to pimp a prostitute, which a lot of cats were doing, then you could *really* make it," especially since "prostitution was legal there." (Emphasis in original.) At one nightspot, "I got into a serious crap game," he said. Those shod in "AAA-width shiny black shoes with long pointed toes," were said to be shorn in "ho kickers." A woman friend of Terry's "called me her 'tennis shoe pimp' because I didn't beat her," he remarked.[116]

Still, marijuana, morphine, and Benzedrine were readily available in Kansas City. Milton Morris, the owner of the Hey-Hey Club, posted a sign on the bar advertising joints for 25 cents each. Despite these hurdles, the "colored" Local 637 of the musicians' union worked both sides of the town's color line, playing more jobs than their "non-colored" counterparts, who belonged to Local 34, leaving them irritated. The Negro success allowed them to buy a two-story red-brick building at 1823 Highland Avenue. However, this success did not prevent Parker from fleeing eastward to presumed greener pastures, this after an automobile accident, a peril of constant travel, caused the saxophonist to depart with intense pain that led to a heroin habit, fueled by the fact that Kansas City had a legion of pushers of this drug. Parker had clashed with gangsters who controlled St. Louis's popular—and aptly named—Plantation Club, which provided little incentive to stay in Missouri. Yet he made his way to 52md Street in Manhattan, already infested by the likes of the mob-connected Morris Levy and his club to be named Birdland.[117]

Given his widespread popularity as the veritable avatar of bebop, musicians imitated Parker, leading Lorraine Gordon of the Village Vanguard to conclude that "a lot of these men," speaking of musicians, "had drug habits," though all were not parallel to that of Parker. For example, "Louis Armstrong lived on pot."[118]

The pianist Randy Weston, present at the creation of the new turn in the new music, argues that "this heroin epidemic was being spread by organized crime,"[119] and given the continuing, if not enhanced, role of those like Levy and Glaser, this supposition is understandable.

Parker was emblematic of the music; he practiced at times for fifteen hours per day and did that over a period of almost four years, although early on this innovative artist was reduced to menial labor, sweeping nightclubs and washing dishes.[120] Ironically, this labor may have had an upside, according to vocalist Jon Hendricks. Parker was a dishwasher at the Onyx Club when fabled pianist Art Tatum was playing there "and he heard Art playing. That inspired him. Art was the father of what later became known as bebop. I know because I was singing all those substitute chord structures when I was 14."[121] In a posthumous tribute to Tatum, fellow pianist George Shearing said, "Whenever I hear Tatum I feel like becoming a plumber or a carpenter instead," quite a feat if executed by one as blind as Shearing.[122] Despite his mastery, Tatum is an emblem of an exploitative industry, given the hard times on which he fell; fellow pianist Hank Jones knew him well when "he worked at the Three Deuces" and was living in a Harlem hotel on 125th Street; "It was a terrible hotel," said Jones, near Eighth Avenue, "but it was the only one that he [could] get at the time" and Jones used to "take him down to work in a cab" soaking up the knowledge of piano wizardry all the while.[123]

Parker was also emblematic in that he was victimized by Jim Crow in a way that could easily induce instability of various sorts. Bassist Gene Ramey recalls the saxophonist "getting beat up by the cops in Jackson, Mississippi," where "there was a curfew for blacks." Bandmates were "smoking cigarettes" on a "front porch . . . and Bird" wound up being assaulted; "They had knots on their head big enough to hang a hat on."[124] In the summer of 1942, he was arrested for breaking a curfew in Jackson, a stricture that according to his biographer was "only enforced on black citizens." Also during the war Parker, Gillespie, and Oscar Pettiford were attacked in a New York City subway by a soldier who stripped the latter two naked. In Pine Bluff, Arkansas, Gillespie was hit in the head with a bottle after refusing to play a request from a Euro-American member of the audience. Parker, says Brian Priestley, was subject to the "normal well-founded resentments of the minority members of an aggressively white society." As a result, Parker (and others similarly situated), "had a grand disregard of law and courts, most probably stemming from the miscarriages of justice towards the Negro." So opined sculptor Julie McDonald, a friend of his, in words that shed light on the fire and passion that drove his music and the companion difficulties that haunted him to his grave.[125]

5. We Speak African!

THE 1940S BROUGHT OTHER TRANSFORMATIVE changes beyond the turn that was bebop.[1] The 45 rpm record was developed by RCA in 1949, followed quickly by the proliferation of a device that could play these discs, followed in turn by transistor radios. Along with the rise of television, these fueled the youth culture, which had been buoyed by the rise of bebop but, as matters evolved, shifted toward a musical form known as "rock 'n' roll" and a predecessor and parent known as "rhythm 'n' blues." Both opened more doors for musicians, though it might have closed a few for those who were "beboppers."[2] All of this was occurring as Jim Crow entered a death spiral. Clarinetist Buddy De Franco was among the practitioners of the new music soured by this turn of events. At the "beginning of rock and roll coming in," he said, "most of the jazz clubs began to fold," meaning "very little work for jazz players, very little."[3]

Aiding this elongated process was the obvious sacrifice Negroes had made in defeating fascism, a close relative of racist segregation. This was not just soldiering, said Louis Armstrong. "During the war," he said, "I played so many Army Camps until I'd begun to feel like I was a Lt. [Lieutenant] General."[4]

This anti-fascist sacrifice was not without cost. The drummer Chico Hamilton, unlike Armstrong, was an actual enlisted soldier. "I got court-martialed," he recalled later, "and had to do some time." He also honed his musical skill in a military band, but this assignment was not as comfy as it sounded. For in "Delaware, some place like that, I couldn't stay in the same hotel my band stayed in"; then "right outside

St. Louis," the crew "stopped to get some gas" and the "dude poured the gas on the ground and he made me pay for it." Salt Lake City was no prize either: "Their religion said the reason we were black [was] because we sinned. That was God's curse on us."[5] As matters proceeded, it did seem that seeking to dissolve the encrusted racism that permeated the United States, not least in a sector, music, where Negro influence was far-reaching, was akin to taking on the Almighty.

"CHARLIE PARKER WAS ONE OF THE FINEST persons you could meet in your life," said percussionist Machito, born in Cuba. "He was complicated, he had problems, mental problems or emotional problems," was his assessment of a man with whom he recorded. "He respected us because we respected him, so you know, it was a complete understanding" with this musician, a "gentleman."[6]

Bebop was not the only turn in the music in the 1940s. Another was the influence of Cuban artists, represented not only by Machito's relationship to Parker but how the percussionist and others influenced a heightened racial consciousness, and even created openings for the descendants of enslaved Africans that manifested itself in unusual ways. When bandleader Charlie Barnet sought to check into a hotel with his prime singer, Lena Horne, he found that "whenever I thought there might be trouble" in getting her a room, he would dispatch a comrade to "the desk, order our rooms, jabber to her in Spanish double talk and then say to the desk clerk, 'our Cuban singers would like a single room with bath.' This worked every time."[7] Interestingly, Horne faced such bias despite the fact that she knew "the nearer white you looked, the better chance you had of having your beauty noticed by those who did the hiring."[8]

Apparently, this privilege did not extend to hotels. The Cuban escape hatch notwithstanding, it was striking how the color line was policed, often on an ad hoc basis. Toby Butler, a drummer with the Darlings of Rhythm, described as an "all-girl orchestra," was detained in Milledgeville, Georgia, after it was alleged that she "was a white girl" and her bandmates were not so endowed.[9]

As the examples of Bauza and Machito suggested, Cuban musicians were becoming more prominent in New York. Perhaps foremost among them was the trumpeter known as Fats Navarro, born in Key West in 1923. Growing up there, he was exposed to Cuban music via radio. Both of his parents were of Bahamian ancestry, though his grandfather came to the United States from Cuba in 1895 and registered as "white" according to the 1900 census. His mother's father was an uncle of trumpeter Charlie Shavers, an early idol of the young horn man.[10]

Navarro left his hometown by 1941 and soon was playing in the band of Billy Eckstine, replacing Dizzy Gillespie. He joined Andy Kirk's band in 1943. "He was the influence,'" said Navarro of bandmate Howard McGhee, born in Tulsa in 1918. So influenced, he went on to star with Coleman Hawkins, while speaking highly of Hank Jones, Bud Powell, Max Roach, Kenny Clarke, and Parker. Navarro performed with Illinois Jacquet and Lionel Hampton too. In some ways, Navarro became the paradigmatic symbol of the new music in the postwar era (along with Parker). This was not only because of his musical virtuosity but the impact of narcotics on his life and of racism upon him.[11]

His warm and crackling tone, his clean notes and his startling technique ranked him with Dizzy Gillespie and Miles Davis.[12] Davis, who once had his own drug problem, called Navarro a "real bad junkie, pitiful."[13] Ironically, it was Davis who replaced Navarro in Parker's band, since by July 1950 the Floridian was dead in Manhattan, marking an era in the new music.[14] One analyst nevertheless concludes that Navarro was "the ideal trumpeter for Parker's quintet" because of "his high standard of dexterity plus his approach to melody, timbre and articulation," all of which "formed the mainstream of jazz trumpet." The two, Parker and Navarro, were said to be "ideal partners in a modern jazz ensemble,"[15] though both redolent of the grim reaper narcotics that bedeviled the music and musicians alike.

Navarro was among the most politically conscious of musicians. As he informed bassist, composer, and arranger Charles Mingus, "If they don't own us, they push us off the scene. Jazz is big business to the white man and you can't move without him. We [are] just work ants. He owns the magazines, agencies, record companies and all the joints that sell jazz to the public. If you won't sell out and you try to fight, they won't hire you and they give a bad picture of you with that false publicity."[16]

Also symbolizing the influence from abroad, which from its inception had marked the new music—which, after all, was rooted in Africa—was the impact of Mario Bauza. Jelly Roll Morton spoke of the "Spanish tinge" of the new music's origins, unsurprising since New Orleans was once under Madrid's rule.[17] Louis Armstrong's 1930 recording of a Cuban song, "El Mansiero," was suggestive in this regard.[18] Bauza was born in Havana in 1911 and by the 1930s was playing with Cab Calloway. He befriended Gillespie and performed alongside Parker. Bauza termed Navarro a "mechanical Dizzy Gillespie," that is, a "mechanical trumpet player" and "without a doubt the best. Nobody fooled with Fats." Bauza's interlocutor said that Navarro "had more understanding of Afro-Cuban rhythms than most jazz trumpeters in the early days because he came from South Florida" and was exposed to a melding of various African musical trends. Another trumpeter, Quincy Jones, concurred, and saw these Cuban maestros as being underestimated in assessments of their influence, because of their mastery of the "Cuban tumbao,"—that is, the basic rhythm played on the bass, at times replicated on the piano and often adopted on the mainland via the conga drum—a continuing staple in popular music.[19] When Art Blakey and Horace Silver adopted Afro-Cuban rhythms, Machito, Navarro, and Bauza could claim partial credit.

But it was Bauza as much as Navarro who was responsible for this development. By 1926, he had arrived in Manhattan, where, he said, "I was overwhelmed by the Negro shows at the Lafayette Theatre in Harlem," not to mention "the jazz" featuring "black men and women doing their thing." But it was his militancy that made Bauza a symbol of a rising epoch. By late 1937, he and other musicians met at the El Torredor Restaurant at 110th and Fifth Avenue to develop a plan to get better representation from Local 802 of the American Federation of Musicians. "I didn't make my living playing Latin music," said Bauza, unlike some other attendees, but he played a vanguard role nonetheless. "I attended the meeting," he said, "and saw mostly white musicians and white bandleaders." So he stood up and spoke forcefully, pointing out that he toiled in the "black jazz world," while adding pointedly, "Why didn't you invite the Afro-Cubans and Afro-Puerto Ricans who you won't give a job to?" And even with the spreading popularity of "Latin" music, he was disappointed, noting that, "I never saw a black musician working in a Latin orchestra in midtown." Thus, he said triumphantly, "I told them off and walked out of the meeting." (He managed to exempt his Euro-Cuban peer Xavier Cugat, who, he claimed, "was not a racist . . . he hired dark and mulatto musicians.")[20]

But it was not just Navarro and Bauza—or Cugat—who were adding resonance to bebop. "We didn't talk," said Dizzy Gillespie of his percussionist, Chano Pozo, "we just looked at each other."[21] Luciano Gonzales, known professionally as Chano Pozo, was born in Havana in 1915. "I've always been interested in Latin music," said Gillespie. "When I formed my big band I told Mario [Bauza] I wanted a tom-tom player. He took me to Chano's furnished room on 111th Street [Harlem], between Lenox and Seventh. We hit it off well," said the trumpeter, "even though he didn't speak English. When Chano joined my band is when the Afro-Cuban innovation in jazz began. At first he clashed with my drummer, Kenny Clarke. This changed when I sang him the melody and the beats." Thus, he continued, "all of my Afro-Cuban songs except 'Cubana be [Cubana bop]' [written by George Russell]were composed by Chano and me. It was Chano's idea and I always added something . . . on one occasion a reporter asked me how Chano and I communicated. Chano, standing behind me, answered him in broken English . . . 'Deezy no speaky Spanish, me no English . . . we speak African!'"

Like many Africans born in Cuba, Pozo found it difficult to accept the indignities of Jim Crow.[22] Machito, the Cuban-born percussionist, recalled that after performing in North Carolina, Pozo returned to Manhattan, purportedly to get new drums: "Chano had his drums but didn't want to play in the South. He didn't like the separate rest rooms and everything else which separated the whites from the black people." He told Gillespie he would join him at a subsequent performance but shortly thereafter was murdered in Harlem, dead at thirty-three, yet another victim, albeit indirectly, of Jim Crow.[23]

Looking back, Gillespie continued to praise his bandmate, though he flashed across the musical sky like a doomed meteor. "When Chano" arrived, "he really opened things up. There are things that he played . . . that I'm just beginning to understand now." Although Pozo "wasn't a writer," he was "stone Africa," that is, he helped to reconnect the music with its taproot. "He knew rhythm—rhythm from Africa." He "taught us all multi-rhythm, we learned from the master." Moreover, said Gillespie, a pioneer in his own right, "my roommate and my best friend in Cab Calloway's band musically besides Milt Hinton [bassist], was a Cuban, Mario Bauza. . . . [He] was like my father" in the manner in which he was "broadening my scope in music."[24]

It was not just their musical ideas that allowed Cubans to influence their African American peers. It was their different experience on the island that they brought to the mainland, as suggested by Pozo's revulsion when confronted with Jim Crow and Bauza's challenge to recalcitrant union practices. It was also Machito naming his band "Afro-Cubans," which has been called a "brave statement of ethnic identity" during a time when, as fellow percussionist Bobby Sanabria put it, many U.S. Negroes had been reluctant to claim African identity.[25] This was at a time when the vocalist, born Lee Brown, who sang with Lionel Hampton, adopted the name Babs Gonzales, a "Latino" identity,[26] which also underscored that those whose surnames reflected possible descent from mainland enslaved Africans, that is, those who had fought the formation of a slaveholders' republic, were subjected to a special persecution,[27] allowing more leeway for arriving Cubans.

Still, as so often happens, the arrival of the Cubans, with their differing ideas about racism and identity, was a product of the times as much as these brave men were shaping the times.

For, after a hiatus with the death of the deported Marcus Garvey in 1940, Black Nationalism began to flourish, along with Islam, when Paul Robeson, a lodestar of the left and once a hero to musicians, came under withering assault, creating a vacuum that demanded to be filled. Coincidentally, these various strands of militancy were then entangled in a Gordian knot of heroin and other dangerous substances. Jackie McLean, who was in Harlem throughout the war, says, "I never knew of any drugs or anything like that the whole time I was coming up until the end of the Second World War," and then, "the minute the Second World War was over, 1946, '47," the community was deluged with drugs (though the co-factor may have been Washington's entente with the right wing in Italy, seen as necessary to combat what was then one of the strongest Communist parties in the capitalist world). "In most black communities," says the artist, "there was an influx of [hard drugs]"—and the cost? "It was cheap, man. It was like a dollar for a capsule."[28] It was as if there were those so bewildered and outraged by the surge of progressive anti-fascism that they launched a counterattack on multiple fronts.

Unfortunately, it was even deeper than this. The U.S. anti-drug czar, Harry Anslinger, an inveterate liar and self-promoting blowhard and a xenophobic racist, was among those who thought even marijuana promoted sexual promiscuity and "interracial sex." The new music early on was associated with both, which led to the 1930s harassment of Louis Armstrong, described as a victim of the "first celebrated marijuana bust." Anslinger, like many, was both fascinated and repulsed by these artists, and this obsession only grew during his career. He established a fund for paid informants to infiltrate the world of these artists and set them up for arrest. They had much work to do since critic James Lincoln Collier asserted that as many as 75 percent of practitioners of the new music by the 1940s and 1950s used heroin.[29]

As one scholar put it, "The rise of Orthodox Islam in the postwar era paralleled the development of modern jazz."[30] It was not simply the "Orthodox," however. Trombonist Curtis Fuller was a product of this developing trend. His father was in Mosque #1 of the Nation of Islam in Detroit, the seedbed of this important religious-cum-political group, though he was only one among many of a rising generation of musicians whose ideas varied from those of their predecessors.[31] Indeed, critic Richard Boyer associated the so-called bebop revolt with youthful musicians with a bent toward militancy and Islam alike, as symbolized by the drummer born in 1919 with the name Art Blakey and later called Abdullah Ibn Buhaina, along with pianist Walter Bishop, Jr., who was also known as Ibrahim Ibn Ismail, born in 1927. Many of these musicians studied Arabic, and some of them could write in the distinctive script and "proselyte unceasingly," according to Boyer.[32] In 1947 the multi-instrumentalist Yusef Lateef, born in 1920, was introduced to Islam in Chicago by the trumpeter Talib Dawud; he "gave me some literature," Lateef said, that had been produced by the Ahmadiyya Movement, an Islamic offshoot from British India. He was also influenced by Buhaina—Blakey—and saxophonist Sahib Shihab.[33]

Like many African Americans, musicians too often felt ambivalent—at best—about the faith that was Christianity. Characteristically, trombonist Slide Hampton, born in 1932, groused, "my dad and mother made us go to church every Sunday and Sunday school. I hated it. I hated it." It was a Baptist church that he found lacking ethically, since "somebody doing something that was unfair to someone else always really just turned me off. Justice and principle and integrity was something always important to me," emphasizing: "Selfishness is a thing that I hate."[34] He found no remedies within the church, which was true for others who then turned to Islam. There may have been other benefits too. Musician Buddy De Franco said that because of religious affinity, "some dignitaries . . . from different nations would come to see Art [Blakey]," boosting his profile and possibly his earnings, though the clarinetist rather archly found this religious tie "was like a reprieve from being a black guy."[35] It was not just that. The critic Mike Zwerin pointed out that "on their police cards, black musicians could be designated as 'Muslim' instead of 'colored' and this could persuade some owners of segregated hotels that they were visiting Arab dignitaries."[36] In brief, other forces were at play were impelling African Americans to convert to Islam.

This religious-cum-political trend filled the vacuum in the aftermath of the eviscerating of the left-wing and socialist trends represented by Paul Robeson. His comrades had shown considerable interest in the new twists in the new music.[37] In turn, pianist Billy Taylor admitted that "one of my heroes was Paul Robeson." Thus, when he traveled to Haiti in 1949, he confessed, "I saw with my own eyes the kind of injustice that people of color suffer the world over, the kind of injustice to which Paul Robeson was passionately opposed."[38]

Dexter Gordon was among the musicians who admired Robeson—
"of course" says his biographer.[39] "Robeson had always been my hero,"
chimed in fellow musician Red Callender, adding, "I always loved the
way he spoke about society."[40]

Southern California musician Coney Woodman, born in 1917,
observed that in the 1940s "a lot of movie stars were Communists.
They wanted us to join the Communist Party. We never got around
to it," he assured, though "we played for Marcus Garvey."[41] "We
used to play for all the Communist dances," was the opinion of
Dizzy Gillespie. Benny Carter played for scale at several fundrais-
ers for "blacklisted" Hollywood workers and later denounced the
witch-hunting House Un-American Activities Committee. After
Fats Waller died, a Communist-affiliated youth group held a memorial.[42] Music producer George Wein speaks of the "influence of Ethel
and Frankie Newton"—the latter a prominent musician—"who had
become active members of the American Communist Party." It was
precisely "Communist organizations," according to Wein, that "provided a lot of work for jazz musicians in the late 1940s; the Party often
hired bands to play social engagements. I remember accompanying
Frankie Newton to a function in Irving Plaza" and there he enjoyed
his "first encounter with Thelonius Monk."[43] Barney Josephson, born
in 1902 and of Latvian ancestry, was in the orbit of the Communists
and founded a popular desegregated club in Greenwich Village that
gained in prominence as anti-fascism roared. In a novel touch and a
breakthrough then deemed radical, racially mixed couples could sit
anywhere within the club. This was the atmosphere in which Billie
Holiday flourished and in which her haunting anti-lynching ballad,
"Strange Fruit," took flight. Columbia Records was reluctant to release
this creation in an atmosphere in which Frankie Newton discussed
Marcus Garvey and the latest permutations of the Soviet Five-Year
Plan.[44] Critic Nat Hentoff compared Newton to Robeson. Newton
too had difficulty making a living because of his outspoken political
stances and had to work as a janitor. This artist also painted, creating
sterling images on canvas.[45]

Pianist Art Hodes, born in the Ukraine in 1904, was also in this
political orbit; thus, he said, "Our phone was tapped for a long time,"

and, likewise, "If you went on a train with blacks, you had problems," and thus "I had all sorts of problems." He visited Camp Unity, the left-wing pastoral setting, and found, "I couldn't dance with a Negro in New York but here I can do it. So it wasn't only dance. It was the free love or whatever it was."[46] In sum, it was revulsion at such episodes that led to a crackdown on dancing and the acceleration of mere listening.

In the postwar era, Negro entrepreneur Sunnie Wilson of Detroit allowed Robeson to speak at his nightspot when he was banned elsewhere. This occurred in the face of serious threats of violence, which called for heightened security led by future mayor Coleman Young, in a helmet; 1,800 amassed and hundreds more were turned away,[47] though soon the great performer and activist would be sidelined altogether.[48] In 1949 Dizzy Gillespie was performing in Harlem and found that Robeson was in the audience. "Dizzy was so impressed," said critic Nat Hentoff. Robeson told the trumpeter, "I would have gone backstage, but I didn't want to get you in trouble."[49] "I always remember Paul Robeson," said Dizzy Gillespie, "whom I loved." After Robeson was demonized, he was loath to visit the trumpeter backstage, but Gillespie instructed him bluntly, "You are me, man. . . . I sincerely meant that."[50]

Not only Black artists leaned leftward. Bandleader Artie Shaw was among those who "had nothing but contempt for hearings," held by the Un-American Activities Committee in Washington, designed to root out real and imagined Communist influence.[51]

But a kind of false dawn symbolized the rise of Josephson's club, Café Society, and the left-wing aroma it exuded, for the end of the war in 1945 featured a fierce counterattack against this trend. In some ways, it was a battle of "Reds" or Communists versus racketeers,[52] and though the former was to be weakened severely, the politics they espoused were not eradicated altogether, while the mobsters received an extended lease on life.

As late as 1950, when the political climate had become more frigid, Lena Horne gushed that she was "so in awe of him," speaking of Robeson.[53] Strikingly, horn man Buddy Collette, born in 1921 in Los Angeles, used the exact word—"awe"—in speaking of Robeson. He also was a reader of the U.S. Communist press, on the premise that "viewing some of the socialist views . . . opened up the mind," since musically, "there's more than one way to play a song," the same holds true for politics,[54] mandating openness toward diverse viewpoints. "Roach also saluted Robeson and A. Philip Randolph [union leader] as models," contended drummer Max Roach.[55] Roach went further, asserting that the exploitation of artists "goes right back to Karl Marx when he talks about . . . always keeping a reservoir of unemployed— that [way] you can control the employed."[56]

Yet, as Reds declined, racketeers ascended further. As early as 1946, trombonist Britt Woodman, born in 1920, acknowledged that the Downbeat, a popular club in Los Angeles, "was owned by a gangster called Mickey Cohen. Our payroll checks were signed by him," which was not unusual since "during that time the mob owned practically all the clubs the musicians played in."[57] Buddy Collette also had dispiriting encounters with the thuggish Cohen.[58]

This was not unique. Saxophonist Frank Foster, born in Ohio in 1928, has pointed out that "northern Kentucky—right across the Ohio River from Cincinnati, are the towns of Covington and Newport"—resembled Southern California at its worst. "Newport was a wide-open town as far as gambling was concerned. They had after-hours clubs that went from 1 a.m. to 5 in the morning. I had to get my mother's permission to work a job in this club, the Sportsman Club," which featured gambling. "We played for black folks. There were not mixed audiences in those days. You either played for all black audiences or all white audiences," though there was a "smattering" of "whites" in the former clubs. "I made max $10 a job," meaning naked profiteering for some. Instead, by 1946 his mother wanted him to attend the Cincinnati Conservatory, "which at the time was not admitting blacks," driving him back across the river into the arms of the mob. In any event, though his high school classes were not segregated, "swimming classes were," betraying a fear of intimacy while clad in swimsuits. In downtown Cincinnati, "black patrons could not go into" certain clubs, though "black musicians played there," while across the river there were sites where "black bands couldn't even play . . . they only had white bands, white patrons." Similarly, the Cincinnati Reds baseball team played at a ballpark where Jim Crow reigned.[59]

Meanwhile in Harlem, fellow saxophonist Jackie McLean was being influenced by Jimmy Briggs, whose "business was the numbers." and said the bebopper, "My dad was controlling the numbers from 155th Street to 163rd."[60]

But during the same time uber-producer Norman Granz organized the series Jazz at the Philharmonic, and forged a program to "mobilize band leaders in a drive against racial discrimination" that was to bear fruit.[61] Granz was a supporter of the left-wing presidential candidacy of former vice president Henry Wallace, defeated in 1948 by former Pendergast machine functionary Harry S. Truman, yet another turning point politically.[62] It was Granz who cancelled a concert in New Orleans when the authorities demanded that Negroes sit upstairs and others below, a typical practice.[63] Pianist Hank Jones is among those who give credit to Granz for the postwar push toward desegregation. "He insisted," said Jones, "that the audience be integrated, even in the southern towns. For instance, if an audience was segregated, he would not take the concern . . . This is something a lot of the Afro-American bandleaders . . . the Duke Ellingtons, the Cab Calloways and others, did not do." Perceptively, he added, "Norman of course was white, so he had a little more power to do things like that."[64]

This Granz initiative was timely in that it came in the midst of an incident in 1946 when Monogram Pictures, a studio soon to be defunct, substituted two musicians defined as "white" for two Negroes when Charlie Barnet's band was being filmed. That is, Negroes played on the soundtrack, they just did not appear on camera.[65] Across the continent in Manhattan, by 1947 there was only one Negro musician working in house bands for the powerful network of radio and nascent television stations. The left-leaning National Negro Congress, soon to be driven into extinction, sought reform. As things stood, the "best" Negro musicians "generally get paid only as much as second-rate white units" and were "excluded from most choice locations" besides: "Classical music was shown to be far more restrictive than the pop field" in that "not one Negro is employed by any major symphony orchestra." At that point, it was reported that there were 10,000 Negro musicians, 2,500 of them in New York.[66]

Los Angeles, which had been the recipient of a tidal wave of arriving Negro immigrants in the 1940s, was also the scene of heightened racist tension, as a partial result. Howard Rumsey, who founded a club, the Lighthouse, in Orange County during this tumultuous decade, observed late in life that "in the early days [Negro] musicians had a tough time navigating around local police officers, who sometimes tailed them through town. . . . Many quit coming and didn't resume for several years."[67] This pattern also held due north in Los Angeles. Buddy Collette was headed to the Westside with a Euro-American woman in tow, and the maître d' at the club's door "just about lost his teeth." Said Collette, "I really got frightened."[68] What Collette was experiencing was a supposed crackdown on crime that was actually a crackdown on Negroes—a repetitive pattern before and since. L.A. cops, frustrated at their inability to solve crimes, began raiding Central Avenue nightspots in Black L.A., strangling business. This was driven, said a reporter, by the alleged "relationship between jazz and crime," meaning "musicians, entertainers, customers (particularly in mixed parties) were arrested right and left."[69]

In retrospect, the dual militancy of Robeson-influenced leftism and nationalist-influenced Islam combined to puncture the walls of Jim Crow that had handicapped so many. As drummer Roy Porter put it, "You see, with the Black Bebop Jazz Musicians, you weren't dealing with no 'yassuh boss niggers.' We were a new breed," willing to confront the point that "all the clubs were owned by whites with blacks fronting in some of them."[70]

Ironically, the satrap of the Pendergast machine in Kansas City, President Harry S. Truman, spearheaded the offensive against Robeson, which altered the political calculus for musicians and Black America alike. During the midst of war, Truman managed to travel in January 1945 to Pendergast's funeral, where he told a reporter that he "owed his political promotion" to the late political boss,[71] an unsettling signal at best.

As one man from Kansas City was turning the ship of state sharply to the right, another (albeit from across the river) continued to innovate energetically in an objectively different direction. Saxophonist Jackie McLean, born in Harlem in 1931, recalls espying his fiery congressman, Adam Clayton Powell, and his similarly progressive spouse, the pianist Hazel Scott, enjoying and drawing energy from a Parker performance at the Royal Roost in Manhattan in 1948.[72] Pianist Duke Jordan, born in New York in 1922, is no doubt correct in asserting that Parker was "bugged by the fact that being a Negro, he could [go] just so far and no farther," while "many whites in postwar America longed for a return to the old values." As late as 1949, a disc jockey in Detroit could be fired from a "white radio station" for broadcasting a "black record" by the mild-mannered singer and keyboardist Nat "King" Cole. At that historic moment, the Jim Crow regime was straining against the leash of global public opinion, which had turned against Berlin's racism during the war and was unwilling to tolerate Washington's, yet it was not clear if the Euro-American majority and the elite that spoke for them would be willing to yield. As things evolved, the popularity of music and musicians may have been a factor in generating a solvent that would serve to erode the most obdurately obsidian bias,[73] a process associated in coming years with Congressman Powell.

The pain and perception that Parker felt was poured into and out of his instrument. During this time, at Minton's in Harlem and other clubs where bebop was being developed, musicians had to "play their hearts out," according to Miles Davis's son, who had reason to know. "The audience had been known to come onstage, drag a musician off, and bodily throw him into the street," while imploring vigorously, "Don't come back till you learn how to play."[74]

This vigor was a reflection of the energy being directed against Jim Crow. Unsurprisingly, when the visiting blind pianist George Shearing traveled across the United States in 1949, he was sufficiently perceptive to note a startling level of racism,[75] though more perceptivity might have detected a rising tide against this pestilence.

This was a promising trend that was to manifest more dramatically in the following decade, but in the short term—1949—Nesuhi Ertegun, a founder of what became Atlantic Records, which was to record John Coltrane and other notables, told co-founder Ahmet

Ertegun that "the demand for Dixieland records is very high right now. . . . We are setting up distributions in key centers all over the country." He then added revealingly, "We want [a] distributor who gives full coverage to white locations especially, and who handles no other Dixie line preferably." In short, contrary to Granz, he was willing to capitulate to Jim Crow rather than combat it.[76] Atlantic had to contend with an unforgiving environment. In a cash business where distributors had to make their own deals with local trucking companies and shippers, no independent record company could say without equivocation that it was free of mob influence, meaning rightward tugs.[77] Just before the words between the Ertegun brothers were penned, a reporter was noting that companies like his were troubled: "Indies losing out in wax race," since the "Big 4 controls industry. 300 indies may soon be holding collective bag."[78] Those labels that were lucky would be bought or subjected to merger.

Even during the waxing of anti-fascism, there were disturbing signs that it would take more exertion to eradicate the horror that was Jim Crow. In the febrile atmosphere that arose, for example, Prestige Records, formed by Bob Weinstock in 1949, a company that Miles Davis equated with a shark, was indicative of the changed balance of forces between progress and reaction, capital and labor. Known to take decided advantage of musicians who were desperate for money, particularly those who had to have cash because of heroin addiction, Prestige signed them to adhesion contracts that compelled them to record a sizeable number of performances in exchange for a tiny advance against future royalty payments, which often did not materialize in any case. Because of such unscrupulousness, according to critic Frank Kofsky, Weinstock was "able to accumulate innumerable priceless performances by Davis, Sonny Rollins, Thelonius Monk, John Coltrane, Charlie Parker, Eric Dolphy," and other masters of the art. Jackie McLean said provocatively that "if you can imagine being under the Nazi regime and not knowing it," you can imagine being under the heel of Prestige. For his part, Weinstock invested handsomely in Florida real estate.[79] In reflecting on the assessment that Prestige was known as "the junkies' label" and "the plantation," McLean agreed that some "independent record companies and club owners knowingly take advantage of musicians who were strung out on dope." It was "terrible," he said. "We were helpless." These "exploitative" labels compelled artists to pay for recording sessions but then "all the music went into their publishing company, so they made a killing there. The recording contract you signed said that you paid for everything eventually: sandwiches, cabs, Rudy Van Gelder [engineer], studio time, the pressing of the records, the design, everything. You got no royalties until that nut [expenses] was met."[80]

Heroin, said critic Nat Hentoff, reduced the genius pianist Bud Powell to begging: "Can I have a dollar?" was his wounded appeal.[81]

At any rate, this was a continuation of a related trend for as cornetist Rex Stewart, born in 1907, observed, record executives often thought "a musician played with more native abandon when he was full of alcohol"; thus at recording sessions there was "always . . . plenty of whiskey or gin" present.[82] Bandleader Harry James was among the major imbibers, said Artie Shaw; he "used to drink five martinis at lunch," a rate that "killed Bix [Beiderbecke]," a fellow musician. Coleman Hawkins was among those who preferred brandy.[83] Ben Webster, Coleman Hawkins, and Lester Young, said one analyst, "each drank themselves to death in a protracted long, slow-moving suicide." The latter, in particular, "suffered a whole lot of Jim Crow," and this doubtlessly contributed to his "alcoholism." Hawkins's father "committed suicide. He walked into the water one day."[84]

The pressure of racism was intense, often inducing such radical reactions. J. J. Johnson, an extraordinary trombonist, born in 1924, observed that racism was "rampant" when he grew up in Indianapolis: "We were a self-contained community," yet the veritable walls surrounding his vicinity were not sufficiently impermeable to exclude noxious external influences: alcohol abuse in the first case. Fred Beckett was his biggest influence on his instrument but, said Johnson, "he had a bout with alcoholism—a terrible, terrible bout with alcoholism. It was a tragedy because he was such a talent. . . . It hurt most of us to see him go down," passing away at the age of twenty-nine.[85]

"When I first came to New York," said Billy Taylor, speaking of the immediate prewar years, whiskey was freely available; it was the "drug of choice" and "you could get a drink in the daytime if you had 15 cents. At night the prices went up to a quarter for a scotch. A double was 35 cents," a price range supplemented by the point that musicians could often get drinks at even cheaper rates—or for free.[86]

Alcohol flowed easily at performance sites. But that was not all. Pianist Jimmy Rowles, born in 1918 in Spokane, found it necessary to wear a "mask" because of cigarette smoke, while adding, "I don't give a damn whether they think I look funny," indicative of an unhealthy climate that could drive a musician to drink, or worse.[87] Revealingly, there were said to be caged birds in Birdland, which did not survive long because of the smoky atmosphere.[88] Trumpeter Joe Wilder noted irritably that "smoke used to drive me crazy" while playing in clubs, a situation worsened since "about 65% of the fellows I worked with did smoke."[89] Pianist Barry Harris, born in 1929 in Detroit, confesses, "I was a cigarette smoker," albeit for defensive reasons. "The only reason I smoked cigarettes," he said, "is that it was my protection against the marijuana and the cocaine and the heroin. You had to do something, you know, so I would smoke cigarettes." Other musicians thought that if you consumed hard drugs "you could play like Bird [Charlie Parker] or something." Harris was subjected to stress too but was able to overcome it. When vocalist Sheila Jordan came to hear him play in Hamtramck—or "Polish town"—close by Detroit, he found that "every eye in that joint was looking at us," notably the melanin deficient vocalist and "when the gig was over—good thing there was a streetcar going by, 'cause we made it to that streetcar, but they [were] coming after us."[90]

Besides smoke, there were loud sounds with the musicians in close proximity to same. For Buddy De Franco this meant tinnitus, which can deliver hearing loss. "It is a hiss," he said. "It's always there . . . [although] sometimes the hiss is louder than the band I'm working with." He blamed drummer Art Blakey, since "for many years I'd stand and play in front of the drummer." Then the constant fingering of his horn contributed to "trigger finger. . . . I'd wake up," he said, "and it would be locked and I'd have to pull it out. I got an injection of cortisone" and was also "fighting the battle now with this jaw and my eyes and I have double vision. . . . I've spoken to a lot of doctors."[91]

Gambling was also an occupational hazard of musicians, worsened

when Las Vegas expanded in the postwar era, a place where this practice was legalized. "Gambling was the only addiction I'd dealt with,"
said Clark Terry. "The thrill of winning was so powerful."[92] By 1948,
pianist Mary Lou Williams's self-described gambling addiction was
feeding excessive drinking, a dangerous habit fed by the venues in
which she performed her art. She began supervising gambling out of
her own home, with what one writer described as "four tables going.
All the hustlers in town came . . . the game lasted almost two days,"
with one intimate complaining that she was "fooling around with
these dope fiends. . . . Dope fiends will rob you." She responded that
"nervousness" was at the root of this overweening problem.[93]

The "nervousness" may have been shaped by the overriding patriarchy that reigned in the business.[94] Horn man Von Freeman, born
in 1923, was among those who felt that "a woman has to be twice
as good as a man to get any kind of recognition, because this is a
man's thing. . . . They had to be great, great, great, great before the
guys would accept them."[95] As Clora Bryant put it, "I never let them
forget I was a female," since it was assumed that "when you play the
trumpet, you had to be a man. That was my main purpose for doing
that. Because when I was in college," said this artist born in Texas in
1927, "we played some of these places. They'd say, 'aw, that ain't nothing but a bunch of lezzies,'" meaning lesbians. "I didn't want to hear
that," she said, "so that's why I dressed to impress. . . . I even played a
place that used to be up on Vermont," in Los Angeles, her residence,
that is, "a lesbian place. . . . I'd see the women in the booths kissing on
each other." Being a woman meant that, a fortiori, she was even more
subject to being rooked by unscrupulous club owners. For example,
there was the club "run by Curtis Mosby. He was a little crooked. He
owed a lot of people money" and ultimately, was jailed.[96]

Billie Holiday born in 1915, endured wrenching experiences while
performing. Artie Shaw recalled a time when she was derided as a
"nigger wench" and "she was really hissing at" the insult, which had
the "makings of a riot," even a "lynch[ing]." This was at "the end of
Billie's southern tour," he said. Another time, she was told to take a
freight elevator in a hotel, a purposeful insult. Another time, "We
painted a little dot on her head with this lipstick. One red dot between

the eyebrows. We called her the Princess Majarani so-and-so. She check[ed] into the hotel," with little difficulty as a result, though she felt it was "kow-towing,"[97] when actually it was a tactic to evade the often violent obloquy routinely heaped upon presumed descendants of mainland enslaved Africans.

Besides rank insult, women musicians had to contend with rank bias. Pianist Billy Taylor recalled "Norma Shepherd," a "very attractive woman who at one time [was] . . . the best jazz pianist in town," speaking of Washington, D.C. "But because she was a woman she didn't get the kind of attention that Mary Lou Williams and some of the luckier women had got."[98] There was a related issue, said Clora Bryant. "Many times the guys have to turn off from me because they are afraid that their wives and girlfriends will get the wrong idea. I've called guys that I've worked with and their ladies would answer the phone and get upset because I was a woman." This complicated the opportunity to land jobs. Moreover, postwar "black musicians were getting the white women to go [for]them," she asserted, "and the powers that be didn't like any of that stuff. . . . They had to break it up. Before long they were harassing folks around Central Avenue on a regular basis. . . . It was a conspiracy to destroy what we had," she declared.[99]

It was not just gender mixing that was subjected to sanction. Clarinetist Buddy De Franco played alongside trumpeter Clark Terry, and recalled, "I was the only white guy and it got to be ridiculous," leading to "phone calls that were nasty or somebody in the audience might [say] 'how come you are playing with [him].' . . . I got a lot of static for being the only white guy in the band." This Italian-American was once playing with Kenny Drew, Blakey, and Eugene Wright, "three black guys and myself," he said, "and the owner came to me and said, 'I see you have colored men in your group. . . . They can stay downstairs in the cellar, we have a place for them.' . . . It was a real personal effrontery to me," he claimed later. On another occasion, playing with Drew, a "white lady . . . wouldn't let him alone and she kept hugging him," while chanting, "I always wanted a black man," perhaps accidentally jeopardizing his life expectancy. On yet another occasion, this time in Chicago, he allowed singer Harry Belafonte to stay in his room, and then "about five or six guys came after me. And

two of them pinned me against the wall and I figured, well . . . this is
the end of my career . . . and one of the guys said to the other guys, in
Italian, 'Leave him alone, he's Italian.' So they walked away. And [as] I
walked away he kicked me in the pants."[100]

En route to Kentucky by train in 1946, Terry and his bandmates
knew that "normally this meant that all colored passengers had to get
up from their regular seats and relocate to the back of the train in the
'Jim Crow' car." Even at a Chinese restaurant in Portland, he found
dismayingly that "coloreds" faced impermeable barriers. His future
wife, Pauline, didn't want to travel with him because "she wasn't too
comfortable among white people. She'd told me how when she was
a little girl, some white men dragged her cousin out of their house,
strung him up a tree, and hanged him right in front of the whole
family." Again, the travel that was a constant of a musician's life was
a source of constant stress. "Cats would go home only to hear gossip
about their wife's new lover or, even worse, catch the clap from their
wife . . . actually *walk in* on their old lady with some sleaze ball."[101]

Vultures like Weinstock took full advantage of the situation presented to them. Art Farmer said that "between narcotics and the
prejudice thing," they fed each other in that racism "might have led to
the narcotics in some cases, just feeling like the avenues are blocked
anyway, so we might as well get high."[102]

And it was not just Weinstock who was preying on musicians. Morris
Levy of Birdland was well-connected to various branches of organized
crime and his club was thought to be a center of operations for these
miscreants, their presence serving to aid the dissemination of drugs to
musicians and patrons alike, facilitating the heightened exploitation of
the former. A good deal of Levy's vast fortune was made by assigning
himself royalties of artists who recorded for the many labels in which
he had an interest, notably Roulette, which in completing of a circle
devoid of virtue had been a front for heroin trafficking.[103] "You were
pressured," said Artie Shaw. "There was a lot of pressure" by publishers,
meaning "you rarely saw royalties."[104] Percy Heath, born in 1923 and
a member of a renowned musical family, recalled that "Morris Levy
and his brother, Irving, and some other, hooked-up, connected Jewish
owners" of clubs were influential in the business. "All those clubs in

New York at that time," he said, "were run by the so-called mob and Morris Levy was connected, otherwise they wouldn't be in business." In contrast, Thelonius Monk "couldn't get a cabaret card" allowing him to play in Gotham because "he had been busted," while Levy, a gangster, meanwhile was raking in cash—"sort of a double standard there. Musicians were restricted from appearing in nightclubs and the owners were all gangster-involved type people."[105]

This racketeer influence hardly dissipated in the immediate post-war years. Indeed, Levy could argue that those like himself revived a dying music scene. By November 1946, *Downbeat*, the bible of the new music, was fretting that there were "worrisome days along the street," speaking of 52nd in Manhattan. "Biz is sad."[106] Weeks later, it was announced tremblingly that there were "four spots left" on this thoroughfare, as "jazz" supposedly "blows final breath on 52nd Street."[107] But soon, Birdland took flight and just as mobsters had fought Klansmen in 1920s St. Louis who wanted to exclude Negro artists altogether, the likes of Levy helped to move bebop from uptown to midtown, better facilitating exploitation. Thus, by August 1949, the turnabout was complete: "Jazz booming again in Gotham," it was announced.[108]

Vocalist Jon Hendricks, born in 1917, began his career as a drummer, but once he heard Roy Haynes he pawned his drums and became a singer;[109] he once observed about his hometown that "in Toledo it was the Niccovoli [*sic*] mob. In Detroit it was the Purple Gang. I worked at the Chateau La France for the Niccovoli mob. I would have to spend my time in the back by the kitchen door. I would watch this big pack of touring cars drive up. These four men would get out with the big overcoats and the big Borsalino hats. They would come in, take off their overcoats, take these big shotguns out from under their overcoats and stack them in a barrel by the door"; at times, "they would rub my head" since "it was considered good luck in those days to rub a nigger's head . . . that was degrading and it was awful. I would feel so mad." Adding insult to injury, then "they would put this wad of money in my hand" in presumed charity.[110]

Even if racketeers were not visibly part of the political economy of the business, their methods and tactics continued to be felt. J. J.

Johnson came to maturity in Indianapolis and in a conversation
with fellow musician and Indianan David Baker was reminded by
him of "an incident in St. Louis when you were with Benny Carter
where you were actually physically attacked by someone." The tactful Johnson replied, "My exposure to violence in any shape, form or
fashion was more exposure to psychological violence than physical
violence," which was similarly damaging.[111] Unfortunately, the violence inflicted on Bud Powell was physical. Jackie McLean noted that
the keyboardist declined mentally after Philadelphia police officers
"started beating Bud over the head" and "knocked him unconscious"
and "he ended up in the psychiatric ward."[112] Substance abuse—or
self-medication—was his next stop.

The threat of murder loomed ominously over the heads of Negro
performers, often compelling assent to edicts that otherwise might
have been ignored. Lena Horne "began to dread mealtimes," deathly
worried that a racist upset with her success might seize the opportunity to poison her.[113] Drummer Max Roach recalled, "I've had
fights, heavy ones because I was with white women" on 52nd Street.
"I broke my thumb. . . . I had to fight my way out of the situation. The
3 motherfuckers broke both my thumbs. . . . [They] suckered me into
a rumble." This was "about '49."[114]

This violence—or threat thereof—helped to keep in line artists who
were generating enormous profits for others. "What is the reason,"
asked percussionist Roach with asperity, "that Duke [Ellington] didn't
have as much money in his estate as Irving Berlin? The conditions
we have to play under are just an extension of the conditions Black
people have to live under."[115]

According to Billy Taylor, these record labels were so busy cheating and addicting artists that they had "no marketing plan," adding,
"many things that they could have done in terms of promotion and
merchandising were not done because that wasn't the way they did
business at Prestige or Blue Note or the Roost or any of those labels."
In sum, the much-touted decline in the music was partially a self-
inflicted wound imposed by ham-fisted exploiters. This critique
brought the pianist and composer into sharp conflict with music
executives. He said, "The idea of being able to control my own destiny

was the one that got me in a lot of trouble throughout my entire career, because I was not averse to speaking to the guys that owned the clubs and other people in ways that they were not accustomed to being spoken to," about sensitive matters, such as working conditions and fees. Taylor, who "read all the black newspapers" and attended university, then went on in coming decades to spearhead struggles for musicians' self-determination.[116]

Taylor, who emerged from a family of dentists and preachers, headed north to Harlem in the 1940s and soon encountered the difficult conditions then endured by other musicians. One of his first stops was Minton's, an incubator for bebop. This, he said, was a "place where a lot of pimps and hustlers and people who live the fast life partied"; they "hung around the bar in the daytime," where they at times encountered Henry Minton, a "former delegate to the Musicians' Union." But since there were "many places" where "you couldn't enter because of Jim Crow," options were limited. One was Sherman Billingsley's club in midtown Manhattan: "They didn't want African-American people there," said Taylor of this posh nightspot. Even Harlem had barriers; at a southern border of this neighborhood, he said, "not only could black people not own businesses on 125th Street, none of them owned any business[es]."[117]

In short, the postwar upsurge of musician militancy marked by various forms of nationalism combining with a declining allegiance to the socialism represented by Robeson was met, quite typically, with a vociferous counterattack, which in turn compelled a number of artists to continue the historic trend of seeking work overseas. John Levy, described by Hentoff as "the first black manager of any kind of substance," reputedly said "there were black contracts and white contracts. The kind of royalties you got and the kind of publicity you got from the company would depend a lot on your color," as opposed to your talent and creativity. This kind of corruption was pervasive. Thus, even the estimable Leonard Feather, viewed as being aligned with the angels, was scorned as embodying "conflicts of interests," according to Loren Schoenberg in conversation with Nat Hentoff, since he was a "composer and an A&R guy," that is, label executive, and a "record reviewer. . . . Musicians must have reacted a certain way, saying, 'Man, you better record this guy's tune, because we know that he's writing reviews in this magazine.' " Hentoff concurred: "The conflict of interest stuff, I thought was tawdry." Hentoff had reason to question Feather in that he questioned himself; he became introspective after his daughter told him bluntly, "How can you write about people's careers when you can't tell one chord from another?" "That hit me hard," the critic conceded. "I was brooding about it . . . I had power. That's what led to my brooding about it."[118] His daughter may have known of the caustic words of flutist and saxophonist Yusef Lateef, who complained bitterly that "the critic might not even recognize the form of the music. . . . Perhaps they really didn't know what they were listening to," for "if you misidentify a form . . . this discredits the person," meaning "there's a danger of being a poor critic." Citing philosopher Arthur Schopenhauer, he offered the dictum that "a critic is one who has no occupation of his own."[119]

J. J. Johnson, was like a number of musicians in seeing critics as "strange birds. I've had problems with what I've read," he concedes. The unfairness he perceived led to his making a fateful choice: "I got out of jazz," and "took a job at Sperry Gyroscope for economic reasons," simply to "have an income and be a responsible husband," and, he confessed, "I was glad that I did."[120]

Thus, it became easier for Prestige Records to ensnare musicians in light of the intractable difficulties endured by many of them. It became easier also, for just as wartime helped to suppress the safety valve that was expatriation, by 1948 Louis Armstrong was reportedly asking, "Why won't you let us bring our music to Britain?" A kind of musical protectionism still reigned, and Armstrong, who was able to escape to Western Europe in the 1930s, was portrayed as disconsolate about this trend.[121] Dizzy Gillespie was allowed to visit weeks earlier, but the Ministry of Labour forbade his playing; an editorialist wailed that "old stagers among us will remember the tremendous fillip given in British dance music by Duke Ellington and his orchestra in 1935. . . . They came over here and they put us right."[122] This obstruction in reaching London was notably significant, for it was there, said Louis Armstrong, that he received the name "Satchmo," an important affixation more important than the name itself suggested.[123]

Still, musicians continued to depart the United States for more favorable climes. Artie Shaw suggested why. Trumpeter Roy Eldridge, according to the bandleader, was the "highest paid member" of his group, yet he was "kept from entering [the] front door" of the club where he was slated to perform. "He came in very salty," said Shaw later, "very angry . . . and his playing was angry," an indicator of how prevailing conditions impacted the music. Afterward, "someone knocks at my dressing room door" and "in comes Roy and he's got a knife. He said, 'Any reason I shouldn't use this on you?'" A startled Shaw was able to convince him otherwise: "He looked at me," said Shaw, "and started to cry. I put my arms around him and said, 'For Christ's sake, get out of this country. You don't belong here. Go to Paris.' "[124]

But even those who concluded that simply migrating to Manhattan was the preferred option had problems doing so. For as Billy Taylor pointed out, often you had to wait six months to get a union card allowing you to play after arriving, precisely to curb out-ot-town competition.[125]

Musicians were being squeezed. Often blocked from exiling, or even moving to Manhattan, they continued to face high hurdles in Dixie, a region that Louis Armstrong, with a dash of sarcasm, referred to in 1946 as "Germany," a reference to Berlin's recent unfortunate history.[126]

This intensely racialized atmosphere ineluctably influenced the music and may have played a role in the movement across the Atlantic, where at least it was easier to choose accompanists without Jim Crow impediments. A historian of the music, William Russell, was told by a musician that "I can't (and have no desire to) listen to anything but the *best* and no (or very few) white men" can meet this standard. "It's pretty impossible for a group of *white* musicians who have never experienced any of what [we have] to approach" his compositions and arrangements.[127] Performing alongside Bunk Johnson, it was reported, "has 'spoiled' me for wanting to play with any other trumpet players (especially *white* musicians) and the more I play, one single fact keeps recurring and that is, that I don't want to play with white musicians . . . at all anymore, especially drummers."[128]

This racial preference expressed in 1940s San Francisco was eased

by the fact that the musicians' union "refuse[d] to allow the [man-
ager] of the Sunday session to hire white members to play with Bunk
[Johnson], so they're using a small colored combo."[129] In other words,
this racial preference was in part a surrender to an enforced reality,
which, as noted, drove the most competent musicians to play together
and mutually reinforce innovation.

The drummer formerly known as Kenny Clarke, who chose exile,
averred that "when I started out black people had their own publishing companies, their own dancehalls and they did their own booking
[but] the Jewish people bought them out. . . . By the late thirties it was
all over. That's why Teddy Hill," bandleader and manager at Minton's
in Harlem, "quit playing music." Accuracy of detail aside, his acerbic recollection was a reflection of a long history of exploitation that
did not seem to cease despite the clamor of antifascism. In any case,
as the historian Mike Hennessey put it, "Certainly it has been my
experience that when they are aware that their comments are to be
published, more black musicians soft-pedal their antagonism to discrimination,"[130] since those defined as "white American," frequently
irrespective of ideology, tend to get upset when this touchy matter is
broached.

Clarke was disgusted with the growing practice of record companies paying artists with narcotics, creating a relationship of
dependency. Promoters responded by threatening to boycott, but he
refused to yield, leaving few options beyond exile.[131]

Yet some of these same objectors were similarly vocal in denouncing the exploitation that was the common lot of Negro musicians. An
epitome of bebop, pianist Theolonius Monk, born in 1917 in North
Carolina, recalled a time when he "worked all over town," speaking of
New York City. "Non-union jobs, twenty dollars a week, seven nights
a week and then the man might fire you anytime and you never got
your money. I've been on millions of those kinds of jobs," he said. The
union hardly objected, and the same held true when unprincipled
record companies employed non-union Negro musicians to create
so-called race records.[132] Horn man Buddy Collette spoke of a time—
"maybe [19]48"—when he recorded for a label run by a man who
"wouldn't pay anybody."[133]

It was not just labels. Saxophonist Benny Golson, born in 1929, once performed alongside Art Blakey and was informed that he would be paid after the "next album." Then after that album was finished, Golson inquired about payment, and "Art looked at him like he had two heads" and replied curtly, "Not this record date." Disgusted, Golson spoke ill of "such shuck and jive slipperiness," a "bait and switch. Promise and temporize," that is, the "artistry of a three-card monte dealer."[134]

Suffused with disgust, a stream and then a flood of musicians migrated to Europe in the postwar years. "European exodus gains momentum" was the summer 1948 headline in *Downbeat*.[135] This chosen exile allowed musicians to be living symbols abroad of the iniquities of the United States, at a time when Washington was determined to corral allies for Cold War goals, creating ever more pressure for a retreat from the more egregious aspects of Jim Crow. This lengthening list included bassist Percy Heath, who fled Philadelphia—"it was like institutional segregation" there, he maintained—for Paris in 1949. "Europeans were very receptive. They were more or less color blind, where in America, it was some kind of race music," he was said to perform, a "degenerate, degradation of the population, degrading of morals" besides. This degradation, he contended, was reflected in common parlance: "Don't give me all that 'jazz,'" which "meant it was insincere." This elevated art form was "only allowed in . . . unsavory places, like in brothels and smoky nightclubs," a degradation that stemmed from the music's evolution "from slave hollers in the field."[136]

Trombonist Slide Hampton, born in 1932, wound up in Paris too, where, ironically, he was exposed to Brazilian music, which did not leave his art unaffected. "I started listening when I was living in Paris," he said later, "because a lot of Brazilian people came to Paris." He migrated for the usual reasons, for example, "The guys that were making the most money in most cases were paying the least." Lionel Hampton was in the first place: "He was the most popular band out there. Paid the least." Thus, it was on to France where he encountered drummer Kenny Clarke, also known as Liaquat Ali Salaam, born in Pittsburgh in 1914. So taken was the percussionist with his new homeland that "if you said something about France, Kenny would really jump on you, because he lived in France for a long time and without a green card," or proper immigration credentials. "They loved him so much there," which was not atypical, since "in every major city in Europe, there is a subsidy from the government of that country to record jazz."[137]

Salaam was exiled in 1948 to Paris after he was cheated by a booker. The booker, taking umbrage at the drummer's discontent, told him threateningly, "You'll never work in New York again," not leaving him with many alternatives beyond exile. It is claimed that he was making a mere fifty cents a night while accompanying Roy Eldridge during these lean days. "It finally made me realize," he said, "that I didn't belong in the States." The drummer, says his biographer, was "extremely bitter about the exploitation of black musicians by white people" and "detested the rampant racism in the United States," to the point where he tried to persuade others, including Charlie Parker, to follow him abroad. "Over here you will be treated like an artist," he insisted.[138] It was not just Clarke in France, according to Nat Hentoff, who found contentment abroad; Ben Webster, for example, was "lionized" in Denmark.[139]

But one past venue was now being closed. "Commies spell doom to Shanghai entertainment," it was said in December 1949,[140] weeks after the triumph of the Chinese Revolution. Months later, war on the Korean Peninsula erupted, heightening the anti-communist wave while hastening the further persecution of Robeson and his comrades. Yet the simultaneously heightened global engagement opened the door for further external pressure upon the nation to reduce its hateful Jim Crow policies. These checkered trends would continue in the coming decade.

6. Lullabye of Birdland

AS THE 1950S DAWNED, the former Cotton Club dancer and co-worker with Lena Horne, Howard Johnson, was a Communist on the lam, underground, evading detention. Then, at a club in Cincinnati, he bumped into Duke Ellington, whom he knew from halcyon days in Harlem. The elegant bandleader played along with Johnson's now furtive identity. He even offered to allow the fugitive from injustice to "stay in his suite," as Johnson recalled, an unsurprising trend given prevailing ideologies among musicians.[1]

Just as there was a dual trend in the immediate postwar era of a United States pressured to retreat on Jim Crow, as it heightened anti-communist interventions abroad—not least against nations such as Korea and Vietnam, not defined as "white"—there was also the con-tinuation of the battering of those perceived as close to Paul Robeson and the U.S. Communist Party, which, in some ways, was at odds with the retreat from apartheid. Those like Johnson, ergo, were bruised, which had the not incidental collateral impact of dulling the ideologi-cal edge among African Americans, to the detriment of this besieged community.

Also besieged was the music itself, for the form known as bebop continued to be subjected to unremitting fire. It was no more than a "narcotic," charged one exasperated critic in 1949. "Today large seg-ments of the working class are being duped by the bourgeoisie into the decadence and violence of bebop." This musical form "started as a revolt—an *individual* revolt by certain musicians against yet within the confines of bourgeois institutions. As such, it could only end like

the cults of existentialism, surrealism and non-objective art, in fleeing from reality." The writer, James Elmer Hutchinson, was well aware
of the external strains pressing on musicians: "Not until 1945—with
Count Basie—did the first Negro band play in a Broadway theatre or
hotel." Moreover, "The musician of bebop is forced to live an abnormal
life. His late hours, the strain of his conditions of work, tend to drive
him to special forms of adjustment. Cultism, alcohol or narcotics can
[mask] the musician's awareness of his hopelessly exploited condition
for a time." Despite this apparent sympathy for the musician, there was
decidedly less for the music. "It is undanceable," Hutchinson cried,
and consequently, "as a formalistic form of music, interferes with the
satisfaction of the social needs of the dancers." Thus "the audience
is forced into the position of passive, uncreative sitter in the static,
non-functional concert hall," not to mention that the music "is not lis-
tenable either!" And "the lyrics [sic] are largely anti-social, anti-labor,
anti-Negro and sex escapist." Despite these alleged flaws, the music is
"big business now. Thelonius Monk. Charlie Parker. J. C. Heard, Tadd
Dameron, Lenny Tristano, all contributed to the formulation of the
stillborn little bebop." This musical form was just "another example of
the fundamental problem of bourgeois art, viz. the separation of form
and content, the attempt to take historically developed form and separate it from its historic function," meaning bebop was "certainly not
progressive or people's music."[2] Another left-wing writer was more
sympathetic,[3] but this aforementioned broadside was a troubling sign
that there were those opposed to evolution of the music, seeing it as a
frozen form and, instead, were bent on forcing it into an impermeable
and crustacean shell.

Conceptual obstacles aside, accomplished artists continued to
produce wealth, largely appropriated by others. Indeed, there was a
postwar boom that involved more income streams including the proliferation of jukeboxes. Union boss Petrillo claimed that this device
was partly responsible for 60 percent of his unions being out of work,
though his own mob ties made it difficult for him to alter what he
perceived. He called jukeboxes "Scab Number One."[4] For in the early
postwar era, there were 7,000 of these contraptions sited in Chicago
alone, a bonanza that unleashed intense rivalries with an overlay of

organized crime muscle. As one racketeer put it, the "Jukebox racket is now the number one racket in the City of Chicago and . . . there will be a large number of gang killings as well as other trouble." The rivalry was vertical, from manufacture of the devices to where they would be sited to what music would be included, or not included, on them. That it was a cash business only increased the allure since this facilitated money laundering, mixing funds from a wholly illicit enterprise such as prostitution and mixing it for purposes of bank deposits with jukebox cash. By 1945, the national "take" from jukeboxes was estimated to be $23 million weekly, providing opportunity for bribing police and state liquor inspectors, politicians, and ward heelers who might be disposed to crack down on illicit businesses. Pressure was also placed on small business—tavern and restaurant owners—to discontinue service with one controller of jukeboxes in favor of another. Unions were tied in insofar as mechanics had to "service" these machines. There were not only songs but "soundies" too, a precursor of music videos, which often featured practitioners of the new music. The "picture," said an analyst, is "sordid and dirty," but it all rested on the disadvantaging of artists.

Even before this postwar profit explosion, these lucrative devices were estimated to deliver almost $5 million in gross income annually. Getting in on the ground floor was James Roosevelt, son of a president, particularly in producing "soundies": by the 1940s there were 600,000 jukeboxes, and what were called "movie-jukes" attained 25 percent of the reach of the former. The younger Roosevelt purportedly controlled a manufacturing plant at 4100 West Fullerton in Chicago that resembled an automobile production line, with a daily output of "fifty jukes selling at the factory for $695 each and to the customer for $1,000 each." An old crony of Al Capone, Eddie Vogel, was involved in this grimy business on Chicago's Northside and in the northwest suburbs, as the gainful business was segmented neatly. Inexorably, what followed[5] were blackjack and lead pipe attacks on competitors. John Pisano, another competitor, was found slain. Arson could also befall the uncooperative.[6]

It was not just Roosevelt who was attracted to this gold rush. Homer Capehart, a U.S. senator from neighboring Indiana, was involved,

but, his power notwithstanding, he was described as having "lost" to
the "Capone gang" in a battle for control.[7] By 1950, said one heated
report, the "battle for control has resulted in murders, sluggings and
stench bombings."[8] This was in the midst of what was described as
a "very thorough absorption of even the smallest operators into the
hoodlum-controlled jukebox business."[9]

Few were the bistros and nightspots capable of avoiding the poisonous snare of racketeering. Jazz Ltd., at 164 East Grand in Chicago, was
among the few that "stayed clean," according to an observant journalist. "They have barred the way to known mobsters, dames, cigarette
vending machines"—yet another gangster industry— "jukeboxes and
a well-known 'kinky' brand of whiskey." When the club opened in the
early postwar era, Bill and Ruth Reinhardt were visited by a "party
of six" who "dropped in, shepherded by a top gangster with a cold
stare and a taste for hot jazz." Thus, "unlike many other liquor licenses
here, they are not mere stand-ins for hoodlum big shots who secretly
control the action," the emerging norm. Strikingly, this supposedly
mob-free club pursued a policy that mandated that "women without escorts are not permitted and even women with escorts are not
allowed to sit at the bar. The waitresses wear skirts, not flimsy or tight
fitting 'harem' outfits."[10]

The latter notwithstanding, the Reinhardts' ability to diverge from
past patterns was due in substantial measure to the continuing impetus provided by wartime anti-fascism. Before the Reinhardts, there
was a not inaccurate stereotype of money-grubbing Loop booze-
mongers, allied with flesh peddlers. There was a veritable wall
separating Northside and Southside musical ventures, which allowed
Negro performers to entertain Euro-Americans, although Negro
customers themselves were restricted. Or there were sites like Chez
Paree where it was policy to seat the two groups separately. As the
Reinhardts were opening their club, the Loop endured a Jim Crow
that was redolent of Birmingham, Alabama.[11] Music promoter Joe
Segal said later that "the jazz center" in the early postwar era "was at
63rd and Cottage and there'd be fifteen, twenty clubs within a radius
of five or six blocks,"[12] but as time passed, this too changed. As one
writer put it, the image of the "jazzman" as a "sporty character who

played only in honky-tonks or speakeasies operated by gunmen who thought nothing of murdering a business rival"[13] began to dissipate, not least because of the altered postwar political calculus.

The proliferation of television sets as a household appliance may have driven more adults into the comfort of their homes, thereby intensifying cutthroat competition among nightspots and those seeking to place jukeboxes in these venues. According to Virgil Peterson of Chicago, who studied this phenomenon, "lucrative Wurlitzer distributorships" had been placed in the hands of leading racketeers, for example, Meyer Lansky: the diminutive mobster who may have been influenced to deepen involvement in Las Vegas and Havana when jukeboxes came under assault. He was not singular: the odious gangster Abner "Longie" Zwillman was also so involved. Zwillman and Lansky were both Jewish American. Raymond Patriarca of Rhode Island was Italian American, but he too was enmeshed in a munificent enterprise whose reach extended eastward to London and westward to Hong Kong. These men were not just involved in siting these devices but also were involved in their manufacture (and, again, there was a Nevada connection in that these same sinister forces were similarly involved with slot machines). In 1951, Lansky told Congress that he had been involved with jukeboxes for "about four years." Near that same time, in 1948, "Sugar Joe" Peskin, one of the largest jukebox operators in Chicago (and long close to Capone), moved to Los Angeles, within hailing distance of Las Vegas, where he entered the jukebox distribution business. By June 1949, the City of Angels was on the verge of a bloody "jukebox war," an indicator of the profits involved.

Again, there was a kind of vertical integration involved in that in Chicago, as in other cities, the bartenders' union, which had a say in what was played on jukeboxes, was also controlled by mobsters. The few Negroes who were able to break into this mob-controlled business were constrained: Ollie Herbert, one of these few, had ostensible ownership of a jukebox enterprise that was actually gangster-controlled and supervised. In June 1951, Theodore Roe, known as the "Negro Policy King" of Chicago was kidnapped by remnants of the Capone gang, then killed, as he was seen as straying beyond his limited lane, by, for example, managing recording artists, seen as the province of the traditional mob since the new music arose in the late nineteenth century. As of 1954, said Peterson, "the Capone gang" was "still powerful," had "long maintained close relations with politicians at every level of government," notably through the person of fixer-lawyer Sidney Korshak,[14] who gained unimaginable leverage because of his purported "successful blackmailing" of Congress's chief crime-fighter, Senator Estes Kefauver of Tennessee.[15] Korshak dug his claws into the music business via his exceedingly close ties to Armstrong's manager, Joe Glaser. The barrister handled Glaser's personal and business operations and would serve as executor of his estate made plump by exploitation of Negroes.[16]

Chicago club owner Frank Holzfeind was bold enough to tell Glaser directly that a comrade "hit the ceiling and told me in no uncertain terms that I was ten different kinds of a damn fool to mess around with a guy like you." Boldly, he continued, "I am ready to pick up the marbles and not play with you any longer," given Glaser's expertise in administering the "first-class runaround."[17] But since mobster Charles "Cherry Nose" Gioe had his claws embedded in hotel and restaurant workers unions, Holzfeind, rather than bold, might have been described as foolhardy.[18] Comrades of "Cherry Nose" were simultaneously profiting handsomely as disc bootleggers, who were "waxing fat on stolen goods,"[19] which was little more than looting of Ellington, Holiday, and other stars.[20]

As the example of Roe indicates, during the postwar era, U.S. Negroes continued their course of seeking entrance into the gainful quarters of the business side of the music, where they confronted organized crime. In Los Angeles, Red Callender, bassist, was present at the opening in January 1951 of an enterprise of John Dolphin, who he described as a "tall, heavy-set, light-skinned black man, dapper in a loud kind of way" with a "cigar in his mouth all the time."[21] The entrepreneurial Dolphin recorded pianist Erroll Garner, born in 1923, and hired Callender as an executive. Other Angelenos, for example, Buddy Collette and Charles Mingus, also worked alongside Dolphin. The crooner Floyd Dixon recalled that Dolphin purported to give him "$30,000," but there was a $50 bill on top and a $20 bill on the bottom,

and in between there were only $1 bills, making for a grand total of
$125. Dolphin could counter by asserting that he was only respond-
ing to the dominant culture. At the same time, the neighborhoods
where those like Dolphin were compelled to function were heavily
policed, making arrest and detention more likely. By 1950, for example, the Newton Division, which included Central Avenue—a citadel
of bebop—consisted of 4.8 square miles and 101,000 Negroes, moni-
tored by 32 police officers per square mile. In contrast, there were
443 officers assigned to 239 square miles of Hollywood, Wilshire,
Foothill, etc., fewer than two officers per square mile. Soon Dolphin
was leading a march of Negroes against what was termed a police
"campaign of terror and intimidation." Not long after, Dolphin was
shot and killed at his shop by a frustrated singer, though the frustrating environment into which Negroes were jammed can be seen as a
causative factor in the unfolding of this tragedy.[22]

Dolphin's entrepreneurial verve challenged the sway of mobsters
like Mickey Cohen. The region stretching from Southern Nevada to
Southern California was among the most corrupt nationally. To cite
one example among many, the chief of police in Burbank in 1950
bought a pricey 56-foot-long yacht with cash. Stars like the comedians Red Skelton and Jimmy Durante were both close to Cohen,
just as Frank Sinatra was close to Sam Giancana, Moe Dalitz, Meyer
Lansky, and other leading racketeers. Their racial and ethnic chauvinism did not create a favorable climate for either Negro entrepreneurs
or artists. This was so even when a similarly illicit figure like Santo
Trafficante controlled a booking agency that favored Nat "King" Cole
and Ella Fitzgerald.[23]

Nonetheless, the postwar era witnessed the propulsion of the anti–
Jim Crow movement, inspiring the likes of Dolphin, but it collided
brusquely with the status quo in the music industry, which involved
hegemony by the unscrupulous, racketeers not least. This contradictory pattern is espied in the 1950 victory won by pianist Hazel Scott in
prevailing in a lawsuit against a Mount Pasco, Washington, eatery that
refused to serve her on racist grounds.[24] This contradictory pattern
is also seen in an Oakland occurrence of mid-1950 when, with Ella
Fitzgerald performing, an observer noticed that for the "first time . . .

[a] color line has been drawn at [a] dance since 1946,"[25] as Jim Crow
erupted where it was thought to have dissipated.

Then, there was the presumably progressive merger of once segregated musicians' locals in Los Angeles in 1953. Yet mergers like this
one often meant that Negroes surrendered an independent base to
the "whites," placing desegregation itself in bad odor among African
Americans,[26] which may explain why in late 1952 Benny Carter was
defeated for the presidency of Local 767 of the American Federation
of Musicians on a platform of merger with the larger Local 67.[27]

Complicating matters further was the reality that the war had left
many U.S. competitors prostrate, creating a postwar boom in North
America that energized capitalists generally. During this era, said
Dizzy Gillespie, "The clubs made money and they all became millionaires," Morris Levy not least, while "we musicians weren't making any
large sums of money," he concluded with a touch of sarcasm, noting,
"Morris Levy was very nice to me."[28]

The postwar era also witnessed a contradictory skein of events
for the music. According to Richard Cook, there were "hardly any
records by recognizable jazz artists [that] made the 'Billboard' album
or single charts in the period covering 1955–1960," which saw the
birth of another youthful music, denoted as "rock 'n' roll," preceded
by yet another blues-inflected form denoted as "rhythm and blues,"
then "soul" (admittedly, this trifurcation reflects the Jim Crow that
has yet to be extinguished. Interestingly, Berry Gordy, a founder of
Motown in Detroit, which capitalized upon the rise of these newer
musical forms, began as an aficionado of the music of Ellington and
Armstrong and, says one chronicler, "stocked his store with jazz
records," but by 1955, he was "bankrupt," a "traumatic event" for him,
and switched course).[29]

Yet despite this constant handwringing about Negroes deserting a
music that sprung from their community, "most of the record buyers"
of the music known as jazz came from Negro neighborhoods. Joe
Fields of Prestige Records said, "What we sold in Boston was nothing
compared to Chicago, St. Louis, Detroit," suggesting that any decline
in music sales may have been driven by inept marketing plans. Yet,
longtime music executive and journalist Dom Cerulli argued that

Cleveland, presumably a sibling of the midwestern bastions noted above, was a "dead town for jazz."[30]

As for the venues where the music was played, Levy's Birdland was viewed as a "Mafia front," and virtually every club was prey to a rampant corruption that included graft and payoffs. Even Max Gordon, whose honesty was unquestioned, and who presided over the Village Vanguard in Manhattan, was said to pay a monthly protection fee to the avatars of corruption.[31] Art D'Lugoff of the nearby Village Gate had to deal with local gangsters and crooked cops, creating conditions favorable to enhanced exploitation of musicians.[32] "We don't work in temples or in a protected environment, like the European classical form or like ballet dancers," groused singer Abbey Lincoln, born in 1930, and once the spouse of drummer Max Roach: "This is by hook or by crook." Actually, in clubs dominated by crooks, hooks were imbedded figuratively into the flesh wallets of artists.

The reverberations also ensnared those Negroes who simply wanted a slice of the lush profit generated by illicit enterprise. The case of Tampa provided chapter and verse in this regard. "Bolita" was the name affixed to what was called the "numbers" elsewhere and the operators, as the Latin name suggests, were mostly of Cuban and Italian ancestry, while many of the low-level runners and bettors were African American. But Charlie Williams decided to break this mold. He was also president of the Negro Elks lodge in neighboring St. Petersburg and second-in-command in the state organization. A former railway porter, he amassed a sheaf of arrests for bolita and bookmaking stretching back to the 1930s. The postwar era, propelled by lingering anti-fascism, promised to buoy him further but on February 19, 1953, his luck ran out; more precisely, a man approached him and fired two shots into this chest. He fell dead on the street.[33]

Investigated by Congress and confronted by up-and-coming Negro challengers, mobsters flexed their muscles increasingly in an arena where they had wielded influence for decades. Clark Terry witnessed an example in his hometown, St. Louis, where Benny Carter was leading a band at the appropriately named Club Plantation (surely, the proliferation of clubs nationally carrying the name "Plantation" is worthy of prolonged consideration). "Somebody insulted this lady, the singer, and [trombonist]J.J. Johnson took up for her," which ignited a tempest. Gangsters proceeded methodically and "pistol whipped J.J." in a manner that extended deep into history. But then Carter "came up and grabbed this cat and pulled his pistol out and said, 'Now pistol whip me,'"[34] a challenge that ended the beating abruptly but also sent a signal about a new dawn descending. Carter, according to bassist and manager John Levy, was "one of the strongest—physically—persons that I know. He and Ben Webster were very strong and showed it at times," as the ruffled St. Louis mobster could have attested.[35] Saxophonist Jimmy Heath, born in 1926, could have used Carter's muscle when in 1952 he performed alongside Symphony Sid's All Stars, then objected to being shortchanged. "Then Symphony Sid brought some Al Capone types with these big hats on, gangsters," in sum, delivering credible threats.[36]

Another indicator of the direction of prevailing winds was sensed by musician Joe Wilder, born in 1922. It was in the early 1950s, he recalled, "when they asked me to [play] *Silk Stockings*. . . . That was the first time they had ever had a black musician play a key chair with a Broadway show, go on the road with a show." But also indicative was his arrival with the troupe in Boston when a man at the Shubert Theatre—he was in the violin section—objected to his presence on racist grounds.[37]

John Levy also benefited from the changing political environment. His surname, he said, was bequeathed by "French Jews" in "Plaquemines Parish" in Louisiana; "My godfather, who was a French Creole, [was] very light-skinned. He passed for white," but his godson, Levy, "had to stay behind that sign" meant for the Negro section on public transit "and he would go up front, then he'd come back and make a joke out of it but I realized there was a difference, that me being black, I couldn't go past that sign. . .. I felt very hurt about the whole thing. . . . It gave you a feeling of rejection." In movie houses too "we had to sit way up top." Born in 1912, he was in Chicago during the fabled racist pogrom in 1919: "They were grabbing people off the street and doing them bodily harm." He became involved in "numbers running" and "got arrested" but righted himself via his musicianship, accompanying violinist Stuff Smith, though by 1944 he was working as a doorman in Manhattan, garnering a hefty $400 weekly. The latter job was arduous, involving "long hours," but he abandoned performing because Billie Holiday, whom he was accompanying, "wouldn't pay me on time. . . . I'm very violent about money, about somebody not paying me," he said with evident pain. "I lose it completely. . . . To be a person that's pretty even-tempered and pretty calm, I've had some outbursts about money that really is scary." So, soon, with the altered political climate, he was the rare musician who switched to the business side and did quite well for himself. Still, he had to confront scoundrels like Morris Levy, who insisted that the famed tune "Lullaby of Birdland," which, said John Levy, had the chord structure of "Love Me or Leave Me," be recorded with Morris Levy's publishing company.[38] Teddy Reig is not far wrong in declaring that Morris Levy "could easily have become a strong-arm enforcer for the mob" and "was seldom above using physical force," a habit that could readily convince a wavering musician to bend to his will.[39]

Certainly, viperish businessmen were reluctant to diverge from the example of Morris Levy. Assuredly, Herman Lubinsky would have agreed. From his perch in Newark, he had attained a crude kind of vertical integration, involving recording musicians and selling and repairing radios where their music was heard. "It wasn't hard to persuade Herman to record white musicians," said fellow producer Teddy Reig, since he "was always looking for white hopes" and found one in Allen Eager, a saxophonist born in 1927. "He had the Lester [Young] stance with the saxophone"—horn askew—"and his tone was reminiscent of Pres [Young]. To Herman, if you could do all that and you were white, you couldn't lose." The musicians' union did little to discourage this bias, he said. Union boss James "Petrillo held Chicago like a gorilla, but that was the white action. He didn't care what the blacks did" or what was done to them, for that matter. "New York was mob controlled. Everything depended on what you knew and you could get around any rule," as "well-connected owners held the scales down for years" and "the union would hand out plums. If a guy was out of work, they'd give him picket duty for $6 a night. But if the club paid off, they never had to worry about pickets."

Naturally, Miles Davis was among the legions who "hated Herman with a passion." Perhaps Davis would have had even more intense feelings if he had known of the machinations in Lubinsky's radio store. "[Eighty] percent of his business in the radio store was black," said Reig. "A customer would come in with a radio to repair and Herman would tell him that he needed a new tube. Then he'd take the radio into the next room, shine up the old tube, give it back and charge $6." Thus, Lubinsky's headquarters for his various enterprises at 58 Market Street in Newark was termed "Devil's Island . . . Herman Lubinsky, warden."[40]

As the seesaw juxtaposing "Reds" versus "Racketeers" tipped in favor of the latter, untoward consequences ensued for African Americans generally and musicians from this group particularly. On the one hand, the postwar era witnessed an expansion of Nevada as a seedbed for the malignant forces that had propelled the new music in the first instance: gambling, prostitution, organized criminality; on the other hand, as Nevada boomed, more jobs for musicians arose. Revealingly, 1950 was the first year, according to historian Michael J. Ybarra, that the state "made more from gambling than from mining; a decade later gambling was almost two and half times bigger than mining." One Negro leader in Nevada argued that during the war and immediate postwar period, left-leaning unions were most helpful to his community. But as "Rackets" rose, "Reds" declined. Suggestive of how far to the right the nation had swung and how Nevada aided this process is the point that Senator Pat McCarran of the state assailed not only Roosevelt but Truman and Eisenhower as well. All were deemed to be insufficiently reactionary. Nevada was also a linchpin of the emerging postwar anti-communist consensus. Not coincidentally, the state's major power broker, Senator McCarran, lent his name to potent anti-communist legislation. He, too, was tied to mobsters,[41] having aided Moe Dalitz, preeminent in this regard.[42]

As McCarran's presence suggests, Nevada was an anti-communist battleground that did not provide a favorable environment for Negro artists. Senator Joseph McCarthy himself accused a prominent Las Vegas publisher of being a Communist, and he responded by charging that the Wisconsinite was a closeted homosexual. The accuser, Hank Greenspun, did have Brooklyn roots and did work in the law office of Vito Marcantonio, a lawyer and politico who was close to the U.S. Communist Party.[43]

Milos Knezbich arrived in Nevada from socialist Yugoslavia in 1954, and Senator McCarran introduced a bill to grant him permanent residence status. His three brothers were already present there and were all U.S. nationals. Yet the ever vigilant officials of the state's Gaming Control Board were fixated on the "possible former Communist connections of the applicant" for a casino license, compelling him to argue, "I am a Serbian, white. . . . I am not now and never have been a member of the Communist Party."[44]

By 1950, mob influence in Nevada exploded. A primary reason was gambling, which soon became a multi-billion-dollar business. Intriguingly, a leading figure was a woman, Dorothy McCreedy, a convicted "white slaver" who had controlled brothels in Honolulu, suggestive of the noxious climate that musicians had to confront.[45] She was just one of many figures of questionable propriety who were employing musicians in this state of sin.[46]

Moreover, one Negro argues that Nevada was less segregated before the 1930s construction of what became the Hoover Dam, when it was sparsely populated and the indigenous formed a larger share of the population.[47] "I also worked in Chinese gambling houses in San Diego, Los Angeles, San Francisco and in Mexico," said Clarence Ray, a man of African descent who was of part indigenous—Creek—ancestry (his grandfather—"Never a slave," he said—was born in Barbados). This was the late 1920s before construction of the dam and when a different set of racial dynamics prevailed in that "it was common for the Chinese to employ Blacks more than anybody else. . . . They hired a lot of Blacks because they usually set up their operations in Black neighborhoods—they couldn't get legally licensed in white neighborhoods." Ray, a professional gambler, first visited the state in 1922 and by 1931 was running a gambling house: the "first gaming license issued to Blacks in Las Vegas," he said. He witnessed the upsurge from a prewar time when there were 180 Negroes in Clark County (Las Vegas) to a time when there were thousands.[48] Then, said a concurring Reverend Prentiss Walker, a U.S. Negro, "There was no such thing as 'Jim Crow', as [we] know it, in the forties."[49]

But then came the postwar turnabout that propelled organized crime. "When I was growing up" in the state in the 1950s,
said Nevadan Ruth Sweet, "they always said that the [Las Vegas]
Strip was owned by the Mafia."[50] The postwar rise of Nevada was
an earthshaking development—quite literally. Lee Henry Lisby witnessed atomic testing above ground that "wrecked some buildings,"
and he felt the underground variety: "[They're] used to a . . . shake."
This Teamster and driver servicing construction sites was kept quite
busy given the boom—even when he became a hotel porter—but
irrespective of employment, he was barred from certain casinos
because of Jim Crow.[51]

True to its historic pattern, organized crime was not a vector of
equal opportunity but, instead, a hotbed of ethnic chauvinism, generally Italian American or Jewish American, sometimes both working
in concert. The mob figure known as "Mr. Las Vegas," Moe Dalitz, was
Jewish American,[52] and he cooperated at the highest level with Italian
Americans, such as Nicholas Civella, a retread from the bad old days
in Kansas City. Thus, when scorned African Americans sought to "do
for self" and in the 1950s open the Moulin Rouge, a Negro-controlled
hotel-casino, they were crushed by their non-Negro competitors, who
simply wielded more influence politically. A study concludes that
these bosses "welcomed if not contributed to its failure"; this Negro
initiative "may have been undermined by those threatened by its popularity."[53] Sited on Las Vegas's west side, the Moulin Rouge was also
where Benny Carter once toiled.[54] The Moulin Rouge was the first
casino to not bar patrons on racist grounds.[55]

Musician Frank Foster was familiar with both Jim Crow and
Nevada. Foster was not a natural for the "gin joints" where musicians were often forced to perform: "I have always been repelled by
the smell and taste of any kind of liquor," said this man who dodged
being drafted for the war in Korea but wound up in nearby Japan,
soon to be a major stop for touring artists. By 1953, he was in the
Basie band playing before segregated audiences in Dixie: "On one
side of the ropes were the whites and the other side were the Blacks."
The latter "allowed to sit in the balcony and the whites were on the
floor dancing." Bandmates "became angry and annoyed at Basie for

accepting" this setup but, he said resignedly, "we might have had to disband if we didn't accept some of these engagements." Soon they were in Las Vegas and still frustrated since the band "had to stay in a section of a town called the Dust Bowl . . . tantamount to Las Vegas's Harlem. . . . We couldn't stay on the Strip." Working conditions were Dixie-like too: "We played two-and-a-half hours straight through, then took half an hour intermission and then came back after that and played the final hour," making about "$160 a week" with only $40 more when he left the band in 1964. Yet "whenever we went to Europe salaries were doubled"—encouraging dreams of Paris—"to $300" weekly. Foster, an arranger, "was making from $35 to $50 an arrangement" for Basie and wrote "between 100 and maybe 120" of these intricate productions. He was working fifty weeks a year—with a two-week vacation without pay—touring constantly to unpleasant sites such as Las Vegas.[56]

The Moulin Rouge and Foster's journey west too were symptoms of the false dawn delivered after the war. It was thought widely that revulsion at the genocidal nature of fascism would lead to questioning its close cousin in Dixie, and that, combined with the blood sacrifice of Negro soldiers, would create favorable conditions for an agonized retreat of Jim Crow. The onslaught against Jim Crow was supposed to be in motion as a result of a May 1954 U.S. Supreme Court decision invalidating the once sacrosanct "separate but equal" principle. Yet the Moulin Rouge closed in November 1955. The site was shuttered, though on the final night of operation, "there was standing room only for the Les Brown show," said singer and activist William "Bob" Bailey. "Pits were making money but the place started getting a lot of pressure from the other hotels because we were taking customers," because of their influence with top-flight Negro artists—and "as the entertainers go, so go the girls, so go the high rollers." Nevertheless, the Moulin Rouge was crushed by a pincers spearheaded by mobsters, competitors, and banks, the latter being important since "they had a lot of short-term notes, and I'm given to understand," said Bailey, "that they put pressure on the purveyors to call some of those short-term notes"; that is, "big hotel owners," said Bailey's questioner, put pressure on their financiers.[57]

The opponents of this casino apparently preferred the 1940s when Louis Armstrong was forced to reside in below-par boarding houses on the west side when visiting Las Vegas, then known widely as the "Mississippi of the West."[58] "Black musicians couldn't even stay at the hotels they were working in," said musician Roy Porter.[59] Abbey Lincoln was not alone in saying disgustedly that she "hated" Las Vegas; "If you're creative, you're like in the manger."[60]

The Mississippi of the West bore the earmarks of its Dixie inspiration. William "Bob" Bailey said of the Silver State that lighter-skinned Negro entertainers were treated better than their darker peers—except for vocalist Billy Daniels, who "for intent and purposes is white," a conflict driven by a pugilistic proclivity: "He got in fights with one of the bosses or customers" periodically. The same held true for bandleader and singer Billy Eckstine. He "got in a fight with a customer and it was fantastic."[61]

Mobsters discovered Nevada early on with Al Capone arriving in Reno in 1930,[62] where he was able to capitalize on an early gambling boom, as Prohibition's end was drying up a lucrative income stream.[63] His fellow racketeer, Frank Costello, invested in the state by 1949.[64] Fortunately, Bill Fong was able to open the New China Club in 1952, and his enterprise was less prone to observe the strictures of Jim Crow, since he did not carry the mark of North American enslavement. This also meant that when leading Trinidadian intellectuals, C. L. R. James and Eric Williams, arrived in the state for "quickie" divorces, they were not barred altogether from recreation.[65] Also known as "Bew Hong Fong," the Nevada authorities seemed pleased that Fong's Reno club had the "advantages of [being] contemplated for colored personnel at Stead Air Base."[66]

Dalitz and his comrades had influence particularly because of their access to ready cash—via jukeboxes, restaurants, and the like—which was critically important when the business cycle hit bust. Las Vegas became a money-laundering capital, a crucial global function.[67]

James McMillan was a moderate Negro leader in Las Vegas, speaking warmly of the butcher Dalitz as a "gentleman" (they golfed at the same country club). He was also Philo-Semitic but asserted that "the Jews who owned the hotels and things could have helped us end this segregation years before . . . but that didn't happen." Later he attained notoriety for associating with the Nation of Islam, generally scorned by Jewish Americans. "I went to [Louis] Farrakhan's first meeting in Las Vegas," he said later, "and sat on the stage with him. Some of my Jewish friends didn't like that. Too bad."[68]

The Negro leader who carried the name Woodrow Wilson was present at the creation of the boom. "From the time that blacks moved to Las Vegas in the early 1940s—I mean the *masses*—it was a confrontation; it was a battle all the way up and down the line," he said.[69] Early on, Nevada Negroes developed close ties with musicians, not least because Jim Crow often compelled the former to house the latter because of hotel restrictions. James Gay of Arkansas arrived in the Sagebrush State in 1946 and quickly found himself present at nuclear explosion sites (it is unclear if this influenced his decision to become an embalmer). This self-described friend of Lyndon Baines Johnson acknowledged that "Lionel Hampton is [a] very dear friend of mine," Duke Ellington too. He "talked" with the vibraphonist and "mentioned that there was no black promotional group in town, a booking agency," and—post-1954—as Jim Crow barriers came under assault, initiatives in this "lucrative field" were launched, albeit with difficulty.[70]

Cora Williams was similarly situated. This Negro woman's roots were in Los Angeles, but she arrived in Las Vegas in 1952. She too was friendly with performers: "I've met Frank Sinatra, Tony Curtis and Sammy Davis, Jr. . . . I've seen lots of stars by being here so long." She also recalled a time when African Americans could not be hired, even as parking lot attendants; "there were no black dealers" in casinos, "except in West Las Vegas."[71]

"Louis Armstrong used to come in and blow all the time," said William "Bob" Bailey, speaking of the Moulin Rouge. "It was the only hotel the musicians could get together and jam. . . . There was no place that they could jam on the Strip where the Black musicians could sit in!"—again illustrating how Jim Crow harmed the ability of artists to sharpen their musical skills. Bailey, a singer of note—"I'd been with Count Basie for three years"—also takes credit for terming Las Vegas the "Mississippi of the West." He admits to having the ability to sing in "five languages,"[72] a handy skill since describing the odiousness of Southern Nevada strained the capaciousness of the English language.

Perhaps it was the familiarity of the Moulin Rouge that induced Armstrong to unburden himself there in August 1955, a few months before this place's unfortunate demise. Scribbling on their impressive looking stationery, he reminisced that "when I was a teenager hanging [with] gamblers, pimps, people of all walks of life, they all loved the way I played my horn." This built his confidence and even affected his diminishing desire for a companionate relationship since "I have my horn to keep me warm." As ever, reassuring his correspondent, the slimily sleazy Glaser, he recounted how "Black Benny" of Chicago instructed him before his departure from Chicago that "no matter where you may be—always have a *white man* (who like[s] you) . . . [who] will put his hand on your shoulder and say, 'This is My Nigger.'"[73] Perhaps the insidiously pernicious nature of Las Vegas, a city overrun by mobsters, may have led him to recall this unctuously malevolent advice. Then again, given the Jim Crow milieu into which Armstrong was born, he may not have perceived viable alternatives, particularly since the postwar climate meant his income was increasing: by August 1956 Glaser was informing him gleefully that the engagement in which the trumpeter was joined by Ella Fitzgerald at the Hollywood Bowl "was an overwhelming success whereby all records were broken there and they drew $32, 000 net."[74]

Still,[75] to destroy the attempt by a growing circle of Negro entrepreneurs to horn in on casinos, other tactics were deployed beyond political influence lubricated by a stream of cash, the specter of mob muscle, and the like. Beginning in 1950, Sarah Ann Knight was a casino owner in Hawthorne, Nevada, after moving there in 1942. She too knew performers, Nat "King" Cole, for example. At first, this Negro-owned enterprise was doing well since the competition barred Negroes altogether. But then, to undercut her, the competition, she said, "built a little small room" at the "back" of their casinos and, insultingly, "named it 'Behind the Eight Ball.' This was for Negroes" and "it really hurt our business because the Blacks wanted to go in this place," and were not sufficiently politicized to confront the insult. "We had a bar, a dice table, a twenty-one table, a poker table, slot machines, jukebox and a restaurant," but the competition often had all of that plus live music performed by adept musicians. As so often happened, a defeat for Negroes, even an entrepreneur, was a defeat for others facing bias. For, as her business was nosediving, all women dealers were dismissed in the midst of a massive counterattack buoyed by anti-communism. "Some of the men got together," she said, "through politics and had this resolution passed" as they were "afraid that the women [were] going to take over. . . . The white women and the Black women formed this little organization to do something about it," though it took a while for them to overcome.[76]

Their ideological flexibility, if not opportunism, also meant that mobsters like Benjamin "Bugsy" Siegel from nearby Los Angeles, were able to develop an entente with yet another religious minority that had influence, the Church of Latter-Day Saints, headquartered in nearby Utah.[77]

Since opium was legal in the state until 1909, leaving the region festooned with opium dens, this meant that racketeers were averse to halting the flood of hard drugs that materialized postwar, a phenomenon that had done so much to destabilize musicians.[78] Given the interlocking directorates linking drug barons and music moguls, it was inexorable that artists would be impacted. In 1952, the lanky saxophonist Dexter Gordon was arrested, convicted, and imprisoned for two years for possession of heroin.[79] Soon he was to flee for exile in Denmark, further denuding his homeland of talent and creativity, a kind of replay of "The Great Migration," which involved a similar process of absconding from Dixie to points northward.[80] Ultimately, Copenhagen was to attract, as well, skilled artists, for example, Thad Jones, Ernie Wilkins, Sahib Shihab, Kenny Drew, and Horace Parlan. There, it was reliably reported, Gordon was to attain "a feeling of confidence and security that he had never felt in the United States."

Gordon's Los Angeles was en route to leading the nation in narcotics arrests by 1954, surpassing the uncrowned champion, New York City, by 50 percent, though it reputedly had about one-tenth as many drug users. His biographer quotes one official as declaiming scorpion-like, "I set out to destroy that crowd," speaking of practitioners of the new music, "and damn near did. I ran Charlie 'Yardbird'

Parker. . . . out of town."[81] Reportedly, one federal official with jurisdiction over narcotics—Harry Anslinger—told the U.S. Congress, that
he wanted to imprison for violations of drug laws "musicians. . . and I
don't mean good musicians. I mean jazz musicians."[82] Arguably, this
was the opening shot in what became a "War on Drugs," which was
to eventuate in a "War on Negroes" that was to fuel what came to be
known as the "Prison Industrial Complex" and led Governor Nelson
Rockefeller of New York in 1973 to compare "[drug] addicts" to an
"invading army" in how they supposedly "effectively destroyed. . . .
whole neighborhoods" en route to "destruction of our society as a
whole," the ineluctable result, he suggested, if they were not squashed.[83]
Intriguingly, this baneful practice of mass incarceration accelerated—
if not began—with a targeting of Negro artists.

Arranger and composer Johnny Mandel, born in 1925 in New York
City, has declared that hard drugs as a proliferating phenomenon
lasted for a decade, concluding in 1955, though this is hard to square
with the Dionysian 1960s.[84] Saxophonist Lou Donaldson recalled
that "when I came on the scene . . . the junkies had everything—and
the recording studios had the junkies. If you weren't strung out, you
couldn't get a record date. I didn't get high so I was kind of an outsider
at first."[85]

The plague of heroin was also invoked when Gordon's fellow saxophonist Wardell Gray was found dead in Las Vegas in a field, miles
from the Strip. His neck was broken, and he appeared to have been
beaten over the head with a club or some other weapon. The official
story was that he was shooting heroin with dancer Teddy Hale, which
somehow led to an accident involving multiple fractures.[86] Murder was
suspected, said the British-based *Melody Maker*.[87] "The talk before,"
said singer Richard Boone, "was that he'd burned the people in power
who supply the heroin. He'd done something wrong, not enough to kill
somebody, but from their point of view they figured that they'd snuff
him out." Vernon Alley, who had employed Gray in his San Francisco
band, also suspected foul play.[88] Drummer Roy Porter said that "some
people found it gangster related," speaking of the death.[89]

Alternatively, it was thought that the stress of the business drove
the unfortunate Gray into suicide. Thus, saxophonist Joe Maini, born

in 1930, was thought to have died playing Russian roulette, though, again, others dissented. But not Clark Terry: he "blew his brains out" said the trumpeter. Terry also believed that vibraphonist and vocalist Gary McFarland, born in 1933, also died playing the same game but with a lethal drink in his case—though here, others suspected foul play: an overdose of his methadone.[90]

The same accusation of murder was made when bass saxophonist Adrian Rollini perished. Born in 1903 in New York City, it was asserted in the April 27, 1956, edition of the *New York Times* that he suffered a compound ankle fracture in a fall, then died. Philip Sillman of Flushing, New York, was not as certain. "The police, suspecting foul play said they found nothing at odds with . . . explanation of a 'mysterious accident.'" But Sillman put more credence in the story that he was "run over by a car on the coral surface of the parking lot of the nite-club [*sic*] he'd just visited . . . He'd gone to the club to discuss a business deal for buying-in or purchase. It seems the local people did not want his competition." There was also the complexity of "Adrian's business with the same bootleggers he dealt with when he had the California Rambler's Inn back in Westchester," New York, during those frenetic "Prohibition days!!!"[91]

On the other hand, saxophonist Stan Getz, born in 1927 in Philadelphia, was on the other end of felonious accusation, when he was accused of seeking to rob a drugstore in 1953 to obtain funds for the purchase of hard drugs.[92] An observer blamed the difficult working conditions under which he labored, which drove him to despair.[93]

The "dope menace keeps growing," it was announced ominously in late 1950, "menacing the dance band industry." Heroin "principally" was at issue with Davis and Blakey being the most recent arrestees.[94] Nevada, which brought together gangsters of various ethnicities and religious backgrounds, also represented a geographical confluence in that these men hailed from sites as diverse as Los Angeles, Kansas City, and Cleveland. This unity hampered the ability of their opponents to drive a wedge between and among them.

It seemed as if the profusion of hard drugs was lubricating the path for a renaissance for the substance that had bedeviled musicians for decades: alcohol. "Jewish jazz musicians were always good drinkers," said Johnny Mandel,[95] though he easily could have dropped the ethno-religious modifier. "I was into cognac," said percussionist Max Roach. "Poppa Joe," speaking of a fellow drummer, was also a "cognac man. He would take a little bottle" but was often outdone by the imbibing Roach who really "was into the bottle. Then [I] would sleep."[96]

"Everybody was a prostitute and a dope addict and a dope pusher in Honolulu when I got there," caviled Abbey Lincoln. Worse, "People would send you the alcohol. I mean it was like free. The drummer who was the uncle to the saxophone player, they were both heroin junkies," but did not seem to turn down alcohol. "The bass player, who was the band leader was a cocaine junkie. It was disgusting and they admired street life. Pimps and whores" abounded, "and I was lonely," making her susceptible to temptation, too. Plus, her primary accompanist, the pianist, was an alcoholic. The Grand Guignol scene was capped when "[Euro]-Americans came and they took the place" and "busted everybody . . . two young guys from Kentucky, they came and they hung with everybody, did everything everybody was doing and then they started to bust everybody and they beat them and they sent them to jail." This scandal occurred "in '52 and '53."[97]

The rise of Las Vegas was symptomatic of the continuing ascension of organized crime with its manifest malignancy, of which con-trolled substances were a part. Lou Donaldson, the sweet-sounding sax man, was well aware of corruption, having grown up in Badin, North Carolina, which was doubly "segregated," as he recalled, and contained an "aluminum plant" with the bauxite arriving from racist South Africa. Born in 1926, in the postwar era he was playing fre-quently in Harlem, at a time when "Malcolm X used to stick his head in the door, but he didn't come in there," given his newly found reli-giosity. "The big gangsters," notably Bumpy Johnson, were not as shy; "all those people, they used to come in," and "another guy named Red Dillon," who was a "dangerous man!" Donaldson was not above pro-curing "used . . . suits from 'boosters'" or those who illicitly obtained this finery in the first place. Surrounded on the bandstand by such characters, Donaldson did not feel intimidated, since, he said, "I was a good boxer," and "in case somebody bothered me, I'd knock them out. But I didn't have nothing to worry about because all those guys were junkies. You know what I mean?" he asked rhetorically. "They couldn't fight." Still, some in this unfortunate category he admired. Charlie Parker "was a brilliant guy," he said. "We talked about politics" and he was a "smart guy." Though he "worked 24 hours a day to get money for the next hit." As for pianist Bud Powell, "he was bad with the money. Because he'd get the money and by the time you got ready to get your pay, he's gone." Donaldson did not think highly of Art Blakey either—a "con man," he said. "Miles [Davis] wasn't reliable with money. . . . I wouldn't want nobody to see me hit him upside the head with a baseball bat," he added menacingly. His recollections could be trusted, said Donaldson, since "I could be called an historian. I met everybody and I was out every night."

Junkies attracted unpalatable characters effortlessly. "There was a woman around there named Hilda and she worked. I guess she worked for the Mob. . . . She had the inside on all the clubs. So any time I wanted a job. I just called her. I got it right away." The Blue Coronet in Brooklyn was a favored haunt and a "tough club" with "fights now and then. . . . Most of the guys that owned the clubs, the ghetto clubs, were like hustlers," that is, "numbers writers, dope sellers," and included within this rogues' gallery was Don King of Cleveland, who became a wealthy boxing promoter.[98]

The quotidian corruption that Donaldson espied had various permutations and may have been fueled in part by the often idiosyncratic nature of musicians. By 1951, the agent for pianist Erroll Garner was moaning that her client was "paying debts, paying debts, paying debts." He had sent her "$600 of his pay from the Blackhawk" in San Francisco, but "$50 goes to a lawyer here against his car debt" and $75 to another creditor, another $75 to another, "$200 on back salary to me . . . $200 [to] tax money" and soon what seemed like a hefty amount had shrunk to nothingness.[99] The manager, producer, and business partner of the pianist Martha Glaser found her client to be a spendthrift. By mid-1952, he "had been behaving like a dream," she said, but "he's still spending more than he should, but considerably less than he has been. He just doesn't understand what the word budget means."[100] Such spending may have made him more vulnerable to signing draconian contracts.

At the same time, the dapper Erroll Garner with the slicked-back hair, then so popular among Negro performers before the steady ascension of the anti–Jim Crow movement, was being squeezed in a way that could be disorienting. In Atlantic City—New Jersey's version of Las Vegas—his agent carped that his "only offense" was "that he was booked on the failure to register as once having been convicted on a narcotics violation" and though his "one and only past violation occurred nine years ago in Los Angeles," she said in 1952. Anyways, countered Martha Glaser—apparently unrelated to Armstrong's manager of the same name—it was unclear "as to whether Erroll was guilty as charged of use of marijuana. . . . How much longer that violation of nine years ago will continue to haunt him, I don't know. But it all added up to a lot of unfortunate press," which, not coincidentally, reduced his bargaining leverage to his financial detriment and to the advantage of those who hired him. Then, there was the often distasteful environment in which he and others similarly situated were compelled to operate. "As Erroll put it," she said, "there isn't an entertainer in the business who doesn't attract a lot of unsavory characters, and if you're around when the chips are flying from these characters, you get hurt." The result was Garner's "bruised reputation," which left the pianist confounded since "he was so [shocked] that anything he does or doesn't do rates headlines."[101]

Thus club owners were "working his fanny off," speaking of Garner, "40 to 45 minutes on every hour, with fifteen-minute breaks . . . they're pretty cheap kids running the club." There was a possible racist edge as well in that the youthful entrepreneurs "took a terrible bath with Charlie Barnet to whom they paid $2,500 a week for two weeks—so they're making it up on Erroll. . . . Unfortunately, both here and in San Francisco we'll be playing opposite Louis Armstrong."[102] Shortly thereafter, the hammer was dropped on the stylish keyboardist. "Erroll has been erased from membership from [Local] 802 for failure to pay" various fees, which would circumscribe severely his continuing ability to work.[103]

Glaser thought that her client was compounding the matter, acting "out of his mind": "It's beyond me. I have warned him repeatedly about his debt, taxes, etc. but he continues overspending. . . . It has

been my headache but ultimately, it will be his . . . he is at the Bellevue
Hotel San Francisco—living in high style with a 'friend.'" [104]

Garner may not have realized that his manager may have been part
of his problem in that she, in a toxic combination of what might have
been class resentment and white supremacy, could be terribly condescending toward him. "I hate to destroy a 'child of my own making,'"
she said of her adult client—but if he continued on his perceived way-
ward path, she felt bound to do so.[105] But Garner did not have many
options. Record producer George Avakian said that the "man who
ran the Olympia" in Paris was a "notoriously tough gangster type"—
Bruno Coquatrix—who sought to compel the pianist "to play these
concerts without getting paid."[106]

There was also implicit competition from the likes of fellow pianist Dave Brubeck, who was surging to prominence alongside Garner
but had the "advantage" of not being of African ancestry, providing
him with more options. By 1950, the Californian was considering
signing with a major label, though he was wary since a "detriment"
could be the "corporation is already committed to push these established groups first . . . [George] Shearing, [Red] Norvo . . . [Lionel]
Hampton, [Louis] Armstrong." Thus, "I absolutely will not sign a
three-year contract with ABC but I will sign for one year with the
intention of renewing the contract after each year that has been satisfactory for both parties."[107] It was understandable why Brubeck
compared himself to a fellow keyboardist, Shearing. The club owner
and producer George Wein admitted that he paid the blind pianist,
born in 1919 in London, multiples over what he ordinarily agreed
to, adding, "I mean I'd never paid more than nine hundred, a thousand dollars," even weekly, "I thought I could lose my shirt."[108] Wein
may have been engaging in entrepreneurial bluster: Hampton Hawes,
a pianist comparable to Shearing in talent, if not star power, said, "In
1956 I was playing the Embers in New York making $1,500 a week."[109]
It was also in 1956 that saxophonist Julian "Cannonball" Adderley
toiled at the Blue Note club at 3 North Clark Street in Chicago for two
weeks—thirty-two hours weekly with a five-day week and Sunday
matinee—for $1,250 per week.[110] Yet Artie Shaw claims that "at the
age of 16 I was making the equivalent of $1,750, close to $2,000 a

week," which, if true, is either an example of deflation in musicians' wages or piercing racial bias—or, perhaps, both.[111]

AS MENTIONED, WILLIAM "BOB" BAILEY of Nevada was also an activist, an equivalent of Frankie Newton or Howard Johnson. This leader of the NAACP affiliate in Reno was accused of being a leader of the Communist Party branch, a charge brought by Alice Smith, once a member of the Progressive Independent Party, tied to the doomed presidential candidacy of Henry Wallace, who was supported by Norman Granz. By the time of the accusation, Bailey was also a mini-mogul, serving as owner-operator of the Harlem Rooming House and Club Room and partner in the China Mint Club.[112]

Due west in Los Angeles a similar process unfolded. Drummer William Douglass was a leader of the Negro local of the musicians' union and was part of the contradictory process that led to a consolidation with its "white" counterpart (a presumed shift to the left) accompanied by an anti-communist purge (an actual shift to the right). "People started playing dirty politics," he said. "They started to name many of us as being 'influenced' [or] 'Communist inspired.'" He knocked on the door of the NAACP "and they were scared to touch us. To this day," he said much later, "I am not a member of the NAACP. I resigned my membership."[113] Just as in Hollywood, the witch hunters targeted musicians, too: "Music Men Named in Red Hunt" was a typical headline.[114] "Music is combatting communism!" cried critic Leonard Feather.[115] Moreover, it remains unclear if the amalgamation of the once segregated locals was a step forward, because the Negroes, according to one scholar, tended to "sign away . . . assets," eroding a base from which white supremacy could be fought, while consenting to being digested by unions where white supremacy was hardly absent.[116] Sounding unalarmed, *Downbeat* announced that "assets were turned over to the former white local," seen as a sign of progress, since by 1953 New York and Los Angeles were the only cities with "one union" across racial lines.[117]

Unsurprisingly, given such adverse conditions, Negro musicians, in particular, continued their exodus, though the snatching of the passport of Robeson showed that any veering from the status quo could disrupt this escape plan. Cab Calloway's band was performing in Montevideo by 1951.[118] "No more white bands for me says Little Jazz," referring to the sobriquet of Roy Eldridge, who contended that it was much different overseas. "You don't even think in those terms over there," he said, while hinting that a dispute with Benny Goodman was driving him abroad.[119] Leonard Feather agreed. "Outside of the [United States]," he said, "the best place in the world to look for good jazz is Sweden," referring to the recent return of Stan Getz and Charlie Parker. "France has the most fanatical jazz fans," as suggested by the fact that "innumerable newspapers and magazines have departments devoted to jazz."[120]

According to Lou Donaldson, there were other reasons to flee the United States. "The best trumpet player around New York during those times was named Idris Suleiman. He could play better than any of those guys," he recollected. "But he knew he wasn't going to get no gigs because all the promoters and all the club owners were Jewish, so he just packed up and went overseas," at a time when the formation of the state of Israel and the conflict with Palestinians, Egyptians, and others in the Islamic world was sharpening. Suleiman was not alone. Sax man Sahib Shihab fled for similar reasons, he said.[121]

As ever, Paris retained a hold on fleeing musicians. By 1952, a Negro journalist reported that "at any time of day" in this city, "one can hear 'New Orleans Jazz' on the radio. . . . The love of jazz in Paris is a fact,"[122] it was reported happily. This attraction was not just limited to men, for example, Kenny Clarke and Miles Davis. According to the informed journalist Rudolph Dunbar, "Colored women in Europe are at a premium and are given the most lavish . . . attention. In these circumstances," he said in 1950, "when they have tasted the allure of freedom and democracy, it is difficult for them to keep their heads in the right place. Very few of them do, but most of them don't."[123] The lure of exile continued to draw artists abroad, where their very existence was a continuing rebuke to Washington as it sought to portray itself as a paragon of human rights virtue, contributing to the momentum for retreat from the excesses of Jim Crow.[124] By 1953, a journalist was asking rhetorically, "Have you been hearing wondrous tales about living conditions for American musicians in Europe and especially for Negro musicians in France?"[125]

But it was not just the City of Light that drew artists. Saxophonist Don Byas, born in Oklahoma in 1912, and a stalwart with Hampton, Gillespie, Basie, and Ellington, moved to Europe in 1946,[126] settled in Amsterdam in 1955, and lived there until he died in 1972.[127] And musicians were not just going abroad to earn income. By 1955, Lionel Hampton had contributed to building a hospital in Israel, a precursor to his deepening ties with conservative Republicans.[128]

Still, there were hurdles to be surmounted abroad too. In 1956 George Avakian of Columbia Records reminded his top performer, Louis Armstrong—via his manager, Glaser—of the "British union's action in threatening to cancel the rest of Louis's tour if he records for an American company." This was "all wrong," he said, "and perhaps even quite illegal . . . after all, our contracts are approved worldwide by the American Federation of Musicians." Yet despite this bold admonition about this demarche being "illegal," with a whimper he concluded, "I am not going to protest."[129] Armstrong should not have felt he was targeted: "Britishers ban U.S. jazzmen," was the 1950 headline trumpeting the exclusion of luminaries like Sidney Bechet and Coleman Hawkins.[130] Moreover, exile abroad did not guarantee work. The critic Eric Hobsbawm estimates that in 1953 there were 19,114 pianists playing the music in the United States alone (not counting amateurs).[131] Even if one posits inflation in his calculation, only a tiny percentage of this number could bank on being hired in Paris.

Some musicians did seek domestic alternatives. But at times it seemed that it might be easier to get employment in historically protectionist London, rather than New York, the city that had always attracted musicians magnetically. Unions in New York City and Los Angeles, said Johnny Mandel, engaged in geographic protectionism: "They didn't want anybody coming in. . . . They wanted to make it as hard as they could for anybody to come in from other towns. And when you came, you couldn't work at your professions for six months" and "they used to send goons around" to enforce their diktat. "I'm not kidding," he said to the unconvinced, "they sent people around to check at your house. they were really rigid . . . which freaked me." He was particularly familiar with the City of Angels, since the "West Coast Jazz" that took off in popularity in the early 1950s was seen as "effeminate," a softer version of the hardcore bebop then rising. "Hollywood did not take very kindly to jazz in those days," he said, referencing the old guard, "especially Dmitri Tiomkin," born in 1894 in Ukraine. "I was one of those interlopers," said Mandel and "they didn't care to know about people like Hank Mancini and me in the late 1950s." Mancini was a multiple Oscar winner and nominee. That Mandel, who was Jewish American, felt this discrimination speaks volumes of what befell Negroes of similar caliber. Thus, he said stellar musicians were playing in strip joints in 1950s Los Angeles; yes, he said, "a lot of that work was there" but "you had really be able to speak on the instrument" and even that was no guarantee of employment. After the ascendancy of Mancini, "for a while they were trying to put jazz scores to everything and it was quite laughable"—though it did combine with anti-racist pressure to open the door for those like Quincy Jones and Oliver Nelson.[132]

Then there were those who sought to organize at home against the evils that trailed musicians. This included fighting against what critic Nat Hentoff termed as the "classical color line" in symphony orchestras.[133]

This suggested that there was a further reason for why the union operated like most unions of skilled workers in the United States, that is, as a kind of "white job trust," locking in benefits for Euro-Americans, especially men of this group, to the exclusion of others. By 1955, of nearly 250,000 members of the American Federation of Musicians, about 72,000 earned the major part of their livelihood from music, with more members of the union holding regular jobs in symphony orchestras than other settings, providing them with leverage to protect the status quo.[134] That is, the domination of symphony orchestra musicians in the union, artists mostly defined as "white," perpetuated the status quo, which included their racial domination of the union. This held true despite the admonition of Artie Shaw that "no classical player worth his salt . . . can play jazz. Itzhak Perlman tried to fool around with it," speaking of the violinist and conductor, "but doesn't come close."[135]

A problem was enhanced competition for a constricted supply of jobs, with racism placing Negro artists at a distinct disadvantage.

By 1952, union boss James Petrillo declared that out of 9,000 U.S. theaters, only thirty-eight employed musicians, quite a decline from past decades, and as Mandel suggested, the major movie studios hardly filled the breach by employing 389 "men" earning an average of $7,000 annually.[136] By 1954, RKO was described as the first major studio to drop its staff orchestra, meaning that for the first time in almost twenty-five years a major Hollywood studio, though soon to be defunct, was without one. This was occurring as records were described as "now a $200,000,000 a year industry," which was hardly compensatory.[137] By 1955, the NAACP was declaiming sadly that "Negro TV, radio jobs" for musicians were "almost nil."[138]

Foremost among these fighters for equity was the horn man, composer, and arranger Gigi Gryce, born in Florida in 1925, who railed against the common practice of royalties routinely stolen from musicians by record companies and other crooks. It was common practice then for original tunes to be illegally purloined by the publishing company of a record executive, who then would not report record sales and retained the composer's as well as the publisher's royalty. There was the related practice of affixing a stranger's name (often an executive's) as co-composer on original tunes, draining musicians' accounts further. William Kunstler, who was to attain fame as a militant attorney, assisted in forming Melotone Music with fellow musician Benny Golson as a partner. Bruce Wright, who went on to become a New York judge, also aided him. Following suit were other musicians, for example, Horace Silver, Lucky Thompson, Quincy Jones, and Thad Jones. It did not take long for Gryce to be seen as a threat to the class- and race-skewed status quo. Soon, according to one study, Gryce "began to look over his shoulder for enemies out to hurt him and his family," which—understandably—left him "clearly terrified" and terribly upset. An accompanist said Gryce became "nervous" and "paranoid," compelling him to abandon him. Gryce was forced out of the business by those with "underworld connections," say his biographers, as "he and his family were harassed, threatened and intimidated." Like other musicians who leaned toward self-determination, he came to adhere to Islam, assuming the name of Basheer Qusim.[139] As of 1955, he was spending more time in France while his partner, Art Farmer, who had been working as a janitor in New York City, was soon to be expatriated permanently to Vienna.[140]

These were difficult times. Saxophonist Benny Golson, born in 1929, played alongside Gryce and recalled that "the record company would record them and automatically take the publishing. Didn't even ask," he said remorsefully. This caused Gryce to "become a rebel" and "I joined him," said Golson. "He didn't trust very many people. It got so bad he and I split up. . . . One day I was at his house. I just happened to see two people . . . checking on the address . . . they didn't see me but I saw them" and they were "from the record company." Gryce, understandably, "got afraid. He said maybe the Mafia's involved in this." Golson may have left Gryce as an accompanist but not in spirit. When he was part of the Jazztet "we had a manager . . . she had taken $50,000 of my money" and "she was engaged to the vice-president of Pepsi-Cola." Undaunted, Golson "had to get a lawyer," instructing "give me my music back" since it "was in her company." The alleged miscreant, Kay Norton, "cost me a pretty penny," he said.[141]

Exhausted and exasperated with such exploitation, musicians in a changed atmosphere brought by the reluctant retreat of state-sponsored Jim Crow sought, in the 1950s, to embark on a path independent of those responsible for their bludgeoning. Their path was smoothed by an altered global calculus, i.e. the need for Washington to improve its human rights record so as to better challenge Moscow. In this changed context, the new music became a vehicle whereby Western European allies—especially France—could express disquiet with Jim Crow while selectively appropriating (like a dinner menu) elements of the superpower's culture: for example, the music of Charlie Parker.[142] Ultimately, this complex process benefited not only touring musicians but African Americans as a whole.

7. Haitian Fight Song

CHARLES MINGUS WAS MIFFED. The Falstaffian bassist, pianist, composer, and bandleader of protean appetites had sought to shake the hold of exploiters on the production of his music, which was becoming ever more popular because of his immense creativity. He was so well regarded as an artist that the talented bassist William "Monk" Montgomery, born in 1921, "felt like going back to the trucks" after hearing Mingus. "How could anybody play an instrument like that," he marveled. "How could I ever get to be like that," he asked rhetorically and balefully.[1] Success has many parents, and the attainments of Mingus were no exception. "I was his original teacher," said "Trummy" Young. "I charged him about two dollars a lesson." But Young revealed the essence of why Mingus was so ambitious and capable: he "practiced 17 or 18 hours a day, *every day* . . . the real secret of Mingus's greatness." The two were close, and Young had reason to glimpse his ability: "He willed me [his] instrument when he died."[2]

The versatile Mingus, born in 1922, took advantage of the renewed dispensation delivered by the official retreat from Jim Crow in the 1950s and continued pressure on Washington to scurry away from the more egregious aspects of racism (so that Moscow could be better charged with human rights violations) and collaborated with like-minded drummer Max Roach in forming Debut Records. Mingus was disgusted with the music business. There was no honest accounting, and he had to find out how many records he sold by inquiring randomly. He would buy $1,000 of his records, but the result would not appear on royalty statements. He was walking in the footsteps of Otis and Leon Rene, so-called "Creoles" from New Orleans—lighter-skinned

Negroes in other words—who arrived in Los Angeles in the 1920s and wound up controlling a record company.[3] Despite the acclaim garnered by the music of Mingus and Roach, on the eve of Debut's debut, the drummer conceded that "nobody was asking us to record so we decided to" do it ourselves.[4] In addition to Debut, it was recommended that Mingus and others form "co-op clubs to be run by musicians" to elude the hegemony of club owners.[5]

"All music," said Roach, "has an improvisational aspect, but black people invented ways to do it collectively,"[6] establishing a new musical form that, even as it was flourishing, was being ignored by all too many, inducing the percussionist and bassist to embark on an independent path.

But by 1955, writing from Boston, a company responsible for getting Debut's records to market was informing Mingus bluntly, "Regarding our not paying you for merchandise, somewhere along the line there was an understanding that merchandise"—meaning exquisite music—"we received from you was to be paid for when this merchandise was completely sold"; thus they were "packing up the merchandise we have of yours, equal to the amount we owe you and returning same for credit."[7] In response "we are quite surprised at the manner in which you conduct business" Debut castigated curtly, telling the company: "You owe us for merchandise."[8]

Mingus's distributor replied with similar castigation: "Frankly we are rather surprised at your indignation" since "in the past, months would go by after we sent you an order without a reply on your part . . . we thought that we were doing you a favor."[9] Despite the mutual irritability, John Sewell of Rochester, New York, a consumer of the music, found a "great deal of interest in Debut Records. The only catch is, of course, there is no place to buy them."[10]

Composing, practicing, and performing, Mingus hardly had the time or energy to compete with single-minded executives in the music business. He had to "labor" and strain to "pack records" for shipping. After the shedding of sweat, his wife—then partner—split and, he claimed, took the company with her and wed Saul Zaentz of Fantasy Records. "Now he owns it," said Mingus, and "they're millionaires." But while he was with the firm, "gangsters" wanted to sabotage him, he said, and thus "I hit one." There were conflicts with the "Gallo brothers," who were "killers." His competition with other record labels was stiff too. "All Bob Weinstock [of Prestige Records] had to do was to find a good pusher, bring him to the [recording] date, keep the guys happy and get some music out. He paid Charlie Parker, he paid Sonny Rollins, he paid practically everybody who was using dope that way. He got better dope than they got white dope."[11]

Undaunted by this setback, a Debut executive was pushing for the "banding together of independent recording companies," like the Mingus-Roach venture, "in order to reap benefits so far only available to the major labels. We have been in business three years," a Debut associate said in 1955, "and have long felt the need for such an association."[12] But Mingus was swimming in a sea of piranhas, which was evidenced early on when he "spoke with Mr. Herman Lubinsky (Savoy Records)," a particularly voracious predator, who was providing advice to this business neophyte, which was akin to seeking advice about heaven from the devil.[13] Like many Negro men of this era, Mingus had reason to be perpetually upset. After witnessing a fiery confrontation the bassist had with the notorious New York City police, pianist Horace Silver commented euphemistically, "Mingus was very adamant about racial situations."[14]

Mingus was an imposing figure, able to implant his will by force of personality, if not by simple intimidation. Dannie Richmond, a drummer born in 1931, who often accompanied Mingus, spoke of him as a "handsome bastard before he got fat. . . . He'd take jobs as a male model when things got tough. I saw pictures of Charlie, half naked with three half naked broads [women] beaming at him in some porno mag. . . . He married four of 'em," he added with apparent flippancy. Suggesting Mingus's reputation, he added, "some he supported, some supported him." Indicative of his ability to implant his will was an occasion in San Francisco when Mingus was speaking to "one of the girls [sic]. . . . Her pimp came up . . . didn't like what he saw . . . words passed. Charlie wasted no time. He swung a right. The pimp pulled a gun . . . Charlie stomped him." Still, he concluded, "Charlie was no pimp. He was a ladies' man."[15] In contrast, Mingus confessed that he "tried" to be a pimp. As early as 1939, Mingus admitted that alongside

Dexter Gordon, he was performing at a "pimp's club."[16] (Mingus was not unique in participating in this sordid business: His partner Roach rationalized that "even that brief episode I had with the pimp thing," that is, enmeshed in this nasty commerce, "was motivated by trying to become more independent.")[17]

Horn man Jackie McLean recalled a time in Cleveland when he gave Mingus notice that he was leaving the band after the bassist shouted at him during his solo. "Bam," said McLean, Mingus "hit me right in the mouth . . . I went in my pocket and took my knife out and opened it. . . . I was going to stab him," he insisted. "In fact, I cut him through his clothes," and the fiery Mingus promptly "fired me." "The union wanted me" to retaliate, said McLean, asserting "he's already hit somebody here in the union office." Mingus, he said, also smacked trombonist Jimmy Knepper, born in 1927. But McLean refused to seek expulsion of Mingus from the union, even though he was injured severely. "I couldn't play," he lamented, since "he'd knocked my teeth back. All those teeth were pushed back facing the back of my throat." But Mingus's fury was not simply directed at musicians and pimps. McLean was with him when the teenager Emmett Till of Chicago was lynched on spurious grounds in Mississippi after an alleged tempestuous encounter with a Euro-American woman. Mingus was furious and immediately dedicated a tune to his memory.[18]

Perhaps contemplating his volatility, pianist Marian McPartland, born in Britain in 1918, commiserated with Mingus and his difficulty in launching Debut Records. "That poor guy. I think it overwhelmed him. He wasn't a businessman. . . . It's a shame because it was such a wonderful idea," as exemplified when others sought to emulate him. Bandleader Stan Kenton, she said, "had a mail order company" too; in fact, "there were dozens of people that did that," as musicians sought valiantly to escape the stranglehold of capital. McPartland sought to break free from these manacles too. "I employed a couple of girlfriends to fill the orders and pack the records up . . . I got as far as putting out three CDs on Halcyon [her label] and then I gave up," frustrated by the ability to market without advertising and an adequate distribution network. She had been funded initially by the wealthy Sherman Fairchild, and she also worked with Hank O'Neal. "I think he was still with the CIA," she said, and "in the end I had to get a lawyer to get rid of him," further illustrating the perils of the business of music.[19]

Despite the bravura impact of Debut Records, a few decades later the critic Playthell Benjamin was posing a question then in the air: "Will Jazz Survive?" he asked in a "Comment on the State of the Great American Art." He pointed to the headwinds encountered by the label of drummer Rashied Ali, born in 1933: "Survival" was the ironic name of his enterprise, while "Philly Jazz" was the name given to that of saxophonist and flutist Byard Lancaster, born in 1942. "Artists often sell their records on the sidewalk outside jazz clubs and concert halls," said Benjamin, as they found it difficult to circumvent existing distribution networks.[20]

IT WAS NOT JUST ADMITTED GANGSTERS like Morris Levy who were a bane to the existence of musicians. Roach scorned Teddy Reig, yet another executive, who—like a plagiarist—"got into the business with the knowledge he got from Otto [Wilkinson]," a Negro mastermind, but unlike the latter, "went right to the top."[21] Of Reig, who worked for both Levy and his fellow exploiter, Herman Lubinsky, it was said by an observer that he "could easily have become a strong-arm enforcer for the mob" as he was "seldom above using physical force."[22]

These avaricious power-hungry hoodlums with close ties to plug-uglies were accused credibly of counterfeiting records, depriving musicians of income through a "black market," all of which required the protection of a muscular bodyguard.[23] Max Roach, an expert on virtually every aspect of the industry, knew that Levy, a "Cuban Jew," was "part of the mob," an association exemplified when his brother Irving was "killed. Somebody shot him," yet another "tough guy" erased.[24]

The up-and-coming saxophonist Sonny Rollins, born in 1930, was subject to similar forces. He was no neophyte in that his parents were Virgin Islanders and his great-grandfather was a doctor in Haiti. Growing up in Harlem, he found "everybody was sympathetic to Garveyites. . . . Garvey was a very sympathetic" figure in his neighborhood. "My grandmother was a Garveyite and I was marching up

and down for the Scottsboro Boys" and "Free Tom Mooney . . . I grew
up in that. . . . It was just something that was normal to me . . . it
made me feel that I was worthwhile as a human being," the latter two
being political prisoners backed by the Communist Party. "In those
days there were a lot of people that were losing their apartments. he
recalled, speaking of the ravages of the Great Depression. "And there
were always pianos out on the street from people who had to move,"
having been evicted. "You'd go walk down the street, here's a piano."
He was surrounded by musicians as he ambled along. The vocalist
known as Babs Gonzalez was "living on The Hill" in Harlem, likewise for Duke Ellington, Andy Kirk, Coleman Hawkins . . . all the top
musicians lived on The Hill, while "on my block there were people
like W. E. B. Du Bois," the premier intellectual and organizer, and
NAACP lawyer Thurgood Marshall. "We would be playing ball and
stuff and I remember" Du Bois "coming home every night." He was
rubbing shoulders with pianists Bud Powell and Willie "The Lion"
Smith, often departing clubs then not "mob owned," but "as you went
downtown" there was a palpable difference as the influence of "Lucky"
Luciano and other racketeers grew. These were "not the . . . people
that you would want to, you know, have dinner with," a malign impact
that he was forced to endure. "I worked many clubs where I didn't get
paid. I've worked places where my overcoat was stolen" in addition to
his labor. "I've got a mental block," he confessed, "so I don't have to
relive those days . . . we just expected that as musicians," particularly
not getting paid after playing. Once a "fight breaks out . . . forget it.
You're not going to get your money. You're lucky if you get your coat
. . . good thing you have your horn in your hand." His neighbor Du
Bois once uttered words with which he agreed, "It's the obligation of
artists to be political," which brought him to the significance realized
by Mingus. But this noble notion was seemingly at odds with the like
desire to excel as a musician: "I had discipline," he said, "I practiced
15 hours a day with not any thought about it," leaving not much time
for politicking.[25]

The competitiveness of the business compelled musicians who
wanted to excel to practice, at times in a manner that seemed excessive. Hank Jones, who started playing piano at the age of ten, said

later in life, "If I don't practice every day, or every other day, I have to put in two sometimes three hours" in compensation, and "if I want to compose something or get into something where I'm doing composition, I might spend the whole day at the piano." Again this did not leave much time for politicking and lobbying, though Jones was among those who defied this logic by being a voracious reader: "I buy too many books," he confessed.[26] Startlingly, in his early nineties, trumpeter "Snooky" Young admitted, "everyday I put in two hours" of practice.[27]

Mingus and Roach were not alone, in other words, in their political orientation. Mingus, in particular, was a fighter, and not just in his pugilistic acumen. Predictably, one of his signature tunes is "Haitian Fight Song," a roaring anthem of resistance that captures the gathering militancy of the 1950s, when it was composed.

Mingus thought of Buddy Collette as "my best friend, my runnin' buddy, we went everywhere together."[28] In turn, Collette gave him credit for the amalgamating of the formerly segregated musical locals for in union battles he "was always fighting the battle of the racial thing." The merger occurred in 1953 and delivered "better health and welfare" and "pension benefits." It led to merit selection of musicians benefiting the exceedingly competent Negro artists—though there was was a downside involved in relinquishing autonomy, no small matter when Negro musicians were more friendly to radicalism. Collette, who influenced the bassist as much as anyone else, admitted to receiving Communist literature. "It sort of opened up the mind," he opined. "I was around Robeson during this time," he conceded,[29] and endorsed "socialist views." No sectarian, Collette also raised funds for the American Civil Liberties Union, alongside drummer and club impresario Shelley Mann, though the group was sympathetic to anti-communism.[30]

The amalgamation was a mixed blessing at best in that it eroded an independent Negro power base in favor of diluting their strength in a mainstream yoke. Purportedly, a colloquy in a car between Mingus and Collette and trombonist Britt Woodman led to this 1953 merger.[31] Still, there was little comparison between the Negro Local 767 building on Central Avenue in Los Angeles and its counterpart on Georgia

Street near Figueroa; as for the latter, said Collette, "It was a fabulous building and it was really stunning." Despite the downside, in other words, it was understandable why amalgamation was sought, particularly when overall union boss James Petrillo objected: "I don't see why we have to get together," he croaked.[32]

The 1950s, in sum, was an era of incipient change, with positivity impelled by changing global currents and deeply-bred Negro militancy. Mingus's partner, Roach, recalled moving from the fabled Dismal Swamp area on the Virginia-North Carolina border—"the area where Nat Turner," heroic slave rebel, solidified his forces "after his rebellion."[33] Roach escaped to New York City in the 1930s, though he brought with him a militant heritage: "My great grandfather is from Barbados," he detailed, "and his are from Jamaica,"[34] both bastions of resistance to enslavement.[35] "I can vaguely remember," he said years later, "standing on those bread lines and they would give you a bag of Midland Meal and some fat back." He made it to Boys' High School in Brooklyn, but "it wasn't until the 1940s that I began to be introduced to reefer [marijuana] and stuff like that." He was present at the creation of the bebop turn, adding that higher taxes and costs for big bands drove musicians into smaller combos, like the ones in which he excelled.[36] "If you had dancing on stage, if you had singing on stage," a tax was imposed during the war. "Big bands, they were finished then. There was no [way] a producer or entrepreneur could afford to do that anymore," shaking the business to the core. "Everybody reduced their bands down and you just sat and people listened," which, in a sense, opened the door for Debut Records to be launched. "There were no big ballrooms," as before, as "people came and they sat and listened."[37] One might as well listen at home on one's record player.

Like Mingus, he found seeking to run a company difficult. "We would have to take pistols to Boston to collect; they'd hold on to the records," Roach said, speaking of those with whom he had contractual arrangements. It was the "Mafia, and we took our records back." Perceptively, his interlocutor, the writer Amiri Baraka, added, "I also think it's because they didn't want that concept of musicians trying to run their own affairs," plus "the black thing made it worse."[38] As for the pistol, "everybody carried" them, said Roach, "it was common" and also included Harlem congressman, Adam Clayton Powell. "I know" him, said Roach, and he too "used to carry his pistol."[39] Yet, despite the sheer terror in embarking on a path of economic independence, Roach was resolute in resisting retreat. "I don't like to think about going back to those periods when we were treated like animals," he roared in 1988—"less than animals."[40] Thus, in addition to Debut, he proclaimed, "I formed my own publishing company, Milma Publishers."[41]

Roach was unsparing in his evisceration of record companies, compelling his entrepreneurial initiative. These barracudas, he charged, "have no mercy. No matter how much you've done and how much money you've made for them yesterday, when you go to see them today, they're going to say 'What have you got new?' " Hence, he said, "you're constantly welcoming new challenges to come up with an idea, so you can stay alive in the business." This, he emphasized, was the impetus behind the constant innovation of his comrade-cum-competitor Miles Davis, which some of his admirers found so maddening: "He knows the business is like that. It just won't permit him to go back."[42]

Working in clubs was even harsher. "When you worked downtown," he said, speaking of Manhattan, "which was in the white part of the city, you worked seven days a week for six weeks straight. The seventh week you had a week off with pay. We worked from nine to three. . . . Then uptown in Harlem we worked from four until eight or nine o'clock the next morning, seven days a week as well."[43]

The pile-driving drummer Elvin Jones had a similar experience. Like other musicians, he joined the military, then a band therein: "It wasn't segregated," he said of this 1946 experience. Next, he worked with Wardell Gray, just before his unfortunate death, then a "piano player named Philip Hill," working from "9 till about 1" in the morning, a condition made worse when he wasn't paid. "So, I went out the door and saw these footsteps in the snow. And then I followed them 2 blocks" before finding the man who "ran off with the payroll" and engaging in self-help to get paid.[44] Quincy Jones had a similar experience in France in the 1950s. The booker "took the advance and disappeared," frustrating him and his bandmates: "You talk about trouble . . . all these people looking you in the eye."[45] The drummer and trumpeter were not terribly unique. Horn man Benny Golson was hired in 1953 to write music for the comedy team of Stump and Stumpy: "I was not paid," he groaned. "The truth was that they didn't have the money," hardly a consolation.[46]

Near that same time, Percy Heath recalled how he performed "six weeks" and "got paid for two," since "these gangsters who owned the club, why they just [put] out bad checks. And one of those guys used to wave this .45 [pistol] around." In another case, "before they paid us . . . somebody else bought the master" of the recording "and "put it out and they didn't have to [pay] us."[47] Drummer Jimmy Cobb shed further light on why musicians might want to arm. "I remember being on a stage once with Earl Bostic in New Orleans," a saxophonist born in 1913, "where a guy pulled out a pistol . . . we were outside. These guys are shooting at each other across the street." They were "like cowboys. Pow, pow. I said, 'Whoa, wait a minute. Get me out of here.'" By then, "Earl is probably up under the piano." It was like the "Wild West."[48]

Perhaps, but such incidents were more likely to occur in the Deep South, where Jim Crow was more inured. There, enforcing racism rigidly generated violence. Paul Williams, saxophonist born in 1915, remembered a time in Dixie when "people in the audience would be fighting one another. I never played a dance where something didn't break out. I saw some people get real cut up." Then in Panama City, Florida, his manager, Teddy Reig, "went to collect the money" after an engagement and "this big old sheriff with the wide hat says, 'You ain't getting' no money here tonight,'" for Jim Crow also bred corruption and collaboration between law enforcement and bosses. Like others, Williams had burned in his memory a time when "audiences were black but a lot of times you had some white people there. They used to have a big rope to divide the races. If someone got out of line, like a white crossing over to the black side, an officer would get up there, stop the music and say, 'Y'all get back where you belong!'"[49]

WHILE HE WAS JOUSTING WITH RACKETEERS in his Debut Records capacity, Max Roach also found time to attend Camp Unity, organized by the U.S. Communist Party for recreation outside of New York City. "[Herbert] Aptheker was there," he said speaking of the Marxist analyst of slave revolts. "Mr. Robeson would come up there and sing." Apparently, the comrades were unaware that Roach's "girlfriend at that time was a madam," and he was a kind of pimp. He was present with Charlie Parker when the now historic engagement took place in Harlem's Rockland Palace; Robeson was there, too, suggestive of the purpose of the fundraiser. "He sang freedom songs," said the impressed Roach, "in every language possible," including "Chinese, Russian, French, Italian" with "no accompaniment," topping it all off with "Water Boy."[50]

"Record companies," oppositely said Roach, used "all kinds of unscrupulous methods dealing with musicians," necessitating Debut—and consorting with Communists for that matter. "That's why Mingus reacted," he said of his partner, though he could have been speaking of himself. "One company took a session of mine, and one of [Art] Blakey's, that were recorded years apart and pretended we were at the same session and called it something like 'Drum Battle' . . . 'Roach v. Blakey.'" Disgustedly, he added, "They've got a million tricks." The "conditions of this business, how we are treated, that contributed not only to Brownie's death," referring to the auto accident that took the life of trumpeter Clifford Brown in 1956, "but to many others" besides. "We had to drive everywhere we went on tour. The money was so light we had to drive everywhere. You'd be tired on the road, speeding, trying to get to the next gig." How to explain why "Brubeck was making more money with that small group than Duke's whole band." Connecting the harshness of racist reality with the psyche of Negro artists, he contended, "When you think about the exploitation, it makes you hard to get along with." He maintained, "Bird didn't make any money. Duke didn't make any money" but Getz, he repeated, "could buy and sell Duke and [Coleman] Hawkins, [Sonny] Rollins, [John Coltrane] Trane together!" He saw "Paul Robeson and A. Philip Randolph as models" but apparently did not realize that the anti-communism of the latter, a prominent labor leader, vitiated in the 1950s the waning influence of the former.[51]

Drummer Chico Hamilton had roots in Southern California. His mother's name was Pearl Gonzales and "up until I was 21 years old, I had never seen over, maybe 100 black people together at one time in my whole entire life." Thus, instead of being attracted to the likes of Robeson, Hamilton "met [California governor Earl] Warren. I met [Richard] Nixon," facilitated since his father was a waiter at an elite club. Thus, he exulted, "I'm a stone-cold Republican." Despite this political proclivity, he encountered difficulties not unlike his more radicalized counterparts. "Saturday night, man, they [customers] get to drinking" and then "they hate the band" and "all us black dudes" besides; thus, we "had to fight our way out of the joint," a not infrequent occurrence. Similarly, he played alongside vocalist Lena Horne, who was part of a "mixed marriage" in that her spouse—also her manager—was "white so there were times when neither one of them could go with Lena to various places," and since "I was the only black dude in her entourage, right," said Hamilton, "I would have to go with Lena and doing so, man, they put all this money in my hand [and] in my pockets," which he was able to parlay to his advantage: "I began to get a reputation as a mac," or what used to be called a "sport." That is, "I began to get a reputation. . . . It was good times," perhaps bolstering his class posture and blurring the racial disadvantage he faced.[52] After all, the drummer could take advantage of the growing popularity of the vocalist: "You put my wonderful mother on the map, as it were," said her daughter, Gail Lumet, then carrying the surname of her husband, famed Hollywood director Sidney Lumet. She was addressing John Hammond, but she could just as well be congratulating Hamilton for his own good fortune as a result of Lena Horne's celebrity.[53]

Lionel Hampton was also a Republican and not in sync with Roach or the developing militancy, but in his case, he and his entrepreneurial spouse held on to money, and, taking advantage of the erosion of Jim Crow, he eventually had his own company.[54]

Hampton not only roughly wrung concessions from those he hired, though playing early on with bandleader Lester Hite he had his own problems in seeking to sell his labor. Later, he hired an Englishman, Jack Hamilton, who cheated him, Hampton claimed, which could mean his tightening up on employees across the board.

From the time he was a youngster in Chicago, the precocious Hampton, by his own admission, had "always been interested in politics." As a newsboy, he consumed what he was selling, the intermittently militant Negro journal *Chicago Defender*. By the 1940s, he made a lifelong and lucrative investment when he helped the young Richard M. Nixon get elected to Congress. Hampton says that 20,000 Negroes registered to vote with his and Nixon's help and that the two became "tight," meaning close. He "made me his assistant campaign manager," says Hampton, who also had a hand in Nixon's pivotal and mudslinging defeat of Helen Gahagan Douglas, the first Democratic Party woman to be elected to Washington. From then on, said Hampton, whenever Nixon called, Hampton instantaneously "drop[ped] whatever I was doing to play for his campaign." Ultimately, George Herbert Walker Bush would attain this same priority. In 1980, Hampton was "elected as a Bush delegate." "I played on the campaign trail for his father," he said, speaking of yet another successful politician, Prescott Bush. Still, he "liked [Ronald] Reagan" and I "used my own money to buy ads in black publications" for the GOP presidential ticket.[55]

Vocalist Jon Hendricks may not have been as far to the left as Collette, but he was certainly to the left of Hamilton and Hampton and more in tune with the times than the drummer. He was at the University of Toledo School of Law, but the soon to be deceased Charlie Parker came to town and Hendricks sang alongside him. "I was going to finish my law degree and offer my services to the NAACP legal department. That was my plan for life . . . but I was married to an Irish girl and I had a son and there was a lot of animosity against that in this legal-judicial system." Then, his financial backing from the "G.I. bill . . . ran out 18 months short of my law degree." Still, he was so distraught with the adverse conditions to be endured in the United States, "I wanted to move to Canada." So, by the 1950s, he was in Manhattan looking for Parker. He was startled by what he found: "Dope, dope, dope. Everybody was shooting stuff." Wages were sparse, so "I had a day job for nine years" as a clerk. "I worked in offices . . . usually typing invoices." However, having access to a typewriter allowed him to write a song a week. "I received

whatever the publisher saw fit to give me, because they were rob-
bing people blind. . . . The way they robbed people and still do in the
music publishing business," he said in 1995, "is something that's got
to be addressed. It's just filthy to take a man's work and profit from it.
I hate it. I hate it with all the passion I can muster." [56]

Duke Ellington was in a category with Collette. In 1943, he supported the successful election campaign of Communist Ben Davis
for the New York City Council,[57] and subsequently started a publishing arm, presumably rescuing him from the thievery of his so-called
manager, Irving Mills, while his son, Mercer, initiated a record-pro-
ducing firm, not unlike Debut.[58] (Quite famously, Charlie Parker
played at a concert for Davis when the latter was under siege in the
1950s; "The Communists paid better than the capitalists," said his
future widow, Chan Parker, "and this was one of his highest paying
gigs." The famed saxophonist, she said, was "unable to forgive the
hurts of the world,"[59] a trait not unusual among exquisitely exploited
musicians like himself.)

It was important for Ellington to develop new revenue streams,
given the need to support a large touring band. The promoter George
Wein said the pianist had an "acute fear of flying," hampering his
ability to reach scattered, large markets. So, said Wein, Ellington was
often chauffeured by his horn man, Harry Carney, the "numbers
runner" for his valuable passenger. Carney, said Wein, "made more
money taking his and band members' numbers than he did playing
the baritone saxophone." After all, "Duke played the numbers nearly
every day of his life."[60]

Pianist Horace Silver also had his own company, Silveto Records,
and quickly found, as did Mingus, that "I had to deal with small distributors, who were not all completely honest."[61] "When I left Blue
Note," he said in 1985, "getting into the record business was something I didn't intend to do," but he quickly found that becoming an
entrepreneur was the most viable option, roadblocks aside. Silver, who
grew up in Connecticut, may have had an advantage over others in
that he was of Cape Verdean descent: "Both of my uncles and father"
were fluent in Portuguese, opening avenues abroad many musicians
did not enjoy.[62]

Unhelpfully, the American Federation of Musicians ruled in 1953 that members were barred from record company ownership, as if the status quo of gross exploitation was preferable to alternatives.[63] Similarly, when Horace Silver had a financial problem with bandleader Art Blakey, he found to his dismay, "the union didn't do shit."[64] It was as if the union heightened class collaboration in order to foil increasingly popular Negro musicians.[65]

An unacknowledged setback for musicians occurred in 1954 when Frankie Newton died prematurely in New York. Born in 1908, appropriately in a town named after an abolitionist—Wilberforce, Ohio—his performance on Billie Holiday's trailblazing anti-lynching hymn, "Strange Fruit," was just one aspect of a richly varied career that amounted to becoming a vanguard thinker among artists.[66]

DESPITE PREVAILING GLOBAL CURRENTS propelling desegregation, a number of clubs dug in their heels and refused adamantly to employ Black musicians. A club in Columbus, for example, refused to hire Negro performers, as did another in Allentown, Pennsylvania. They would not hire "mixed units" either, said Nat Hentoff; moreover, there were "musicians and booking agencies who go along with this."[67]

That is, despite the U.S. high court ruling in May 1954 that Jim Crow would no longer obtain, it would require more militancy before this edict reached fruition. Artists were not escaping unscathed either. Louis Armstrong was attacked by the Negro press for having played at a venue in Indianapolis where Negroes were barred; said the observant reporter, Satchmo denied that he was "undisturbed by [the] racial barrier."[68]

In short, the continuing malevolence of Jim Crow, combined with the opening against this abomination, delivered by official moves toward desegregation, meant that more musicians responded in the manner of Mingus and Ellington: seeking to grab financial and artistic control over their creativity.

Still, it was not just those like Mingus and Ellington who had sensed new opportunities. By September 1955, John Hammond announced that "20 odd years ago there were exactly three record companies in America: Victor, Columbia and American . . . which owned the Brunswick, Vocalion and 25 cent labels," but by 1955, there were "upwards of 40 labels bringing out some form of jazz consistently." Norman Granz and his popular Jazz at the Philharmonic, was seen widely as being in a category all its own in terms of exposing the music and compensating the artists accordingly.[69]

Still, even the progressive Granz was accused of being unable to resist the pervasively corrupt climate, fueled by racism. Pianist Dave Brubeck was told in 1954 that there should be a "nationwide investigation and subsequent exposure of the 'jazz impresario and booking racket' starting with the methods of . . .Granz," since, it was stressed, "musicians *and* the public must be protected from aspiring monopolists (like Granz) and their ruthless methods."[70] Ellington had his own beef with Granz, as they exchanged sarcastic rejoinders.[71] For various reasons, Granz was subjected often to scurrilous criticism; for example, Chan Parker—the widow of the Kansas City saxophonist extraordinaire—referred to him contemptuously as a "screaming faggot."[72]

But even Norman Granz, a counterpoint to Morris Levy and Bob Weinstock in terms of being less shark-like in his dealings with musicians, was still dealing with artists soaked in the brine of the odious past. Lester Young was among those, says his biographer, who "found it hard to trust people, especially white people whom he didn't know well." Tellingly, while touring with Granz, Young rarely stayed in the luxurious accommodations on offer but, instead, retreated to small Negro-run hotels, where he felt more comfortable. Still, these were among the better-paying engagements he endured in that a six- or seven-week tour would bring him about $5,000 compared with about $800 (minus expenses) at clubs over a similar period. The acerbic Young continued to maintain then that "they want everybody who's a Negro to be an Uncle Tom or Uncle Remus or Uncle Sam," and he was unwilling to portray all three roles—and then suffered a nervous breakdown.[73] The disc jockey, Daddy-O Daylie, thought he knew what happened to Young: "When he went to the war," meaning the Second World War, "something happened to him . . . he was never the same . . . when Lester talked about working conditions he was actually

fearful."[74] Max Roach felt similar pressures. "I was a replacement for
Buddy Rich" on a Granz tour, he said. "Rich is mad because he's only
getting $17,500 while [Gene] Krupa is getting $25, 000. But I got a
$1,000 a week for the whole tour!"[75]

In some ways, Young was among those buffeted by the contrasting winds of an official retreat from the more egregious aspects of Jim
Crow in the 1950s, accompanied by a still regnant regime of racism.
Yet, as ever, it was not just racism that was bedeviling artists: there
was also an illiberalism that generated various ills. At the tip of the
sword, as ever, was Joe Glaser, whose claws were sunk into many artists. Pianist Mary Lou Williams was told crudely, "Yes, I would say
you blew your top. Yes, I would think you were crazy," further igniting the ongoing trend of fomenting angst among Negro artists. Just
days before the U.S. Supreme Court on May 17, 1954, invalidated Jim
Crow legally and constitutionally, Glaser was insulting Negro artists as
usual. He also—seemingly offhandedly but likely warningly—spoke of
"my friend on Downing St., Mr. [Winston] Churchill," a pro-colonial
hammer who continues to be revered among U.S. grandees, would-be
and otherwise.[76] But Williams was not alone in being bashed by Glaser.
Promoter George Wein was taken aback when he heard Glaser refer to
Ellington as a " 'crazy nigger' . . . how this agent could label him with
the pejorative N-word was incomprehensible . . . I was astonished,"
said the New Englander. [77]

By 1953, Dorothy Donegan, singer and pianist born in 1922, was in
uneasy straits. It was not just the fact that as a woman she continued
to face barriers peculiar to her gender. She was also to have a dishon-
est manager—"Corkscrew Gervish"—was her name for him: "He was
crooked" and "thought 10% of a dollar was 60 cents," a frequent mis-
calculation visited upon Negro artists. "They take a commission off
the top and one off the bottom" for good measure. Her then spouse
was "into numbers," another drain of income. Still, when she came
before a judge for the inevitable divorce, the judge declared, "She
makes more money than you," reinforcing her core belief that "men
stick together usually."

Like caring parents before and since, she felt "very bad" when
she had to leave home for lengthy periods to perform: "They didn't

deserve that" she said of children left behind (an infrequent admission made by male parents). "I shouldn't have had no children" she said in 1998, weeks before expiring. "You have to earn a living, if you don't have a husband," leaving narrower options, she felt. She admired her own mother who "didn't marry a man unless he stayed gone all the time. They must stay gone," she stressed, speaking fondly of railway workers.

Like Mingus and Roach, Donegan and her ex-spouse sought to break the stranglehold over performing held by non-artists. They opened a club at 45th and Western in Los Angeles. Yet romance and finance clashed. "He didn't want to pay me and then he wanted to [be] with every girl in the joint." The harsh taskmaster (some might say simply sexist) "made me play, even when I was having a baby," which was "common," she said. Otherwise, "it was like a pregnant prostitute out of business, the women stopped working." Anyway, "show women" like herself too often "get nothing but pimps usually." Their club, the Morocco, named for a North African nation with much purchase among U.S. Negroes, was funded in large part "by his sister and brother-in-law," who chose to "front it."

The club opened in 1953 as the war in Korea was winding down and the United States, because of the press of global pressure, would be compelled to retreat from the more horrid aspects of Jim Crow. But, in many ways, Negro pressure aside, it was not easy to say if this epochal maneuver had mass support among the Euro-American masses. This was creating swirling winds of change—and reaction too.

She was no novice, having been in Chicago in the 1930s when "Joe Sherman who worked for Joe Glaser . . . beat up Lips Page. He hit him in the mouth," she said of this once celebrated vocalist, trumpeter, and bandleader, born in 1908. The wise Donegan was able to snag gigs snatched from the similarly creative pianist and vocalist Hazel Scott, especially after her partner, the mercurial congressman Adam Clayton Powell of Harlem, came under pressure. On the other hand, Donegan, who many thought was as attractive Scott, also carried a cross of penalty as a direct result, as when Lionel Hampton's spouse said bluntly, "You ain't gonna hire no broad in this band." She remained unhappy about the fact that "men don't want to hear women play anyway" and unhappier still about disparities in fees based on gender: "I should make the same money [as a man] if I'm playing better or as well," a novel thought for much of her career. After she joined a Negro local of the union at $30 annually, a "white" guy collected the dues nonetheless. She knew the once heralded Mayo Williams, one of the earlier and rare high-level Negro music executives, but his class position still meant that he paid "as little as possible" to artists like herself: "You never get royalties." This was occurring even as she practiced twelve hours a day. "Joe Sherman," Glaser's enforcer, "Joe Sherman wanted me to stay a slave for life." But the feisty performer replied, "I'll stay with you for a certain while but if I get a raise, I got to go." But she went from the skillet to the fire when she then signed with the "greedy . . . Corkscrew Gervish" whose maladministration dwarfed that of Sherman. She knew the game: "I understand that if they don't steal, they won't book you," but her motto was simple: "I don't want no pimps," the man as parasite. Despite her obvious skill as a pianist, she regretted that she had to shake her hips while performing, unlike her peers, Art Tatum or Ahmad Jamal for example. Based in Los Angeles, she managed a minor breakthrough in Hollywood but "if you're in a movie," she recalled, "if you play a Lena Horne" type, which she could do easily, "you can delete it for the South or for [homogeneous] Southern audiences and the plot would not be disturbed." Like other Negroes of that era, notably those who were also rather light-skinned, she thought that "in Europe a darker skinned woman has a better opportunity than a light one." In the United States too, she believed, "they want the entertainers to be dark, especially on TV," so pressured executives could better make a case and because of a perceived unease brought by those once called "mulatta."

Her former husband was no prize, she thought, speaking of her five-year marriage—"too long," she said—to John T. McClain, Sr. But she was proud of her son, a "great music producer—he produced Janet Jackson and Dr. Dre and people like that," referring to popular music stars, with the latter soaring to the top heights of the economic elite. Her next marriage, to Bill Miles, lasted briefly after 1965 and her third, to Walter Eady, came soon thereafter. As a musician who did better than most despite difficult barriers in her path, she summed up

her varied life by saying, "I should have stayed single and just practiced the piano."[78]

Donegan was not the only artist singing the blues about fees and
payments not determined by skill alone. This was also a repetitive
complaint of Max Roach, who found it hard to understand why
"Brubeck owns radio stations across the country, they make a lot of
money just for being white," just as Donegan espied some men who
profited on a similar basis. Yet, when "Duke died," groused Roach, "he
didn't have zip . . . nothing." Why "compare Benny Goodman's estate
with Louis's," meaning Armstrong. "The real money goes to these
latter day minstrels," he complained.[79]

Vocalist Betty Carter joined the long list of artists upset with Morris
Levy, who decided not to give her credit as composer and publisher
for her own compositions, thereby denying her royalties. This led to
her actually informing her many fans not to buy her record.[80] She
faced problems endured by no man. George Wein was dismissive
of her: "She acts like a man, too butch for me." On the other hand,
of another vocalist, Dakota Staton, manager John Levy (a Negro)
said that if she had been better known when he met her, her record
company would have recommended a "white manager." But just as
Lester Young, as an outgrowth of Jim Crow, had developed a distaste
generally for those defined as "white," Staton's partner, Talib Dawud
(formerly Al Barrymore), a former trumpeter with Gillespie, "didn't
like white people," according to Levy, "and really hated the Jews."[81]

Inexorably, as the formidable edifice of Jim Crow began to crack
in the 1950s, attitudes that had been suppressed began to be asserted.
Art Farmer, then working with the Euro-American pianist Bill Evans,
born in 1929, was told bluntly by him, "Art, I'm not able to finish the
gig. I'm gonna go home . . . because some people were saying that I
don't deserve to be here because there are black guys who play just as
well or better than I do who don't have a job." Recalled was the plaint
directed at Miles Davis: "What are you doing recording with those
white guys," speaking of Gerry Mulligan and Lee Konitz.[82]

Apparently, Ella Fitzgerald was not on record in expressing such
questionable ideas; yet, it was during this same time, in 1955, when
the authorities in Houston suddenly burst through her dressing room

door, guns drawn. One noticeably aggressive officer, she said, "put
the gun in my stomach," all in aid of trumped-up gambling charges.
Fitzgerald also was exposed to racist jokes by fellow singer Frank
Sinatra, about Lena Horne and "watermelon rinds."[83] Black musicians
did not always respond ecumenically to such: pianist and bandleader
Horace Silver spoke of his sideman Tyrone Washington, saxophonist
born in 1944, and his "making anti-white comments out loud in the
club and that just tore the band apart."[84]

Is it possible that the stress generated by racism was then directed
toward related ills? Gambling, for example, a kind of occupational
hazard for musicians that seemed to increase as Nevada boomed
in the 1950s, frequently drained the coffers of musicians. This left
Martha Glaser, the manager of Erroll Garner, frequently exasperated.
In 1955 the diminutive pianist with the slicked-back hair "refused to
answer any questions" and was "vague" besides and "very upset" after
she pressed him about gambling debts. He managed to blurt out that
he had "lost over $4,000 in the past period gambling and must have
$1,600 at once to repay these gamblers." She was "extremely weary
from these pressures, conflicts, and from Erroll's unaccounted for,
excessive spending habits."[85] What she should have contemplated is
if the onerous racism and official bigotry to which those like Garner
were subjected routinely may have been a factor in forging a disas-
sociating gambling habit.

In sum, the United States still barely contained a poisonously
racist atmosphere that official anti-Jim Crow decrees hardly vitiated.
Thus, in 1955 the Board of Liquor License Commission in Baltimore
effectively moved against the practice of segregating nightclubs. In
response, August Blume founded the metropolis's "Interracial Jazz
Society."[86] Yet, near that same time, drummer Panama Francis, born
in Miami in 1918, was confronted with an episode that continues to
persist. He bore a political resemblance to Sonny Rollins (his father
was Haitian, mother was Bahamian) in that, as he recalled, "when I
was 8 years old I joined the drum and bugle corps at the UNIA," the
troops of Marcus Garvey. "I played my first gig—it was on the Fourth
of July, at the UNIA Hall in 1931," which led to a gig in a "juke joint .
. . where all the bad type of people used to come." Ironically, "this was

where I formed that fondness for upright pianos because many a night when they got to shooting, that was where the whole band could be found—behind the piano." (Why the term "juke joint"? "Whenever we played like a slow blues," he responded, "the women would be out on the floor like they were having sex, only they were standing up then and had their clothes [on] . . . that's why it was called a juke joint.") His father, a "bootlegger," left the Roman Catholic Church after joining the Garveyites, since the "movement had a church that they started of their own." Francis's father "spoke English with a heavy French accent," thus he said sardonically he was viewed as "not an ordinary nigger, he was a different kind of nigger" in that "there were a lot of stores that my father was able to go into and shop that blacks could not go into," yet another slap at perceived descendants of enslaved mainland Africans, the real and imagined foe of the republic. This was occurring in Miami, "not the nicest town," in fact, it was "very bad," featuring "lynchings and everything else." The indignities did not stop then, for "when intermission time came, we had to line up and they'd let all of the white men out of the toilet and then we went in one by one and relieved ourselves." Rude patrons would "come up to the bandstand and say, 'Hey boy, do you know 'Sweet Georgia Brown' or 'when are you niggers gonna get hot?' " The indolent atmosphere of the venues when he performed meant "my mother would spend all my money playing numbers" and "loved to gamble and . . . used to lose my money a lot of times" (substantiating the supposition that racism may have fueled gambling). Moreover, his spouse "had a problem with the bottle"—drinking—and "we got into the violence . . . which I deplored." Seemingly on the path of Lester Young toward a breakdown, Francis "could be sitting down holding a conversation and I would just bust out in tears." Eventually, in response, he married a psychiatric social worker. "I got married to my psychiatrist," he mused, perhaps a response to the accumulation of tensions brought by racism and a sudden turn to anti-racism. "She used to sit and work with me when I was going through my problems."

However, like other artists he had his own run-ins with the likes of Glaser, who once yelped at trumpeter Roy Eldridge, no shrinking violet himself, who then responded angrily to his erstwhile manager,

"I tell you what you do—you play this God damned trumpet . . . if you want to run my band." Francis was accustomed to confrontation, recalling a time in the 1950s when he was trying to flag a taxi in Manhattan with a drum set in hand: "They're passing me like I wasn't there," he said of the cabs. And it was "raining." So "I stood there and stood there, waving and waving," so like darker-skinned men before and since, he began to walk. "I'm cursing, I'm mad; you could fry an egg on my head I was so mad." Fortunately, since he had also played with Cab Calloway and Duke Ellington, he had the wherewithal to buy a car and learn to drive. Eventually he fled to Uruguay: "I was a star down there." Though, he concluded bitterly, "I often say to my friends that in Europe I'm a king and in my own country, I'm Panama who?" And like other musicians, the harsh conditions in which he was compelled to operate led to a diminishing of self-regard: "I usually look upon myself as a prostitute," he said with astringency in that "wherever the money is, that's where I'm going."[87]

It was also in the 1950s that the pianist Horace Parlan fled to Denmark, frustrated by this state of affairs.[88] But for roadblocks, more might have followed the path eastward. London remained hesitant to ease the entrance of more musicians, even as the "British invasion," just over the horizon, led by the Beatles and the Rolling Stones, mimicking the blues of Negro artists, was about to transform the entire music market. In 1955 Whitehall acknowledged the "possibility of more British entertainers being allowed into the United States. British commercial interests in the United Kingdom, who are anxious to increase the flow of American artists here, have said that the Americans are now pursuing a freer policy on such matters," which conceivably called for reciprocity. But, it was noted, "the practice here will be largely governed by the views of the Musicians Union who, fearful of the preponderance of American musicians who would be suitable for employment here and of unemployment among our own musicians would be reluctant to agree to anything more than a head for head exchange." Recalled was the reciprocity with Louis Armstrong and his band, given visas to perform in Britain on "an exchange basis with Freddie Randall," English trumpeter born in 1921.[89]

"We couldn't play in England because of union rules," said saxophonist Bill Holman, speaking of Stan Kenton's band in the 1950s. "We could do some U.S. airbases and stuff like that. So we played a concert in Dublin" to great acclaim: "In the street, it looked like the French Revolution down there. All that was missing was the torches. It was just jam-packed with people. They're all yelling and cheering."[90]

As Kenton's mates were being cheered, George Wein pointed to the "ultra-left-wing English Musicians Union which was a tough organization. The union often made it difficult to get groups into England,"[91] which sent exiles to Copenhagen and Paris and Vienna instead.

Flugelhornist Art Farmer was among those blocked in reaching England. "We didn't play in London," he said, "because there was a union problem there." He wound up in Europe anyway, a step up from New York City. "I was working as a janitor in theaters . . . money was very low. I was making like $28 a week, $24 after taxes. I was paying $6 a week." Before heading to Europe in the 1950s, he had moved west to Los Angeles and wound up as a hospital worker, an "x-ray clerk." After these dispiriting experiences, Europe was a tonic. "I recall no racial, negative situations at all. None at all." Whereas in Dixie there were "no black hotels" then: "we stayed in first-class hotels" in Europe, unlike in his homeland, where "you wouldn't think about staying in the white hotel because they wouldn't let you in there anyway," meaning tossing and turning sleeplessly on buses cruising through the darkness. In the South, it was "hit and run": play, get on the bus, and race to the next town. Like others, he was unhappy in Lionel Hampton's band. "Lionel always had a very negative reputation for paying people, very negative." Pay? "$17 a night," and "out of that $17 you had to pay your hotel rent and everything." Complaining to the union, Local 802, brought no remedy since the bandleader was close to Glaser, who, in turn, pulled strings with "Caesar [James] Petrillo who was the president" of the union and nothing happened. Like other younger musicians, he was inspired by the example of Gigi Gryce, "one of the first young black musicians to have his own publishing company," along with Quincy Jones. Corporate honchos "didn't like it," especially when this led to a challenge to "union scale" of "$41 for a three-hour [recording] session."

Thus, Gryce was a "paranoid" who had real enemies, Farmer said, a trait not alleviated by an unhealthy diet: he "loved fatty foods," especially ice cream; he "used to eat a pint of ice cream every day," a habit that may have contributed to a "heart attack." He "didn't trust anybody," was "compulsive," and "was not a relaxed person," though ironically, none of this "showed in the music"; he had a "money belt" in which was tucked "all of his money." He "got fed up with the system. He always felt that people were going to steal from him. . . . He was always looking to be cheated" and was rarely disappointed as a result. "They're out to get me" was a pet phrase. Thus, he abandoned the usual routine of musicians, especially performing for peanuts, and "became a teacher" at his Queens home. "He built a room inside of a room in the cellar with big concrete bricks where he could go in there and nobody could come in without his permission," since "he thought that people were gonna go so far to come out there and go into the concrete room that he had to kill him or something." It was a "tragedy" and a "pity," said Farmer accurately, that a man of talent was so blocked by racist and economic exploitation that he felt compelled to retreat to a bunker. As for Farmer, he wound up in Vienna and learned German. "The beat is the foundation of life," he philosophized, "starting with the heartbeat," but in his erstwhile homeland the "beat" was constrained by a strangulating exploitation. In Austria, Farmer felt freer: "Quality of life . . . you gain on quality of life," he declared in assessing exile. In the place of his birth, on the other hand, "sometimes you're in this take it or leave it situation. . . . There's a lot of competition," meaning "some musicians will undercut you." It was "beneficial to get outside the United States," he said, echoing generations of musicians past, "because when people here [Vienna] find out that you make it over there, then they give a little bit more respect over here, when they know that you don't have to stay here."[92]

Max Roach concurred about the value of travel, arguing that "the Europeans are more cosmopolitan than people here. Maybe because they're closer to Africa"; Europe, he said, was "different" than the crusty United States.[93] Trumpeter, conductor, and composer Quincy Jones, born in 1933, could sense the opportunities opening then, particularly abroad. "I was 19 years old," he said, and "studied

Serbo-Croatian, Farsi . . . Turkish, Greek, French, Swedish, Russian."
Yes, "girlfriend[s]" helped too, though this would have been for
naught but for his own initiative.[94]

Also fleeing the United States was singer Myra Taylor. By 2000, she
was eighty-three, but in 1932, when she was fifteen, she tired of working as a maid for $5 a week and became a nightclub singer in Kansas
City, where she encountered the typical: a gangster entered the club
where she was performing armed and pointed his gun at the drummer,
insisting, "I told you I didn't want to hear any more music. But since
you want to play, play 'Sophisticated Lady.'" The drummer promptly
complied with a smooth segue, "as the rest of the band cowered." Yes,
"of course, I was working for gangsters," she averred. Disgusted, as the
second half of the twentieth century dawned, Kansas City was slowly
perishing as a hotspot, so she headed south of the border. There, she
recalled, she "played to a packed house nightly for a decade—and
made a lot more money" than during her last years in the Show-Me
State. From there, she made connections in Hawaii, Japan, Australia,
Vietnam, and Malaysia—her next stops.[95]

Taylor was fortunate in being able to pull up stakes and head to
another continent. George "Big Nick" Nicholas, born in 1922, singer
and saxophonist, on the other hand, recalled all the talented musicians forced out of the business. Saxophonist Hilton Jefferson, born
in 1903, became a bank guard, and trumpeter Jonah Jones was thinking along similar lines "before he got his big break." Nicholas's spouse
"told me to go to the Post Office and get somethin' steady." Speaking
in 1980, he noted that trombonist J. J. Johnson was "still in the Post
Office," while drummer Roy Haynes "became a whiskey salesman."[96]

Guitarist Monk Montgomery seemingly would have opted for a
similar career path, even though he was working regularly at the apex
of the profession with Lionel Hampton's band. "The routine of traveling, making one-nighters and going through all the aches and pains
that go with a big band, especially during the time you were traveling
by bus, sleeping on the bus," was enervating. Moving to Los Angeles
for a more sedentary lifestyle was his alternative. For in his hometown
of Indianapolis in the mid-1950s, he was "working at a place out on
the Avenue on 16th Street, at a place called the Tropicana and we had

JAZZ AND JUSTICE

to go through the back door. There [were] no blacks in the club," as "patrons." Trumpeter Freddie Hubbard "used to come out to play"; born in "Naptown" in 1938, he was treated similarly, ditto for multi-instrumentalist Roland Kirk, born in Columbus, Ohio, in 1935, who "used to come down from Cleveland." Seemingly on the path of Lester Young and Panama Francis, he was "very depressed."[97]

Montgomery's fellow Indianan David Baker—composer, conductor, performer, and expert teacher—knew the bassist. It was probably in a club in Indianapolis where Baker was playing with a "very fast" tempo—bebop style—and Montgomery was right along with him. The bassist's more well-known brother, guitarist Wes Montgomery, born in 1923 in "Naptown," was "really the mild one," said Baker. Their brother, Buddy Montgomery, born in 1930, was humming on the vibraphone at this memorable gig. Typically, a customer—"dude was drunker than a skunk . . . kept messing with Buddy" and in a final flourish "reached up and grabbed one of Buddy's . . . mallets," and "while [the assaulter] was holding the mallet," the incensed Montgomery "reached over and knocked him unconscious. I don't think he missed more than 2 measures," said an admiring Baker of the accompanist who hardly skipped a beat.

Like too many Negro musicians, Baker continued to endure racism even as there was premature boasting about the erosion of this harmful tendency. At Indiana University, he studied classical bass trombone, but when he auditioned for the Indianapolis Symphony, the man in charge, Fabien Sevitzky, born in Russia in 1893 and highly regarded as a conductor in his U.S. home, sternly told Baker that he "was probably the best bass trombonist that they were going to hear and certainly the best one that they had heard up to that time," but, sorry, he could not be hired. "I realized this was an exercise in futility," said a sober Baker, that the higher-ups, the Board of Trustees, were not "going to hire a black in a symphony orchestra . . . any more than they're going to do that now if they can avoid it," he said in 2000. "It was a dose of reality for me," he said, as was the case for too many victims of racism then.

But Baker "knew that I could make it as a jazz player," then migrated to this competitive field. Even in the supposedly liberal college town where he was stuck—Bloomington—he encountered crusted bias; it was "completely segregated," he said, as he "couldn't get haircuts" or other basics. Then, he committed the ultimate offense when he married a woman defined as "white" in Illinois, then returned home to find the "vigilantes were looking for us. I'm serious," he contended. "I was very tense." As he was enduring this 1950s drama, he suffered a car accident and was "in a coma for a week." He started "having trouble with speech" as an outgrowth, meaning "trouble with trying to play the horn," since he was "playing on a dislocated jaw for almost seven years." The "pain," he exclaimed, was "just incredible." So this musician of versatility switched to the cello and teaching, reaching the summit of the industry. "I starved a lot" for a while, he said, before emerging as a redoubtable artist.[98]

There was a related "pain" involved when Baker contemplated the furious reaction to his interracial marriage, a flashpoint, considering musicians often possessed more than adequate income and thus the class cachet that was found attractive. "I've had fights," said the physically attractive Max Roach, "heavy ones because I was with white women" on 52nd Street in Manhattan, the hub of the business. Though officially Jim Crow was in retreat, individual attitudes were not always in sync. As the 1950s were unfolding he didn't find it surprising at all that "music preceded the sports world in [racial] integration," though his industry was hardly avant-garde attitudinally on the racial front.[99]

Perhaps unsurprisingly, saxophonist Bill Holman, born in 1927, thought that Stan Kenton, bandleader, often surrounded by out-of-sorts musicians battling depression, harassment and worse, "always had a secret desire to be a psychologist" or "psychiatrist. So he practiced on the guys in the band." Perhaps Kenton should have paid more attention to the working conditions of his bandmates than their psyches. For it was in the 1950s that his band was on the Pennsylvania Turnpike, when, recalled Holman, the "bus driver nodded out and ran into the back of a truck. . . . The whole trombone section had been lying down in their seats. So, when the bus stopped, they went and hit the seat in front of them and they got all their chops smashed," a condition not conducive to adept playing. Kenton also should have paid more attention to the makeup of his own band when engaging in amateur psychology. For his sideman, Holman noticed that with the development of "West Coast" or "cool" jazz in the 1950s, "there was the fact that it was almost totally white. With all the good players in L.A.," he said, "they only used the white ones that were in our group—in your community—your pals."[100] In other words, just as bebop was a product of the hothouse created by segregating talented musicians, "West Coast Jazz," he suggested, was a kind of counterrevolution, engineered on racial grounds, mimicking the founding of the slaveholding republic in 1776.[101] Wordsmith and drummer Roy Porter said, "black jazz artists were left out in the cold because this so-called cool school of playing was too narrow a category for us to fit into."[102]

Perhaps it was a case of "physician heal thyself," for it was Kenton who seemingly required psychological aid after he claimed that polls ranking musicians were skewed in favor of Negroes.[103]

Also on the move was Nat Hentoff. By 1950, he was in Chicago toiling on the staff of *Downbeat*, the bible of the business, but he was in conflict with ownership. He was fired. Management, he said, was "hostile to blacks," but ownership was "anti-Semitic as well, or didn't like Jews, let us say. . . . I did something that led to my termination. I wondered why we didn't [have] any black people on the staff. . . . I never saw a black by-line on the magazine." When he hired a dark-skinned Egyptian aide, the tipping point was reached.[104]

Yet those like Hentoff were coming under increasing fire because of their critical judgments and their ability to make—and break—careers, making their working lives all the more unstable. "What is a jazz critic?" asked Martha Glaser, Erroll Garner's aide, dismissively. "Who elected him? How does he get there?" Irritably, she concluded, "Jazz critics are terribly fickle."[105] Her client, she said reproachfully to one reporter, was not a "sideshow freak,"[106] which is how he had been portrayed (in a manner that her off-the-record remarks buttressed). Bob Thiele, label owner and producer, was equally dismissive of critics since "they certainly do not understand how music is performed or created."[107] Max Roach found it "very funny . . . that this is mainly a black music and that almost every book that has been written on it has been written by white people," and "that is unfortunate," said the drummer who early on dismissed peremptorily the very term "jazz."[108] Sadder still, he said, "Black intellectuals don't give much credence to the music. Du Bois didn't deal with the music . . . there are no black critics in any major publications on the music," he said in 1996, including "no daily newspapers. It is amazing that these people," that is, employers, "still don't consider themselves racists."[109] Shirley Horn, singer and pianist, argued that "few writers" in the United States "know what they're talking about that I respect," since "the majority of them will look at your bio . . . and take from that" rather than dig deeper. They were derivative and tended to perpetuate "mistake[s]" effortlessly and relentlessly.[110] Concurring, Yusef Lateef said, "I go along with something that Miles [Davis] said once. He said . . . 'I'm my best critic. I don't need anyone to tell me.'"[111] Davis had a point. Some critics had screwy ideas. For example, Gene Lees of *Downbeat* once cited the similarly boneheaded novelist Ayn Rand, a favorite of conservatives, and vociferated "to hell" with those who disagreed.[112]

Yet Glaser and other formulators of sweeping condemnations of critics were a bit unfair. Flaws aside, critic Leonard Feather had a more insightful comprehension of the matter of "race" in the United States than most who were defined as "white."[113] The fact that he toiled in an industry dominated by African Americans should not lead the unwary to conclude that this insight was understandable, even inherent, since others so situated were not as perceptive. Nevertheless, Dave Brubeck was informed bluntly that in writing about music, as opposed to racism, Feather's "standards of criticism are a disgrace" and was told that this critic was little more than a "charlatan."[114]

Irrespective of the merits, or demerits, of Feather, the critic Frank Kofsky has a point when he says, "All but a handful of those who have written books, articles and even advertisements about it, as well as those who have owned and edited the periodicals and published the volumes that have dealt with it," meaning the music we call "jazz," "have been white men," and they have "served to deny, obscure, rationalize, or otherwise defend the single [most] glaring iniquity with the production of the music: that black artistry has created it while ownership has profited disproportionately from it."[115]

MIDWESTERN GUITARIST KENNY BURRELL, born in Detroit in 1931, had similar dispiriting experiences in his hometown. He admitted that because of the dominant automobile industry, the Negro working class often had more income than comparable communities and thus "were able to buy some instruments for their children," accounting for the plethora of notable artists emerging from Motown. "I went to Miller High School," he said, "where Al McKibben," bassist born in 1919, went, along with Milt Jackson, vibraphonist born in 1923. But racist tension meant that growing up there were "lots of fights" and a "lot of violence. . . . I witnessed so many things where gangs were involved and it would just turn your stomach it was so bad," he said with sadness. "So many of the friends I had went to jail or got killed." Complicating matters further was the reality that at Wayne State University, a lodestar for up and coming Negroes, "the word jazz [was] not looked upon very fondly," meaning "negative experiences" for those like Burrell. Traveling to Jim Crow Virginia brought no surcease; in 1955, he was on a golf course with bassist Ray Brown and was told crudely, "We're sorry . . . we can't have colored people here." Despite these setbacks, Burrell was able to take advantage of the changing racial climate. The attorney of vocalist and pianist Nina Simone aided him in publishing his compositions. Fellow Michigander Thad Jones, born in 1923, had "suggested I get my own publishing," and he did so, though it "takes a lot of work to run a publishing company." In this, he was following the lead of the much besieged Gigi Gryce: "I always admired him," said the guitarist.[116]

So did pianist Horace Silver, born in 1928. "I still carry with me a few emotional scars from Norwalk," he said later, speaking of the casual bigotry he encountered in Connecticut. "The things that a black person had to endure in those days," he sighed, "were a pain in the ass." He found that biased police officers—the "vice squad"—hounded musicians because of suspicions of drug habits and a desire to augment their arrest statistics. There was also the casual sexism that did not leave him unaffected. The curiously named King Pleasure, born Clarence Beeks in 1922, was a regular at a club in nearby Hartford and "sold drugs and had a lady trickin' for him too." He also found that "some of the white women only went for really

dark-complexioned black musicians" while "some of the black musicians only went out with white women," while "the black women like
light-complexioned black musicians with straight hair like mine," he
said. When he was dating a Euro-American woman, her ex heard
that "she was going with a black man and threatened to take the kids
away from her." Yet despite playing early on with stalwarts such as
Stan Getz and J. J. Johnson, Silver maintained a "day gig in a defense
plant," making him appreciative of the ducats he accumulated finally
from publishing. Both "Gigi Gryce and Lucky Thompson," saxophonist born in 1925, were the "only black musicians" he knew who "had
their own publishing companies. . . . Gigi turned me on to publishing," he confided, a real plus since "the music business is filled with
unscrupulous people." Silver had varying experiences with record
companies, including Blue Note, Prestige, Savoy, and various executives including Lubinsky, Orin Keepnews, and Bill Grauer, and was
thus well placed to comment on "unscrupulous people." Weinstock
of Prestige and Lion of Blue Note were "always feuding," providing
arbitrage opportunities for the wiliest of musicians.[117]

Among the more masterly musicians is Ron Carter, also born in
Michigan in 1937. Though during his youth the renowned conductor
Leopold Stokowski instructed him that he could not be hired because
there would be racist objection (a common offense by those defined
as "white," as Mingus discovered in his encounters with Red Norvo).
By eighteen, the skilled bassist was involved in "heated" disputes with
pianist Harold Mabern, born in 1936, about how to play. "For a long
time we didn't speak," he said, "it got out of hand," which was a not
infrequent descriptor in a highly competitive and intense climate.
"We were gonna go outside," he moaned, meaning fisticuffs. But all
was not dismal for Carter, taking advantage of the defeated and occu-
pied Japan, like other African Americans similarly situated, he found
that he was "big over there" not least in lucrative "commercials."[118]

Carter could have also mentioned Canada as a factor explicating
why so many Michiganders played a prominent role in the music.
Pianist Hank Jones was among those who listened to CWOW radio
there. "They used to put a lot of Fats Waller records on," which shaped
his own pianism.[119]

Like enslaved Africans in the previous century, Roach was among the artists who also found sanctuary in Canada. As Jim Crow was on the cusp of retreat in 1953, the drummer joined Mingus, Parker, Gillespie, and Bud Powell at Massey Hall in Toronto in a bebop extravaganza. Roach and his bassist, comrade Mingus, "clandestinely," said the percussionist, arranged to bring an engineer to record, allowing future generations to enjoy their masterwork. "We didn't know that Norman [Granz] or Dizzy or Bird especially were part of the Birdland Mafioso syndicate. They own Bird," meaning Morris Levy,[120] which meant problems of all sorts, though these thugs like the dastardly club owner presumably had less influence in a foreign jurisdiction.

The increasing popularity of the music Roach performed also meant that new avenues for performing were opening. By 1954, the soon to be iconic Newport Jazz Festival was launched in Rhode Island, a former slave port. "Given the Gilded Age aristocracy and heavy naval presence," said George Wein, the moving force for this event, Newport "could be as tough for blacks as a Southern town."[121] The dialectic of a Dixie atmosphere well north of the Mason-Dixon Line was symbolic of the difficulties experienced by artists, even as Jim Crow was supposedly crumbling.

8. Kind of Blue

THE POSTWAR ERA WAS NOT ONLY marked by the May 1954 official exodus from the horrors of Jim Crow; this epochal turning point was followed by the mass uprising against school desegregation in Little Rock, Arkansas. These events were countered by the independence of Ghana, West Africa, which placed Washington in the difficult position of seeking to capture "hearts and minds" in Africa and Latin America, while those of African descent in the United States itself were treated like third-class citizens. When Moscow launched a satellite into outer space in 1957, it appeared to some that Washington was even more on the defensive, compelling more concessions at home. More openings were thus created for musicians. In 1959, Harold Battiste sought to organize a "Musicians' Cooperative Records, Inc." in his native Jim Crow New Orleans. Next, the composer and arranger and teacher, born in 1931, tried to form the appropriately named "All for One Records," then the National Association of New Orleans Musicians, and in a final burst of self-determination joined the Nation of Islam, which pursuant to the deft guidance of Malcolm X was growing in spurts.[1] "He was always championing jazz musicians," said an appreciative Ellis Marsalis, pianist and patriarch of a renowned family of artists.[2]

Times were changing. It was not so long ago that Charlie Shavers, trumpeter born in 1920, was said to have sold the hit "Undecided" for a mere $25. Fats Waller sold wonderful tunes for a like amount, and Clarence Williams, born in 1898 (pianist, composer, vocalist, producer and one of the earliest of the Negro publishers of music), found it necessary to depart the business in favor of a used goods store. As the dam of iniquity was breached, a flood of opportunities emerged and, predictably, resistance mounted simultaneously.[3] These opportunities included being sponsored by the United States, as Washington raced to sanitize its soiled Jim Crow image abroad by sponsoring legions of musicians in worldwide tours, which benefited the musicians by opening more markets for their creativity.[4]

But even here, Washington could not escape Jim Crow altogether. Saxophonist Phil Woods, born in 1931, often felt insecure, since, he said, "I'm a white guy" in a music where this group did not dominate. Dizzy Gillespie suggested that in order to learn and become a better craftsman, he should "steal" from his betters. Thus, when the trumpeter invited him on a State Department tour abroad, it was due in part because Washington said "they couldn't send an all-black band as a representative of America . . . they had to get some white faces. . . . They needed an ofay [white] so I was hired to play an alto," a kind of "tokenism" that benefited those like himself.[5]

Yet, despite the service to the state executed by Negro artists, they continued to be denounced by some. U.S. senator Allen Ellender of Louisiana was so concerned with the impact of these sojourners in socialist climes that he denounced the music of Gillespie and others after they arrived in Eastern Europe. He demanded that only "choral groups" be sponsored by the government.[6]

Jim Crow and its poisonous legacy erected barriers that were harmful to all, including those like Woods who could have benefited from more exposure to more talented musicians. Trombonist Curtis Fuller recalls that "I wasn't allowed in one part of downtown Detroit. I wasn't allowed to go out there. In fact when I went to Pepper Adams' house," speaking of the baritone sax man born in 1931, "a couple times I had to go into the trunk of the car" in order to arrive safely. "I couldn't be seen riding in town with him," which was not just harmful to Fuller.[7]

The attempt by Washington to deploy the music on its behalf was breathtaking in its chutzpah, though not without precedent. After all, as critic and historian Eric Hobsbawm articulated, it had not been so long ago that "the aristocrats and the middle class first began to borrow the waltz from the 'lower orders' and the polka from the peasantry."[8]

No better example of the contradictions embodied in this era was the example provided by the Republican Party activist and bandleader Lionel Hampton, the labor-crushing boss. By 1957 he was to be found in London performing a benefit concert alongside John Dankworth and Humphrey Littleton for the benefit of Nelson Mandela and his comrades then on trial for treason to apartheid.[9] This was just after the so-called Suez War, featuring a piratical attack by Britain, France, and Israel on Egypt. Of Israel, soon to be a byword for human rights violations, Hampton rhapsodized about this settler colony as his "beloved" and "spiritual homeland."[10] Contradictorily, Hampton emerged as a premier backer of the Republican Party, which eventually was to emerge as a major barrier to Negro progress. His acumen, however, led him to form two music publishing companies, a record label, and the LH Development Corporation, which built a 355-unit building in Harlem.[11]

Trumpeter Jimmy Owens, born in 1943, began his career at the tender age of fourteen—"I'd practice all day," was his subsequent reminiscence. He wound up with Hampton's band: "125 a week" was the salary, "six nights a week and your day off you were always traveling so it wasn't a day off. . . . We had to pay our own hotel" at "$7 a night" and "if we doubled up it was three and a half dollars a night." The bus that transported them had a section called "Skid Row" where "guys were drinking and smoking," while in the front of the vehicle sat Hampton royally, the "goodie-goodie section where he was reading his paper, the *Christian Science Monitor*." At times, they were on the road eleven months annually, quite useful in enhancing the bandleader's bottom line.[12] Vocalist Annie Ross, born in 1937, also performed with the rotund bandleader, whose face, seemingly fixed with a perpetual grin, belied his hardline methods with musicians. "If any one of you make a record," he once belted, "you're fired!" Rebelliously, she said, "We all made records because we weren't getting paid that much. He fired the whole band," she said, sounding stunned years later, "which was hysterical. It was actually Gladys who did it," speaking of his spouse and manager. "So Gladys was rich. She was rich," she emphasized but so was he, as a direct result of his anti-labor praxis.[13]

Saxophonist Marshal Royal toured Dixie with Hampton during the world war and found the only place worse was apartheid South Africa where he visited in the 1970s. With Hampton "the money really wasn't that good," just "eleven dollars a day," a "starvation circuit." Yet "money was being made because Gladys [Hampton] was buying a thousand-dollar war bond every week."[14]

Hampton was not the only Republican who attained more wealth as time passed. Frank Sinatra was earlier seen correctly as a kind of "New Deal" Democrat, but that began to change as his bankroll fattened. By October 1953, he obtained 2 percent of the Sands Hotel in Las Vegas, then upped it to 9 percent. A few years later he obtained 25 percent of Park Lane Enterprises, which controlled the Cal Neva Lodge in the Lake Tahoe region, even though the authorities knew that he "catered" to mobster Sam Giancana.[15] According to the Chicago authorities, by 1958 Giancana was "now the top dog of the pinball machine and jukebox rackets in Du Page County with possible headquarters at Bensonville, Illinois" and was spending more quality time in Las Vegas. He was also the "man behind the scenes" in a "distributing company . . . dealing in counterfeit phonograph records and underselling the market."[16] Besides being a cash business that mobsters preferred, jukeboxes created more leverage for them since taverns and others were often hostile to the collection of royalties.[17] Likewise, said one analyst, "because records sold for cash, it was always a business that interested the mob."[18]

Giancana's confederates were implicated when young toughs using axes, acid, and hijacking fought to gain control of these coin-related businesses. One reporter said this was "associated with a group that tried to monopolize the distribution of phonograph records to jukebox operators."[19] (Pinball machines, cigarette machines, and the like were also part of these coin-related rackets.)[20] Counterfeiting of records was an essential part of this tawdry business, and forcing jukebox operators to buy them meant facing a pincers maneuver from politicians tied to racketeers.[21] By 1958, future U.S. attorney general Robert F. Kennedy, then Chief Counsel of the U.S. Senate Select Committee on Improper Activities in Labor and Management, was told of the "muscling tactics of the Capone syndicate" in the jukebox business.

Kennedy was told of Diamond Records in Los Angeles, owned in part by Joe Sica, who was tied to both Mickey Cohen and Jack Dragna, paramount gangsters.[22]

Producer Teddy Reig was quite familiar with these scams, having worked for Bob Weinstock at Prestige Records, well known for paying musicians with drugs. One involved "free records. The distributor would buy a thousand records and get five hundred free. Then he'd sell the five hundred and send the thousand back. Then the accountants came up with Chinese arithmetic [sic] about royalties" to disguise the fraud. "It was Herman Lubinsky all over again," he marveled, speaking of the disreputable entrepreneur, "only much more sophisticated."[23]

Corruption was not limited to the Chicago vicinity. A "cabaret card" was needed by performers in New York City to play at clubs, and police were seeking to manipulate the process to extract corrupt payments from desperate musicians. At a public hearing, a reporter noticed that the proceedings "nearly came to fisticuffs" because of contention.[24] By 1960, a cabaret was defined as a site where drinks, food, and live music were on offer, and New York City had a reported 1,200 such venues, supposedly fifteen times more than in Paris. The police department assigned about 1,000 officers to inspect each and every one of these clubs, which created the possibility of bribe-taking and corruption to the detriment of musicians.[25] To their credit, Quincy Jones, Nina Simone et al. brought suit against the cabaret card system leading to reform.[26]

The 1950s were also the time when Atlantic Records, which became an industry giant, gained liftoff. Founder Ahmet Ertegun, the son of a Turkish diplomat posted to Washington, had in 1935 been withdrawn from the posh St. Alban's prep school because they insisted on instruction in Christianity.[27] The younger Ertegun was transformed in any case when he witnessed a performance by Cab Calloway and Duke Ellington at London's Palladium. A few years later in Washington, he organized so-called "mixed-race" performances at the Turkish Embassy, which was technically not subject to the republic's Jim Crow jurisdiction. Then, more conventionally, he organized sessions with nothing but Negro artists. By 1949, his business breakthrough came with the recording of "Drinkin' Wine Spo-Dee-o-Dee," a curious production by one raised as a Muslim.[28] Ertegun actually met his partner, Herb Abrahamson, in what he termed a "Communist-front" bookstore in Washington, D.C., where his brother Neshui was lecturing. However, when he hired prostitutes for a confab of disk jockeys in Washington, D.C., it indicated that he too could not escape the corruption that permeated the industry.[29]

As Jim Crow bars eased, not least because of global pressure, the once stigmatized music was able to penetrate more markets. "Australia is starved for good jazz" was the message transmitted to pianist Dave Brubeck in 1957, the year of Little Rock, Ghana, and Sputnik; there was a "tremendous appetite" for it, he was told, though it was unclear if a similar warm welcome would be extended to the progenitors of the music—those of African ancestry, for example— given that continent's official policy of racialism.[30] Another member of the "Anglo-sphere," Robert Larimer, cited the increasingly sainted Winston Churchill for the idea that "nothing brings back to him so well the memories of past years—with all of their mental pictures and moods and heart-warming associations—as hearing again or humming the popular songs of those years," providing musicians with a powerful psychological lever that could be wielded profitably abroad.[31] But just as Little Rock and Ghana were juxtaposed, so was the open and closed doors for the music: "Jazz in Toronto has been on the downgrade recently," Brubeck was told in 1957.[32]

The example of Brubeck, quickly becoming the "face" of the music, was symptomatic of the contradictions then emerging. The contradiction was sensed by the pianist himself, who mournfully asserted in mid-1955 that "ever since the *Time* article" anointing him as the music's savior, "I have had a barrage of unfavorable criticism (such as [Ralph] Gleason and [Leonard] Feather)."[33] He was an able musician to be sure, but it was hard to gainsay the point that his European ancestry was of benefit to him in making his mark musically. Fortunately, Brubeck was principled in this racial minefield, to the detriment of his bottom line. "Your cancelling a concert in Dallas because of the policy of segregated seating," he was told in 1957, heartened one fan in Waterloo, Iowa. "I want to thank you," was the message. "I am luckier than the majority of Negroes," he wrote, adding, "It is impossible to be completely untainted. This whole core of rottenness" that inhered in Jim Crow, "affects everyone"; thus, Brubeck's correspondent tended to "swing between feelings of great hope and deep bitterness," a not uncommon feeling as the United States strained to change in the face of massive resistance. Brubeck was told, "You can never know how much it means to me to know that there are people [who] react positively to injustices."[34]

Brubeck was in the vortex of a gathering storm. Those in Dixie who appreciated the music at times found its presentation by him more appealing than, say, by Oscar Peterson, the Afro-Canadian piano master, born in 1925. As ever, Joe Glaser was embedded in the controversy. His Manhattan-based firm informed "Dear Dave" that they had arranged about "25" engagements at "colleges and universities in the South and Southwest during the month of February," but the organizers "just called" and "wanted to know if you had any colored boys [sic] in your group, which you do. My purpose in writing you," it was announced without subtlety, "is to see if you could arrange to have an all-white group to play these colleges and universities because they will not accept you as a mixed group"; the fee was not negligible: "25 dates for $1,500 per concert" and this was "not to be sneezed at. This should be considered seriously," "as college concerts are the backbone of your income."[35] Brubeck's refusal to play in Jim Crow venues was costly.

Adhering to principle was expensive, in other words. The very system of Jim Crow dictated such, which also enabled incorrigibles like Glaser. Brubeck's attorney once said that "Mr. Glaser appears to be a liar," a gross understatement. James Bancroft grouped the slimy Manhattanite with "the critics" and "the financial opportunists" who were "beginning to consider you the target" for plucking. This was "part of the price of success," he said, "but it is too bad things work out this way."[36]

Even with opportunities abroad, Brubeck sacrificed by ditching Dallas and like-minded venues. Near that same time, fans of the pianist said that they were "rather concerned in recent months about the apparent lack of promotion of Columbia Records," with which he was signed. "In the Chicago area," it was stated, "air play for Columbia jazz . . . is at the present time practically nonexistent. Why?"[37]

But what was the alternative to these monopoly concerns, which, after all, had advertising budgets and distribution networks that Debut Records was finding the hard way were all too necessary? Brubeck's attorney told the similarly small Circle Records of San Francisco that it was "perfectly ridiculous to expect Dave to pay a portion of expenses over which he has no control," since "half of the expenses listed on your memorandum are for advertising"; besides, "he was not consulted" before being billed.[38]

But as one window closed, another opened, though at times ill gusts blew in unabated. Hugh Hefner, the myrmidon of smut, who accumulated a fortune through the commercialization of sexism, made Brubeck's music an essential part of the seductive armor wielded by his "playboys." As early as 1955, he informed the pianist about "The New Jazz Audience" of which Brubeck was a key attraction; "25% of our audience is collegiate," he said, "the biggest percentage of any magazine in the nation," making it a difficult venue for Brubeck to ignore.[39]

Thus, by the late 1950s, Brubeck ranked with Ahmad Jamal, Erroll Garner, Jonah Jones, and the Modern Jazz Quartet as the top-selling recording artists in the music that was their specialty. But since Brubeck was the only Euro-American in this group—even setting aside Miles Davis and Thelonius Monk who were close behind—it was not unrealistic to expect that in a still apartheid society, Brubeck had an advantage over competitors, whether desired or not. A typical album of Dinah Shore or Rosemary Clooney, said critic Ralph Gleason, sold 10,000 units, which was in the vicinity of what Quincy Jones was then selling, although he could sell 8,000 more in France alone, unlike these singers. Davis was also outselling those singers at home. At that time. the rising sales champion, Elvis Presley, was selling 100,000 units, said Gleason. Even then, Jones was complaining that the ubiquitous Morris Levy "wants to own you," as if slavery had not been abolished.[40]

Entrepreneur Bob Thiele once worked with Roulette Records and admitted the existence of mob ties. Coyly, he said that it was "impossible to be in any part of the industry—distribution, talent, management, retail, performance venues, etc.—without an instant awareness that there are 'goodfellows' [mobsters] among the good guys and bad guys." This made it "impossible for most independent labels to survive," as Mingus and Roach could have attested, for "whoever controls the distribution controls the cash flow." And all roads led back to Morris Levy, who "became incalculably wealthy by funding performers, music publishing, record manufacturing and distribution companies," leaving Thiele queasy and uneasy: "Everyday I felt I was improbably and inescapably trapped in a grade-B gangster epic," an opinion magnified since Roulette also had ties to the gangster-connected International Longshoremen's Association.[41]

Arguably, Levy felt empowered by the historic discrepancy in bargaining power, enhancing capital rather than labor, a trend that was bolstered postwar as unions were weakened and the situation was not assuaged by the official crumbling of Jim Crow. Indeed, the latter, as the violent reaction to Little Rock suggested, may have excited a counterrevolution capable of eroding any gains delivered by desegregation. "During and right after the war," said trumpeter and singer Clora Bryant, born in 1927, "before all the m[e]n had really [come] back . . . we had our pick," speaking of women artists like herself, then busily organizing bands. But, she said, "the Caucasians started taking over the scene and creating categories," for example, West Coast jazz or rock 'n' roll, "and started making themselves the kings of those categories," meaning she said wistfully, "we lost a lot of camaraderie."[42]

These new "categories" were a kind of secession—not unlike the secession from London on anti-abolitionist grounds that created the republic in the first instance[43]—a revolt against preexisting categories where Negroes, men and women alike, had been dominant. Assuredly, some musicians fought back vigorously against right-wing influence. Vibraphonist Terry Gibbs, born in 1924, spoke disparagingly of right-wing leader, Gerald L. K. Smith: "I'd like to go into a room with a life[like] dummy of him—made of good rubber though—and wail the hell out of it."[44] However, his was a voice not echoed sufficiently.

Shirley Horn, born in 1934, was comparable to Dorothy Donegan in terms of being a singer and pianist, and to Bryant in terms of her perceptivity. Her two brothers, both "hoodlums," assisted her early in her career in her hometown, Washington, D.C. "I got $175 for five days, five days a week and two hours," a "whole lot of money then." But then her "dad and mom" objected—"they just acted ugly"—and she departed hastily. Sadly, male musicians objected too—"why do they treat me so mean?" she asked plaintively. "I was always nice to the guys," she said with befuddlement. "You know, come to my house. I'll feed you," but the anger did not subside. In fact, "when they got on the bandstand, it was mean, it was ugly" as their gender-segregated domain was pierced. "And I made up my mind," she said firmly, "I said 'whoa,' I said, 'one day I'm taking over the whole Washington, D.C.'" This was an ambitious mission that was only thwarted partially. "I had the first integrated band in Washington and that was in Maryland over there with the rednecks and stuff, right." It was "The Wheel," a "joint . . . out on Bladensburg Road, definitely a redneck place"; and then "a couple of my girlfriends came in. Both of them were dark-skinned," unlike herself. "They looked at us kind of funny," speaking of the patrons, "at first" but did not react violently, which could not be ruled out. "The music got hot, and they were dancing and everything. It was great. But the drummer, I mean the bass player didn't feel very comfortable. But I enjoyed it." Horn "didn't realize" the historic weight of the occurrence, "until my musicians' union said, 'You have the first integrated band in Washington' " in terms of personnel and audience.

She also performed at the Bohemian Caverns in Washington, though then "we weren't making no money," it was "slavery time. We played Tuesday from nine-thirty until two"—ditto from Wednesday-Friday and on Saturday, a "matinee. Then there was a break, then we played until whenever that was. Then there was a matinee on Sunday. That was eight something [until] something to twelve. That's what I called slavery time stuff and we did every week, every week," she repeated. "But you know one thing? It made us strong."

There were some men who did not object to her presence, one of whom was the much-reviled Miles Davis, who told Max Gordon, Manhattan club owner, "I'm not going to play unless she opens." "That was something," she said recalling the startling incident in 1996. "It knocked me down" that "my sweet love," meaning the trumpeter, intervened. "The same night that I did that, opening for Miles," she said, "it was the opening of *A Raisin in the Sun*" in 1959, yet another breakthrough for a Negro woman, the youthful playwright Lorraine Hansberry in this instance. Also bathed in a halo of admiration with Davis was the manager John Levy, the former bassist. "He cared about me," she said with conviction. "I just wanted to be one of the guys"; he understood, and, as a result, "he's my friend right today and he cares about me." Levy "was a dream," a "good friend and I trusted him . . . we never had a contract." He understood her dilemma, for "ever since day one when I came on the scene, number one, they don't know how to package me, number one, right, because . . . I play the piano like a man . . . now that stops them right there." Critics say, "No, but you've got to stand up and sing," and "I said 'No, I'm going to sit down and play.'" Inevitably, she was denoted as a "diva and I want to punch him right in the snoot. I hate that . . . I mean I'm bebop. I'm a musician," meaning "I get the respect that lady divas, don't get because I'm one of the guys" in that "when I sit down and play, I've got the control," the "boss" in other words. "I control the money."

But even the enlightened Levy said "I was too fair" or light-skinned "for the movies, you know, I'd rather he told me 'you can't act.' But don't tell me it's because of my color, you know." Her management also could not save her from an unpleasant experience in Chicago, a "wrong booking. I shouldn't have gone in right behind this woman named Dusty Springfield. She was a risqué woman. She'd done the dirty songs," prompting one guy to shout, "give the nigger bitch a ten-dollar tip." Again, it was Glaser who "put me in a lot of joints that I didn't like, that didn't suit me. Above all, I tried to be a lady," but he simply wanted to profit lucratively. "I didn't belong in Savannah," she said, "at least put me in Atlanta." Ultimately, Horn was so disgusted with managers that she decided, "I'm going to produce my own stuff." She was alienated by Richard Seidel, "Oh man. He thinks he discovered me," though "it's all about getting his name on as a producer" on one of her productions. "He came all the way to Boston" to that end. "He came to bribe me and he did bribe me to put his name, bribe me with a little machine so he could put his name on as producer." Her response? "Any time that you want to be a producer, I'm going to lend you my wig and my red lipstick and you do it, baby," otherwise, she would handle this duty herself. "I'm just kind of like a rebel," she maintained, "I'm too old and I'm not going to let them push me around." She was not driven by the need for notoriety, "not that being famous is that important, but you've got to have a certain amount of fame in order to make money." As for her attorney, Joel Siegel, he was "more bitchy than I" and "really not my friend" besides.

"I don't need to make any more money. It's not about money in the first place." So she was able to evade what the more famous Washingtonian, Duke Ellington, did not with his manager, Irving Mills. Recording with Verve, she had an experience with a man with a "secretary," apparently the man in question was her attorney: "She thinks her name should go on everything that's recorded. I said 'not on mine.'" The approach was to bury her in pages of a lengthy contract: "They'll send you all these papers . . . papers and papers," and "if you tried to understand and read all that crap, you'd be crazy" and then hope she would not read the document with care. Another important tip was supplied by another performer, Carmen McRae: "One thing I can tell you baby is get the money up front" before performing, not after "and that's what I do."

Like Donegan, she found a contradiction between seeking multiple childbearing experiences and a career simultaneously. "I didn't want a lot of children because I remember my grandmother talking about you if you have too many children it's not good." Thus, "after four years of marriage I had one child and that was it. He thought I was going to have a whole lot and be barefoot and pregnant but I said to myself, oh-oh. . . . I'd seen [over] the years, I've seen women, mean, leaving their children and I've seen what happened with the children . . . the kids suffer . . . kids all screwed up." (Interestingly, women musicians were typically asked about family matters, while men, not so much.) But she did have to deal with a jealous spouse. "He has a problem, because you know people in show business. They hug and kiss. . . . I had to stop him from coming to clubs where I was performing, right away . . . early on, because he was just jealous of everybody. . . . He kind of doesn't like to share me." Once, enraged, he tossed a man down the steps of a club who seemed to be paying inordinate attention to her. She concluded: "You're going to find this to be true, a black man cannot handle a successful woman, wife or woman, and I see that."[45]

AS THE INVOCATION OF ELVIS PRESLEY suggests, another contradictory irony of the era of Jim Crow's official retrenchment was the rise of Euro-American artists who mimicked the performances of Negroes, a trend that reached a zenith with the so-called British invasion featuring notably the Rolling Stones. In sum, audiences defined as "white" found it easier to swallow Negro music when it was not performed by Negroes. The man known as "Magnificent Montague," who rocketed to fame in Black Los Angeles during the 1960s tumult,[46] initially objected since "black labels weren't paying shit royalties to begin with," facilitating the rise of "white companies" who were seeking to "co-opt what little we had." Then they were joined by the likes of Presley, Pat Boone, and the like (e.g. Wolfman Jack, "blacking up his face with makeup stealing Howlin' Wolf's dialect") who "practically before we got it out of their mouths, they took it," and by 1957, Montague charged, "it would get even worse, because the master robber, Dick Clark," would "take his *American Bandstand* TV show nationwide. . . . You wonder why black folk talk about conspiracies where white people don't see them," but exploit their handiwork. Clark aside—referring to the TV host featuring Euro-American teenagers aping Negro dancers—Montague found it difficult "not to notice the number of Jews who ran independent companies specializing in black music. Art Rupe; founder of Specialty Records in L.A.; the Chess Brothers, Phil and Leonard in Chicago; Syd Nathan, who owned King Records in Cincinnati; the Mesner Brothers in L.A. with Aladdin Records." Simultaneously, there was the discouraging story of "how Black Swan," Negro owned, formed in 1921 in Harlem, "was squeezed out by the major record companies." A surface analysis found it simple to equate ethno-religious heritage with exploitation of Negroes, a tendency that accompanied the postwar rise of the Nation of Islam and the concomitant waning in influence of the class ideology of those like Robeson. Still, Montague admitted that "just about the only white people who'd ever given me a break in this business were Jews." Then, there was "payola," companies illicitly buying access to radio airwaves, which further advantaged the giant firms.[47] Perhaps Montague was too tactful to mention Ted Brinson, a proficient Negro guitarist in Los Angeles who once played alongside Lester Young and arranged for Mary Lou Williams but then became a mailman and wound up recording "white surf groups" and singing with them too, aiding their escalating popularity.[48]

Though much has been made of the formal retreat of Jim Crow in the 1950s, too often this has not been linked with the simultaneous retreat of unions and class-based groupings, which hampered class solidarity and created fertile ground for the rise of racial and ethnic sensitivities. "Most of the clubs in Hollywood and toward downtown were Jewish-owned," said Clora Bryant.[49] Shirley Horn, singer and keyboardist, spoke of Sheila Mathis at Verve Records, who was "smart" but "thought they were going to fire her, because . . . they got rid of all the Jews at some point. Anybody who wasn't a Jew, fired them, right."[50] Even Jerry Wexler, journalist turned music producer, was offended that the Chess brothers of Chicago, ill-famed exploiters of blues musicians, sometimes referred to contracted artists as *chaya*, which in Yiddish meant "animals," indicative of their "plantation mentality."[51]

Shirley Horn captured the sentiment of many beleaguered musicians when she spoke of this era contemptuously: "So much fighting between the musicians and the record companies," she groaned, "so much fight, fight, bite, scratch," with the performers often left vanquished, victims of unequal bargaining power. "They were crooks," she said of the executives, speaking in 1996. "Steeplechase [Records]," she said, "right today, they owe me money. It's a kind of joke."[52]

If she had been more expansive, Horn might also have cited the social double standards as further afflictions of women artists. Max Roach conceded that songstress Dinah Washington "was playing the field, like we were," speaking of his fellow male rakes, but the latter were not castigated as frequently as she was, placing inordinate pressure on her as a result.[53] Thus pianist Marian McPartland was of the opinion that her comrade keyboardist Mary Lou Williams "was known to be tough . . . the men respected her. Some of them were afraid of her,"[54] but her toughness was often misinterpreted.

Tragically, the barriers leapt by Horn were not only amassed in her difficult path. Vi Redd, saxophonist born in 1928, had to moonlight as a schoolteacher because of diminishing opportunity. Said Feather, "She talks with very little rancor of having been resented as a female, of being passed up for jobs, of seeing men walk off the bandstand as soon as she walked on." Arguably, the seamy sexist origins of the music in brothels and the like had not disintegrated even as the music gained acclaim as a distinguished art form. Feather boasted, quite earnestly and without irony in the pages of the journal of the *Playboy Jazz Festival*, that "during the 1940s and 1950s most of the recordings led by female instrumentalists were instigated and produced by me and that of the all female sessions, I was responsible for nearly 100%." Whatever the case, Feather's admirable intervention could not rescue Redd and other women artists from having to cope with a never-ending flow of words laced liberally with sexual overtones made by bandmates and fans alike. Soon a rising feminist movement, buoyed by anti-Jim Crow measures, was to change things somewhat but not soon enough to heal damaged careers.[55] The budding music mogul Nesuhi Ertegun told "Dear Leonard" that "as a result of your enthusiastic recommendation," Redd would receive a recording contract; Ertegun had "never heard [of] this artist"—further vindicating Feather's industry.[56]

Clora Bryant and others had difficulty developing what was thought to be the correct political line given the other matters occupying space in her imagination. "They don't even let me gig near the studios," she lamented, speaking of jobs in Hollywood. "Name me one female horn player who gigs in the studios," though there were "female violinists, pianists, flutists . . . only a few if any trombonists, saxophonists, or trumpet players because the men guard these jobs." Inferentially, it was evident that she was not blaming all men for this paucity. "When I speak with someone black," she said, "it's a different feeling, I'm more comfortable. I don't say certain things to white writers for fear they may take it the wrong way or edit something I've said to suit their viewpoint (which has happened)." Thus, "every time we get together as a group to do something," she said, speaking of African Americans in 1985, "they make a big deal out of it. But when they do their thing no one else says a word." This pinched attitude had financial impact. "The jazz music business has become a real political business. I have many problems with it, one of which is the money paid musicians," which was "very bad actually." There was a spatial dimension as well, in that "for years there has been a systematic movement in the Jazz scene here from the inner city to the suburbs," meaning that if you resided in South L.A., especially without a vehicle, it might be difficult to work in Laguna Beach, Hermosa Beach, or West Hollywood.[57]

Women artists may have been hit disproportionately, but the cesspool of iniquity generated by capitalism left few unscathed. Critic Frank Kofsky once argued that there was a "pattern of exploitation of black musical artists—and, by extension, of white artists who . . . perform in black idioms—that extends at least from the 1920s," and the harassing of artists for drug possession leading to imprisonment suggests that he is largely correct.[58] Red Rodney, a trumpeter born in 1927, got swept up in a phenomenon that disproportionately snared Negro men: mass incarceration. It was almost as if those who strayed across the color line, irrespective of intent, merited punishment.[59]

In the 1950s drummer Roy Porter was imprisoned because of drug possession and found himself alongside saxophonist Dexter Gordon, who, he said, "organized a jazz band" that included "altoist Fred Walters, Chris White on trumpet," in a group so highly regarded that "that band played in a movie that featured" football star Elroy "Crazy Legs" Hirsch, speaking of *Unchained*. On the one hand, one response to the pro forma retrenchment of Jim Crow was a crackdown on prominent Negroes, especially jazz men with drugs; on the other, incarceration helped to create a music school of sorts. It was while imprisoned that Porter "learned how to voice chords properly, to write and compose"; he "immersed" himself "completely in music while I was there," he recalled. But to his dismay, when he was released from prison as the pivotal year of 1957 approached, he found "clubs leaving Central Avenue," once the stronghold of the music, while remaining jobs were being gobbled up by "white musicians . . . just starting that 'Cool School' of jazz. Most black musicians couldn't fit in that narrow category," perhaps not coincidentally.[60] This was even more ironic since the ebony-hued Miles Davis was a founder of this school of sound and the very term "cool"[61]—detached emotionally, shuttered behaviorally, and projecting an abrupt masculinity—was symbolized by the enigmatic trumpeter responsible for many twists and turns in the music. Yet even Davis could not claim sole paternity for this phenomenon, as Lester "Pres" Young could also claim parentage,[62] not to mention African Americans as a whole who were compelled to project "cool" in the face of lynch mobs and less difficult crises too. The often-neglected downside to the ascension of this complex phenomenon was that detached emotionality and abrupt masculinity did not enhance the health of intimate relationships.

Lee Konitz, saxophonist born in 1927, with roots in Europe and often associated with the "Cool School," did not dissent. He was part of Stan Kenton's band and acknowledged that "the problem seemed to be that he didn't have many black players coming through the band. There were some, Ernie Royal," for example (just as Konitz himself was part of the paradoxical *Birth of the Cool* sessions inaugurated by Miles Davis). But, says Konitz, there were "not significantly enough [openings] for black guys," meaning bandmates. "I don't know what disagreement Dizzy [Gillespie] had with Stan but he really put him down strong" too.[63]

As Kenton's bankroll fattened, the brickbats tossed at him increased in velocity. The bandleader continued to be upset by polls that he felt did not reflect adequately his own presumed qualifications as a musician. "There is a new minority group," facing bias, he charged, "white jazz musicians." This brought him a sharp rebuke from Leonard Feather: "Nobody heard a peep out of you when real prejudice existed back in the early 1940s." Refusing to holster his weapon, Feather asserted further that the graying Kenton, born in 1911, was "riding your white charger to defend white supremacy" and ignoring that "almost every major development in jazz history has been the work of Negro musicians."[64] As early as 1950, it was Feather who argued vehemently that such polls "show a definite discrimination against Negro musicians" since "most or all of the first-place winners" were white. Ironically, he found *Melody Maker*, the music bible of Britain and their French counterpart, did not exhibit the same tendency, but instead tended to favor European-born artists such as George Shearing.[65] The spunky

Feather also broke ranks when he reamed fellow critic Stanley Dance for various transgressions, perceived widely as violating unwritten rules of the fraternity of critics. [66]

Because their creativity generated so much wealth in a society grounded in white supremacy, Negro artists were noticeably vulnerable. Erroll Garner's agent upbraided Baronet Records because of "your unauthorized manufacture, sale and distribution" of the pianist's "improvisations."[67] Giant company Columbia Records was accused by Martha Glaser of "illegally releasing" Garner's music "from the inventory."[68]

"Trummy" Young was aghast at what befell Garner: Timmie Rosenkrantz, an associate of the diminutive pianist, "had very expensive equipment" in New York City, "and he used to bring Erroll Garner down there and just record him by the hour, and he'd give him all the liquor he wanted and anything else he may want, have chicks for him down there and food. And when Erroll got popular, man, all of [that] stuff came out in Europe, man. This guy made a fortune. All of these things started coming out in Europe," and "it kind of really hurt his own recordings," depleting his income. "His albums were selling for five, six or seven bucks," and "this guy was putting these things out for $3" featuring a "lot of the same tunes and a lot of the same things." This travesty occurred, though "they were supposed to have been friends," leaving to the imagination what an enemy would have done. And it was not just Garner who was being shafted. When Young was "with Louis [Armstrong] in Europe, they used to find trucks out in the back with all kind of electronic gadgets, picking up the whole concert" for pressing discs for sale. This outrage was conspicuously occurring in Germany. "Louis played the best concert halls in Europe where the acoustics were perfect," making him an obvious target for bootleg recordings.[69] Companies, perhaps accidentally, undermined their productions: John Hammond is among those who found engineering to be inferior on jazz recordings, which simply opened the door for selling bootleg records, which may have been better engineered.[70]

Most exploitation was more mundane. Lee Konitz "was always in debt to that band," speaking of Kenton's orchestra. "I drew money for family needs," he said, in a kind of musical sharecropping, driving him deeper into a financial hole, and he was hardly alone.[71] But just as anecdotally, Euro-American football stars—a minority in a professional sport dominated by African Americans—seem to find more opportunities in broadcasting and executive ranks today than their melanin-rich counterparts. Leonard Feather, echoing Max Roach, found it remarkable that Shelly Manne, in some ways the epitome of a color-coded "West Coast Jazz," owned six valuable horses, acres of land in Northridge (the heart of the valuable San Fernando Valley in Los Angeles), a jazz club, and more.[72] Tellingly, one of the few musicians associated with this musical turn who actually hailed from the Golden State was Mexican American drummer Chuck Flores, born in 1935, who played with bandleader Woody Herman and, insultingly, was termed a "wetback" or so-called "illegal immigrant" even by bandmates.[73]

Again, there was a discrepancy between the easing of Jim Crow barriers and the continuation of a rancid status quo. The contradictory winds brought by the 1950s were also reflected when Miles Davis, becoming ever more popular, was beaten and bloodied by New York City police officers in front of Birdland in August 1959.[74] Just before then, in a less publicized episode that his son recalled, a Chicago club owner wanted to dock Davis $500 because he did not follow orders and went on first. "I was standing there and I saw him," meaning his dad, "get real mad. He just reached over this desk and pulled the dude out of his chair. Before I knew it, Miles had him on the floor and was whipping his ass."[75] With every blow inflicted, this was a metaphor for the past pummeling of Jim Crow delivered by generations past, allowing Davis to act without fear of lynching.

Unfortunately, Davis's bloody experiences were not unique. Trombonist Curtis Fuller was accustomed to hard times, having resided in an orphanage and having endured bias in a military band. Yet this did not prepare him for an encounter in New Jersey when a state trooper pulled him over and bleated, "Get out of the car." Unhappy with Fuller's perceived dearth of alacrity in responding, "he pulled me out of the car," said the startled artist. "He put his boot on my back. He took out his Magnum. I said, 'What's wrong officer?'

'Shut up,'" was the hard-bitten reply. Then he unleashed a fusillade of racist epithets: "n word, n word, n word, n word," was how Fuller daintily put it. "He's terrified of a man on the ground?" the artist asked rhetorically. "It's raining and I'm cold. He said, 'What's in that case?' I said, 'My instrument, Sir.' He took it, open[ed] it and looked in it and took it apart. He threw the bell one way and threw the horn over the bridge on the New Jersey Turnpike." Still dissatisfied, the officer was "shaking" and quivering. "He's got the gun and the club," but he was the one "shaking like a leaf." Fuller was ecstatic to escape to tell the tale. But he knew well that "[that] color line is still here for us."[76]

THERE WERE OTHER FACTORS BEYOND police terror shaping the overall environment for musicians. The triumph of the Cuban Revolution on January 1, 1959, was one such factor. Even before Fidel Castro and his comrades arrived to take power, Havana had become risky for casino investments, and thus Las Vegas and Reno skyrocketed. Nevada was a magnet, attracting speculators from Cuba. William McPherson had been licensed to run a casino as early as the 1940s in Cuba. "I put the first gambling in there when I bought into it," he claimed of Cuba.[77] But he too came to the Sagebrush State: "I sold out in the fall of '46," he said, as Las Vegas was taking off. Others followed him from the Caribbean after Castro's rise. Weeks after this turning point, the Nevada authorities were told that one investor found the "situation in Cuba" so parlous, "that I do not know at the present time whether I will be in business in Cuba or not," no minor matter since it was "impossible" to dispose of his "holdings."[78]

With investors fleeing Cuba one step ahead of revolutionists, a number could either deepen their holdings in Nevada or start same. This could be good news for musicians seeking work but, as evidenced by the contradictions of this era, this could also mean more opportunity to exploit Negroes, often unprotected by unions. Thus, in the prelude to the Cuban commotion, Hugh Duncan of the Silver State's Esquire Club sought vociferously to "protest his innocence," having "no idea how the marked cards happened to be in the club," it was reported. "They were planted," he asserted. Interestingly, it was

also said that "although Nevada gambling laws and regulations provide that illegal cards or dice cannot be used in games, they do not
specifically prohibit their presence in casinos."[79]
    In 1958, months before the Cuban overthrow, the Nevadan
authorities were probing "Cuban gambling" and the "ramifications
and implications of Nevada licensees participating in Cuban operations. . . . There are eight Nevada licensees presently holding interests
in Cuban casinos." The list included the infamous Moe Dalitz, for
there was the "general impression that Nevadans are running Cuban
gambling and are synonymous with it." Carson City was seized with
the idea that "the gambling element in Cuba, many of them ineligible
to hold Nevada licenses, have become an issue between revolutionary
parties and the [then] Cuban government." Inevitably, the migration
of thuggery to Las Vegas from Cuba, post-1958, would introduce
more instability, to the disadvantage of musicians. This "tends to lend
credence to the oft-repeated criticism of national racketeering syndicates which, by virtue of the factors developing in Cuba, now takes on
an international aspect and implies that Nevada represents a hub in
the alleged nefarious network," raising the "possibility of co-mingling
of funds in Cuban ventures of Nevadans and others."[80]
    Though these authorities were concentrating on the backwash of
events in Cuba, Negro activists—for example, former Basie vocalist "Bob" Bailey—were urging them to focus more on Jim Crow.
Drummer Jimmy Cobb, born in 1929 and best known as an accompanist of Miles Davis (on some of his bestselling albums, including *Kind
of Blue* in 1959), could have served as an expert witness. No stranger
to bigotry, he recalled playing alongside Billie Holiday and "at that
time black people couldn't be out—I don't even know that black
people could be in that club at that time." This was "like Las Vegas
where you could go in behind the bandstand and come up on the
stage in the lounge," then play, but exit quickly, avoiding discomfiting Euro-American patrons unaccustomed to having Negroes in their
midst—except when these artists were performing. "When I was with
Dinah Washington," Holiday's logical successor, "you had to do that. .
. . We had a trailer out in the parking lot" that they had to use instead
of lounge facilities. "There's a [lot] of things that happened," he said

dismayingly and mysteriously, "that a whole lot of people don't need to know about. So, I'm going to keep it like that."[81]

As matters evolved, post-1959 Dalitz and his comrades were ousted from Havana, bringing more capital repatriation to Nevada along with more expansion of casinos and clubs, but this was not necessarily a step forward for artists. In any case, artists were often paid better in Cuba than Nevada. When songstress Eartha Kitt appeared for the first time in Cuba—this in the 1950s—mobster Meyer Lansky paid her a small fortune to perform at the opening of his new casino.[82] She was not alone, as, according to one observer, the Tropicana in Havana became a necessary stop for "many American jazz musicians."[83] There were sad similarities between the sinks of sin that were Las Vegas and Havana. "I was in Cuba thirty-eight years ago," said Max Roach in 1989 and, typically, "I wasn't allowed to go into [certain] clubs" unless performing.[84]

Gambling had taken off in Las Vegas in 1931,[85] and now in 1959, it had reached yet another turning point. Institutionalizing a game of chance opened the door for all manner of underhandedness. Typically, "considerable time" was devoted in Carson City to "discussion of conditions in the gambling industry" and "ways of controlling cheating and thieving games,"[86] product of a culture that could easily capture unwary musicians. "Loaded dice"[87] and "edgework"[88] performed on dice were among the many tricks of a state overrun by grifters.

The rise of Castro also led to a severe counterreaction. Cuban exiles in the United States did not take kindly to any sympathy for Havana, nor those the new regime were thought to support, making particularly vulnerable musicians from nearby islands. Seedy elements in the business often compelled musicians to seek alternatives to the status quo. Eddie Palmieri, a pianist of Puerto Rican ancestry born in 1936, recalled the influence of the man known as "Symphony Sid" (Tarnopol) born in 1909, often credited from his perch on radio in popularizing the bebop genre. "He was controlled by the record company," said Palmieri, and "I recorded with [same] and so he put it [his music] on rotation." This helped to rescue him from the crassness of the Palladium Ballroom in midtown Manhattan. "Fridays you had all the gamblers and their ladies," present but, despite their affluence, pay was minimal. "You played 16 shows in four days for $72 and [they] took out taxes. And you needed your cabaret card" too, documentation from the authorities that you were above board, but this entailed "racial profiling" against those like himself, "because there were too many blacks and Hispanics working downtown," it was said. "As long as you stayed uptown, Minton's," for example, "you were fine." So, like others, he headed overseas, France in his case. "That's why I have a special thing for France," he said, "even though they can't stand any American." Besides, "I was accused of being a Communist" because of avant-garde ideas, and the "CIA and FBI went to see my record company." In a companion maneuver, the ubiquitous Morris Levy "brought me and said, 'Mr. Palmieri what did you record for me?'" He was referring to his composition, "Mambo con Conga Equals Mozambique," seen as an affront to the U.S. ally in fascist Portugal, the colonizer of this African nation, which became independent in 1975. The well-connected Levy was "backed by the Big Mafia . . . [the] Gambino family" and the "Columbo family." So Palmieri had to take it seriously when the gruff Levy barked, "Don't record that shit any more." But there was a related problem in that Cuban exiles in the form of Alpha 66, known to deploy terror, were upset with him and were threatening "to blow up all the radio stations that played my music." He hired progressive Negro attorney Bruce Wright to protect his interests.[89]

Bigots still plagued a state where somehow the mascot of the campus at the University of Nevada-Las Vegas was a treasonous Confederate rebel, though this state was far from Dixie, at least geographically. When Negro customers were admitted to certain clubs, they were charged more for drinks than others, hardly creating an atmosphere favorable to Negro artists.[90] On the other hand, the man known variously as Bew Fong or Bill Fong, a rare club owner in the state who was not defined as "white," paid for a lifetime membership in the NAACP and was even saluted by the group.[91]

The rights leader, former Basie vocalist, and accused Communist William "Bob" Bailey accompanied fellow singer Nat "King" Cole when he was rudely turned away from a club on the "Strip," with a fistfight ensuing that both singers managed to avoid. Bailey well knew that in order for a Negro musician to be hired in the thriving clubs in Las Vegas, one had to be a "really jazz giant, really a giant of some type," and "still today," he said in 1978, "I doubt if half of one percent, or a half or an eighth of one percent are blacks . . . playing in the house bands." At once, this infuriated Black artists and hampered class unity when those defined as "white" did not object strenuously, or at all. Despite being red-baited, it was Bailey who, by his own admission, subpoenaed people to testify about racism before official bodies. "I've signed more subpoenas for owners of hotels here than the Kefauver Committee," a reference to U.S. senator Estes Kefauver, whose klieg-light investigations became a staple of early television. "That's a fact," he boasted with justification. "That's an absolute fact," he emphasized. "This was the Nevada State Equal Rights Investigatory Commission . . . appointed by Governor Grant Sawyer." Yes, he said with satisfaction, "we did the job and got it off the ground and finally got the law. Finally got the law," that is, the "State Equal Rights Law," a landmark. Still, in a thinly veiled reference to the potent Church of Latter-Day Saints, he remained "very concerned as to the future progress of coexistence in a town where you have a very respected religion that by virtue of its own religious patterns, discriminates against a person because of the color of his skin. . . . This is a rough road," he said.[92]

While the musicians pouring into a booming Las Vegas had to pay attention to the chiselers and gougers who were rampant, as ever, New York City presented a different problem. As the Cuban Revolution was triumphing, a report was issued detailing "widespread discrimination against Negro musicians" in the "symphony orchestras, Broadway shows, and radio-television networks." The heralded "Philharmonic Symphony and the Metropolitan Opera orchestra never have employed a Negro professional musician," and there were "no Negro musicians on the staff" of NBC, a major television and radio network. And since 1943, Radio City Music Hall "has never hired a Negro musician on a permanent basis." All this was documented by the National Urban League.[93] Near the same time horn man Ike Quebec, born in 1918, was driving a taxi, a job frequently taken by capable though unemployed musicians; not long thereafter one of the most highly praised pianists of his era, Cecil Taylor, born in 1929, was washing dishes in a restaurant in order to survive.[94] Drummer Philly Joe Jones, born in Philadelphia in 1923, while stranded in Munich had trouble finding work so he found a job "dubbing movies into English. It was fun," he exulted.[95]

Travel abroad was customarily the option pursued by Negro musicians blocked at home. This remained true. Clora Bryant observed that "Dizzy, Blakey and others have told me if it wasn't for Europe they wouldn't be able to make it." But given the nature of the republic, she suggested, Negro artists had few alternatives: "They took this land away from the Native Americans," and the racist pattern was established from the inception.[96]

Among those fleeing to Europe was saxophonist Johnny Griffin, born in 1928. "The government puts a lot of money into the arts," he declared in 1986; there were "radio orchestras all over Germany, Denmark and Holland." Since he had "been through some very hard times" in the United States, exile agreed with him. "I live in the middle of the country in Southern France,"[97] said the satisfied musician, exemplifying a pattern that stretched back to the music's origins. Shirley Horn, like many, was enthusiastic about Japan; "They respect the musician. . . . I make a lot of money in France and Japan and you don't have to work, work yourself to death."[98]

However, unlike Tony Scott, who traveled to apartheid South Africa in 1958, Negro artists were circumscribed generally in seeking to gain access to this lucrative market. "I did make a profit financially," said the clarinetist happily.[99] (When Clark Terry noticed Mingus assaulting Scott—"choking him to death" with the clarinetist "turning green and blue"—it was (apparently) not an inspired anti-apartheid protest.)[100]

Nevertheless, the Cape Town pianist then known as Dollar Brand, born in 1934, was often found playing alongside saxophonist Kippie Moeketsi, born in 1925, who was said to possess "an encyclopedic grasp of Charlie Parker's work as well as South African folk traditions." Their music was a breakthrough for what was called "South Africa jazz" and credit was given to the keyboardist eventually known as Abdullah Ibrahim, viewed as a "scholar of Duke Ellington and Thelonius Monk," who found decades later when he was exiled to Manhattan that Ornette Coleman and Don Cherry were among his "fans."[101]

Just as Brand—or Ibrahim—moved across the Atlantic, so did the Nigerian percussionist and bandleader Babatunde Olatunji, and just as the South African was a living symbol of anti-apartheid with wider repercussions, the Nigerian was a living symbol of anti-colonialism, both transmitting undulating ripples. Olatunji arrived in the United States in the early 1950s to attend Morehouse College, the alma mater of Dr. Martin Luther King, Jr. "We used to organize and ride the bus dressed in African clothing" in Atlanta, a powerful message in itself, given the then reigning negative attitudes toward most matters African. "We would sit anywhere and the driver would not move the bus. We would end up at the jailhouse" in Atlanta. Undaunted, he reached out to Du Bois, Ghana's Kwame Nkrumah, Julius Nyerere (founding father of Tanzania), Sékou Touré (founding father of independent Guinea-Conaky). He had heard Duke Ellington on BBC in Nigeria before leaving home, leaving a deep impression. Reciprocally, Olatunji left a deep impression when he began to collaborate with Randy Weston and other musical leaders.[102]

Stanley Turrentine, saxophonist born in 1934, might have done well by purchasing "African clothing," since he admitted, "I had to literally think about my life when I was traveling down South, [because] when they had separate things, you couldn't stay in hotels" and "had to stay in those ragged buses." Perhaps with the proper garb and a phony accent, he could have taken advantage of Washington's desire to court a decolonizing Africa. "It affects the way you think and the way you approach it, it really affects your playing," he moaned. "I mean," he insisted, "you might have seen somebody killed that day" and in "reaction, you play that. You can't probably verbalize it, but you play it."[103]

Crossing the Pacific in 1956 was Toshiko Akiyoshi. Born in 1929, her father controlled a textile plant in Japanese-occupied Manchuria, now part of China. She admits, "we were segregated [from Chinese]," though she railed against the comparison with Jim Crow. After the war, she moved to Japan, the land of her ancestral roots, and continued her piano study with Teddy Wilson (once known as the "Marxist Mozart" because of his advanced study of the piano and politics alike) and Bud Powell as her recorded guides. A few years after her arrival, she was married to saxophonist Charlie Mariano, born in 1923. However, she became a fount of information for the many artists who began reversing sail, finding fame and fortune in Tokyo. Art Blakey, she stresses, was "really popular in Japan." She was struggling, however, until Mingus, she says, "asked me to join" his band. "I was really alone and struggling," she emphasized, "barely paying the rent. . . . I decided maybe I should quit, because the world doesn't need another piano player." Fortunately, her fortitude prevailed and the world was not deprived of yet another excellent piano player.[104] For though she spoke movingly of what she termed "sexual prejudice" in her homeland (what might be termed "gender prejudice" here), in the United States, she found both "sexual and racial" bias, "because Orientals [sic] were not associated with jazz." Shockingly, she said, "I didn't meet one first-generation Japanese-American who liked jazz," unlike Japanese, "and very few second generation either—they associated it with black people and found it undesirable in terms of their desire for status,"[105] suggesting assimilation to hegemonic white supremacy, the price of the ticket for admission to a certain status in the North American republic.

Akiyoshi could have added that many of Japanese ancestry in the United States had been singed when Tokyo was perceived in the pre-1945 era as being overly militant in speaking out against lynching and other racist ills, and the backlash bruised Issei, Nisei, and Sansei alike, contributing to their mass incarceration during the war.[106] As for "sexual prejudice," Von Freeman, saxophonist, argued—it is worth repeating—that "a woman has to be twice as good as a man to get any kind of recognition, because this is a man's thing. They had to be just great, great, great before the guys would accept them,"[107] an analogue of the Black Experience generally.

Speaking from Oppama, Japan, Dave Brubeck was informed that "imitators are the rule" in this Asian archipelago "and the Toshikos the exception," in that the former pursued a "literal transcription of both arrangements and solos . . . note for note." This lack of creativity "applies mainly to hornmen and guitarists," whereas the rhythm sections, for example, drummers, "seem to be more individualistic, although few pianists seem to have much chord sense." Yet indicative of why Japan was becoming a fecund outpost of the music was the conclusion that "one can hear jazz here much more readily than in the United States." Though "rock and roll has made its inroads . . . jazz hasn't the public opposition it has in much of the United States."[108]

As Akiyoshi was arriving in the United States from Japan, pianist Hank Jones was arriving in Tokyo. The U.S. State Department brought him there in 1956, and by 2010 he had been there "maybe 15 times," in his recollection. Born in Jim Crow Vicksburg in a horrid era—1918—he found "Japanese audiences" to be "more attentive and they seem to have a greater knowledge of what you are doing."[109]

Though African musicians were escaping colonialism in the United States, African American musicians continued to flee abroad. By 1958, Britain featured seventy clubs sponsoring live "jazz" seven nights a week, and increasing dependence of London on Washington in the aftermath of the disastrous Suez War of 1956 created a possibility for African American artists to grab some of these jobs. By that year, said critic Eric Hobsbawm, there was "probably no major city in the world in which someone is not playing a record of Louis Armstrong or Charlie Parker," which at least created even more jobs abroad.[110]

Compared to the United States, Europe proved to be an oasis for Negro musicians. "I have not had a single bad racial experience since I've been in Europe," said Art Farmer. "No one has ignored me as people will do here," in his homeland. Jon Hendricks began in Toledo as a drummer, and began singing. Similarly, once he landed in Europe, he made yet another fateful transition, spending more time performing in the nations of the "old continent." Even serving eleven months in the brig after deserting the U.S. military in France did not sate his appetite for exile. "In America we're still viewed as ex-slaves," he said, "they're thinking in terms of racism all the time. They don't want no music that brings people together without thought or differences. . . . The Europeans never had us as slaves"—at least not to the same extent—"so they can accept it for what it is," meaning the music and the performers, too.[111]

NEGRO MUSICIANS CONTINUED TO BE dogged by the drug epidemic, though the changing political climate was opening more opportunities abroad. Producer John Hammond, testifying before the New York state legislature, scoffed that "the union has closed its eyes on this," leaving their membership further unprotected.[112] Thus, when Charlie Parker finally expired, his mother was distraught in recollecting that a woman who "worked for the Italian Mafia" was egging him toward hard drugs.[113]

This was not the only way in which unions left their members unprotected. Drummer Jimmy Cobb recalled a time when a recording was slated to be made with Columbia Records: "You make a date. Then you have to wait [at] the union for two weeks or three weeks to get your money." Cobb managed to make a date to record *Kind of Blue* with Miles Davis, arguably the best-selling "jazz" record of all time. He received "under $500, way under $500" and "that would take you even a few weeks to get that. . . . The record is still selling a lot of records," he said accurately, but sadly, "I don't have no money to fight them. They got the advantage there," which was similarly accurate. "If they [were] giving you what you was supposed to get, I probably wouldn't have to work as hard." At that point, his spouse added, unprompted, "Sidemen don't get paid in this business . . . they don't. Jazz musicians really like to play. They don't like the business end of it too much usually," and the union was seemingly unable to compensate. Thus redoubtable artists like Lucky Thompson, saxophonist born in 1924, left the business, said Cobb. "He just got disgusted with it for some reason."[114]

Agreeing, producer Gus Statiras, who also worked as a disk jockey, noted that "you paid the musicians for three-hour sessions. Right after the war, scale was $21.25 for a sideman, $42.50 for the leader." But even that sparse payment was too much for the likes of Herman Lubinsky, who "never went by the union rules. He paid ten dollars, fifteen maybe," but that was too much also, so "he'd pressure the [executive in charge] to get that extra tune out of the musicians."[115]

George Coleman, saxophonist born in 1935, was more critical of Davis, whom he also accompanied regularly. He found the trumpeter "vindictive," contributing to his "high blood pressure," unhelpful since he was "diabetic" too.[116]

But even Davis's purported transgressions could have been handled better by Coleman if the union had been keener to protect all its members. Instead, in 1956–57 the "white Local 6 in San Francisco" vetoed a move to desegregate and join ranks with "Colored Local 699" by a vote of 799–554, leaving the latter on the outside looking in. As their members were often the most competent artists, effectively this created a Shangri-la for unscrupulous employers of musicians, able to feast with little pushback. In a stunning display of exclusion, the "Colored" local not only had Negro members but Chinese, Japanese, Portuguese—and others who could easily have been defined as "white." But this local had only 350 members, while Local 6 had a whopping 4,000.[117] (Alert readers may have noticed by now that white supremacy was so deeply entrenched in the republic that neither integration nor segregation, absent a dedicated strategy of mass education and global pressure, were sufficient to bring equity to the otherwise beleaguered.) This veto vindicated the opinion that unions often were acting as racist job trusts for certain Euro-Americans than class-based groupings fighting for the class. But the dilemma of being Black in a white supremacist society did not provide many viable alternatives; for when the locals merged due south in Los Angeles, the Negroes signed away assets, eroding an independent base, leading one scholar to term it a "bum deal."[118] Unfortunately, the ascending liberalism encountered difficulty in navigating the tricky currents of desegregation, leading to one "bum deal" after another.[119]

Nonetheless, with the changing political atmosphere—Ghana, Little Rock, Sputnik—U.S. imperialism adapted by sponsoring junkets abroad by even Negro musicians under the banner of "jazz," the once derided music being a symbol of supposed U.S. democracy, sharing, improvisation, and "freedom." Yet this now familiar discourse ignored the point made by self-styled pianist Romano Mussolini, born in Italy in 1927: "My father"—a founding father of fascism—"was not against jazz"; indeed, during the world war he helped to engineer, "in Italy jazz was a symbol of revolution" and "progress," and the keyboardist himself "played Fats Waller records in the house," invoking no irritation from his busy father.[120]

The wider point was that as the stigma of Jim Crow came under increasing assault, it was even more likely that the art form would find ever wider audiences. Billy Higgins, drummer, was among those who found that "the thing about this music is that it is appreciated in other places more so than here," meaning the United States, making it a potent political weapon, especially against those who had been in solidarity with the domestic foe that was Robeson, who just happened to be a musician himself.[121]

The state broadcaster Voice of America, which reached via radio virtually every corner of the planet, sponsored the music too, which had the benefit for artists of opening new markets in which to display their wares. Willis Conover, a Euro-American born in 1920, became the voice of the music abroad. He and the music quickly became wildly popular. John Chancellor, a leader of VOA and former leading television broadcaster, captured the sentiment among the U.S. elite when he claimed that Conover presented the "most effective piece of American diplomacy," stressing that he represented the "*finest* message about the United States that we would possibly send."[122] This brought more positive exposure for U.S. imperialism's bloodstained Jim Crow record, but when Louis Armstrong—who in 1956 joined the Royal Philharmonic in London for a benefit for anti-communist rebels in Hungary,[123] performing free of charge[124]—reproached Washington for the depredations perpetrated against Negro youth in Little Rock,[125] the downside of this new musical diplomacy was now evident, along with the contradictory tensions of the era: Armstrong was aiding and reprimanding Washington from month to month.

Conover claims that his employer "dropped all [jazz] music during the Joe McCarthy period," but this was an exaggeration depending upon a narrow view of this era.[126] By 1959, Conover was heard daily by 30 million people in eighty nations, making him one of the most popular broadcasters of that era, and his overall message was clear: "Jazz corrects the fiction [*sic*] that America is racist," he claimed.[127] Thus, when he arrived in Warsaw in 1959—"behind the Iron Curtain" in the anti-communist parlance of that epoch—all seats were taken for his appearance, fans were standing in the back, crowding the edge of the stage in a manner that would have called for the fire department to intervene if such a scene had materialized in Washington. The "applause overwhelms me," chortled Conover.[128]

Warsaw was not unique. Across the oceans in Brisbane, Australia, Geoff Atkinson told Conover that his program "has a very handsome following there. I know of at *least* 450 people that would listen at least twice a week" (emphasis in original). [129] Bandleader Stan Kenton told "Dear Willis" in 1957 that "during our recent visit to Australia I spoke to a great many fans who listen to you regularly," adding patriotically, "you are doing a great work for the State Department"—"as well as for jazz."[130]

Given his sensitive post, Conover was dogged by detractors. George Wein, the promoter, said that Conover—and producer George Avakian too—"were jealous and envious of me" and "wanted my job. . . . They were not friends," Wein emphasized. He was upset at the aftermath of a failed 1950s attempt to organize a jazz festival in New Orleans, mimicking Newport. "New Orleans . . . wanted me to do it," but then "they found out that I was married to Joyce"—an African American woman—"and so they said it was embarrassing to the mayor," that is, that he "might be embarrassed if you're married to a black. Willis grabbed that job as fast as he could,"[131] the global symbol of U.S. imperialism's new turn toward democracy via the music opportunistically taking advantage of Jim Crow, a resonant symbol of a conflicted era.

9. I Wish I Knew How It Would Feel To Be Free

THE 1960s, ACCORDING TO ONE ANALYST, was "one of the worst periods for jazz in its history." Actually, this premature burial of the music became a staple with the rise of television's popularity, the "British invasion," and the companion "invention" of a new form—rock 'n' roll—which some saw as a whitewashed offshoot (in the manner of "West Coast Jazz") of what had been colorfully called rhythm 'n' blues. It was true, however, that what was demurely termed "racial strife" erupted periodically, as had been the case since Little Rock in 1957 and Oxford, Mississippi, in 1962,[1] then a turnabout of sorts with Los Angeles in 1965.[2] The federal government enacted civil rights legislation in 1964, followed by the Voting Rights Act of 1965, which, ideally, should have broken the back of Jim Crow, but this system of iniquity was too deeply embedded to disappear readily and touring bands often still faced rough injustice, particularly when passing through Dixie.

Likewise, the music's sponsor-cum-exploiter—Organized Crime—was hardly squelched as a progressive anti–Jim Crow movement arose, complemented nicely by vibrant feminist and antiwar movements. By 1960, the Nevada authorities—with oversight over Las Vegas, a rival of New York and nearby Los Angeles as an employer of musicians—were engaged in a typical exercise: vetting an employer's credentials that were soaked with illicit ties. In 1960, the target was the curiously named "Nig Rosen . . . closely associated with Meyer Lansky," the reputed brains behind the entity popularly denoted as

"La Cosa Nostra." They were business partners in Miami Beach, as well as Las Vegas. Rosen was no minor figure, in other words, and was thought to be implicated in the gangland-style execution of Lansky's erstwhile comrade, "Bugsy" Siegel, subjected to cinematic treatment in Hollywood. There was also Herman Taylor, "connected" with the ghoulishly named "Murder Inc." He was a "mob fighter connected with the Capone syndicate" in a "gambling setup" and along with "associates over the years has been the worst possible . . . front man for nightclubs."[3]

The problem for racketeers was their ability to continue—or escalate—their lengthy record of exploiting musicians shamelessly was being confronted aggressively not only by various initiatives by musicians to halt same but also by energized artists often radicalized by experiences abroad, for example, in Vietnam, where they often received firearms training too. Such was the case for the drummer known as Majid Shah, once known as Jimmy Hoskins, who played alongside Miles Davis, at the apex of the profession, and Los Angeles piano legend and bandleader Horace Tapscott. Then there was percussionist E. W. Wainwright, an Air Force veteran and member of the "Jazz Pioneers," denoted as "the revolutionary band of SNCC" (Student Non-Violent Coordinating Committee), the shock troops of the anti–Jim Crow forces.[4]

Musicians continued streaming abroad, though at times more was promised than delivered. Japan had assumed mythic status in the minds of many musicians, but agent John Levy argued that the "promoters" he encountered there in 1963 were "gangsters . . . domineering, almost arrogant."[5] However, sax man Sonny Rollins represented the gathering concensus in being taken with Asia—India in his case.[6]

Singer Annie Ross recalls being in Paris with James Baldwin: "He and I used to collect milk bottles, cash them in, buy some food."[7] But that was during a time when the city as a whole was still reeling from wartime occupation. By the time the the erudite saxophonist Marion Brown—born in 1931 and educated at Howard University and Wesleyan—arrived, things had changed. He proclaimed with enthusiasm in the 1960s that "I only pay about 55 dollars a month for a large studio with a bath, kitchen and lots of space,"[8] not in Manhattan but Paris. Being in France meant he was more likely to be influenced by the radical currents there, much more manifest, even in 1968, than in his homeland. Also moving to Paris was pianist Mal Waldron, born in 1925 (and passing away in Brussels in 2002). Educated at Queens College in New York City, he had experienced difficulty at home, with a heroin habit driving him in 1963 to a hospital, followed by (probably unnecessary) shock therapy and spinal taps. "The white musicians got the jobs and the black musicians didn't get the jobs even if they had more talent," was his sour assessment of a dire situation that was hardly unique to music. "In America," he said, "if you were black and a musician at the time," speaking of his pre-1965 existence in New York, "it was two strikes against you," whereas in Europe, he said brightening, "it was two strikes for you." Thus, on the old continent he found "so much respect and love" that he "didn't need any drugs." Hence, after expatriation, Waldron "never looked back." However, he did not forget the United States, illustrating how exile did not mean forgetting to influence the place of one's birth. One of his better-known compositions was "Of Pigs and Panthers," homage to the epitome of the militant 1960s, the Black Panther Party, and a rebuke of their presumed porcine foes: police officers. Like other African American artists, he found Japan comforting too: the archipelago, he said, with heartfelt sentiment, would always have a special place in his imagination. And in 1995, he was there on an official invitation for the fiftieth anniversary of the atomic bombing of Hiroshima and Nagasaki,[9] one of the most profound crimes against humanity in world history. (Tellingly, Coltrane visited Nagasaki in 1966 and insisted on visiting the hypocenter of the atomic blast before decamping to his hotel. He placed a wreath on the site—then prayed. The next day at a press conference he was uncharacteristically loquacious in denouncing war. With his own time on earth rapidly expiring, he insisted, "I want to be the force that is truly for good.")[10]

Settling in Copenhagen was Dexter Gordon. By 1969, the rumor was afoot that he was seeking Danish citizenship. He assured his fans that "jazz gets much more exposure on radio and TV in Europe," while he termed his life in Denmark as "very civilized," in apparent contrast to his erstwhile homeland across the Atlantic.[11] He was not alone in this thinking. A few years earlier, critic Leonard Feather had found "about a hundred leading jazz men . . . now settled abroad, mostly in France and in Scandinavia," with Sweden bearing "the best and longest reputation."[12]

James Moody, saxophonist and flutist born in 1925, was also among those choosing exile. He was in France for three years: "People took you for what you were and they . . . didn't discriminate against you," unlike his homeland. "I pledge allegiance to a flag who wouldn't let me go into a restaurant and eat . . . who would do what it does to people that . . . are of a so-called darker hue?" The United States, he charged with incendiary fury, has "double, triple, quadruple standards" based on hue. "If you're a certain hue and you do something . . . you become more rewarded for that than a person who is another hue." "That's a drag," he sighed, "but it's a fact." He knew the vocalist known as Babs Gonzales, born Lee Brown in 1919, from his days in Newark, and understood fully why he changed his name: "Because if you don't look like a Negro, then, like they figured, well, you could get away with a little more, you, if his name was [Hispanicized] not [Lee] Brown, " that is, meaning "he wasn't a n-gg-r."

Moody departed unceremoniously, because "the government is wrong . . . I was just angry at the system, the way it was," but unlike others similarly situated, his craft allowed him to be mobile. He also spent time in Stockholm, where he created his signature hit "Moody's Mood for Love" (undermining the old saw that exile sapped creativity in that it supposedly removed artists from the fount of their artistry). He was energized musically by his exile. "America's a land of mediocrity," he asserted, compared to a "European audience, even an Asian audience," in terms of appreciation of artistry.

Like many leading musicians, Moody had been soaked in the deadly brine of Jim Crow and fled in anger as a result. At the age of eighteen, he had joined the military and was stationed in segregated Greensboro, this after being born in segregated Savannah. "They had the regular Air Force band but they wanted a so-called Negro Air Force band," and he joined. He was stunned to find that German prisoners-of-war could eat where he could not. "I had a little complex," he said shudderingly, "saying, 'I wonder why people hate me? What have I done?'" His conclusion was simple: "The minority is intelligence and the majority is ignorance." Then it was on to Newark, New Jersey, well above the Mason-Dixon Line, but "we would have to sit in the balcony and the Caucasians would sit on the first floor." Even "when we'd go to a Chinese restaurant, we'd sit on one side and the Caucasians on one end." Performing in Jim Crow locales, predictably, there was a "rope across . . . the dance hall and on this side, the Caucasians would be dancing" and on the other side, the Negroes and "you'd have white spectators" but "at a white dance, no Negro spectators." He seemed to suggest that the rigidity of the binary also led to segregation on the bus transporting musicians: "divided into two parts: the hooch hounds and the pot hounds" . . . "the back of the bus drank alcohol, the front of the bus smoked pot." Moody left Dizzy Gillespie's band after "I took an overdose of Benzedrine . . . I was kind of paranoid after that," he said.

However, he was determined: "I wanted to be a musician," so he practiced and practiced. "I had no thoughts or anything about making money. It didn't dawn on me." But the travails that ensnared him took their toll. "I don't hear high pitches," he complained late in life. "I can't hear it. That's why you never hear me trying to play high on a flute." Then Bell's palsy claimed him, meaning that he "couldn't play my horn . . . I had no control over my lips . . . my eye was closed" and "I had to wear a patch."[13]

"We have to go to other nations for our careers," said Abbey Lincoln with sagacity, agreeing with Moody. "If there wasn't Europe, I don't know what we would do." Certainly, staying stateside was a virtual guarantee of immiseration. "When I started to make $100 a week in Honolulu, I thought wow," what a bounty, which it was for one of her ancestry. "I [had] worked as a maid and I had made like $30 a week" and now—seemingly—had ascended economically. But while performing, "I would be sometimes the only black person in the room. They didn't want black people . . . in Miami. A black man would frighten them," and the presence of women like herself did not necessarily bring a different level of unease.[14]

Musicians were also exiling from Dixie. Charles Lloyd, born in

Memphis—an unacknowledged hotbed of excellent musicians—in 1938 remembered his early career performing there: "Those white girls would go crazy, you know," since "they had a thing at the theater where one night a week they'd have an after-hours show or something for whites only." Then "one of the guys who worked down at the jailhouse and heard them sayin' they were gonna come that night to arrest us all" as a result of this unsolicited feminine attention. "It's the South and white girls and stuff like that," signified explosiveness. "They liked us," Lloyd said, speaking of these Euro-American females. "My mother woke me up, put me on a train to California," where he then established a long-term residence. "I was eighteen and I was just getting ready to graduate from high school," he said and escaped one step ahead of the sheriff. "They arrested Willy [sic] and put him on a 72-hour secret docket," speaking of trumpeter and bandleader Willie Mitchell, born in nearby Mississippi in 1928. "They ran us out of town essentially," says Lloyd, which could be said for other musicians who fled to Europe, Japan, or California.[15]

Musicians also headed to Manhattan, as it contained an infrastructure in the form of paying gigs at clubs surpassing those of other metropolises. Yusef Lateef arrived in New York City in 1960. These were "rough years for me," he said, having "$35 when I got [there]." He "had some . . . property" in Detroit, from whence he departed, "and I couldn't keep up the payments," and "lost it." Chastened, the intellectual artist, perhaps preparing for moving further eastward, "studied French," then "literature" at the Manhattan School of Music. "I've written two or three plays and I've written a novella, a book of short stories"—and more.[16] (Regrettably, the intellectual candlepower of these artists is often neglected. Jackie McLean, for example, was a careful reader, speaking openly of "my hunger for history. . . . I'm interested in history from so many different levels," including being "very fascinated with the Second World War.") [17]

As musicians streamed abroad, their music did too. By early 1961, the future famed writer and director Maya Angelou was informing "Dearest Abbey and Max," speaking of Lincoln and Roach, that at a meeting of African exiles in London, where she was then visiting, Louis Armstrong was denounced for various transgressions, including doubtlessly his affect, which included incessant smiling (apparently they had forgotten or were unaware of his critique of Little Rock). Understandably, Roach was praised. She also mentioned in passing that when Billie Holiday died, she was mourned in South Africa, at least among Africans: "They had a day of quiet" there. Like others, Angelou "would never have known that Billie was liked or known or anything."[18] She may not have known that African American artists were hailed in southern Africa. Roach's fellow Brooklynite, Randy Weston, also discovered that his scintillating album, *Uhuru Afrika*, was banned in South Africa.[19]

Weston notwithstanding, the easing of Jim Crow allowed some to open their ears and receive the sweet sounds in a renewed way. Pianist Ahmad Jamal, born in 1930, released an album in 1958 that sold 5,000 units in one day at a time when an album that sold 15,000 units all told was considered significant. One analyst argues that artists of Jamal's caliber—and Miles Davis's and Gillespie's—"had more formal education than the blues artists [and] were careful in their business dealings," allowing them to retain more wealth and accumulate more power as a result. By 1960, this same analyst asserts that there were "some six hundred labels in existence," with "one hundred single records and one hundred LPs . . . released every week," allowing arbitrage opportunities for more musicians—playing off one label against another—to their benefit.[20] Moreover, by 1961, Quincy Jones crossed over and became what agent John Levy called the "first black executive" at a major record label (a slight exaggeration but indicative of the perception of the widening opportunities). This was during a time when Levy told Nat "King" Cole that the only Negro he saw at Capitol Records was a janitor. Thus, the rise of Black executives was more than a cosmetic alteration. These executives were a reflection of the changing times, which propelled them.[21]

Also suggestive of changing times was the journey to Washington, D.C., of Buddy Collette, there for the 1961 inauguration of the newly minted president, John F. Kennedy. He journeyed at the behest of Sinatra, who had not yet moved as far to the right as he would eventually. Symptomatic of the difficult path ahead was the rancid bias the horn man faced in neighboring Arlington, Virginia.[22] By 1963 the massive March on Washington featuring Dr. King had occurred; accompanying the cleric were musicians such as saxophonist, John Handy (born in 1933) and Billy Taylor. Invidiously, Leonard Feather wrote that after a racist incident in Britain, the journal *Melody Maker* assembled twenty-seven leading artists, including Ronnie Scott and John Dankworth, to protest, and ask accusingly, "Why has there never been a simple organized gesture like this on the part of the U.S. jazz world?" (Dizzy Gillespie was among the exceptions to this reproach, he noted. The trumpeter "spent most of his time at the 1963 Monterey Jazz Festival selling CORE [Congress of Racial Equality] buttons at $1 apiece; he had voted to collect $1,000 to turn over to Martin Luther King." Meanwhile, the American Federation of Musicians was rebuked for "sluggishness" in tackling a key issue: "job opportunities for Negro musicians in general [were] growing worse.")[23]

(Dankworth, visiting Manhattan, engaged in a typically white supremacist escapade with Clark Terry. When Terry ducked into the shadows, aware that he would not be picked up by a taxi, the Londoner, born in 1927, emerged curbside to secure a taxi to transport them both.)[24]

Critic Ralph Gleason was displeased with what he saw as the dearth of participation of musicians in marches. "I don't think any of the musicians are doing as much as they can" in that regard, he said. "To the best of my knowledge, the only jazz musician in the Washington march was John Handy," refuting Feather's assertion to the contrary. "Where were all the 'Freedom Suite' composers?" he asked, a dig at Roach. It has "never been my experience," he said, that "jazz musicians of any color mixed in any movements outside of jazz."[25] Gleason may not have heard that just before the March on Washington Monk played a fundraiser for the Negro American Labor Council, one of the organizers of this protest.[26] Gleason may not have known that Nat "King" Cole was then in touch with the NAACP in an effort to back the "most important forward movement that is taking place in the world today. You have my deepest admiration, gratitude and fullest support . . ." However, Cole did not like the "dissension and disagreement" that had been vocalized among anti–Jim Crow leaders. Hence, to cement their fraying ties Cole "announced a giant benefit performance" to subsidize the NAACP, CORE, SNCC, and Dr. King's grouping, all at his "expense." Writing from his home in Beverly Hills, he was bent on "utilizing the tremendous pool of talent in this area in the presentation of an annual affair" to benefit the movement.[27] As promised, days before the March on Washington, a concert was held featuring Pearl Bailey, Dorothy Dandrige, Steve Allen, Burt Lancaster, Sugar "Ray" Robinson—and Stan Kenton.[28] Prior to this event, there was a star-studded "Jazz for Civil Rights" benefit concert at Manhattan's Hunter College with Miles Davis as the headliner, joined by Art Blakey, Kenny Burrell, Babs Gonzales, Philly Joe Jones, Dakota Staton, Randy Weston, Billy Taylor, Horace Silver, et. al.[29] And after the massive Washington march, Mingus organized a benefit concert for NAACP youth.[30]

Given the gravity of the moment, Gleason may have had a point; however, the fact remained that musicians spent so much time practicing—and scrambling to make a living—and the union was so deficient in providing political education, that at times it did seem like they were asleep at the switch. Still, Dave Brubeck, one of the more politicized artists, was a moving force behind a federal bill, HR 4347, which, he said, "will give substantial relief to many composers, particularly those who have never been paid for jukebox performances of their music."[31] Marching on Washington inexorably provided impetus for such legislation designed to benefit scrambling musicians.

Still, Gleason may not have known what pianist and singer Aretha Franklin told record executive Clive Davis subsequently: her father, she said, "was the area leader for the Detroit area's great 'Freedom March' with the late [Dr. King] in Detroit [in] June 1963 which *preceded*," she stressed, "the March on Washington. My dad's dynamic leadership abilities and charisma have been credited with assembling over 500,000 people."[32] She grew up knowing and listening to Art Tatum, Duke Ellington, and Oscar Peterson, all of whom flocked to her Detroit home.[33]

There was much to protest. Earlier, Feather claimed that the "percentage of Negroes in radio, TV and movie studio jobs is actually lower than it was 10 or 15 years ago," which he associated with a perceived "alarming upsurge of anti-white prejudice," which "found its outlet in the conversion of Negro musicians to Islam." The music had generated a "bitter fringe of hard-core haters," though he saw the "primary cause" as "the genesis of the whole chain, Jim Crow itself." Indeed, he said, "most of the talent agencies, night clubs, theaters, and other avenues of employment have been controlled by Jews, some of whom have built this holier than thou wall around themselves."[34] He also predicted the imminent downfall of the Nation of Islam, which today continues to persist.

Willis Conover, U.S. imperialism's prime evangelist touting the virtues of a music once scorned, was an influential player as this music transitioned to Cold War weapon. One of his supervisors termed him the "single most well-known personality of the Voice of America," the U.S. propaganda megaphone. His was the "single most popular program" on these airwaves, and it was thought that Conover would be essential as the United States moved to place "jazz men" on postage stamps, another signal of their transformed status.[35]

Leonard Garment, a key White House adviser, was reported to have asserted that Conover was the "second-best-known American in the Soviet Union," exceeded only by Richard M. Nixon, which was probably not an exaggeration.[36]

Thus, it was Conover who informed the White House of Lionel Hampton's comrade, Richard Nixon, elected in 1968, that these artists could be quite helpful in sanitizing Washington's often ugly image, countering "riots" and rebellions in cities and war in Southeast Asia. In sum, Collette's invitation to Washington at Sinatra's behest was an indicator of what was shortly to come. Said Conover, invite Ellington to the White House and Bill Evans, pianist, and the Modern Jazz Quartet (which carried a sophisticated image). "Much of the liberal-intellectual artistic establishment," he advised, "will be surprised into applauding the President," desperately needed at that moment. "Magazines like *Downbeat* will surprise you" with their praise too; it "reaches more than 85,000 jazz enthusiasts in 124 countries including the USA. I'm their unpaid international correspondent." This journal of record, said Conover, was critical, since "often the most pro-American people in every country" were reached by it. Then there were the "28, 000 members of my 'Voice of America Jazz Listeners' Clubs' in 90 countries." Conover dismissed peremptorily the "lower-class and lower-middle-class Negroes" in the United States, because "the sophisticates of jazz are outside their taste." Still, with a worried eye on urban unrest, Conover argued that the "[frustrating] steam could be drawn off right away by presenting such 'soul music' performers as Aretha Franklin, the Supremes, Sam and Dave, Joe Tex, Muddy Waters, James Brown or B.B. King." As for the "militant black intellectuals . . . their musical deity is Sun Ra," bandleader born in 1914, though he was "not a militant himself." Europeans upset that U.S. imperialism did not honor the music more—a frequent complaint of the artists themselves—would be pleased, even co-opted, by more attention paid to musicians such as Duke Ellington.

Conover's nine-page, single-spaced missive was a blueprint for how Washington could reverse field and honor those previously ignored, a measure needed desperately as imperialism was besieged ferociously by national liberation movements and protest at home.[37] It was noticeably ironic that the music identified with African Americans was deployed in part to subvert liberation movements in Africa, along with their allies, to the ultimate detriment of African Americans.[38]

But with more opportunity arrived more competition. Willis Conover, who had as good an understanding of the global dimensions of the music as any found in 1961: "5,000 traditional jazz bands in England . . . 5,000 amateur jazz musicians in West Germany." And though "jazz activity languishes in the Arab world," he reminded, "in Tunisia the government radio station begins a program of jazz by Negro American Muslims for Muslim listeners."[39]

Still, this association with U.S. imperialism at a time of Washington's marauding in Southeast Asia and elsewhere did not exempt artists from protest. Singer Annie Ross recalls a time when she and her trio, along with Count Basie's orchestra, were performing in Berlin. She detected an "anti-American feeling" and admits openly, "I couldn't understand [it]," especially since those at the concert were "rude. They booed us off the stage" in a "terrible experience," though she also admits "it was a political thing" rather than a reaction to their artistry.[40]

As Jim Crow came under assault, Negroes—make that Blacks— were encouraged. Frank Foster was as well-connected as any musician.

The first cousin of his spouse, Cecilia, was Elvin Jones, that is, her father was the uncle of the drummer and his musician brothers, Thad and Hank. "About this time," he said years later, speaking of the 1960s, "the black awareness, civil rights activism was getting to its height. I wanted to be in on the new revolution," he asserted unabashedly. "I wanted to be on the cutting edge of things . . . I was angry at the so-called white backlash to the black civil rights movement, I was angry at Governor Faubus," who railed against educational equity in Arkansas. "I was angry at George Wallace," the governor who emulated him in Alabama. "I was angry at Senator Bilbo and Senator Eastland," their Mississippi counterparts. And he acted accordingly. Simultaneously, he was "being pressured" by his first wife to "get off the road," adding to the pressures upon him. Then there were his bandmates, "most of them were black, because I was laboring under the philosophy that not too many black musicians get a chance to play with big bands," and, suffused with the spirit of the era, "I thought I would single-handedly try to [remedy] this situation," so that "they would be well equipped to deal with studio and Broadway gigs" then opening up, after years of exclusion. Combining art and activism, he "kept hearing about the Silent Majority. . . . I got so sick of hearing about that," since "I was heavy into the social reform thing, black civil rights" to which the purported "majority" had taken exception. Thus, his counterpoint was a band called "The Loud Minority." Then he got caught up in the "Jazz and People's Movement [JPM]. That was a brainchild of the late Rahsaan Roland Kirk," the multi-instrumentalist born in 1935, and they grabbed headlines when "they successfully disrupted a television show" in protest of exclusion from these profitable jobs—and others. "They started making these musical noises in the middle of the show and they disrupted the entire show." With Jimmy Owens, he also col-laborated with the allied "Collective Black Artists."[41]

Marching to a similar beat was the multi-instrumentalist Bill Dixon, born in Nantucket in 1925, who in the Fall of 1964 organized a series of concerts which they termed the "October Revolution in Jazz," a seeming salute to Moscow at a time of Cold War tension. These were exceedingly well-attended and were seen as a way to circumvent the stodgy American Federation of Musicians. Dixon was also part of the Jazz Composers' Guild that also included other visionary artists, such as Sun Ra, Archie Shepp, Cecil Taylor, Paul and Carla Bley, Mike Mantler, and Burton Greene.[42]

Their venturesome was extended to their music too, as those within their ambit experimented with sound and instruments alike, with the latter especially expressing a form of internationalism that had buoyed the music since its inception. Those within their ambit, such as Albert Ayler, played bagpipes; others played the shehnai, a kind of Indian oboe. Don Cherry, a fellow traveler, played Indian flute and dabbled with the gamelan, the traditional ensemble music of Java. Sunny Murray experimented with the balafon, a kind of xylophone, whose roots in Africa stretched back centuries. Perhaps more traditionally, Joseph Jarman, yet another experimentalist, played the oboe and bassoon while Alice Coltrane played the harp. Yusef Lateef experimented with music from the Arab world, while Sun Ra's band often featured tympani or kettle drums.[43] This experimentation, again, was also, in a sense, a rejection of a homeland status quo that highlighted Jim Crow and its torturous legacy. Hence, Foster had a point. Jim Crow richly deserved to be placed on the defensive. If anything, JPM was long overdue: as of 1965, according to Buddy Collette, the blockbuster evening featuring presentation of the Oscars for movies had yet to hire a Negro musician.[44]

Max Roach asserts proudly that he and his spouse, Abbey Lincoln, were "heavily involved in the Civil Rights Movement," contrary to Gleason's recollection. This was not simple altruism either. He said, "I had a rough period with major [record] labels," which soured him further, engendering militancy. "It's like gold mines. We're the material"—akin to "gold and diamonds"—that "they [go] into South African [for]. . . . They take it and process it and sell it and make billions," leaving crumbs for the actual creators of wealth.[45]

Roach's musical response was the *Freedom Now Suite*, a militant musical intervention that he recalls playing at the NAACP convention in Philadelphia almost sixty years ago.[46] It was composed, said the percussionist, "to celebrate the centennial of the Emancipation Proclamation"; the "'Triptic' section grew out of a statement of [Marcus] Garvey's—which actually linked the civil rights movement

with the liberation struggles in Africa, Asia and Latin America."[47]
According to the staid NAACP leader Roy Wilkins, addressing his
troops, the performance of this piece at the Philadelphia convention
of his organization was a "smash success" that "aroused tumultuous
applause, shouts and cheers"; the assembled were taken by the "fantastic modern and African drum duets in songs of piercing intensity,
in thrilling dance sequences and in big screen projection of NAACP
young people in action"; it was a "stupendous dramatic performance,"
he gushed, that merited an encore nationally as a "moneymaker for
your branch and for the national office . . ."[48]

The enormously significant cultural contributions by Roach and
Lincoln were not necessarily embraced warmly by critics. Lincoln was
outraged by the response to her politicized lyricism: "I wrote a lyric
to Julian Priester's" unjustly neglected composition "Retribution" that
was scorned by the critic Ira Gitler, whom she retitled "Ira Hitler." He
"called me a professional Negro," she said later, still smarting from the
intended insult. Undaunted, Lincoln acknowledged what was obvious: "Dr. King, Malcolm X, Elijah Muhammad were making a great
impression and many of the artists came [to] help forward the so-called
revolution." Thus, the justly praised *Freedom Now Suite* represented a
takeoff from work created by similarly progressive Oscar Brown, Jr.
(This Chicagoan was born in 1926 and was well regarded as a lyricist
and singer and ran for office repeatedly.) She knew that "when you're
getting ready to do something that's really valuable and important,"
the "opposition is always great." Lincoln was a figurative descendant
of Robeson, in the aftermath of his sidelining. "I did know Malcolm
and we did things for him at Town Hall and sometimes uptown." Her
career was on the upswing despite this radicalism, leading to a choice
movie role starring alongside the rising actor of the era, Sidney Poitier.
"After I made *For Love of Ivy*," in the 1960s, she said ruefully, "all I
had to do was heel like a dog and I'd have made some other things,"
exploiting her looks and carriage. But she chose to traverse a different
road, meaning fewer riches but more self-respect. "A prostitute is not a
romantic character. She's a victim," was her conclusion.[49]

Roach and Lincoln were not just benefactors of the movement
through their incessant fundraising, supplying musical services free

of charge, they were also becoming actors in the militant wing of the movement, as evidenced by her sojourn in Conakry. One of the leaders of the Revolutionary Action Movement in the United States, Max Stanford, to be known as Muhammad Ahmad, briefed the "Dearest Roaches" in April 1964, as if they were fellow commandos about the activity of the man then known as Stokeley Carmichael, who was "in charge of ousting neo-colonials" in one sector of West Africa while another comrade was disrupting their "seats of comfort in Ghana." As for Stanford, he was headed to New York and wanted to confer. While praising the ongoing "Socialist" project, he mentioned T. D. Baffoe "and his wife . . . personal friends and his paper always puts forward the Afro-American point of view." As for Malcolm X, already assuming sainted status even before his murder within months, he "sounds like the best thing that has hit Cullud [Colored] Town since Marcus Garvey."[50]

The Roaches unfortunately subsumed the identity of Abbey Lincoln. It was during this tumultuous era that she made her way to Conakry, Guinea, at the behest of the famed South African chanteuse Miriam Makeba. It was there that paramount leader Sékou Touré, as she recalled it, rechristened her: naming her "Aminata for his mother and sister" and the surname "Moseka." This was more than a cosmetic alteration, reflecting a deepening commitment to a decolonizing Africa, with a good deal of the southern part of the continent then involved in armed struggle against U.S. allies in Lisbon and elsewhere. Lincoln most notably observed that "the NAACP . . . didn't like us" and "I can't stand them either." Yes, "we performed the *Freedom Now Suite* one time for the NAACP in Philadelphia. When I started to scream," the epicenter of this riveting work representing the pain inflicted on Africans historically and contemporarily, "the guards broke into the room with their guns drawn because they thought something terrible had happened," which, in a sense, was accurate. Thereafter, "we would do things for CORE. We did things for the Muslims," adding, unnecessarily: "We were radical," a descriptor applied to the NAACP only in the dankest precincts in Dixie. "The NAACP didn't want nobody like us. They still don't," she said in 1996. "I never was a fan of theirs either."[51]

Roach's fellow Brooklynite, pianist Randy Weston, was similar to her; he was disgusted after joining the military and finding it "segregated . . . you couldn't play in the band if you were black." He then worked as a cook in the Berkshires and on the staff at Riverside Records. A turning point arrived when he joined Langston Hughes, Lionel Hampton, Booker Ervin (saxophonist, born in 1930), and others in a rhapsodic tour of Africa. So inspired by 1961, he joined with fellow pianist Sadik Hakim, born in 1919, to form the "African American Musicians Society." Why? "We were disgusted with our situation and our conditions," Weston explained. "We picketed and we protested and they were frisking us," as they pressed to reshape the "discrimination clause and union contract at Local 802 in New York." Musicians, he argued, "were the victims of night clubs" in particular.[52]

Musicians, in sum, were hardly exempt from the strictures of Jim Crow, nor the protests against it. Drummer Roy Porter, like thousands of others, was caught up in the Watts Revolt of 1965, a truly tumultuous hinge moment, and was jailed; he was among those "crowding the cells" where "plumbing hadn't worked for years . . . I saw people drink water out of toilet bowls."[53]

Jimmy Owens's experience was typical. As a young man, said the trumpeter, "I'd practice all day," this after having "worked at Lincoln Hospital in the Bronx" as a "stationery clerk" for a good deal of the day. While traveling in Dixie in the 1960s, "we had a plan if we ever got stopped by those racist cops . . . who would shoot who" and "we got stopped a number of times" in a manner that was "quite frightening." Owens, like Shepp and Weston, and the more politicized musicians, observed, "I was bold and whatnot until the Emmett Till incident happened," referring to the teenager slain in Mississippi in 1955 on racist grounds. "That's what changed my mind."[54]

Even when not as explicitly militant as Roach's creations, the music since its inception had not been immune to change and, predictably, when musical transformation occurred in the midst of a challenge to a Jim Crow based on centuries of racist oppression, peals of outrage were emitted. "Coltrane was a bloody bore," howled Leonard Feather, in a confession to John Hammond, "I had to run out half-hysterical before the first set was over."[55] Critic Ralph Gleason recalled having a "long discussion . . . with a highly intelligent man, an executive of a large corporation dealing with the news" who argued passionately that Coltrane was "playing hate."[56] For his part, Hammond confessed to Feather after listening to Mingus's pianistic improvisations at the Village Vanguard, that it was "one of the grimmest experiences of my life and interminable."[57]

It appeared that disgust with the turn in the music was inseparable from disgust with the political impulse propelling it. Hammond, for example, was upset with "1960s black supremacy [sic] and [the] black nationalism . . . being shouted."[58] Saxophonist Branford Marsalis was moved to dismiss the critics. "Jazz reviewers don't have any power," he contends. "They say this is the greatest record in the world, it sells a hundred copies. They say this is the worst record in the world, it sells a hundred copies. So, there is nothing to fear from them."[59] Maybe so, though Marsalis's acerbic dismissal may downplay the ability of "jazz reviewers" to shape critical reception. On the other hand, critics often disagreed among themselves, as exhibited by Whitney Balliett's attack on the aptitude of James Lincoln Collier, which captured the attention of Leonard Feather.[60]

In short, the ascent of a kind of Black Nationalism was then reflected in a musical turn that certain critics found disconcerting. An embodiment of this trend was the writer once known as Le Roi Jones, then Amiri Baraka. A fellow critic answered affirmatively his own inquiry: "Is Le Roi Jones a Racist?," a charge rarely leveled at the bevy of club owners, executives, and critics of European ancestry.[61]

Dan Morgenstern, born in Munich in 1929, was not conservative, openly expressing distaste for the fact that at *Downbeat* "We were always conscious of the fact that there were very few black writers who got into writing about jazz." He repeated the widely held opinion that John Maher, the publisher, "was a racist," the dearth of diversity on the staff not being accidental. But the 1960s delivered a new twist in that he faced "probably the most pressure that I had" encountered, mostly "from the people who saw themselves as the champions of the avant garde which identified itself at that time with civil rights," a combination in its then form he found to be "specious reasoning." Singled out for critique was Archie Shepp, saxophonist born in 1937, and the exemplar of the politicized intellectual as artiste. But for the Munich-born critic, he was simply the "most verbose spokesman of the avant garde."[62]

What may have been at issue was that African Americans like Shepp were more than willing to confront U.S. imperialism abroad— its weak point—which may have been irksome to those who saw the republic as a refuge. It was at the height of the anti-imperialist upsurge of the 1960s that Shepp arrived in Algiers, then the exiled headquarters of the Black Panther Party, alongside other politicized musicians, such as Graham Moncur III and Sunny Murray, among many others. There, Shepp embraced BPP leader Eldridge Cleaver, then on the lam before his ideological reversal. After performing with Touareg musicians and experimenting with their unique instruments, the stunned saxophonist exclaimed, "I have just lived one of the most profound experiences of my life."[63] Shepp's embrace of the BPP was not unique to him. When party founder Bobby Seale arrived in Copenhagen, exiled saxophonist Dexter Gordon joined him at a picket line at Washington's embassy there, just as Gordon was no stranger at picket lines in Denmark protesting the war in Vietnam.[64]

Leonard Feather was not conservative either; yet he charged that Algiers' close ally, G. A. Nasser of Egypt, was an "anti-Jewish dictator whose government swarms with former Gestapo officers."[65]

These critics' peer, Willis Conover of Voice of America, was well-positioned in that he too was a key figure in determining whose music would reach ears. He was importuned by the U.S. legation in Belgrade to send more artists to Yugoslavia. The festival organized there attracted "professional" men and women from the surrounding region. The most recent festival could only attract Buck Clayton and Big Joe Turner, but the former's "interest in liquor and women apparently exceeded his interest in his own or other musical performances," while the latter was an "authentic illiterate" and unable to "converse," thus not useful for propaganda purposes.[66] Conover, in short, was at the center of the music—not unlike Hammond and Feather—and thus denounced left-wing critic Frank Kofsky, a promoter of Black Nationalism, and Coltrane alike, finding him a "pain in the ass" who "sees villains everywhere"; he was "pathetic," with a "footnote fetish" too. Invoking Moscow, he called him "Lysenkofsky," equating him with a defrocked scientist. The reviled Kofsky, he said, was swimming in "remarkable self-contradictions," though he was "dogmatically, blindly sincere."[67]

Conover and the music he was said to admire would have benefited immeasurably if he had deployed his rhetorical arsenal and vast array of connections to improve the conditions under which musicians had to labor. For assuredly, Conover exerted vast influence because of his weight on the global stage. Iola Brubeck told him in 1958 "that among the jazz fans we met behind the Iron Curtain" were devotees of his broadcasts. The "constant use of Dave's records on your 'Voice of America' program" inspired "gratitude" on her part; she also mentioned in passing that English was being learned from Conover because of his slow and steady cadence and simple broadcast vocabulary.[68]

By 1960, Louis Armstrong had spent four months touring in Europe, partially sponsored by the U.S. State Department. "He played Israel, Lebanon, Yugoslavia and one or two other places," was the message to Iola Brubeck, who helped manage her spouse's career, and the pianist too would be inclined to follow in Satchmo's footsteps. Although, according to the trumpeter's aide, "After all the sweat and tears, we were not paid off entirely, plus the fact in both Yugoslavia and Lebanon," he noted with a veritable shout, "THE MONEY IS STILL RESTING IN THE BANK THERE IN THEIR CURRENCY and we haven't a chance in a million of getting it out."[69]

Meanwhile, the increasingly popular *Playboy* Jazz Festival—founder Hugh Hefner had adopted the music as part of his repertoire of seductive sophistication—informed Brubeck in 1959 that the pianist's performances were "one of the highlights of the greatest weekend in the 60-year history of jazz."[70] Hefner, a self-described aficionado of Brubeck's oeuvre, also congratulated "Dear Dave."[71] Brubeck, said Hefner in 1960, was a "winner of the *Playboy* Jazz All-Star Poll," and besides, a "favorite of our almost one million readers."[72]

Yet, despite this enhanced popularity, Brubeck was informed irritably in 1960 by his attorney, Michael Maloney, about the opaque dispersal of royalties by his record label. "I am more disgusted than ever with ABC accounting, it was said. There is so much money involved that one would think they would take pains to be accurate."[73] Brubeck's lawyer was exasperated to the point that he rebuked Alfred Lorber of Columbia, wondering why this profitable enterprise "finds it necessary to try to haggle its way out of paying a fair mechanical royalty on a promising record by [one] of its best recognized artists," noting that "it is a puzzle to me. . . . We have no choice except to request that the Brubeck-[Leonard] Bernstein record," a reference to the composer and conductor, "be withdrawn from sale and that all distribution cease."[74]

Then Maloney declared himself "incensed about . . . basically unfair royalty treatment." His client was "most unhappy that Columbia has charged another $5,148 to him . . . in addition to approximately the same amount charged on his previous royalty statement." It was "wholly incomprehensible to me," said the eagle-eyed lawyer, "that such a fine recording" being discussed, "listed regularly as a top-selling jazz LP by Billboard, could result in financial loss to the artist as well as to the composer and publisher,"[75] absent terribly creative accounting procedures. At issue was Brubeck's classic tune, "Take Five," an "instrumental single" which to that point had sold "200,000 copies" and its parent album, Time Out, then "pushing sales of 200,000 too," which was "more than slightly impressive."[76]

Despite Brubeck's individual heroism, he continued to have rivers to cross. His label, Columbia Records, an imposing giant in the field, was, according to Iola Brubeck, "afraid of a Negro cast" for the pianist's proposed musical. "Forget about Louis Armstrong," he was told in early 1959, "stay away from Negro cast—or at least do not emphasize [the] color line," still a sensitive topic (particularly for those who might have benefited from it). She was dumbfounded by this response. "Sorry I cannot agree," she replied. "I don't think [Columbia] gets the point that the show is a mixed cast," she stressed.[77] The production, added the pianist, was a "jazz musical" that was "specifically written for Louis Armstrong and Carmen McRae," vocalist, born in 1922, and had a "mixed Negro and white cast" that was, in fact, "required."[78]

Unsurprisingly, there was less resistance to other Brubeck productions. Brubeck's "shows on the subject of theology and jazz have been one of the most exciting ways of getting Christian faith across to high school youth" was the conclusion delivered from tony Grosse Pointe, whose overt religiosity did not preclude vigorous attempts to bar African Americans straying from nearby Detroit.[79]

Iola Brubeck, who superintended her spouse's career, was also provoked as a result of her dealings with Joe Glaser's firm, ABC, which handled the pianist's 's bookings. "Frankly," she told him in 1960, "my biggest problem is in the handling of ABC commissions and deposits," that is, "sometimes there is a delay before we receive the money," allowing the sly entrepreneur to invest it on a short-term basis for profit. "Sometimes we are paid in cash at the engagement," inconvenient and making one vulnerable to robbery. "Sometimes all the money goes to ABC," again allowing for short-term investments. "Sometimes there is a deposit and there are three ABC offices with different methods of handling commissions," a fertile basis for all manner of chicanery. "Hollywood bills me, Chicago deducts from the check usually, New York deducts commissions from deposits." The pianist wondered about the "difficulty" in a new system of ABC grabbing "all money earned," then doling it out accordingly; thus, if a "'shaky' promotion" occurred, he wondered further if the "promoter could be trusted to mail you the money due immediately after the engagement is played." For "at this moment," she said, her team was "trying to track down over seven thousand dollars," reputedly "mailed to us but we have no record of having received" and with all that, "it took us one year—and a tax audit to discover this discrepancy."[80]

It was not just slick bookers and finagling record labels that dogged Brubeck, one of the more financially successful musicians performing the music. In 1963, he performed at a "free concert with Benny Goodman," clarinetist, born in 1909, and the results were "recorded and Benny kept the entire tape," the pianist complained. "Knowing Benny," he said, he will send to engineer Teo Macero "the one track . . . where he sounds good and I sound bad," enhancing his reputation and eroding Brubeck's. "Knowing Benny," he continued, "we will never get a copy," though it was promised.[81]

(Trumpeter Joe Wilder, born in 1922, also had trying experiences with Goodman when he toured with him in 1962. "He seemed to regard any of the talented people he had working for him as a threat. He seemed to delight in hiring people who were qualified and then trying to denigrate them in whatever way he could." In addition, he cheated bandmates out of money.[82] Wilder might agree with trombonist Tom McIntosh, born in 1927, who argued that being a "musician is the second most insecure profession in the world," just behind acting, with applause and critical acclaim so necessary for the survival and flourishing of both.)[83]

Thus, Dave Brubeck, despite his prominence, continued to endure manifest problems in the 1960s. It was "almost impossible for Dave to be with the family more than a week or so at a time," groused his overworked spouse in May 1960, speaking to a correspondent in Warsaw, because of the incessant touring he had to abide precisely in order to support his growing brood. "The boys have now reached the stage where they definitely need a father as much as, or perhaps more than, a mother."[84] Gene Lees, of *Downbeat*, doubtlessly captured the sentiment of her spouse when he announced that "every creative artist needs a wife like you."[85]

It may not have been coincidental that Iola Brubeck was addressing Poland since Brubeck's staunch stance against Jim Crow was circumscribing his audiences at home. It was also in 1960 that a student at the University of California was effusive in praise for the pianist because of his "strong stand against segregation. It was rather upsetting for me to learn," said his correspondent, "that ten 'centers of higher learning' would not accept a jazz band because it contained a Negro. However, your commendable action partly erased the cynicism that I was beginning to acquire."[86] Days earlier, NAACP leaders saluted Brubeck and expressed "deep admiration of your courageous stand against [Jim Crow]."[87] Then justly celebrated playwright Lorraine Hansberry and her then spouse, Robert Nemiroff, gave effusive "thanks" to "Dear Dave" since his concert at Manhattan's Carnegie Hall, a "Salute to Southern Students" then mounting the barricades in Dixie, had garnered a profit of $8,000 for their activism, with 1,500 "turned away."[88] Union leader A. Philip Randolph, then on the verge of sparking the monumental March on Washington of 1963, enthused about "your great generosity and human involvement in helping to raise hundreds of thousands of dollars for the civil rights movement." Now he wanted the busy pianist to do the same for the event that catapulted Dr. Martin Luther King's "I Have a Dream" speech.[89] Brubeck may have known that Dr. King was a "lover of jazz," according to Billy Taylor, and was a devotee of the paradigmatic tune, "I Wish I Knew How It Would Feel to Be Free."[90]

Brubeck's progressivism was comforting to those in Dixie who harbored deep resentment of the apartheid there. Ginger Kuhle found that there were "times when I feel that Lincoln should have just let the South go—strange words for a white living in East Texas."[91] J. M. Haynes told Brubeck that "Negroes everywhere are grateful" for your "great courage and farsightedness. My limited knowledge of jazz prevents me from judging you musically," he admitted, "but no one of goodwill denies the soundness of your principle."[92]

Negroes were less resistant to hosting Brubeck's heterogeneous band. "We are aware," said an admirer in 1960, that Brubeck's "is a mixed group and [we] are proud to present him at our college," in Petersburg, Virginia. "This being a Negro college they were well aware of this fact" of heterogeneity "before the date was ever consummated." "However, thanks for calling it to our attention as I also would certainly not want any last minute mix-ups,"[93] more likely in nearby Charlottesville, for example. Still, critic Ralph Gleason was among those who was told that Brubeck's music "is considered a radical departure from Dixieland and traditional style of jazz" and the latter increasingly was associated with a kind of cultural conservatism, just as, for example, Coltrane's music was tugging in an opposing direction: "This might have entered into his canceled tour in the South . . . because of the presence of Negroes in his quartet."[94]

It is probable that Brubeck, because he was Euro-American, may have accumulated more plaudits for opposing Jim Crow than, say, Max Roach. Perhaps it was thought he would inspire more Euro-Americans to evolve progressively; perhaps it was just another aspect of Jim Crow, privileging the "pale male." Whatever the case, Brubeck's posture was welcomed by those suffering from the lash of bigotry.

Nevertheless, drummer Chico Hamilton found it necessary to apologize to Brubeck, as the pianist was featured prominently in

reportage concerning the increasingly cited neologism Crow Jim[95]—
or, somehow, bias against those defined as "white" in a musical form
where they were a minority as artists but not necessarily as club
owners, managers, record executives, critics, and so forth. Hence,
even after it was thought that Jim Crow was buried and interred
safely, the great bassist Milt Hinton approached Conover to "send a
reference that would attest to my qualifications [and] experience,"[96]
not vice versa, a reflection of the dynamic of power and influence in
a society still stained by white supremacy. It was those like Conover
who pursued a kind of affirmative action in sponsoring the music of
certain artists abroad, just as some of the same forces were opposing
this policy at home in other spheres. "Most of the State Department–
sponsored tours," says pianist Randy Weston, "kind of specified that
there had to be a white musician somewhere in most of the bands,"[97]
as Phil Woods had attested.

Thus, though Glaser seemed ecumenical in his shameless exploitation of artists, as Iola Brubeck might attest, the fact that society
had been formed on the basis of enslavement of Africans made it
appear that he had more leeway in bludgeoning black musicians.
"You seem to feel that I and my associates do not have the interests of
Charles Mingus at heart" was Glaser's unabashed message to the Jazz
Workshop in 1962.[98]

THE MINGUS-ROACH VENTURE, Debut Records, had tough
sledding, encountering especially roadblocks in distribution. By
1961, sensing exhaustion, a competing record label offered Mingus
a new deal, citing the "many advantages of affiliating yourself with
Frank Sinatra," a performer who because of connections, mob ties,
and white supremacy had encountered fewer difficulties in establishing a record label. Reprise, the crooner's label, offered a seemingly
sweet deal, including "booking you at the top nightclubs" and for
added appeal, inclusion in "his TV specials and in scoring music for
his new Essex Film" business. "All this is very possible," it was said
tantalizingly and "incidentally," it was noted in passing that Sinatra
"is deeply impressed by your works." As for the competition, Sinatra's
consigliere, Mo Ostin, "ridiculed [the] information that John

Coltrane receives $15, 000 a year from ABC Paramount," a hefty sum then. "They claim that he only receives $5,000 advance per album and a total of $10,000 for two albums a year." Sinatra, the bassist was told, "pays Elmer Bernstein $25,000 for scoring a feature film," speaking of the award-winning composer and suggesting that Mingus could expect something similar. "Frank has surrounded himself with the top 'tough' pros to build a successful company," speaking euphemistically of the singer's less-refined partners. The competition was also repudiated. "Don't forget the lousy way [Columbia] treated you in the past," not inaccurate but self-serving. Then there was the prospect of rising in rank in the much scrutinized Downbeat poll: "When we get into the big-time money," Mingus was told with a flourish, "I will buy five hundred copies of Downbeat and fill in the ballots like Lionel Hampton used to do every year," which obviously paid off handsomely for the vibraphonist.[99]

Sinatra had leverage that Mingus or any others so concerned could hardly ignore. The Nevada authorities knew, for example, that the singer was quite friendly with Sam Giancana, well known as a racketeer, who often resided at a Silver State site controlled by Sinatra with the latter's "knowledge and consent." The sinister Chicagoan was lavished with "food and beverages by employees" of Sinatra who "for a number of years last maintained and continued social association" with this disreputable character, "well knowing his unsavory and notorious reputation and he has openly stated that he intends to continue such association" in "defiance of the law." So bolstered, Sinatra was not above seeking to intimidate the Nevada authorities. On August 31, 1963, the actor and charter member of the aptly named "Rat Pack," called Edward A. Olsen, chairman of the State Gaming Control Board, the putative overseer of casinos, and who "used vile, intemperate, obscene and indecent language" that was "menacing [to] the extreme" and was "designed and intended to intimidate and coerce the Chairman."[100]

By then, Sinatra's investment in the Sands Hotel in Las Vegas was worth hundreds of thousands of dollars and he was seeking to expand his vast empire,[101] hence the reaching out to Mingus. Unvarnished, Sinatra's words were surveilled when he exchanged insults with the

Nevada authorities in vile terms: "Don't fuck with me," he shouted; he was "emotionally overwrought," Olsen noted understatedly. There was speculation that the Rat Pack leader had been imbibing his favorite alcoholic beverages, inducing his vitriolic logorrhea.[102]

Apparently, the backing of the likes of Giancana emboldened the bantam rooster crooner. By 1967, the Chicago authorities continued to assert that the "jukebox racket has been able to flourish through collusion between trade associations dominated by underworld characters and representatives of labor organizations" influenced by gangs shaped initially by Capone in collusion with the "record business," giving these mobsters a prominent role in determining musical tastes.[103]

Besides Sinatra and Giancana, it was well known that Sidney Korshak, a close comrade of Glaser, wielded immense influence in the music industry. By 1962, those in the know in Chicago knew that this attorney was a shill for "gangsters and was then currently in touch with Capone syndicate members." The tricky Korshak even made the concession to prevailing winds by reaching out to J. B. Martin, that rare bird: a Negro with capital who reportedly "set up a drug store in Memphis, and it became one of the largest drug companies in the South"; then "he owned the Chicago American Giants baseball team and for fourteen years had been president of the Negro American Baseball League," a business that generated mounds of cash, which watered the appetites of money launderers.[104]

But reaching out to Martin or Mingus should not be interpreted as manifesting a kind of merger of entrepreneurs in the manner that Negro locals were being cajoled into marriages with "white" locals. Although lionized, Mingus, one of the more entrepreneurial musicians, continued to receive negative publicity, which undermined his value as a keystone artist. He was negotiating with *Playboy*, a growing player as a promoter of the music, to publish his autobiography; McGraw-Hill had paid him a $12,500 advance, then assigned the prominent Negro author Louis Lomax as his amanuensis, but he "wasn't up to the task," Mingus was told bluntly, and Hentoff was then considered. Yet even *Playboy*, the merchant of smut, seemed to be taken aback by the many lurid sex tales spun by the bassist.[105]

EVEN IF MINGUS HAD BONDED with Sinatra, it is unclear if the singer-actor-businessman would have served as a savior. Capital was hardly interested in demolishing the "Great Wall" that often separated them from Negro capital, and unions were hardly predisposed in that direction either. That was the dilemma of the musician as a new era dawned with Jim Crow in ostensible retreat. In a pattern that would be replicated nationally, segregated locals of the union merged in 1966 in Chicago. Previously Local 208, according to one scholar, "could count more members than any other black local in the AFM [American Federation of Musicians] and the majority of white locals as well." Their 1,500 members included such eminences as Ahmad Jamal, Willie Dixon, Bo Diddley, Howlin' Wolf, and Buddy Guy.[106] By 1960, Jamal was asking, and getting, a substantial $3,500 weekly for engagements, after performing for $350 only recently. Still, the closing of Chicago's Blue Note club was an ominous signal, losing $38,000 steadily by early 1960, perhaps inducing Local 208 to run up the white flag.[107] The merger was certainly in tune with the emerging ethos of "integration" or even the analytically distinct "desegregation," but practically it eroded an independent base of power controlled by African Americans with their potency swallowed whole by a more influential "white"-dominated union in a society in which retreat from Jim Crow and white supremacy was both agonizing and grudging.

Still, it was a kind of package deal that brought more customers to desegregated settings to pay to hear musicians and the concomitant liquidation of Negro locals. Jamal was not singular. Fellow Chicagoan Ramsey Lewis, pianist, born in 1935, hit the jackpot after his rendition of the hit "The In Crowd" climbed the charts in September 1965. "Our income jumped sky high," he declared, "maybe we were making $13, 14, 15 . . . $1,700 . . . a week." His trio, was "getting offers" soon of "making $2,000 a night. Oh boy," he exclaimed. Yet more money delivered more problems; by November "there were grumblings in the group," known after all as the Ramsey Lewis Trio, underlining the dispensability of the drummer and bassist. "Their attitude had changed" once "the wives had put pressure on them" and "our relationship got worse and worse," and "we broke up." Like others, he credited the popular disk jockey known as Daddy-o Daylie, who was a mass popularizer of rhyme in a manner that foreshadowed the rise of rap—"He was tops, Pops"—for providing him sound counsel that allowed him to avoid the fate of too many who recorded with Chess Records: "He was the man," says Lewis, though he could have added that the changed environment of the 1960s made it easier for sound advice to be followed. "Money is owning the masters," he said, speaking of the source from which copies of the final mix of an album are made and which often were not controlled by creators of the underlying music. "The money is [also] accumulating masters" in addition to controlling "marketing, promotion, selling [of] merchandise," that is, the "business side of the record business . . . becomes very important." Sensitive to the political economy of the nation in which he resided, Lewis concluded querulously, "Why are jails now Big Business? And as Big Business, who are [the] majority of the people in those jails: blacks and Latinos . . . why are blacks and Latinos . . . put in jail for having an ounce of cocaine on them and white-collar guys on Wall Street can cause this country to almost fall to its knees because they found a way to sell fraudulent instruments," yet escape unscathed?[108]

Moreover, there might have been more squabbling and scrambling in the music business because the stakes were not as munificent as in other branches of the culture industry, igniting more furor and recriminations. As Moses Avalon, a notorious producer, put it, "The entertainment industry is like a big casino. Motion pictures are the backroom baccarat tables for the millionaires with the $10,000 gold chips. Television is the $100 table for the yuppies, theater the $25 table and the record biz is the $2 table, essentially for the bargain shoppers," where racial and ethno-religious minorities rumbled for small stakes.[109]

This scramble for bucks, as was the case historically, continued to afflict artists. Abbey Lincoln remembered a time when she "shared the bill with Nellie Lutcher," singer, born in 1912, at the Say When Club in San Francisco. "The club owner ran off with Nellie's money. Some of it was ours too," she added sourly, in a manner in which the very memory fueled enhanced militancy. "We never saw him again." The overall environment did not aid the attempt to improve wages and working conditions. "I'm jealous when I see ballet dancers in their settings and classical musicians in their settings," she said with rancor. "That's when you bring your best not when you're in a smoky dark funky room without a dressing room. Okay," she confessed, "I railed and railed about that," which did bring plaudits from cabaret operators. "Jazz rooms were . . . [originally] brothels where people with shady characters come and pick up each other," she said, speaking as a historian. "The sound is an abomination," and "there's nothing romantic about poverty and that's what jazz joints are."[110]

Yusef Lateef concurred, "I don't think the music belongs in the club with all the smoke and the smell of alcohol" for "too much blood, sweat and tears and labor has gone into music for it" to be there, that is, "put into what Albert Heath calls 'the smoke cellars.'"[111] Lee Konitz agreed, adding that "Most musicians I know find the club setting difficult to function in," influencing the music negatively, in light of the noise and the drunks who often could be found there.[112]

Saxophonist Charles Lloyd also concurred, adding the ultimate exploitative factor: child labor. "I played every night of my life growing up from age ten or twelve," he said. Yet, after escaping from Memphis to California, he encountered another kind of exploitation. "When I was away all those years in the Big Sur," he said, "my record company had blackballed me. I couldn't record for someone else because they said . . . 'We still owe him and he still owes us,' and they offered me another glorified ten cents to record again and I said no," with his career and bank balance suffering as a result.[113]

Jimmy Owens reflected on a perilous moment when he was performing alongside Hank Crawford, saxophonist, born in 1934, then returned to his hotel, but then the leader "went and disappeared. Actually, they didn't pay us. They went and disappeared," he repeated as if he still could not believe it. They "unhitched the U-Haul trailer, took the station wagon, drove someplace and came back," though the culprit leaders "wound up spending the money, a whole lot of money." Expectedly, the "guys in the band were pissed that we weren't getting paid. . . . This is the kind of stuff that used to happen with some of the black bands. Guys would go out and party and didn't have the money to [pay] the band." he said with disgust.

Some of the rigor to which musicians were subjected was ostensibly self-inflicted. Jackie McLean says that John Coltrane died prematurely in 1967 because he played his horn too much. "He was playing for an hour and fifteen minutes on one tune," then "go home and continue to practice at home at night," then "get up the next day, practice . . . all day. Very hard," not just faking exertion.[114] Was McLean accurate? Was this self-inflicted harm? Did Coltrane love his horn too much? Or did the stiff competition and strenuous working conditions drive musicians over a cliff? Or was the sensitive artist unduly and negatively impacted by the racist tumult then erupting, which was reflected in his 1963 recording of "Alabama," a heartrending dirge recorded just two months after white supremacists bombed a Birmingham church, slaughtering children?[115] Fellow saxophonist Branford Marsalis tends to agree with McLean. He opined that the brain is only able to absorb about four hours of serious practice a day. By all accounts, "Trane was practicing eight hours a day . . . toward the end of his life," and his "mouth was bleeding. You can't practice eight hours a day without having physical repercussions. . . ."[116]

Still, Coltrane notwithstanding, the pro forma retreat of Jim Crow may also have improved, if only slightly, certain otherwise onerous conditions endured by artists. By 1956, Jackie McLean was playing alongside Art Blakey, and it was during that time that he lost his "cabaret card" authorizing him to perform in New York City. He was "without it" for years, he said, but, coincidentally, he got it back in 1965, as anti-racist rumblings roared. "It took a long time," he said, though this Pyrrhic victory then allowed him to reenter "smoky cellars." Coincidentally, 1965 was the year he chose to abandon drugs, with which he had a difficult experience. Like others, he had been influenced by Charlie Parker, who was expiring as McLean joined Blakey. The Kansan "pawned an instrument that I was using—he and I were both using," he added. He too had sparred with Bob Weinstock of Prestige Records; it was "like a factory," in that "they didn't approach recording the music the way they [did] at Blue Note. At Blue Note they were more considerate," unlike the shady Weinstock, who was not above "doing two dates in one day," which was "incredible" with a "$300 advance" for a "leader" of a group being normative for this "junkie's label." (Even Blue Note changed, he said, when George Butler assumed the helm in the 1960s.) Thus, McLean "wasn't making a lot of money" and was reduced to going to a store, and buying "cigarettes and candy and malted[s] and cream" and "then I would sell it at Slug's," a then popular club on the Lower East Side of Manhattan, after his gig ended. He was even jailed for a while. On Riker's Island in New York, where he was jailed, "there were a lot of musicians," including Ike Quebec and "Freddie Douglas, a great alto player" from the Bronx. A forced connoisseur of imprisonment, he found that the Tombs, another jail, "had no music," but even Rikers was "like slavery."[117]

On the other hand, the formal retreat of Jim Crow was a boon to Black singers of various stripes, which also meant it was a boondoggle for the legions of exploiters. Consider Sam Cooke, for example, born in 1931, but as he lay dying in 1964 in a seedy hotel in Los Angeles, his manager, Allan Klein, instead of seeking to preserve his musical legacy and attending to the needs of his heirs and estate, instead managed to acquire the rights to his catalogue and rolled the assets into the company he founded. Klein routinely structured deals so that he held artists' assets, paying the musicians fixed accounts while keeping profits on the float or subject to short-term investments for his benefit. He was accused of shafting the Rolling Stones, leading to decades of litigation. He was finally prosecuted in the late 1970s on charges that he had conspired to sell promotional copies of Beatles records off the books, the Beatles being a group he also managed.[118]

Lashed by contrasting currents of still stinging racism and official pronouncements lauding the (premature) burial of Jim Crow while continuing to be beset by still difficult working conditions and shameless exploitation, musicians found it difficult to survive both materially and psychologically. The manager John Levy ascertained that songstress Dakota Staton, born in 1930, "had a mental problem" in that "she did a lot of crazy things and then she became very anti-Semitic, very strongly," in fact.[119] As the *Freedom Now Suite* was premiering, Max Roach, its primary creator, was enduring depression, enveloped as he was in a "nervous breakdown" induced, he said, by "either alcoholism or something else."[120] Artists often tend to be sensitive, allowing them to identify with the suffering of humanity to our benefit but making them more susceptible to unfair critique. After a critic slammed pianist Phineas Newborn, born in 1931, in a manner that Marian McPartland deemed to be "very inflammatory," even she was upset in the treating of him like "he really wasn't a [jazz] player . . . it was a bad thing." The result? "That was at the point [that]Phineas became weird."[121]

There was also a fair amount of isolation involved in reaching the summit of musicianship, which was antithetical to forging the kind of social bonds necessary for sound mental health. Hubert Laws, born in 1931 and part of a family that rivaled the Marsalis clan in contributing to the music, seemed like a slacker when he said, "I can practice my flute 8 hours at least." This was a family tradition, since his father worked "two jobs," he said, fifteen hours daily "for 35 or 40 years" consecutively. (Unfortunately, bias prevents a keen analysis of the impact of a history of enslavement in shaping the often excessive work habits of African Americans; in fact, the stereotype steers toward the risible claim of their alleged laziness.)

Certainly, the toxicity of Jim Crow in Houston where Laws spent his early years was sufficient to induce unsteadiness. There were "separate locations on the bus," he said; "you had separate drink-water fountains, separate facilities where we could eat and drink." Touring Dixie in the 1950s, "we couldn't stop and use the bathroom," placing tremendous pressure on the bladder—and the psyche. "We had to have . . . bottles to pee in," an emblem of disrespect. Then there were the horrific working conditions: "you played late hours and I'd tear my em [embouchure]," deadly for a flutist. It "would always kill me sometimes, playing those gigs" with torturous "long hours"; exuding angst, he added, "it took so much out of me," comparing it to exhausting "manual labor." "It wasn't that gratifying," he said grimly, "we were just doing it for commercial purposes." Drummer Nesbert "Stix" Hooper, fellow Houstonian, born in 1938, a charter member of the most financially successful of combos, The Crusaders, was "politically minded" and influenced those around him, including Laws. He too charges rampant theft of the work of others, enough to drive creators batty. Both "Bridge Over Troubled Waters" (associated with Paul Simon and Art Garfunkel), now a U.S. classic, and "Let It

Be" (associated with the British Invasion and the Beatles), he recalls hearing growing up in Houston, decades before both were released to acclaim: "[The] name was changed to protect the guilty" he added acidly.

Finally, in the 1960s, driven by global trends in the first instance— especially national liberation movements allied with a socialist camp—Washington reluctantly began to yield. It was then that the flutist conversed with Leonard Bernstein, rapidly gaining notoriety in Manhattan as a conductor, about "blacks being hired in orchestras. . . . They had hearings about it, where black musicians felt . . . like they were being overlooked when it came" to hiring; "It was during that period of time that they actually got hired," a real breakthrough. "They even offered Richard Davis," bassist, born in 1930, "a gig without even having him . . . audition." But those halcyon days rapidly disintegrated to the point that by the time of his speaking in 2011, Laws concluded unhappily that "even now, it hasn't changed that much in these orchestras"; indeed, it was "pretty much the same thing all over." Thus, the "L.A. Phil[harmonic]," a leader musically, was a laggard otherwise: "There aren't too many blacks" in their ranks, he said. "There are maybe two or three . . . but what can you do," he said resignedly. Speaking a bit of Spanish, betraying his borderland origins, he accused "conventional religions" of being the "main culprit for keeping people enslaved . . . Why?" "Because it's counterfeit," he said subversively. "But the central issue is government." However, music was culpable too, since "bad music can create bad behavior," particularly since "music has deteriorated . . . and it's caused society to be deteriorated" as well.[122]

Clark Terry benefited from this mass pressure. By the early 1960s, he had become the first Black musician to be hired by the giant broadcaster NBC. The salary was $350 a week, "plus the double overtimes," a not infrequent occurrence. This hiring was not only the product of his talent as a musician, but ratcheted pressure exerted by the National Urban League. Each network had about 175 musicians on staff and when Aaron Levine of NBC threatened to fire his comrade, Snooky Young, a fellow trumpeter, born in 1919, Terry threatened to leak the news to the press, and Levine swiftly changed his mind. But even then, "there were not a whole hell of a lot of black musicians who were doing the jingle business," he said, speaking of commercials.[123]

Once that golden door opened, Jimmy Owens walked in. In the 1960s, he was making $55,000 yearly working on the widely broadcast television program hosted by David Frost, the "equivalent of $375,000 or $390,000 per year," by the first decade of the new century. The conscious artist had joined the union in 1959—"You have to audition to be in the union, yes"—and wisely made his first pension contribution that same year. He said that most were not as wise as he in this regard. This, he understood, since the union "was not about protecting jazz musicians, especially black jazz musicians." He understood fully why "many musicians are not in the union—I can't blame them," he said with commiseration. By the time of this 2011 interview, he acknowledged that "instead of paying $210" in dues annually, "I only pay $80. I'm a life member." Despite the inadequacies of the union, Owens persevered, seeking to emulate Gigi Gryce, which brought him grief. "Maybe I knew too much, I was passing on too much information to too many people. I went many years without a recording contract," at times a kiss of death for a working musician.

Despite the hurdles, Owens took the next step from Gryce when he and other artists decided "we can't wait for Columbia or Blue Note" to produce and distribute their creations. Besides, "there were many, many issues with musicians who had recorded with record companies and their publishing rights had been given to the record company and they had very little control over anything," and "they knew nothing about copyright." Thus, in the late 1960s he was joined by pianist Stanley Cowell, born in 1941, and bassist Reggie Workman, born in 1937, to form Collective Black Artists with dues of "$2 each" per artist, "per week." That was the nucleus from which Owens, Cowell, and trumpeter Charles Tolliver, born in 1942, began a record company, to be known as Strata East. More ambitious than Roach and Mingus, they also "put together what was called an institute of education," including "classes on the business aspects of the music industry," the "history of African art," and other topics designed to forge a musician of the new type. The need was real: "Here I'm working with musicians who are full-time musicians who never made $5,000 in their lives in one year. They were supported in general by their spouses," contributing to the hoary saw: What do you call a drummer without a lover? Homeless. More seriously, artists were selling hundreds of thousands of records and taking home next to nothing. CBA continued until 1977, and by then Owens was collaborating with music aficionado Congressman John Conyers of Detroit, a founder of the Black Caucus on Capitol Hill, along with trumpeter Donald Byrd, Baraka, and David Baker on various initiatives to uplift the art and the artist.[124]

Yet another New Yorker, Randy Weston, near the same time organized the "African American Musicians Society" in conjunction with the sadly unheralded Gigi Gryce, John Handy, and Melba Liston, trombonist, arranger, and composer, born in 1926. They picketed the site of the rising Lincoln Center in Manhattan, a glaring example of exclusion in that it displaced a once thriving Negro neighborhood and then for years excluded their music. "At that time," he declared, "there was hardly any work for us," allowing plenty of time for picketing. "They didn't want blacks in symphony orchestras, they didn't want blacks in society orchestras. When you worked in a jazz club, if you were a leader, you might make $125 a week, with sidemen getting $90 a week . . . and I'm talking about top clubs." Then this inimitable crew organized an important conference to plot future moves, though Ornette Coleman, saxophonist, born in 1930, "was the only bandleader who came to our conference. We missed Max Roach, we missed Charles Mingus," he said sadly. The "Jazz Guild, an integrated musicians' organization," fared little better. "The Sixties," concludes Weston, "were a hard time for all jazz bands."[125]

Why the Jazz Guild, and Strata East, and CBA, and JPM were needed was reflected in the continuing travails of the pioneer, Charles Mingus. In 1964, he was selling his albums at $10 a unit, which could only be obtained via his good offices and unavailable in stores. Now he was backed by his old friend Collette and basketball star Wilt Chamberlain, another beneficiary of the eroding Jim Crow. "What would you do," asked the bassist and composer, "if you made more money in four months by mail order than you did in eight years with regular record companies?"[126]

Like so many others, before and since, Mingus was emulating Gryce, a trailblazer in the difficult business of artists reclaiming control of their creativity. He was a "real warrior," said Weston of Gryce, "but he dealt with a lot of racism. He tried to get all of us to protect our music, but the establishment didn't want to deal with that, so a lot of pressure was put on" him as a result. Weston absorbed the lessons imparted by Gryce when he negotiated with Morris Levy's Roulette Records after the pianist had created the wonderful *Uhuru Afrika* album. "He wanted a certain percentage of the publishing, higher than normal," said Weston of the gangster/businessman. So, Levy, who owned the premier club, Birdland, countered by threatening, "You guys are never gonna work Birdland again, forget about it." Then he executed and "put the freeze on," barring him from this prime outlet. Gryce, the horn man, composer, arranger, educator, and organizer, also continued to encounter barriers. He "died rather mysteriously," said Weston, speaking of the 1983 demise of this man born in 1925. "There was speculation among musicians that he was actually killed."[127]

10. Song for Che

ORNETTE COLEMAN AND CHARLIE HADEN WERE STUNNED.
The saxophonist and his bassist, born in 1937, were performing in
Portugal, alongside other musicians. It was 1971, a scant three years
before the fall of the dictatorship, an event that would in turn contribute mightily to the liberation of Lisbon's beleaguered colonies,
Mozambique in 1975 and Angola, once a hunting ground for Africans
to be enslaved, by 1976. However, benighted forces still maintained
tight control over this European nation. There were about 10,000
in the audience when Haden boldly decided to perform his stir-
ring "Song for Che," a brilliant homage to the Argentine-born hero
of the Cuban Revolution. Coleman gave the okay to proceed, but,
said Haden, "before I'd finished the dedication, pandemonium broke
out. At least half the audience applauded . . . and the applause lasted
through the number." Haden had been "warned there might be repercussions," and predictably, the "next day's concert had been cancelled
by the police." A comrade suggested that they depart forthwith. They
raced to the airport, and Haden was then "taken to the security room
and told I would have to come with the policemen . . . I began to get
scared," he said. At the police headquarters, he was "interrogated for
some five hours," before somehow being rescued from further misery
by a representative of the U.S. embassy.[1]

TIMES HAD CHANGED, THOUGH NOT ENOUGH. Jim Crow
was eroding, but barriers to equity persisted stubbornly. Musicians
continued to stream overseas, yet, as Haden discovered, even there

hurdles were strewn about. Fortunately, Max Roach and Archie Shepp encountered no such difficulty a few years later when the Chinese leader Mao Zedong died and they were asked to perform a benefit concert on behalf of Soweto in apartheid South Africa. This led to their recorded performances of "Sweet Mao" and "Suid Afrika '76," and they were invited to France to re-create these works. Roach scoffed at the remonstrance of critics, declaring, "Leonard Feather hasn't been able to hear any music since [Louis] Armstrong and [Coleman] Hawkins."[2] Roach, in contrast, was proud of his handiwork. "It isn't taboo to be on the left like it is here," he said of Italy and France. "The Italian Communist Party," then a giant, "invited us to participate in a huge manifestation in Rome," while he also "wrote a suite for Mao and this was only released in Paris." The music "trace[ed] the history of Mao" and his "Long March" to triumph.[3] During this time, Lee Konitz was also importuned by the Italian Communists to perform.[4]

Roach was nonplussed by his alignment with those frowned upon by some. The music aficionado Jay Bregman, for example, was beyond furious at Shepp, saying the saxophonist's "aim is to either sow strife among musicians both black and white"—or he is "misinformed."[5] It is likely that this angry critic was also displeased with Shepp's active support for freedom of the radical Michigander, John Sinclair, who had received a lengthy prison sentence because of possession of a small amount of marijuana.[6] Roach was more concerned about the generally accepted posture of musicians aligning with the powerful, citing the deployment of Noble Sissle's and Eubie Blake's "I'm Just Wild About Harry" as a campaign ditty on behalf of President Truman, not to mention the recruitment of bandleader Lionel Hampton and multi-talented performer Sammy Davis, Jr., by President Nixon. These latter instances, he said, were examples of music "used as a political and social depressant," akin to "apolitical message songs," then so fashionable, and "opposed to music for enlightenment," the form he preferred.[7] Roach knew of what he spoke. In 1972 his *Freedom Suite* was adapted for film by the Italian cineaste Gianni Amici and won top prize at the heralded Film Festival in Lucarno. "It sneaked into South Africa," said Roach, "until they heard the words [Oscar] Brown, Jr., put to it. Then it was barred."[8]

What was changing was the spectacle of artists invading the inner sanctums of the elite, hoisting the banner of liberation. That's what Leonard Feather detected in 1971 when he turned on his TV for the *Ed Sullivan Show* and watched agape as Shepp and Rahsaan Roland Kirk reaped the victory of the Jazz and People's Movement (JPM) and performed Mingus's combative hymn, "Haitian Fight Song." The dumbfounded Feather wrote accurately, "January 24 was a unique night in the history of jazz on the small screen."[9] In an apparently unrelated occurrence, Mingus received a handsome grant from the Guggenheim Foundation, this after JPM besieged their tastefully decorated office.[10]

Roach was no dilettante or even a simple purveyor of radicalism while safely abroad. The activist then known as Max Stanford of the Revolutionary Action Movement, best seen as a formation similar to the Black Panther Party, reached out confidentially to Roach in 1972 on the stationery of the allied African People's Party, headquartered in Cleveland. "I need a base in Africa, preferably Algeria," in aid of "consolidating the interna[tionale]," (that is, his global movement) while informing the drummer that "you can help on the Algerian asylum aspect. We will need to raise lots of bread [money] for what must be done [and] you could probably help on this." Unreservedly, he implored, "we need your help on economic matters" since "we have the potential of another Garvey Movement but on a higher and more scientific level."[11]

Roach was not alone. Multi-instrumentalist Clifford Thornton, born in 1936, was barred from entering France in early 1971 on the questionable grounds of being a Black Panther Party "suspect" and placed on a plane heading back to New York. However, later that year he appeared in Paris in a benefit for the BPP and from then on was working with greater frequency in Europe than at home.[12]

Buoying the musicians and their music was its continued popularity in defiance of the repetitive proclamation that "jazz is dead." By 1970, trumpeter, composer, and bandleader, the appropriately named D. Toussaint L'Ouverture Byrd—otherwise known as Donald Byrd—was teaching a class at Howard University in Washington, D.C., the self-proclaimed capstone of Negro education. "One of his classes," said a student journalist, that focused on the "History of Jazz" was "the largest in the University" in terms of enrollment.[13] "This is the only Black Music Department in the country," said Byrd, recently installed as "Chairman of the new Afro-American Music Department." Byrd, said an inquisitive journalist, "had worked with such greats as . . . [John] Coltrane, Coleman Hawkins and Charlie 'Bird' Parker."[14]

This vibrancy at Howard may have been difficult to ascertain because of ideological blinders. Disconcertingly, the dominant ethos in the United States promoted a liberal form of "integration"—at times at odds with the increasingly radical bent of artists—and which often meant disbanding longstanding affiliates of musicians' unions dominated by African Americans (or ignoring trends at Negro colleges, for that matter), depriving these artists of an independent power base, won against tremendous odds, in favor of consolidated unions dominated by Euro-Americans, often leery of these competitors, often seen as more talented and more able to compete for a finite number of jobs and worthy of being blocked at every turn. Thus Black musicians, in particular, continued to seek work overseas, and though this provided a kind of haven from the indignities of the United States, the experience of Coleman and Haden in Lisbon demonstrated that there were no pristine safe harbors—at least not yet. A poignant moment arrived just after Haden's escape, when trumpeter Lee Morgan, born in 1938, suffered the ultimate hazardous working condition when he was slain on the bandstand in Manhattan, a victim of intimate-partner violence.[15]

Intriguingly, in what was billed as his "last interview," Morgan sounded notes that were to resound loudly in coming years. He lamented the fact that the music in which he specialized was admired more abroad than at home, signaling the continuation of exile; he was seeking to purchase a club himself in California—the Lighthouse—and hailed the JPM, of which he was a leading member.[16]

Further punctuating the harrowing encounter endured in Portugal was the vicious attack on Haden and his Liberation Music Orchestra in the pages of *Downbeat*, enunciated even before his startling performance, indicating the uphill climb yet to be traversed by musicians of unquestionable integrity.[17]

IN EARLY 1970, IN NEW ORLEANS, putative birthplace of the music that had now swept the planet, there was taking place the merger of two locals of musicians after three years of negotiations. There was "acceptance of the merger by members of the predominantly white local 174 and rejection by members of the predominantly black Local 496," according to *Downbeat*. The latter had "greater per capita wealth," unsurprising, given the well-recognized creativity and artistry of the musicians; moreover, there was the fear of "possibility of loss of black representation due to the greater numerical strength of the white local" in a town where Jim Crow lingered angrily. There was an alternative: the "two-union system could have continued in a manner similar to the setup in the city's longshoremen's union."[18]

In Pittsburgh, another center of the music—as Art Blakey, Stanley Turrentine, Billy Eckstine, Mary Lou Williams, Erroll Garner, Ahmad Jamal, George Benson, and Billy Strayhorn could well attest—a similar scenario unfolded. The two segregated locals signed a merger agreement in 1964 at a time of undue racial optimism, and at the end of a five-year period the unions were supposed to have integrated their members. However, in 1969 it became painfully obvious that the merger had not benefited Black musicians. In fact, they had lost by just about any measure. They were underrepresented among the leadership of the merged union. In response, Black Musicians of Pittsburgh—BMOP—was formed, and a lawsuit was filed against the union and its officers. After five years of litigation, BMOP lost when the suit was denied.[19] This unfortunate result ensued though top-flight attorneys Melvin Wulf and William Gould (soon to be a law professor at Stanford University and a leader of the National Labor Relations Board in Washington), pointed to a "statistical exclusion from Executive Board positions" of the union.[20] A distraught Gould admitted to his clients, "I am most disappointed. . . . The situation vis-à-vis the union is a lost cause from a legal point of view," though, as was typical of the times, he added incautiously, "I hope that you will not lose faith in the process."[21]

The merger was a bigger loss than had been thought initially. More distraught than Gould was close observer Shakura A. Sabur, who lamented that "when we merged with the all-white musicians' union,

Local 60 . . . our records got lost, somehow, after we turned them over to the white union. Now we have to prove our membership to get our benefits," a difficult task at best. "Some black musicians have even died without insurance; it just hurts." Moreover, "segregation in Pittsburgh prevented black musicians from performing in the higher-paying sections of town. But when segregation ended"—formally—"nothing changed" in that regard. Class collaboration had been a byword of the settler colonial regime in North America from its inception, and, unsurprisingly, "major white club owners" wound up "sitting on the executive committee of the white union," and wielded undue influence on the merged union to the detriment and dismay of Black artists. "The all-white musicians disciplinary board would increasingly impose 'discipline' in the forms of suspensions and fines against Black musicians who defied the unspoken 'ban' against performing in all-white clubs." Also unsurprising, where the major sports team was called "Pirates," the city at the juncture of three rivers "had its fair share of gangsterism too." Unsettled, Sabur dazedly proclaimed, "How we lost our case, I'll never understand. We even lost our appeal," he said, apparently laboring under the illusion that a sound legal argument was sufficient to prevail in an adverse political climate. "The court maintained that we were active participants in the negotiations that limited us to three years of representation on the merged union Board of Directors," though "there was no mechanism in place, then or now, to undo discriminatory practices. All the white union had to do was wait us out," which they craftily did. "That's essentially what happened," that is, "they waited until the 'transition' period ended was over and went back to business as usual. When the 'integration transition period' ended in 1971, so did black representation on the Musician Union's Board. We run for office but we don't get any votes." The "biggest tragedy," Sabur said resignedly, "is that too many black musicians have also stopped playing," frustrated, as they were, with a rigged process. It was quite a comedown from the heady days of 1960 when the "Afro-American Musical Association" was chartered, preceded in 1908 by the now defunct Local 471.[22]

Musician John Hughes, born in 1924, joined 471 in 1940—"we started young in those days"—and spoke movingly of their building as a one-stop shop for legal aid, food, and other amenities. An arriving musician from out of town could stop by for briefings and fellowship. Educated at Duquesne University, this educated artist also regretted the compelled merger.[23]

"I didn't like the idea" of the merger anyway, said Joe Harris of the former Negro local, "because it was like we were merging with [Local] 60, 60 wasn't merging with us, we were merging" and "that affected me." Harris, a drummer who was to perform in Europe, continued, "I felt that we [should] have just stayed [in] 471." His interlocutor, Charles Austin, reminded him, "The federal law mandated that we merge" in response to the mania for integration, and "we were one of the last cities to merge . . . we didn't want to merge, and it was an abrasive time." After all, "we had a $1,000 death benefit" and "they only had $500 on theirs. So when the merger came up, in some kind of way, then everybody got the $1,000 coverage, which was a plus for them" but, at best, a standstill for the Blacks.[24]

Herman Hill was also sour about the merger. He did not see Local 802 of New York City, a desegregated affiliate, as a model. Like others, he had honed his craft in a military band, playing trombone and other horns, before decamping to Lionel Hampton's draconian band, then to the band of the singer Lloyd Price. Bitterly, he recalled about his hometown, "I played in a nightclub over there [on the] Northside with all them faggots." Yet even this epithetical experience hardly prepared him for the rigors of the merger. It was "so abrasive," he said, using that frequently cited adjective for the process, since "we didn't want to go, so everything we turned in they put on the third floor in boxes and left them [to] sit. They didn't go through it . . . they pitched everything out," destroying records and puncturing memory.[25] More than this, this painful process also served to discredit "integration," if not "desegregation," which advantaged the Nation of Islam.

A similar controversy concerning merger of segregated locals also erupted in the other seedbed of the music: Kansas City. By early 1970, *Muhammad Speaks*, the organ of the ascendant Nation of Islam, detailed the fracas in what it termed the "union of Charlie Parker," that is, "KC local musicians union chooses not to integrate with white group." The observant journalist saw the music as a legacy of Africa—Congo more specifically—and objected to what was seen to be the hijacking of it. Richard Smith, one of their sources, concurred, averring, "We can stand alone," speaking of African American musicians, not least since "we have been here as an organization since 1918." There was fear that a merged union would not protect the essential integrity of the music. Also in this newspaper was an account of the farewell address of Benjamin Mays from the leadership of Morehouse College, where he mentored Dr. King; he predicted that a new battle was then emerging with "liberals" in light of the undetected conflict between desegregation (which was supportable) and integration (which was problematic).[26]

James McConnell of Kansas City "found the merger of Locals 34 [white] and 627 [Negro] not to be in good taste for the black musician," since the latter was "not treated fairly." Consonant with the national trend, he said, it was ascertained that "black musicians are farther away from playing the nice, decent jobs than ever in history . . . Why aren't there any black musicians playing in the Police Circus Band? Why aren't there any black musicians playing in the American Royal Group? Why don't black musicians play some of the good jobs? . . . Why and who started the lie [that] black musicians are never on time?"—one of the canards deployed to prevent their being hired. "Why and who started the lie [that] black musicians can't read music?" He could have asked also why non-Black musicians who might have an interest in undermining stiff competition could be depended on to refute canards leveled against that same competition. "Why are the black musicians beginning to feel that the merger was the worst thing to ever happen to them? Why do black musicians get less jobs now after the merger?" McConnell had first-hand evidence of what he was alleging: "I have never been called for any job from Local 34-627," the merged union. "I am a college graduate with a major in instrumental music." Yet McConnell was blocked from employment repeatedly. Addressing pointedly the parent body, the American Federation of Musicians, he instructed, "analyze this letter carefully . . . before all black musicians lose complete confidence in *our* so-called Local 34-627." With biting sarcasm, he ended his astringent message with the word "Musically."[27]

Yet despite the manifest difficulties thrown up by these mergers, there were those who were wedded ideologically to "integration" and tended to overlook the downside. Among this group was critic Ralph Gleason, who complained that "some of the leading local jazz musicians who were Negroes were against it," meaning the merger, and "many white jazz musicians didn't vote at all." He attributed this to the point that "all jazz musicians are apathetic on political and social issues."[28]

As in Pittsburgh, where an overlay of "gangsterism" complicated union politics, the same held true in Kansas City, perhaps more so. These thugs exercised influence in clubs where musicians played and were not known to be equal opportunity employers, placing their thumb on the scales in favor of Euro-American artists, with the latter often insufficiently politicized to object. A few years after the merger, Clarence Kelly, then heading the FBI, asked tellingly if organized crime was worse in western Missouri than elsewhere.[29] Kansas City, said the paper of record in this metropolis, "tolerated the presence of a powerful organized crime group for 50 years"—and counting.[30]

One of the key men in this cabal was Carl Civella; by the late 1970s he was, like many of his comrades, described as "wealthy," a turnabout from the time at the age of ten when he was deemed to be "incorrigible" in his lust for the fruits of crime. A decade later, he was viewed widely as a hoodlum and a suspected but—to that point—not convicted robber. He was also close to City Hall, not unusual, and useful in securing ill-gotten gains. Thus, he was identified early on in the machine-gun killing of a bank messenger and the theft of hundreds of thousands of dollars. He was charged in dealing morphine illicitly, as an epidemic of drug addiction coursed. For the latter, he was convicted, but his sentence of a year and a day was seen understandably as a veritable slap on the wrist. Afterward, he fled to Chicago, citadel of gangsters, after hometown comrades threatened to liquidate him, before returning after an interval. In his absence, racketeering displayed its malleability in welcoming into its leadership Max Jaben, described as a "Polish-born Jew"; he joined other Eastern Europeans, and Syrians too.[31]

The expansion of criminal ranks also meant an expansion of business interests, all of moment to musicians, including alcohol, vending machines, bars, taverns, and restaurants.[32] Through their influence within the Teamsters union, a conglomerate of workers and racketeers extended their tentacles into far-flung pores of the political economy. Many of the top leaders of this influential union actually came from Kansas City, including Daniel Tobin, who once drove a horse-drawn streetcar and was elected the leader of the union in 1907, and Roy Williams, undisputed chief of the Kansas City affiliate (the city's largest union) for more than a quarter of a century, before climbing the greasy pole to the top of the union. Williams was tied to Civella.[33]

Kansas City's fashionable "River Quay" district, once the site of car bombings when mobsters first began flexing their muscles, had by the 1970s become a bastion of their influence. It was estimated then that almost 80 percent of the bars and entertainment businesses were owned outright by mob associates or subject to their hidden ownership. Inevitably, the scene featured "go-go girls and prostitutes" and rampant money laundering.[34]

The Kansas City Teamsters were the connective tissue linking mob capital, Chicago, to mob paradise, Las Vegas, with all three sites seen as loci of hiring of musicians.[35] Their influence was not limited to those three cities. And, as well, African Americans wondered why they should be barred from scooping up this filthy lucre. Thus, in Cleveland, Don King—a Negro—was one of the biggest numbers bankers there by the late 1960s and, smartly, was seen by a critic as "close to Italians in the traditional Mafia." King owned a tavern at 78th and Cedar where pianist Erroll Garner often performed. And King often played what sterner critics derided as the "race card" when he asked why those of his ancestry should be excluded from lucrative income streams, an unanswered question that then propelled him to the top ranks of boxing promoters and unimaginable riches.[36]

Meanwhile, back in Nevada, rapidly developing a reputation as the premier state of crime—and a home for entertainers, musicians especially—mobsters did not relinquish their tight grip on affairs. Indeed, mobsters were extending their reach. Ralph Gleason commented that a pivotal figure in this unholy business, Frank Sinatra, swapped "Charlie

Lucky," a reference to the paramount gangster, Charles "Lucky" Luciano, "and the other mobsters for Spiro Agnew and Ronald Reagan, and who is to measure the difference?"[37] Contributing to the less than resolute approach by the authorities to crush organized crime was the romanticizing of these cutthroats. By 1972, there was an "Al Capone Memorial Jazz Band" in Chicago and, said a journalist, "members of the group are businessmen" bent on memorializing a disgraced figure.[38]

Also applying for a casino license was Abe Phillips, once arrested under the name of Sam Golden. "[I] met Mickey [Cohen]," infamous crook, "when I was about 10 years old," he confessed. "Next time I met him was about 1956. . . . I was his personal bondsman" and then his "personal companion. . . . We were friends as kids and it's pretty hard to ignore somebody because they want you to have dinner with them," he rationalized. But it was not just Cohen; this prospective club owner was on intimate terms with a murderers' row of Los Angeles gangsters, including John Roselli, known to have connections to U.S. intelligence agencies at the highest level: "I met [him] at the Friars Club," said Phillips/Golden, "and every time I went [there]," lo and behold, "he was there and I'd talk to him like I talk to the rest of them." Yes, he said, "I knew Allen Smiley," yet another racketeer, accused in the murder of a founding father of modern Las Vegas, Benjamin "Bugsy" Siegel (he was sitting on a couch beside him when he was slain by an unknown assailant).[39] Other unsightly men, including Robert Sunshine, a convicted perjurer and embezzler, were making applications for licenses, too.[40] Lyle Stuart was questioned about the "obscene" books he was known to publish, along with "pornographic literature" when he applied to invest in the Aladdin Hotel. "I am certainly not in any way mixed up with gangsters," he contended: "I have never violated the law." He was disbelieved when the State Gaming Control Board "moved and seconded that the application of Mr. Lyle Stuart be denied on the grounds that he has an unsuitable background"—"Motion is carried unanimously."[41]

Jobs for musicians in Las Vegas continued to be coveted. Organized labor was coming to play a preeminent role, and by 1970 Leonard Feather was marveling that "even on the lower echelons, casino employees do well. Musicians make $246 per six-day week."[42]

Due west in Los Angeles, complaints proliferated not unlike those from musicians in Pittsburgh and Kansas City. "When I first came out from Omaha," said saxophonist Preston Love, "I felt sure that as one of the very first Negro alto men I would be able to specialize in lead alto work as numerous white musicians do," but this proved not to be the case. "For actual livelihood," he told Leonard Feather, "I was forced to take rather menial employment outside of music while I watched musicians of less ability than I reaping a bonanza through being in a clique." His furor rising—possibly in distortion—Love pointed the finger of accusation at fellow artists: "Paradoxically the worst enemy of Negro musicians," he charged, "has been certain other black musicians who as arrangers, contractors, producers and A&R men discriminate [against] Negro musicians" in a manner "worse than any white leader or contractor"; in fact, he said accusingly, "they practically decide who will [perform] about 40 percent of the recording in Los Angeles"; this stitch-up was "controlled by certain Negroes (mostly arrangers)," with Quincy Jones fingered, along with Oliver Nelson, horn man, arranger, composer, and bandleader, born in 1932.[43]

Seeking to escape the clutches of the smoky cellars where the music was often performed and the barracudas, sharks, and other predators that operated same, artists began seeking income elsewhere. Cecil Taylor, pianist, applied for funding to the Rockefeller Foundation in order to subsidize a residence at Antioch College in Ohio. "I do not think of CT as a Black Nationalist," said an evaluator of his proposal, Howard Klein, a descriptor seen as negative. "He may be open to the inclusion of white jazz musicians," it was said, as "race" by Rockefeller was seen at least as important as talent. Yet, "since he sees jazz as basically a black art form it is reasonable to suppose that white involvement would be minimal." For, Klein announced irritably, "in the middle 1950s many black jazz groups began to practice what was called Crow-Jimism, the ostracizing of whites from their groups." Less attention was paid to the exclusion of African American artists from various venues, including film studios, Broadway, and symphony orchestras. Still, "black innovators such as CT, Ornette Coleman and others [are] going begging for chances to practice their art," though "the important white musicians who gravitated in the jazz field have also run against a wall of indifference. Such performers as Stan Getz, Gerry Mulligan, Paul Desmond, Lee Konitz and other sensitive players [sic] have dropped from the scene or else become entirely commercial and have lost the desire to experiment." There was a related fear that a "Black Nationalist" musician could provide succor to likeminded students, creating further problems—for some. "There is a strong militant group at Antioch, the Afro-American Studies Institute, which would like to capture this Jazz Project." Fortunately, the student Bill Brower—who went on to become an expert and promoter of the music in Washington—was seen as "being extremely bright and a natural leader."[44]

Despite the sympathy for Taylor, there was apprehension, as the Rockefeller Foundation was informed, that those from "inner-city ghettoes," the target audience seen as disruptive to the status quo and in need of assuaging, might not find the pianist's performances appealing since they "respond to music which impels them to dance" and Taylor's music was not seen as conducive to this manner of frolicking. Thus, the impulse was to fund music with "more grassroots appeal."[45]

The overriding fear, however, was that "Black Nationalists" at Antioch might be bolstered by a Rockefeller grant, and thus, the application was rejected. Yet these funders' skepticism may have been vindicated when Taylor lectured at the University of Wisconsin-Madison in 1971 and proclaimed "my being here is a result of the Black Student Strike in 1969," this in the midst of lambasting the "1820 sharecropper mentality" among club owners.[46]

Facing rejection from munificent foundations, musicians also turned to themselves and their ancestral community for support. Brooklyn, which produced both Max Roach and Randy Weston, was a hotbed for this strand of "Black Cultural Nationalism." The site of choice was "The East," a shrine to this trend, which accommodated performances by such musicians as Pharoah Sanders, McCoy Tyner, Roy Ayers, Rahsaan Roland Kirk, Dewey Redman, Sun Ra, and Lee Morgan. There were also lectures by the likes of the activists once known as Stokeley Carmichael and H. "Rap" Brown.

More controversially, the proprietors were also close to the regime of Forbes Burnham in Guyana, seen by Washington as a reasonable alternative to the Communist-backed Cheddi Jagan.[47] The East was joined by "Boomers," a nightspot for the music at 340 Bleecker between Christopher and Tenth Streets in Manhattan, billed as the "only black-operated club in [Greenwich] Village."[48]

By 1975, vocalist Joe Lee Wilson, born in 1935, was reported as joining the "growing list of musician clubowners with the debut of the Ladies Fort at 2 Bond Street" in Manhattan.[49] The reference may have been to Sam Rivers, horn man and pianist, who by 1975 was the proprietor of Studio Rivbea on Bond Street."[50]

Further uptown, a *Guide to New York Jazz Clubs* listed "Salaam No. 7, 115 Lenox Avenue" in Harlem, "part of a Black Muslim Mosque," providing "dinner jazz by top musicians."[51] Critic Stanley Dance knew that during this era it was "quite hard to discover who is playing uptown without phoning the joints or taking the A train," which Ellington memorably characterized as the "quickest way to Harlem."[52] By 1972, Billy Taylor and his partners were able to buy what was described as a "black radio station" in Savannah, the fifteenth out of 7,000 stations to be controlled by African Americans, though it was unclear if the format would allow for more playing of the kind of music that characterized Dr. Taylor himself.[53]

"Collective Black Artists," yet another agglomeration of musicians, continued to stir then, receiving praise from bassist Richard Davis, born in 1930, and his fellow master of the instrument, Ron Carter, who asserted that the group sought to "replace them," meaning "agents, promoters" and their sort and to "give the black artist a bigger share of the take, to obtain better conditions to work under."[54]

Artists continued heroically in their ongoing attempt to seize control not only of their creativity but the means of production too. Iola Brubeck recalled a time when "the first four sides Dave recorded . . . were peddled to every label small and large and no one was interested. By paying for the records himself, Dave got them on a local San Francisco label owned by Dixie-land musician Jack Sheedy. When the records started to sell, Dave was able to buy the masters back and started his own record company . . . with Max and Sol Weiss."[55] By 1970, the entrepreneurial and

well-connected Quincy Jones had formed Symbolic Music Productions
with bassist Ray Brown, born 1926, which was involved in record production and management.[56]

IN SHORT, MUSICIANS CONTINUED TO BE attracted to politics,
embracing various parts of the spectrum. The "Panther 21"—Black
Panther Party leaders and members on trial in Manhattan during
this tempestuous era—were able to escape a dire fate because of the
energetic fundraising of artists such as Wynton Kelly, Cedar Walton,
Jackie McLean, McCoy Tyner, Elvin Jones, Pharoah Sanders, Alice
Coltrane, Graham Moncur III, Freddie Hubbard, Anthony Braxton,
Leroy Jenkins, Steve McCall, Leo Wadada Smith, and many more.[57]
John Hammond tried to get singer Nina Simone, born in 1933, to do
a benefit for the Panthers in New Haven, then facing ghastly travails:
"God knows," he said accurately, "this is about as controversial as any-
thing can be in this day and age but I thought it might stir some fond
memories of the past."[58]

In a similar vein, pianist Herbie Hancock's pulsating composition
Ostinato (Suite for Angela), was a musical salute to Angela Davis, who
maintained ties to both the BPP and the U.S. Communist Party.[59]
Pianist Horace Tapscott released an album in league with BPP leader
Elaine Brown, but as so often happened, their rousing rendition faced
severe challenges in being distributed in record stores. Multi-talented
singer and songwriter Eugene McDaniels, collaborated with horn
man Eddie Harris and keyboardist and vocalist Les Mc Cann on their
still powerful *Compared to What*, which reprimanded lyrically the
"President" and "his war," referring to the bloody conflict in Vietnam
then unfolding. It was the protean Mc Daniels who collaborated
with Tapscott on compositions in homage to slain BPP leaders John
Huggins and Alprentice "Bunchy" Carter, and, again, it was the very
same lyricist and pianist who wrote music in honor of yet another slain
BPP leader, George Jackson. Mc Daniels also worked with bassist Ron
Carter, perhaps the most recorded musician ever on his instrument, in
writing music critiquing President Richard M. Nixon.[60]

A similar group of artists emulated Hancock and raised funds for
the trial of Angela Davis, including Harold Battiste of New Orleans,

who was to join the Nation of Islam.[61] Trumpeter and bandleader
Gerald Wilson, born in 1918, organized benefit concerts for the
NAACP.[62] Raising funds for the Congress of Racial Equality were
Thelonius Monk, Ben Webster, Brubeck, Roy Haynes, Weston, and
many others.[63]

Vocalist Nancy Wilson, born in 1937, was proud of her assistance to
Dr. King: "Being there for Martin's lieutenants," she said, "making sure
that they were housed and fed and going to the Justice Department to
make sure that they were protecting blacks running for elected office
. . . going to Selma," to protect voting rights. "I remember the rifles
that pointed at my head. But I had to do it," she insisted. "I was the
hostess for the first UNCF telethon," she boasted justifiably, referring
to the United Negro College Fund, which performed yeoman service
in raising funds for higher education. What was her inspiration? "I
got the first Paul Robeson Award too. That was special for me." She
was also "vice president of the French Club" in high school, providing
her with the linguistic acumen to advise musicians interested in exile.
And, like many women artists, she had to endure the discomfiting
disruption of some elbowing aside of her spouse as they sought to
reach her.[64]

Other innovative artists, finding it difficult to survive in an adverse
climate, fled to other occupations. Pianist McCoy Tyner, who had
seemed to rocket to fame after accompanying the sainted Coltrane,
was reduced to driving a taxi after Coltrane's passing in 1967. His
comrade, drummer Sunny Murray, born in 1936 and who would die
in exile in Paris in 2017, did the same. Those were the days, said Tyner,
of the "starvation band," an ironic accoutrement of the celebration of
the demise of segregated union locals and the supposed new birth of
freedom that was expected to ensue.[65] According to Tyner, before his
career took off Coltrane was considering becoming a construction
worker,[66] ironic in light of the wealth the saxophonist generated.[67]
Also, driving a taxi and toiling for years at the post office, providing him with the sobriquet the "Wailing Mailman," was saxophonist
Roger "Buck" Hill, born in Washington, D.C., in 1927.[68]

Likewise hustling for fares was saxophonist Dave Liebman, born
in 1946, who eventually hit the jackpot with Miles Davis. "I realized,"

he said later, "that the only way I'm going to get good, is playing man hours spent on the horn," that is, "serious eight-hour-a-day practicing" was his path to Davis. Back then, he said, "everybody," meaning those like himself, "was driving a taxi or [working as] a bartender or whatever." This was during the late 1960s and early 1970s when "jazz [was] at a very low point." He hooked up with Ten Wheel Drive, a rock band, and garnered "$125 or $150 a week," then with Elvin Jones, which allowed him to quit his job as a substitute teacher in the Bronx, rescuing him from "death."[69]

Bassist "Monk" Montgomery became a construction worker in Los Angeles, building swimming pools, and found that this setback affected his confidence in his musical ability, generating "insecurities." Then, the career of his brother, guitarist Wes Montgomery, ascended skyward, which had the opposing problem of adjusting to stardom. The bassist had to adapt with difficulty to being an accompanist of his younger brother, and there was speculation that the resultant tension may have contributed to the latter's heart problems and premature death, though, said the bassist, he was a "chain smoker and he was smoking these cigarettes made out of lettuce." Then, the bassist had to "fight the system" when he sought to organize a music festival in gangster-infested Las Vegas. "I had posed a threat to someone," he said ominously, and, undaunted, he "made a big issue out of that" and "there was a big scene." He "got threats on my phone," but, wisely, "knew I couldn't go it single-handedly. That's why I formed the Jazz Society" in 1975, organized in conjunction with comedian and drummer Bill Cosby. Soon it boasted of a membership of "500" as the beleaguered music received a boost.[70]

Yet Nevada was not altogether reflective of national trends. Pianist Andrew Hill, born in 1931, surveyed the landscape in 1973 and lamented, "I see some of the best musicians in the world on welfare. And that's really a shame"[71]—and an outrage too, he could have added. Nonetheless, it was undeniable that the erosion of Jim Crow had opened opportunity for those in a position to take advantage. Trumpeter Eddie Henderson, born in 1940, had a profitable sideline as a physician and psychiatrist,[72] as well as touring intermittently with keyboardist Herbie Hancock,[73] born the same year. Stride pianist and composer Lucky Roberts, born in 1887, was able to do sufficiently well enough that his grandson, Charles Willis, was running for an elected post as a judge in New York City—"one of two black judges in upstate New York" was the message conveyed to John Hammond.[74]

The pitfalls befalling musicians were no better illustrated than the experience of Ornette Coleman, not just being harried in Portugal, but later he admitted that there had been furious disapproval of his musical innovations, which did not enhance his bank balance: "I've had people come up to me" he said in 1973, "and spit in my face and try to beat me up."[75]

A sturdy perennial had yet to disappear, erosion of Jim Crow aside, as drummer Roy Porter ascertained: "In my experience," he declared, "most managers, book agents and accountants (black or white) will steal from their clients if they can." His comrade Charlie Parker "died a pauper," yet the "record companies that recorded him are still making money off of his records." He was particularly harsh in assessing record producer, discographer, writer, and radio presenter Bob Porter, terming him a "fast talker" who "creates a good deal of animosity with his egotistical and heavy-handed work methods. In fact, I heard from others who were involved" with various projects involving him that "they never received a cent." The besieged drummer was sufficiently concerned that he began packing a pistol. Nowadays, he concluded wearily, "sad to say, the jazz musician is treated as a third-class citizen in the world of music."[76]

Composer, bandleader, and multi-instrumentalist Don Ellis was of like mind. Born in 1934, this native Angeleno told John Hammond that "you are one of the few people in this business that is completely honest and fair and that can be trusted." Earlier, he had signed a deal with Irving Mills, ill-famed for cheating Duke Ellington repeatedly. That accord, said Ellis, deprived him of "50% of my royalties . . . I only signed this agreement," he explained, "because he promise[d] to back the band to the tune of twenty-five thousand dollars which he soon reneged on."[77]

Mills, who could be grouped with Joe Glaser as a dominant exploiter of musicians, apparently bought the mega-hit "Caravan" from Juan Tizol of the Ellington band for $25, which was not extraordinary, said the Puerto Rican composer and trombonist, born in 1900. He was asked, "Things with you and Duke [Ellington with] Irving Mills's name . . . he didn't write any of the music, did he?" Tizol responded, "No, no. I don't think so. No." His spouse said of Mills, "He didn't write the music—Juan wrote the music." Tizol was ill-positioned to object, given his colonial status in the United States.[78]

Charles Mingus had a similar experience, though his was not with Ellington. "I hardly played one year with Lionel Hampton," he said. "I wrote a lot of arrangements," but "he never paid me. That's why he's a millionaire, I had a copyright on 'Mingus Fingus' myself . . . but his wife said they wouldn't record it unless I assigned it to their publishing firm. A lot of people do that."[79] Mingus's partner, Max Roach, was similarly vociferous in his denunciation of "club owners, agents, promoters," all of whom "provided only bad contracts, low salaries, inferior working conditions and cultural discrimination."[80] Of course, club owners faced their own pressures, for example, in 1968, when a club in Raleigh was targeted by white supremacists with the threat of violence, this after Thelonius Monk was slated to perform.[81]

Dexter Gordon may have concurred with this dyspeptic outlook when he returned to Los Angeles in the 1970s from his sinecure in Copenhagen. "I was shocked that there was no press interest in Dexter in Los Angeles, especially since it is his hometown. I noted that they had a Chick Corea Day and he is from Boston." Such was the dismaying message conveyed to Gail Roberts of Columbia Records in words that likely influenced how Gordon would be promoted and how his album sales would eventuate.[82] (It may not have been recognized that Corea had an advantage in that he was a member of the Scientology religion, which was known to boost well-known believers so as to attract others. Lee Konitz also was part of this group in the early 1970s: "The only time I really played with Chick Corea," he said, "was in the Scientology connection at different places."[83] Dave Liebman, saxophonist, also "did Scientology" for a while, though he said he was Jewish.)[84]

Perhaps more concerning was the message to Gordon's Danish attorney that his globetrotting might mean that he had tax liabilities in more than one nation.[85] These manifest problems notwithstanding, the lanky horn man could be comforted by the support he received from fans like Lou De Caro, who told him that "your music has really contributed to my emotional well-being, amidst loads of study and pressure." Moreover, he said, it "seems to proclaim the majesty of God."[86]

During this conflicted era, the U.S. ruling elite continued to build bridges to practitioners of a music once scorned. President Nixon, whom Leonard Feather had reason to believe had organic connections to racketeers,[87] invited an elderly Duke Ellington to the White House and bestowed upon him the highest civilian award of the republic— the Medal of Freedom. The visibly touched bandleader responded by bussing the smiling politician four times on both cheeks.[88]

This was a belated recognition of the luminosity of the resourceful composer, an example of the "best of times, worst of times" dialectic of the state of the music during this era of contrast, with the latter often exacerbated by inexpert marketing. Shortly after the White House ceremony, producer Norman Granz recalled that "some years ago . . . when I was managing Duke Ellington, I had a long meeting with Goddard Lieberson, president of Columbia Records," and suggested that they should "record everything [the composer] wanted to put on tape" and added that it "shouldn't cost more than $100,000 a year and for a company grossing more than $100,000,000 (and with its parent [CBS] close to a half billion) and considering that half of this would be borne by the U.S. government by way of tax deduction," this would be a profitable venture indeed. Lieberson "flatly rejected the idea, saying that the sales figures of Ellington didn't warrant this project." This unfortunate decision was made "three or four years ago," circa 1967, though the negative vibrations of this monumental omission continued to reverberate, arguably to this day.[89]

This sin of omission was compounded by sins of commission to which the bandleader was subjected, raising the disturbing point that if one of his stature could be rooked systematically, one can only imagine what befell others of less elevated status. Poring over his files, John Hammond found that "the first sign of domestic royalties" that he found "in any of the correspondence in the Ellington files" at Columbia Records did not appear until 1939. "Who knows what kind of side deals there may have been between Irving Mills," his alleged agent, "and the American record company," that he supposedly faced across the negotiating table. "I worked for Irving Mills, in 1934" said Hammond, and found that the "artists themselves ended up by owning 1/3 of themselves," a helter-skelter retreat from the 3/5 of a person that was the designation for Africans at the Republic's founding. "After 1939," said Hammond, "Ellington broke away from Irving Mills," whose name remained on a number of the pianist's compositions nonetheless, meaning the deprivation of Ellington heirs.[90] Apparently, the executives at Columbia did not consider Ellington's continuing fashionableness overseas, a trend assisted by his own generosity, such as when his orchestra arranged a well-attended benefit concert in Japan and donated over 900,000 yen after a devastating earthquake.[91] When Togo, the small West African nation, placed Ellington on a stamp, it was clear that it was folly to ignore his fame abroad when contemplating record sales.[92] The failure to capitalize on Ellington's evident popularity was even more troubling when one considers his parallel role as a tastemaker, suggestive of his having a thumb on the pulse of commercial appeal. Iola Brubeck pointed out that "Duke Ellington heard them," speaking of her husband, Dave Brubeck's, group, "on the West Coast and was the first person to recommend them for a job in New York in the early 1950s."[93]

(Fellow producer George Avakian argues that Hammond "never liked" Ellington and, thus, his comments should be viewed with this in mind. "Ellington and Armstrong were the musicians who wouldn't talk to him," not least because he was a "strange person, very eager to grab credit . . . peculiarly self-centered and insecure."[94])

And if Billie Holiday is a guide, those that exploited these artists systematically remained in a position to profit from their art eternally. By 1972, she had been dead for years, but then new interest was stirred by a new movie and play about her storm-tossed life. "Just one minute of Billie on record," said Hammond, "is worth more than anything in either the play or the movie," and since "all of the best Holiday material is on Columbia," this company was destined to profit handsomely. "Bad as they are," Hammond continued, "both the film and the show are going to do business and are going to make people want to know how Billie really sounded."[95] Hammond knew of what he spoke. A few years later, he was determined to produce a record with Helen Humes, the "best jazz singer around," in his opinion. "I want to do an album," he told Bruce Lundvall of Columbia, "and feel I can bring it in for under $7,000," a bargain since there "won't be any arrangements" and a "maximum of seven musicians."[96] This stinting was bound to produce a bonanza, given the growing popularity of this vocalist.

Miles Davis, the son of a dentist, was able to do relatively well financially, despite the negative publicity that often attached to his stage persona and offstage disputation. Abbey Lincoln recalled a time when he was taking home "$5,000 a week."[97] (By way of example, in the early 1970s at the height of his popularity, Thelonius Monk still could be paid $2,500 per week for club engagements, minus his booking agent's 10 percent commission.)[98]

Davis's sideman, Jimmy Cobb, recalled a time when the trumpeter bumped into Sly Stone, then a keen purveyor of wildly popular music, who said, " 'Yeah man, I worked in . . . Madison Square Garden last night. I made 83 grand.' Miles says, '83 grand!' Right after that I went by Miles's house. He had a closet full of funny-looking little suits and hats and all that stuff. I say, oh, wait a minute. So he went into the music," meaning Stone's variety. "He had the wah-wah pedals. Boy, he went all out."[99]

Enhanced income did not curb Davis's disputatiousness. Producer Teo Macero, with whom he frequently collaborated, took note of an article detailing the trumpeter being shot in Brooklyn.[100] Given the rebelliousness of the era, Davis's bad boy image might not have harmed his record sales. In 1970 John Hammond pointed out that "an artist like Miles Davis usually does around fifty thousand albums domestically and still is a tremendous name in European countries." Davis's chameleon quality, adapting to emerging trends, was wise, according to Hammond. "Miles has been smart enough to maintain contact with the young," he said, referencing Fillmore East in Manhattan and Club Baron in Harlem. Thus, his profile was heightened, though "sales of old-time artists in jazz such as Willie 'The Lion' Smith and Eubie Blake are disappointing to say the least" and "big bands like Basie and Buddy Rich usually make their costs, although sales are by no means spectacular." Interestingly, the British invasion—"thanks to the pioneering work of the English group," as he put it—had given a boost to the catalogs of those like Bessie Smith, Robert Johnson, and other blues performers. However, the popularity of these Europeans might have sliced into the overall sales of Davis's peers. There were then "about ten spots with decent jazz in New York," said Hammond, and "even artists like Bill Evans and Gil Evans are having trouble getting either engagements in clubs or on records," and "except for Newport and Monterey the festival outlook is dim." The hopeful sign was the fact that increasingly trendy chat shows hosted by Dick Cavett, David Frost, Johnny Carson et al. tended to hire house bands that were then pressed by JPM and other groups to diversify the ranks of musicians hired.[101]

It was not just chat shows that created paychecks for musicians. "Trummy" Young spoke of the "hundreds of shows I've done, starting with *Life of Riley* and *Gunsmoke* and *Hawaii Five-0*," though these television shows brought no residuals or continuing payments when rebroadcast, which happened with these programs that were often shown worldwide. He also worked with comedians Flip Wilson and Carol Burnett. The absence of residuals irked him: "The band gets nothing. That's one of the beefs we've had," since "our [union] leadership is really not on our side." The myopic union boss, James Petrillo, at the outset of this new medium opined that "he really didn't believe that TV was going to last," indicative of his dearth of vision. "That's a fact!" Young insisted, speaking of this wrongheaded prediction. "Consequently, the musicians' contract with the TV networks regarding filmed shows was ridiculous. We get nothing." Still, spending "three years" in Hawaii was not exactly stressful. Besides, said Young, "I didn't start to make any money until I disassociated my name from jazz" and migrated to TV and movies. Here he had advantages and disadvantages. "People always thought jazz musicians couldn't read" musical notation, especially in Hollywood, yet another excuse for excluding Blacks," especially "typical black musicians or typical black people" but "sometimes I didn't fit the typical role because I had red hair and freckles, so they'd stick me way in the background.[102]

Clark Terry also made his mark in Hollywood, but when Skitch

Henderson left the *Tonight Show* with Johnny Carson, one of the most profitable shows on the small screen, "it was rumored," said the trumpeter, "that I was up to lead" the band. "But the word came down that if they had a black person in front of the band, it would ruin the ratings in the Southern market." Justifiably, Terry exclaimed, "I was . . . pissed" at this "racist crap."[103]

Hammond was sufficiently sagacious to combat "racist crap" when he helped to produce an album by enlightened folksinger Josh White in 1939. Bayard Rustin, the activist who happened to be gay and who was to aid Dr. King, "was one of the singers in that group" and Hammond "almost lost my job at Columbia because of my insistence on putting this album out." But with the onrushing anti–Jim Crow movement flexing its strength, there was "absolutely nothing that we cannot put on record having to do with protest or injustice."[104]

Near the date of Lieberson's unfortunate decision, Louis Armstrong's agent, Joe Glaser, exposed a reason why the business was suffering—poor management decisions—when he said the trumpeter and singer "made records 20 and 25 years ago that are still selling and bring in thousands of dollars today and more than new ones other people have made more recently."[105]

Glaser had a point. The record of Dave Brubeck, not generally viewed as a pathfinder in the music, unlike Armstrong and Ellington, helped to prove the point (though, arguably, his not being Black may have aided his sales, trailblazing aside). In 1969 Iola Brubeck declared that "if you measured success by the number of single records sold, then the 'apex' for [his] Quartet would have been about 1963," with the "middle fifties" being the "years of rising popularity. Dave signed with Columbia in 1954 and before that had recorded only on his own label, Fantasy, which incidentally cost more to run than was ever made" and "had small distribution for promotion. Dave's 'rise' in the fifties was not due to phenomenal public relations," she said. "As for the time and money spent on actually recording," she continued, "a great deal more goes in to a [Miles] Davis record or Monk's sessions, because of the way in which they work and their temperament. Ask Teo Macero," she said, speaking of the recording producer. "So I do not think any favoritism is played within the jazz ranks at Columbia," a frequent accusation. Thus, "if you care to measure commercial success by the contract price per engagement and the size of audience, then 1967 was undoubtedly the peak year" for Brubeck. Serving to propel Brubeck into the stratosphere of popularity was the endorsement of such stars as "Bud Powell, Charlie Parker, Cecil Taylor, Willie 'The Lion' [Smith], Louis Armstrong," all of whom "at one time or another put in print . . . remarks to reporters their admiration of the group and for Dave." She did not say so, but, like Elvis Presley and the "British invaders" who were thought to gain popularity by performing African-derived music even though they did not share this ancestry, Brubeck's popularity may have been propelled by the imprimatur placed on him by those seen as the originators of the music. Brubeck paid his dues, in any case, she said, since "he worked his way through school by playing in Negro joints in town and [during] summers he was a cowboy on a large cattle ranch."[106]

It was true, as noted, that Brubeck was on the side of the angels when it came to disregarding the strictures of Jim Crow performance, and he risked lucrative engagements in order to do so. It is also possible that the evident difficulty that proficient pianists like Tyner had in surviving financially during this same era may have been a result of a backlash against Black artists, driven by anger at the erosion of Jim Crow and assisted by the companion rise of those like Presley and the "British invaders," factors that may have impacted Brubeck to a lesser degree. Max Roach discerned, for example, that British-born pianist and singer Elton John was by 1976 one of the biggest, if not the biggest, earner among musicians.[107] Though Black musicians could benefit from these new musical trends—Panama Francis was a drummer on Buddy Holly's tune, "Peggy Sue," which climbed the charts—he still saw this cultural turn as derivative. Francis was in a position to comment since he also drummed on "Bobby Darin's first big hit record, 'Splish, Splash.' . . . Listen to Presley," he said, "you will hear Otis Blackwell because he sang 'Don't Be a Cruel' and 'All Shook Up' exactly like Otis Blackwell sang them—note for note." But after Darin's tune "became a big hit, that's when he did the album," and "they used the all-white band," he said dolefully, and "I met him a couple of days afterward and said to him, I said, 'Look, Bobby, man, why didn't you call me to do your date?' He replied, 'Well, you know, when you move up in the world, you change company.' " Yet Francis had a deeper sense about what was at play. "When the bebop era came in," he said reflectively, "the music made a change. Instead of jazz being the music they would . . . dance to, it became music that they listened to," and, presto, "rock-and-roll was able to have such a foothold because people were able to dance to it." Jazz "will never die," but it would and could evolve, as it did in the 1940s.[108]

Saxophonist "Big Nick" Nicholas encountered a different problem with the rise of Presley and Darin. With this new twist, he said, arrangers "decided they wanted the tenor to sound like a cow and sound like a hawg [sic]. In other words, prostitute yourself, you know," discarding "all the years that you've studied and tried to create a beautiful sound. They didn't want that; they wanted noise" and he was uninterested in "demeaning" himself. The reduced market for horn men like himself led to more intense competition for remaining jobs, meaning that those once seen as "brothers" were now seen as competitors, to the detriment of close ties.[109]

But it was not just migrants from Europe who managed to do well. Jimmy Knepper was born in Los Angeles in 1927 and died in West Virginia in 2003, but this Euro-American trombonist conceded that when times got rough and tough he became "involved in landlordism in recent years,"[110] an option generally unavailable to most African-American musicians, most likely to muddle along as tenants.

Whatever the case, it was evident that Brubeck risked popularity by refusing to accommodate the backlash. After passage of federal anti–Jim Crow legislation, a spokesman for the Department of Music at the University of Alabama-Tuscaloosa, still struggling with state-sanctioned racism, recalled an earlier time when Brubeck had braved the brickbats of outrageous misfortune by daring to perform in the heart of Dixie with a desegregated quartet. "The program presented by you and your musicians was the first time that the box office at our main auditorium had been integrated," Brubeck was told. "We had a number of colored people at that program in spite of the fact that there was considerable threat on the outside by representatives of the KKK [Ku Klux Klan]." Thus, Brubeck was told, "the reception given you and your trio including the Negro musician was so enthusiastic that it took the minds of the worried few off the problem of admitting for the first time Negro patrons."[111] Expectedly, Brubeck's group did not spend considerable time touring Dixie; in one random month near the time of the Tuscaloosa event, the Quartet toured in Mexico, California, Hawaii, Japan, Hong Kong, Carnegie Hall, and England.[112] In other words, the Brubeck group should be recognized for its vanguard role in refusing to accommodate bigotry.

The pressure-packed venues in which the Quartet performed may have exacerbated preexisting tensions within the group. Saxophonist Paul Desmond, born in 1924, was essential to the popularity of the group and, said Iola Brubeck, contributed to "personality problems within the Quartet. Dave must be extremely careful that his actions do not displease other members of the group. Paul . . . is very uncooperative when it comes to doing any recording project and especially one that is different."[113]

Perhaps assuaging Desmond and keeping him on board in the group was the ability of Brubeck to monetize the popularity of his music again, at a time when other talented artists were being reduced to driving taxis. Nevertheless, Desmond's obstinacy may have been fueled by the fact that as a Euro-American artist in a musical form dominated by those not of that ancestry, he may have enjoyed opportunities unavailable to more typical musicians. By 1970, for example, Stan Getz was performing in apartheid South Africa, where scuttlebutt suggested that musicians of European ancestry like Getz could do quite well financially. According to *Downbeat*, he was "playing for whites only in Johannesburg, Cape Town, and Durban," reputedly the first jazz artist to visit the land of apartheid since the earlier performance of Bud Shank, horn man, born in 1926, and former accompanist of Stan Kenton.[114] Interestingly, in Getz's 1991 obituary, it was observed that unlike many musicians he was "well paid throughout his career,"[115] an indication perhaps of this utter flexibility, politically and morally.

Still, the German critic Joachim Berendt instructed Brubeck that "your music is white and I wonder why you are afraid of making 'white' music. There is nothing wrong about this," said this man who was apparently unfamiliar with U.S. history. Purporting to peer inside the pianist's brain, he told Brubeck, "you like the 'popularity' for its advantages but hate it for its artistic implications." One point he made was closer to the mark: "If your music proves strong, all the bla-bla-bla of us critics will vanish like ice cream in the sun."[116] Maybe so. Despite the blather about "Crow Jim," or purported discrimination invidiously targeting Euro-American musicians, less attention was accorded another trend exposed when a writer asked plaintively: "Is the white cornet style dead?" Accompanying a portrait of Bix Beiderbecke, born in 1903, was a quizzical comment about the "Negroid influence" in the music and the "essential heat of Negro jazz."[117]

Nonetheless, the Euro-American saxophonist Dave Liebman, who accompanied the mercurial Miles Davis, found "lots of tension" then, "a black white thing, a Black Panther thing. It was all Black Panther colors . . . and here's a whitey standing there." As for Davis, "I got along with him," he said, though he compared the experience to a "plantation system, in a way . . . . I've got to tell you something about the black guys," he confided. "I believe this. They—with each other, man, they were like, 'that's my property' . . . you were an indentured servant. That's actually—that's very true." He also found an over-heated bacchanalian climate in the business. With A& M Records, for example, "they meet you" on tour and "they're like, 'you want girls? You want dope?'"[118]

According to John Levy, it was the opinion of Larkin Arnold, an African American and one of the most influential entertainment executives and attorneys of the modern era, that "black artists were not getting the same treatment or support as the white artists."[119] If so, this too may have worked to Brubeck's advantage. Similarly, what John Gennari has called "white hegemony in the jazz business" also might have benefited the California-based pianist.[120] The crusade by the aide to Dr. King, the Reverend Jesse Jackson, to press Chess Records and other firms to hire more Black executives should be viewed in this light.[121]

Songstress Betty Carter in the 1970s reflected on this particular deficit. "Don Robie . . . was the first black man to have a record company; he recorded all the gospel groups in Texas years ago" and had died recently, spurring her eulogy. His "was the first black company, Peacock. ABC Paramount bought everything he had, when he died," adding to their considerable assets. Adding to the aforementioned analysis of Jackie McLean, she declared that because these companies paid so little to musicians, and often compensated them by feeding their drug habit, meant there were "so many records out today," depressing the value of their output. Still, there were a "few independent record companies" limping along "which have come to the forefront in the last four or five years," though it was "not easy to compete with the giant corporations like Columbia and Warner Brothers and ABC Paramount." This she knew because she had her own record label, "Betcar." She added, "nothing is easy, especially for black people in this country."[122] Drummer Jimmy Cobb laments the dilemma faced by those like himself: "Black people couldn't record for those companies," meaning Columbia and the like, "so, if they got a hit on the small companies," like Betcar, for example, "it would be repeated by the white artist in the big companies, exact same thing, the arrangement and everything." The disparity also extended to performance. Cobb's spouse, Eleana Steinberg Cobb, bitterly remembered when "in the '70s, the Bottom Line," a nightspot in Greenwich Village, "wanted to pay Larry Coryell," guitarist, born in 1943, "$5,000 and Jimmy $150 for the same gig, the same night."[123]

Panama Francis would have agreed. After playing on dates for Atlantic Records and watching founder Ahmet Ertegun become wealthy, he too decided to start his own record label but did not become successful. That's when he exemplified Carter's axiom for life not being "easy, especially for black people," for financial distress occurred "when I was having my problems at home, and I started walking into record dates screaming at people."[124]

It was left to the militantly named trumpeter and educator D. Toussaint L'Ouverture Byrd—Donald Byrd in short—who sought to add sustenance to the German critic's controversial assessment. "It's not talked about very much, but every orchestra was built along ethnic lines. The New York Philharmonic . . . was a German orchestra. One reason why [Arturo] Toscanini had the NBC Orchestra was because he couldn't get through as an Italian—they had to give him an orchestra and then he brought all the Italians in on the scene. The Boston Symphony," he asserted, "was a French orchestra," referring to conductors Henri Ribaud and Pierre Monteux.[125] (For some reasons, this did not bring peals of strident objection from popinjay critics with their knickers in knots crying "Crow Jim.")

Nevertheless, it remained true that often more opportunity was available overseas for practitioners of this musical form than at home, underscoring Byrd's dismay at opportunities for artists like himself at home. "I'm seeing a totally different lifestyle over here," a correspondent of Dexter Gordon said of his adopted Danish home. "Things move at a more relaxed pace. I can see why you lived in Copenhagen for so long. The people here are very friendly."[126] Thad Jones, trumpeter, might have concurred since when he died in 1986 of cancer, after a fruitful tenure as an arranger and composer for Danish radio, a street in Copenhagen was named after him.[127] Violinist Stuff Smith, born in 1909, also resided rewardingly in Copenhagen before expiring in 1967.[128]

Niranjan Jhaveri, in the city then known as Bombay, remembered fondly that Coltrane was "deeply involved" in his country and was hopeful that Gordon would act similarly: "While jazz has come that much closer to India," he said, "so far nothing has been done from India to welcome that trend and to assist in the process of moving Afro-American Music towards Indo-Afro-American Music."[129] Despite this oversight, he was elated to observe that "due to the deep interest most jazzmen have for India, its music and culture, we have been fortunate to have many great jazzmen in our concerts."[130]

Despite the obvious reality that jazz was appreciated deeply in India, for example, the foremost U.S. conservative intellectual, William F. Buckley Jr., an architect of the right-wing resurgence embodied by the rise of Ronald Reagan on a television broadcast asked the astonished Billy Taylor why the music called "jazz" was "so slow in crossing international boundaries." The pianist countered aptly, "It always fascinates me that people from other countries have an enormous appreciation for jazz and they recognize its power . . . much more rapidly than we tend to do here at home."[131]

Perhaps Buckley, who earlier had expressed deeply felt sympathy for apartheid South Africa,[132] allowed his racial blinders to over-whelm his anti-communist sympathies. His ideological confrere, Willis Conover, was as late as 1976 still marveling about his 1959 visit to Poland: "Hundreds of Poles met me at the airport," he recalled, and "today Polish jazz may be the best in Europe."[133] Tomasz Stanko, trumpeter, born in 1942, was clear evidence of what he said.[134] Stanko was preceded in residing in the United States by guitarist Gabor Szabo, born in 1936, who departed his native Hungary in 1956 for a stint at the Berklee College of Music in Boston and an extended stay in the United States.[135] "VOA here is effective," was the message about Conover's Voice of America, which was transmitted by U.S. envoy in Prague Thomas Byrne in the 1970s; this was so, Conover said, "since the Government" there is "unhappy with its programs." In fact, VOA was of "crucial importance in Eastern Europe," which was no exag-geration.[136] Prague aside, Conover thought he had reason to believe that Warsaw was miles ahead in terms of acceptance of the music he broadcast. Of the countries that had especially lively jazz scenes in Eastern Europe, "certainly Poland's first."[137]

Conover remained close to foremost anti-communist mouth-pieces, including *New York Times* columnist and former Nixon staffer William Safire, who once thanked him for his "friendly comments."[138] Still, Conover remained a figure of controversy: even the *Washington Post*, not hostile to his political outlook, found it significant that somehow by the 1970s he exercised a "monopoly as principal jazz consultant for several federal agencies,"[139] as this music came to be a tool particularly wielded abroad to sanitize and rationalize the otherwise racist image of U.S. imperialism. (Predictably, critic Dan Morgenstern rose to Conover's defense.)[140]

Nonetheless, musicians continued their flight abroad, though at times the tensions of home overcame them before departure. Such was the sad case of saxophonist Sonny Criss, a reported suicide in 1977 just as he was to start a concert tour in Japan. He was a mere fifty years of age.[141] (Also meeting a sad and tragic end was bassist Jaco Pastorius, born in 1951. By 1986, he was hospitalized and diagnosed as bipolar. Despite having reached the zenith of the profes-sion, performing with the band Weather Report, soon he was living in a park, then died of a brain hemorrhage after being assaulted by a manager in a nightclub.)[142]

Impelling their exile were numerous factors, escape from the uniquely pathological form of U.S. racism most notably, which carried special animus for descendants of mainland enslaved Africans.[143] Certainly, the fact that the radical left was in retreat in the United States, as Jim Crow was receding, was not helpful in forging class consciousness. This may help explain why in 1970 the drummer Kenny Clarke, then residing in France, informed his fellow percussionist, Max Roach, that he had "been on the 'Black-List' of Jewish promoters for the last twenty years," which was "one of the reasons I left the States. And they have all but followed me here," and had continued to persecute him. "I just can't seem to make any money. I work very hard but nothing happens." Yet, he insisted, "I'll find a way."[144] Unfortunately, this attitude was not Clarke's alone, raising searching questions about provenance. It was left to Leonard Feather, a former vice president of an NAACP chapter, to reprimand Austrian-born pianist Joe Zawinul for anti-Semitism after he attacked "Jewish people" in their relation to Black music.[145] Oppositely, Feather was reproached since—supposedly—he was "unable to give a fair review to the performance of white musicians" and was "conducting [a] one-man black superiority crusade and [was] convinced that [the latter's] success depended on ignoring or putting down white musicians. Racism is racism," said Leo Walker.[146]

Thus, though Europe was a refuge for many escaping the United States, hindrances did not disappear at times. "Slam" Stewart, bassist, born in 1914, observed in 1979 that "when I appeared in France and different parts of Europe, even in Germany, Denmark, Switzerland, when we were appearing and performing, we'd run across situations where we were being recorded by someone in the audience," that is, "bootlegging" and depriving artists of income.[147]

There may have been an accelerating flight—ironically with the dissipating of rigid Jim Crow—because as Max Gordon of the Village Vanguard put it, "The '60s were tough because of lack of interest in jazz."[148] Buddy Rich, the drummer and bandleader born in 1917, might have agreed. Once he earned as much as $2,500 per week playing alongside Harry James, regarded as "the highest salary paid to a sideman at the time." Yet by 1968 he declared bankruptcy.[149]

It was also in 1968 that Art Farmer, who had been toiling as a janitor in New York City, decamped for Vienna. "Young black musicians caught hell in Los Angeles in the late forties and early fifties," which he experienced firsthand, while "white musicians had the work at the few clubs sewed up." Thus, while he was compelled to work in menial posts at home, whereas in Austria he was exultant: "I have not [had] a single bad racial experience since I have been in Europe," he said. "No one has been rude, no one has ignored me, as people will do here," speaking of the United States.[150] Lack of work drove saxophonist and composer Steve Lacy from the United States during the same decade that Farmer fled. He spent time in both Rome and Paris, and, though he was not Black, he was loath to uproot and return to the States since "my drummer and piano player might not want me to come," since they were African Americans.[151] Again, this was not new. According to Dan Morgenstern, Coleman Hawkins spent the years from 1934 to 1939 in Europe, which he termed "perhaps the happiest of his life."[152] Arriving about a decade later in France, Howard McGhee, trumpeter, born in 1918, was ecstatic to find that the "people in Paris were so nice that I couldn't hardly believe that they were sincere," particularly compared to the United States, which he found "*horrible* . . . the way they treat Negroes."[153]

11. The Blues and the Abstract Truth

AS THE TWENTY-FIRST CENTURY APPROACHED, then unwound, the music that had originated decades earlier continued to endure setbacks and attain successes. Wealth continued to be generated, with the lion's share appropriated by those who deployed capital—as opposed to artists. Yet, as legends like Ellington passed from the scene, the bitter squabbling over his estate, indicated that the anti–Jim Crow movement had succeeded in ensuring that a modicum of riches would be bestowed upon creators. However, as the premature death of Oliver Nelson, musician and composer suggested, a paradox remained. African American artists continued to be whipsawed by the ills of society with a renewed malady added: death from overwork. African-Americans continued to encounter barriers, as well, in entering the managerial side of the business, not least in invading the inner sanctum of Organized Crime and forming rivals to giant record companies' domination of sales, marketing, and distribution. White House invitations to esteemed musicians had become au courant nonetheless. Unions continued to be wracked with tension, making it difficult for them to push aggressively for changes in the law to protect their members—charter members of the inherent insecurity of the "gig" economy that had ensnared a growing segment of the entire work force. Yet, below the summit of top-flight artists, there continued to be a growing number of amateur musicians, guaranteeing—at least—profits for manufacturers of musical instruments. Musicians continued to flock overseas too, a process now facilitated by the rise of supersonic air travel. There were those like Dexter Gordon, who reached a new measure of success by crossing artistic boundaries as an actor, reaping critical acclaim in the process, as he portrayed a troubled musician in exile in France. Nevertheless, as a Parisian might say in translation, the more things changed, the more they remained the same. For racism continued to mar and mark the political economy of the music.

BY THE 1980s, AHMET ERTEGUN'S WAGER on the viability of commodifying music had paid off spectacularly. Henry Kissinger, a former U.S. secretary of state, now en route to untold wealth himself as he commodified the insights he had gained in office consulting with corporations on "risk" to their global investments, told "Dear Ahmet" cheerily, "I cannot thank you and Mica enough for being such thoughtful hosts and entertaining travel companions" during his recent sojourn in Ertegun's commodious estate in Turkey.[1] Ertegun was by then a favorite in the most elevated ranks of the U.S. ruling elite. Dr. Kissinger perhaps did not know that the profitability of Atlantic Records, the Ertegun vehicle, was based heavily on the artistry of African American artists. Just before the diplomat's missive, Atlantic artists were running the table, sweeping accolades as the best in their respective fields. *Downbeat* judged pianist and vocalist Roberta Flack to be "best female singer"; Rahsaan Roland Kirk as "best clarinetist" and "best miscellaneous instrumentalist"; Gary Burton as "best" vibraphonist. Joe Zawinul, keyboardist, born in 1932 in Vienna—and voted as "best composer"—was an Atlantic artist who was not African American, though he made his mark accompanying Miles Davis and Cannonball Adderley, who were.[2]

Ertegun was not alone in cultivating the high and mighty in politics. By 1990, Steve Ross of Time Warner was informing Ertegun that the wider "company" of which Atlantic was a part had "never faced more important challenges in Washington than we confront this year. We have had no choice but to become totally immersed in the legislative and regulatory processes," which "requires us, of course, to make campaign contributions,"[3] placing capital's thumb on the political scales to the disadvantage of the artists.

It was not just Atlantic that was profiting from the creativity of Black artistry. By 1975, John Hammond, then at CBS Records, was told what he likely knew already: "Your company has probably the largest and finest collection of the Big Dance Bands and Jazz." Much of the "best was now on defunct labels" such as "Brunswick, Master, Vocalion, Epic, Coral, etc. to just name a few," with their rich catalogs now available for swallowing. "There are legions of collectors willing to PAY top dollar for some of these treasures," said A. F. McNaughton, Jr., who "over the years amassed in excess of 30,000 78-RPM records."[4] In other words, companies could profit from long-dead labels and artists, with many of the latter having signed adhesion contracts, leaving their estate and heirs bereft. Moreover, these exploitative deals, consummated in an earlier era when labor and Negroes alike suffered a deficit of rights, allowed companies to promote the music by these dead labels and artists, and, correspondingly, downplay younger artists to the overall detriment of the art: what this could entail took place in 2018 when with grand fanfare a 1964 recorded performance of Erroll Garner was reissued. The diminutive tinkler with the slickly pomaded hair had stopped recording for Columbia in 1958, in the midst of a protracted, bitter legal battle over payments and unauthorized release of his early work. Still, by the year of the 1964 performance, Garner was viewed widely as being as popular abroad as the supreme Louis Armstrong. Typically, in this elegant performance he used his right hand to play the melody in octaves with two or three notes filling in to emulate a brass section, while his left hand played the lower keys as if he were strumming a guitar. Nevertheless, it will be intriguing to track if this recording outsells those of today's first-rate pianists, for example, Jason Moran.[5] On the other hand, Duke Ellington albums continued to sell by 1990, long after he had expired, although it was then that Ertegun complained of the "dismal sales" of this late titan's records.[6]

McNaughton was among a coterie at the pinnacle of U.S. society who appreciated the music, though it was unclear if their influence was perpetually benign. For example, there was Edwin A. Ashcraft III, descended from an old Chicago family. He was a lawyer, as was his father. He lived in a sizeable and comfortable home in the posh suburb of Evanston. There he was often visited by musicians performing in nearby Chicago; this Princeton alumnus also played piano and was friendly with Bix Beiderbecke. Still, he served a lengthy tenure as a U.S. intelligence operative, including tours of duty with both Naval Intelligence and the Central Intelligence Agency, and it was unclear what he might have gleaned from musicians who toured abroad. He also spent considerable time in Washington, D.C., yet another mainstay of the music. Hank O'Neal, who for years was also responsible for promoting international jazz cruises, also was an intelligence operative who collaborated with him.[7]

Even Hammond had to object to some of the hardball tactics used by corporations to denude further struggling artists. "One of the problems in holding up payments to Alberta Hunter," he said in 1981 of the elderly vocalist, "is the fact that you want to have a five-year clause forbidding her to record the same material again within a five year period. Alberta is eighty-six," he said with exasperation, "and a five-year clause [is] obscene for an artist of her age. When I recorded [pianist] Eubie Blake in 1969 when he was eighty-six," he reminded, "CBS was happy not to insist on this clause."[8] But back then, there was a surging political movement. By the early 1980s, the counterreaction had begun to ossify, placing artists at a distinct disadvantage.

This was part of the paradox of the music as the late twentieth century unwound. On the one hand, there were some who were profiting handsomely from this relatively new art form; on the other, there were artists who were doing quite poorly and, in fact, abandoning the art altogether. One would have thought that Ben Riley, drummer, born in 1933, was at the apex of his profession, but he left Thelonius Monk's band and chose to withdraw from the music scene altogether. He took a job at a Long Island school working in the audio-visual department and worked for the YMCA.[9] As Riley was mothballing his drum set, Harold Mabern, Jr., a pianist and composer born in 1936, was complaining that "'even today if you go . . . to borrow money . . . and put down 'jazz musician' as your occupation, right away you won't get any cooperation [since] the stigma is still there.'"[10]

The miasma of profiling extended beyond the cosseted confines of banks. That same year, 1971, the instrumentalist Rahsaan Roland Kirk, coincidentally a political activist with JPM, was accused of "skyjacking" or attempting to hijack a commercial airliner, an act generally attributed to political dissidents. He faced these charges in Cleveland based on an anonymously rendered telephone tip and when searched, it was found that he was armed with a tear gas pistol and knife. The visually impaired artist said that he was a "student pilot" and said further that the knife was ceremonial and the pistol was for protection since he carried cash frequently.[11]

By 1980, one would have thought that Dave Liebman too was at the apex of his profession: how many musicians could boast of touring with Miles Davis? But by 1980, he was asking himself, "How am I going to make a living? This jazz thing is not going to pay" forever. "I'm not a star," he confessed candidly. So he migrated to teaching, declaring, "It saved me." He still performed, to be sure, though "80, 90" percent of his work was in Europe but not east of Vienna since the "Communists" despised the music, he opined, "because it's completely anti-authoritism [*sic*]." His peers, Herbie Hancock and Chick Corea, dominated the "Japan market . . . which is burgeoning into Korea, Manila" and outward; the "Japan-Australia thing" was the term he used. He was left with "one" market, Europe, "but without America, it's tough. It's tough." In his homeland, "we're at 1,500, 2,000 a night for the band," he said in 2011, "but not 8,000 a show," the going rate for certain peers, his assessment in 2011. "[Joe] Lovano's a low-level A," referring to the sax man born in 1952. "Herbie, Chick, McCoy—Wynton [Marsalis] of course," referring to the trumpeter and bandleader born in 1961: this quartet "was A top level. That's money," said Liebman. "I'm talking about money. I'm talking about filling the hall with 800 people. I cannot get 800 people in San Diego," he conceded. "I cannot get 800 people in San Francisco. It's not going to happen." The same could be said for Lee Konitz, who was "not making any more money than me, not really."

Still, there was yet another reason for his fateful 1980 decision. Liebman set aside his tenor saxophone and picked up the soprano, "basically to escape Coltrane . . . I couldn't escape Trane"—his style established a pattern that made others seem like pale imitators. A few years later Liebman "let the flute go" too since "you have to play every day to get a good sound. I just couldn't do it." By the mid-1990s, he started the "tenor again. But thinking of stopping again" was a preoccupation. For then he was having trouble handling the soprano, a "wild beast" of an instrument: "It's a hard instrument. It's high. It [has] a small mouthpiece" and thus "can be an annoying instrument" and "it can hurt your ears" too. Max Gordon of the Village Vanguard "couldn't stand it," for example. Being self-described as "Jewish" in an art form dominated by African Americans apparently shaped Liebman, even beyond the intimidation of seeking to excel or equal Coltrane. Late in his career, he heard the plaint, "I don't want any white drummers . . . we got to have some validity." It had to be Billy Hart or "Tain's great," referring to Jeff Watts, especially if "we can't get Jack," meaning DeJohnette.[12]

While Liebman was mouthing his complaint, the saxophonist known as Kenny G was telling Clive Davis, the record executive, "I heard you were in L.A. last week during the riots" of 1992. "It really does give one a strange feeling doesn't it? Lyndie and I were isolated from it but felt strange about living so well while others are living so poorly. That is why it is essential to be grateful for the good fortune that we all have."[13] Of course, this fabulously wealthy horn man was deemed to be part of the "white majority" in the United States that purportedly was subjected to "Crow Jim" or alleged discrimination against Euro-Americans. By 1999, Kenny G was so ensnarled with the contradictions of his anomalous position that he told Davis that "as jazz critics will undoubtedly have a 'field day' with this album" because of its hoary quality, "one way to offset this" was to "'give back' . . . as the forefathers of this music were mainly black, what better way to make the right kind of statement." That is, "why don't we sticker the album with something like 'for every record sold Kenny G and Arista [Records] will donate $1.00 (or whatever amount)" to a well-known charity. "Let's launch this story on a major show," he said excitedly. "Oprah would be the perfect place to tell this story" and, perhaps, sport star and entrepreneur Magic Johnson could be co-opted.[14] The saccharine-sounding saxophonist was emulating Ahmet Ertegun, who by 1990 admitted that "Atlantic Records makes a contribution to the United Negro College Fund at the end of every year, as well as on other special occasions, like my late brother's funeral," a gesture that reaped rich dividends.[15]

Kenny G aside, the more talented Liebman had sought to rescue his career of full-time performing by signing with drummer Jack DeJohnnette's Creative Music Agency, sited in Woodstock, New York. "We deal mainly with colleges and jazz societies," then proliferating as reliable performance venues, and sought to avoid charging "fees" for bookings, as it signed up Sam Rivers, Lee Konitz—and Liebman.[16]

Liebman was reflecting yet another trend. By 1980, the inexorable counterrevolution asserted itself with the election of Ronald Reagan as president, inaugurating a fierce pushback against the militancy of the recent past. Thus, Euro-American producer Teddy Reig used to travel to Harlem regularly and, according to his colleague Peter Spargo, the closer he got to this neighborhood, magically his "voice would change. He would actually take on a black accent!" But by 1982 "it wasn't possible to walk around up there anymore," as tensions mounted.[17] A decade later, the Negro critic Albert Murray was reproached. "My first warnings of the current racial jazz wars," Leonard Feather was told, were "when one day three summers ago . . . Al suddenly started calling me 'white boy' after almost eighteen years of friendship."[18]

Perhaps it was unavoidable that in a white supremacist society—and charges of "Jim Crow" followed in metronome fashion by shouts of "Crow Jim"—racial tensions would rise. By 1975, promoter George Wein had another target in his riflescope when he charged that African Americans were not supporting the music sufficiently, but Euro-Americans were,[19] a claim made without scrutiny of differing socioeconomic outcomes. For his part, Branford Marsalis espied another kind of bias; speaking of his quartet in 2012, he remarked that "there's some white people who come to the concert and just love the fact that there's a white guy up there," an analysis, which if true, could well contribute to a kind of "affirmative action" for Euro-Americans (or disadvantage for more qualified African Americans).[20] In other words, this suggested the precise opposite of "Crow Jim."

Still, it was unclear if the counterreaction would wipe out altogether the progress that had been made in entrenching the music in the previous century. By 1973, for example, there were about 175 "jazz festivals" occurring in the United States and Canada, with the average number of jazz bands participating in each festival amounting to twenty-five, with an average of twenty musicians per band—and 4,500 different bands involved in all the festivals.[21] These festivals required teachers and administrators and role models, too, which tended to benefit top-flight artists. By late 1973, it was estimated that there were 390,000 instrumental musicians currently involved in jazz education in all private and public schools.[22] As of 2013, pianist Billy Taylor found 40,000 jazz bands nationally, with each containing about twenty musicians, which, minimally, was a bonanza for manufacturers of instruments, who would have been wise to direct some of their profits to exemplars of the music.[23]

Whatever the quantitative figure, Clark Terry's qualitative analysis was difficult to deny. "No matter what," said the trumpeter, "racism was on the scene,"[24] continuing to handicap an ample cohort of musicians. Terry was stating an axiom. Still, malodorous conditions that beset Black artists also beset those who were not Black but were forced to toil in a profession dominated by them. Thus, Pepper Adams, born in 1930, was regarded as "jazz's most brilliant baritone saxophonist," yet the "last time he enjoyed a steady job as a leader was back in the summer of 1956," and by 1982 a report indicated that "he averaged about four full weeks of work per year, which never earned him more than two thousand dollars" annually, thin gruel indeed. "If it had not been for the generous support, respect and devotion of the European and Japanese jazz fans . . . jazz as a living art would now be dead" was the sobering conclusion and perhaps Adams's career along with it.[25]

As difficult was the route traversed by composer and trumpeter Woody Shaw, born in 1944. Legally blind, he fell onto a subway track in New York City and emerged with a severed left arm. He suffered complications in the hospital, possibly worsened by use of heroin, and he died of kidney failure in 1989.[26] Eddie Palmieri may not have suffered as much as Shaw, but he experienced grievous pain nonetheless. After a fiery dispute with his record company, "I suffered dearly," he recollected, "in those six years" at the height of his popularity. "I locked myself up in my house, without working . . . with no communication, nothing." His "family went through hell" coping with him and "financial things were very bad" too. He was suffering from an acute "depression," worsened by "tremendous problems with the IRS [Internal Revenue Service]." How did he survive? "We'd sell male and female prostitution, we'd sell every drug you could think of," and he would bounce from "one shylock to the other" obtaining funds for a perpetual emergency.[27]

Pianist Gene Harris, born in 1933, led a band sufficiently popular to make it to the august pages of the *Wall Street Journal* by 1988. Yet to make a living, he retreated far from the beaten track to the tiny capital that was Boise, Idaho. His guitarist, John Jones, could only survive by working in a pawn shop, while his bassist, Rod Wray, worked as a chef; his saxophonist, Charlie Warren, was a part-time construction worker; while Gib Hochstrasser, his drummer, had a band all his own.[28]

By 1975, Grover Washington, Jr., was well on his way to a chart-topping career, exemplifying his signature tune, "Mr. Magic," yet that lofty perch did not protect him from the casual indignities that routinely beset musicians like him. "We have to stay at the cheapest hotel [close] to the club," he complained of his rigorous travel schedule. "As soon as you say you're a musician at some motels, they immediately cancel you. They think you're going to be shooting drugs in your room, having four ladies in there, having a wild orgy," and otherwise trashing the room. Instead, he contended, musicians would practice their art, talk music, write music, listen to music.[29]

By 1975, McCoy Tyner seemed to be en route to the stardom that ultimately claimed him. Yet he found it hard to forget the difficult days when he earned a few bucks giving stranded pedestrians rides during a subway strike in New York City.[30] That same year, Stanley Turrentine was residing in Tyner's Philadelphia and recalled how he was barely making it. Then one day his wife "went shopping with my gig money and came back loaded with packages and an envelope was in her mouth." In it was an application for work at the post office. "I was so hurt," said the startled musician, "tears ran out of my eyes."[31]

Also on the scene was Exhibit A in Terry's hall of infamy: Irving Mills. "Irving Mills Music" was a thriving enterprise still in the 1970s, and it was then that Paul Mills, general manager of the company, told Earl Hines, the pianist, that "we acquired the Hi-Cue catalog and I would say that we are honored to be able to add your illustrious name to our roster of great artists."[32] It was difficult to shed copious tears for "Fatha Hines," however. In 1978 Stanley Dance, who operated as both critic and agent, á la Leonard Feather, said that "last year you paid me $5,700 on engagements I negotiated amounting to $150, 000" and now he was demanding "5% on all bookings made through agents" and "10% on all those we get ourselves," including recording dates.[33] Like Ellington, Hines too was invited into the inner sanctums of power. In 1967, President Johnson and his voluble spouse, Lady Bird, invited "Mr. and Mrs. Hines" to lunch.[34] By 1976, President Gerald Ford hailed Hines for the "superb musical program" he provided for the head of state of France.[35] By early 1980, Hines was a member of Artists and Athletes for Carter-Mondale, the Democratic Party presidential ticket subjected to a crushing defeat that same year.[36] However, Hines may unwittingly have given propulsion to the forces that triumphed in 1980. Earlier, he had agreed to perform in the land of apartheid, before accepting a hefty $9,000 in "settlement" for "cancellation of the South African tour."[37] Monk Montgomery, unable to refuse the emoluments offered, chose to perform in apartheid South Africa and accepted the contractual proviso that he would play only with African artists before racially segregated audiences.[38]

Hines also suffered the perils of popularity in the form of "bootleg"—or illicitly manufactured—recordings, for example, a performance featuring Coleman Hawkins on a "label called Pumpkin," according to the pianist's delegate. "Mr. Hines is concerned about this," it was said gravely by Hines' representative, "because he has already been the victim of other bootleggers."[39]

Like other musicians similarly situated, Hines had difficulty in maintaining his marriage, necessitating more income to pay alimony. By mid-1976, "dissolution of [his] marriage" was on the agenda. Despite his various lucrative income streams, his soon-to-be former spouse was cautioned about her "demands," given the "very shaky and unpredictable music business as it now exists" and "shaky financial position of Mr. Hines," as his representative put it. Like the classic hit by Little Johnny Taylor, the argument for all sides was that it was "cheaper to keep her." Hines "wishes to offer to reconcile with Mrs. Hines" in that "greater financial security can be obtained for the parties if a single household were maintained." Moreover, since she was considerably, younger than Hines, there was more "potential benefit of Mrs. Hines of being a widow rather than a divorcee,"[40] as the parties stumbled toward reconciliation.

Hines was not the only musician doing reasonably well financially. The Marsalis clan of New Orleans had attained a distinguished status musically. Yet interviewed in 2010, the patriarch, pianist Ellis Marsalis, was unembarrassed to admit that "when I was growing up, I had a certain resentment for club owners" and their exploitative ways. His son Branford had an early band, The Creators, which he said "made more money than me," though he had a growing brood to support.[41] Branford Marsalis, saxophonist, composer, and bandleader, was born in 1960 and, consonant with his parents' consciousness, continues to carry the middle name "Iweanya" chosen by a friend of his father from Kenya when that nation was mired in what was called the "Mau Mau Rebellion." His impressions of his hometown are congruent with national trends in that a "lot of the musicians in New Orleans were thugs" and "tough guys . . . cutthroats" in sum. "There was a tradition of that in New Orleans and it's carried over," he said, harking back to the turn of the twentieth century. "So that the idea of musicians being effeminate," he said quizzically, "that wasn't part of my experience growing up." Confirming his father's memory, he concurs that as a teenager "we got paid well" for performing. "We got paid more than my father did. . . . He was making forty, fifty bucks a night. We [were] out there playing other people's tunes and [were] making a hundred, a hundred and twenty-five dollars a night" playing "night clubs, fraternities, dances, proms, weddings." Ultimately, Terrence Blanchard, trumpeter, composer, and educator born in 1962, "played in the band. Wynton," his younger brother, also "was in the band."

Perhaps driving him further into the clutches of performing were desiccating experiences in school. "Mrs. Dewey, my fourth-grade teacher, she loved reading Mark Twain but she didn't like black people, so she would always have me read the pages with the word 'nigger' on it in a class full of white people." This happened "constantly, constantly" and "it was a drag." His father reminded him that the "buses you ride on everyday to public school, I used to have to sit behind a cage that said 'Colored Only,'" reinforcing the perception of perpetual bigotry. Outraged, his mother "went to the school and cursed Miss [sic] Dewey out," a woman who "really resented having to teach black kids."[42]

Marsalis's younger brother, Delfeayo, trombonist and educator born in 1965, also experienced a Jim Crow New Orleans. When his older brother, Wynton, was in school there, "they gave him a stuffed monkey for Christmas," says the younger brother.[43]

Fortunately, teaching and the institutionalization of "Jazz Studies" at leading universities such as Princeton, Columbia, UCLA, and elsewhere arrived not a moment too soon, Hines's success notwithstanding. For by 1971 the American Federation of Musicians declared that "high-echelon . . . studio work" dropped "30 to 40 percent" in the United States during the past year; the 300,000-member union blamed "runaway production," that is, "recording overseas under cheaper wage scales."[44] By 1980, CBS Records conducted "analyses of net billings, talent expense, recoupment and roster turnover for jazz acts on the Columbia and Epic rosters" and found that in 1979 there were thirty-nine artists signed, twenty-five by 1980, and twenty-two projected by 1981.[45] The "Jazz Roster" as of July 1980 included what were called "A artists," meaning Weather Report (featuring Zawinul and former Miles Davis accompanist Wayne Shorter) and Herbie Hancock (also a Davis alumnus), along with "B artists" including bassist Stanley Clarke and trumpeter Freddie Hubbard and "C artists" including saxophonist Arthur Blythe.[46] If a heavyweight musician like Blythe was bringing up the rear, this was an indication of the parched climate endured by others. Thus, "Jazz Artists dropped/Potential drops" as of July 1980 included luminaries like Billy Cobham, Stan Getz, Bobby Hutcherson, Cedar Walton, and Lonnie Liston Smith; those slated for potential axing the next year were Eric Gale, the Heath Brothers—and Freddie Hubbard.[47] Despite this purge, CBS knew that "in the first six months of 1980, the Jazz Repertoire had net billing of $8.5 million contributing," about a fifth of "pre-tax profits" overall. "The month of June," it was said proudly, "proved highly successful mainly due to releases by Bob James, Al Di Meola, and the continued success of Stanley Clarke and Herbie Hancock . . . jazz profits were

17.2 percent of total pre-tax profits."[48] Thus, George Russell was not being idiosyncratic when he said in 2004, "I have nothing to say about American recording companies," at least "nothing good to say."[49]

Coincidentally, as CBS was surging from strength to strength, competitors were suffering. This was particularly the case for those who had emerged from the halcyon days of the anti–Jim Crow movement but by the 1970s were falling victim to the counterrevolution. Such was the case for Stax Records of Memphis, an unheralded fountainhead of Black Music. By 1973, it was ensnarled in a grand jury investigation of what was termed "underworld influence in the record industry."[50] Like its counterparts in the mainstream, Stax also sought to construct cinematic portraits of gangsters—except that Black mobsters were not viewed benignly and thus their attempt to make a movie about Frank Skinner was unsuccessful: he was a burly bar owner of Brooklyn, Illinois, a town that had been run by hoodlums, but then was transformed as he became police chief and chased the thugs out of town.[51] Earlier Stax had signed with CBS to distribute its records, and then charged that the larger firm was seeking "'to destroy'" the smaller, meaning Stax.[52] By then, though relatively small, Stax was considered the fifth-largest Black-owned business in the nation, just behind Detroit's Motown,[53] which was also facing pressures it would be unable to escape. By late 1975, Al Bell of Stax, an African American pioneer entrepreneur, was indicted.[54] By 1976 Stax was defunct. It had been founded in 1959 on the cusp of the rising anti–Jim Crow movement, then fell as this movement was receding.[55] Though it represented the inter-racialism that purportedly was the beau ideal of the republic (co-founder Jim Stewart was Euro-American), the fact remained that its roster of musicians, not to mention central executives, were Black, and Stax had been located in a heavily African American neighborhood besides, marking it ineffably in racial terms.[56]

Curiously, it was Stewart who made the explosive allegation that CBS sought to destroy Stax after his half of the company had been purchased by Bell in 1972, which occurred after the deal with CBS had been consummated.[57] By mid-1976, as Bell stood trial on charges of bank fraud, details emerged of a plot involving "getting all the niggers out of Stax . . . especially the head nigger, Al Bell." This charge was made by a consultant to United Planters National Bank, which Bell was accused of defrauding.[58] Bell was acquitted but his company did not survive.[59]

His competitor, Detroit's Motown, also did not survive, at least not in the form initiated by founder Berry Gordy. One analyst contended that "Motown itself . . . had developed its own Mob connections that protected the label," and a critic maintained that "if you're holding a Motown label pressed since 1966, you're looking at a Mafia product from start to finish." Motown executive Michael Roshkind, who happened to be Jewish, was seen as the key man in this setup.[60] (Interestingly, the insanely wealthy singer Barry Manilow hailed the success of record executive Clive Davis in 1986 with "Whitney [Houston], Aretha [Franklin] and Dionne [Warwick] . . . you've become the Jewish Berry Gordy! Congratulations.")[61]

As artists and companies alike were being squeezed by increasingly monopolized record labels, the outlet overseas that had proven to be so bountiful over the decades was coming under pressure. With the retreat of settler colonialism in southern Africa, musicians headed there too, with Darius Brubeck, son of the fabled pianist, starting a department of the music at the University of Natal in South Africa[62]— though the simultaneous retreat of the socialist camp thwarted the ability of the African National Congress-South African Communist Party government to make as much progress as had been envisioned, contributing to tensions nationwide.[63]

It was true that a number of artists continued to see Denmark as a kind of oasis, with "Stuff" Smith, Ben Webster, Oscar Pettiford, and even Mercer Ellington either permanent or partial residents there. Billy Moore, pianist and arranger, born in West Virginia in 1917, died in Copenhagen in 1989.[64]

Also departing for Scandinavia was George Russell, composer, born in 1923, and one of the premier theoreticians of the music.[65] Though defined as Black, his mother, he said, was of "German ancestry . . . she was nearly white." Like many, he was disgusted with what was antiseptically termed "race relations" in the United States, recalling the story of "Fitz, [a] white fellow, played bass" who was beaten into a bloody pulp at the behest of "white detectives," "because he was white, playing

328   JAZZ AND JUSTICE

with a black" in Russell's native Cincinnati. The victim insisted all along "I'm black," but his ancestral cry was unheard. The city became "ugly to me," said Russell. "I hated it then. I really couldn't stand it." In Chicago back then, "you'd be walking down the street" and notice "two guys in a car, wearing hats and they'd be slowly behind you. . . . They'd pull up in front of you and ask, 'What's your nationality?' I was always Spanish and Irish," he countered. Disillusioned, he wound up in Sweden and became a devotee of George Gurdjieff, a mystical philosopher and spiritualist. By the 1970s, he found "definitely an anti-American feeling over there," speaking of his new home, especially "about the Vietnam War. So I decided to come back," for just before expiring in 2009, he had become a fan of George W. Bush, praising him for the invasion of Iraq.[66]

Kenny Drew, the smooth-sounding pianist who died in 1993 at the age of sixty-four, was, in 1989, said a comrade, "celebrating his 25th anniversary in Denmark. He came in '64," but the "Danish tax people are after him" since "things ain't what they used to be in Old Denmark. . . . Times are tough in Denmark these days."[67] When Curtis Fuller, trombonist, was arrested on drug charges upon arrival in Japan, even this purported refuge was questioned.[68] Simultaneously, Mingus's widow was carping about receiving royalties due from Mexico, a persistent problem globally.[69] Earlier, Jim Stewart of Stax Records exclaimed that "you can make more money writing songs than you can performing,"[70] but the maltreatment of those like Mingus challenged this truism. In fact, in the 1970s the American Guild of Authors and Composers reported morosely that "unless we wish to see AGAC become moribund and die of senescence, we simply must get the writers of today's music on our rolls." Detected by AGAC were "real inequities in both BMI and ASCAP," which did maintain "writers of today" on their "rolls" and acknowledged the reality that major writers "didn't need the functions that we presently offer."[71] For its part, ASCAP dragged CBS into court in an attempt to protect the rights of composers and managed to snare conservative lawyer Robert Bork as counsel.[72]

Gunther Schuller, horn man, composer, and author, who, despite his attainments, admitted to being a "high school dropout," was also irate about the structural inequities of the music business. He denounced Marvin Hamlisch for exploiting the music of Scott Joplin for the award-winning and immensely profitable Hollywood movie *The Sting*. "In fact," said Schuller, "'The Maple Leaf Rag' of Scott Joplin came to be called 'The Sting'" by Hamlisch. Schuller was "mad as hell," and no doubt, so were Joplin's heirs. Schuller was even more furious about the ransacking of Joplin's arrangements, more so than the plundering of his music.[73]

Benny Golson was also upset with routine practices in the business that reeked of illicitness. He recalled when the overworked Oliver Nelson died in 1975, which led him to assert that the studio for which he was working was "disloyal," that is, "you write the scores, you turn it in and they copy it and the musicians have their individual parts. This guy had been there 25 years. He had to go to the hospital for an operation. That was the end of his job. I couldn't believe it. I just couldn't believe it," he said, still stupefied decades later. At the time, he confronted a "bigwig" and ranted accusingly, "They killed my friend Oliver Nelson. You're staying up late at night and drinking, trying to get the music out," blankly "looking at the empty page," and then the beleaguered composer "went home one night and he was so tired he couldn't even drive his car"; then he crawled into the "bathtub and never got out."[74] Nelson famously composed "The Blues and the Abstract Truth," but the concrete truth was that his life symbolized the still continuing travails of Black artists.

Stewart's implicit downgrading of performance continued to be reflected in the praxis of the Lionel Hampton band. In 1989, the GOP crony was charged with unfair labor practices by the National Labor Relations Board in that "improved wages and working conditions" were "conditioned upon [performers'] refusal to participate in union activity."[75] According to the union, Hampton "offered so little money for a trip to Japan that the musicians would have lost money by working," and, in cruel retaliation for their objection, he was "offering to pay the replacements"—or scabs—"more than he was willing to pay his regular musicians."[76] It was also in 1989 that members of his band went on strike, refusing to board a flight for a two-week tour of Europe in objection to being paid $100 per performance.[77] On the other hand, staunch defenders of the roly-poly bandleader could argue that his purported good deeds, such as building a housing project in Harlem, justified, if not rationalized, his misdeeds in the sphere of labor.[78]

Hampton apparently agreed with this analysis, since in 1985 he was contemplating a race to become president of the New York City Council.[79] Hampton and his spouse were pictured as being close to Governor Nelson Rockefeller, and fawning press coverage stressed his devotion to "Bible and Christian Science Lessons."[80] In 1984, the Hamptons were raising campaign funds for the presidential ticket of Ronald Reagan and George H. W. Bush.[81] Evidently they had money to spare. A journalist portrayed him as a "real estate tycoon with numerous holdings in the United States and Europe."[82]

Yet Hampton's wealth was built on the backs of musicians often fiendishly exploited. It would have been well if the orchestra had added to its vast repertoire, "Work Song," the tune by trumpeter Nat Adderley, born in 1931, who said it was inspired "from remembering when I was a little boy, watching the guys on the chain gang who were paving what is now Pensacola Street" in his Florida hometown.[83] "I don't believe that money will bring happiness," said Sonny Rollins, saxophonist, "in fact the contrary may be true." He was referring to his recording contract at Milestone, which brought him "artistic control" whereas, he said, "if I went off with some of these bigger guys . . . sleazy characters" he might be paid more in the short term but suffer overall. Rationalizing, he said, "I may be better off without a bigger audience."[84] Perhaps so. But Hampton's band sacrificed both pay *and* artistic control and suffered doubly.

Predictably, a scandal erupted when it was alleged that Hampton deployed "political influence to get lucrative rent subsidies," casting a shadow over the alleged philanthropy of his Harlem housing project.[85]

Rollins was in a uniquely advantageous position but still suffered financially. By 1992, his spouse and manager complained that "we don't want to do any recording for Polygram—particularly with this money" since "we have been underpaid." Yet, like Rollins himself, she insisted "we have many weird things we want (money strangely is not the most important . . .)."[86] This was easier for Rollins and his spouse to say because of his demonstrated popularity. Earlier Lucille

Rollins was stunned by the turnout for an Evanston concert: "2400 per show . . . Sonny sold out 3 nights . . . audience is all young, sit on the floor . . . this has become the norm." In Boston his combo "packed 5 nights (almost without exception . . . 18-25 year old audience", part of a "string of 10 sold-out college concerts . . . last year [there was] a sold-out two days in advance Carnegie Hall concert" and the "audience there was also young. . . ." Typically, she was remonstrating the inadequate marketing prowess of executives at his "record company" who did not seem to "be aware of where the artist's career is going and where his audience is . . ." [87]

Rollins chose to retain a newspaper clipping from that time which argued that "jazz is the savior of the [music] business" and was so fecund that it "could choke on its excesses" in light of the proliferation of genres: "crossover pop/jazz, pure modern jazz, avant garde jazz and vintage, nostalgia jazz. . . ." Indeed, said this writer, there had been an "expansion of the jazz market" which "began in 1969 with Miles Davis' free and open rock tinged, *Bitches Brew*." [88]

Also attaining a modicum of wealth was George Benson, guitarist and vocalist, born in 1943. His upbringing in Pittsburgh was typical, involving incidents of police harassment of his grandmother, because, he said, "my uncle" was "bootlegging liquor out from the basement" of a hotel "to their customers in the rooms. He used to pay the police to stay off his back," to no avail. "They put her in jail," since she was a perceived confederate. "She got sick and she died." Simultaneously, "gangs began to form" in his hometown. "You either belonged to this gang or that gang," and, speaking elliptically, Benson said, "I belonged to a little club. It wasn't big-time," referring to the "Junior Cavaliers." It was "trouble all around" nonetheless. "What broke it up was one of my cousins was killed. They had a gang fight and he was stabbed" and "that changed our whole lives. We—it ended the gangs for us for all time. I had been getting in all kind of trouble. I went to a reform school for six weeks." But he found this life difficult to elude, recalling that "I got into a gang fight and got shot" and "the police came with their guns. Pow, Pow. We're running everywhere. They shot one of my friends in his ankle," in an episode that "was like the movies." Benson escaped with a "gash on my forehead. If you look real hard," he said

in 2011, after accumulating fame and fortune, "you'll see the indenta-
tion or the skin ruffled." The gunshot "flipped me over because that's
what 38s do, I found out later," referring to the pistol caliber. "So I
went to reform school" where the chastened youth wound up. There
a Euro-American man "lifted me out of that chair with a slap. There
was blood everywhere . . . the whole six weeks I was there taught me
a lot about life. I'll never forget. Every day we fought. Somebody was
going to make you fight him. So I got used to it," a never-ending battle
that prepared him for the tribulations and privations of the music
industry. "You made sure you got the first lick in," a life lesson. "All
we did every day was fight." He was only fourteen and "turned 15 in
jail," and when he departed "I got into—I got a fight the first day. After
that my cousin and I started a singing group. It changed my whole life.
I learned everything you could know about doo-wop groups," then
migrated to the guitar. As when incarcerated, in music, too, Benson
said, "first I made enemies and then I turned them into friends."

This method was tested in one of his early engagements in Ottawa
and Montreal. "It was volatile. They had gangsters up there who used
to charge ten percent to 'protect' you." Unmoved, one of Benson's
comrades "put his gun on the table. He said, 'Protect me from what,
man?'" The racketeer responded, recalled Benson, by replying, "I
guess we better get the hell out of here." "I remember that very well,"
said Benson of this further life lesson.

Benson's roughhousing unfortunately invaded the domestic
sphere, as he spoke freely of the "rumble I had with my wife. We'd
only been married 11 months," but, he confessed, "I didn't hurt her
but I roughed her up pretty good." He was then only nineteen. Then,
he accompanied drummer Joe Dukes, born in 1937 and "we fought
over women all the time. . . . He would come by my room, bang on
my door in the middle of the night, boom, boom, boom, and he'd call
me a name." Similar disputes arose with organist Jack McDuff, born
in 1926: "He'd grab the microphone and cuss me out on the bandstand." Then one day Benson "threatened to beat everybody up" and
bandmates began "taking out their switchblades," but the good news
was "they finally got off my back." Finally, Benson was able to escape
this rough and tumble and attain a kind of stardom as a singer and

instrumentalist, especially with his album *Breezin'* and the hit "This Masquerade."[89] Music mogul Clive Davis once told Aretha Franklin, "As you know, big hit songs aren't easy to come by,"[90] and Benson would have concurred.

Mingus's former business partner, Max Roach, continued to encounter hurdles as well. In 1995, he was complaining that in New York City "there are literally about four places that you can work. Only one of them pays enough money for you to get over with, so you better stay on the road." Almost wistfully, he remarked, "Segregation was a different ball game. During the period of the Big Bands you worked 365 days a year doing one-nighters," while "the black communities all over the country are not independent whereas during segregation we had entrepreneurs with people owning stores." Almost tauntingly, he added, "for me my inspiration comes from being right here, that's why I never went to Europe."[91]

More than a shadow was cast over the legacy of Morris Levy when in 1988 he was sentenced to ten years in prison and fined $200,000 after conviction for conspiracy to extort in purchasing of what was described as "cutouts or discontinued recordings."[92] Passing away in 2006 was Bob Weinstock of Prestige Records,[93] though not perishing with him was the malevolent tendency of dangling addictive drugs before hungry musicians in order to ensnare them in adhesion contracts to record. Adding to the hall of infamy was the expiring of Joe Glaser. When he died appropriately the chief mob mouthpiece, Sidney Korshak, assumed control over the deceased's "Associated Booking Company" (ABC) and was listed as the executor of his will, which doled out millions.[94] "I direct my dear friend, Sidney R. Korshak," to "make all arrangements for my funeral and burial," said Glaser's will; even the "coffin shall be selected by Sidney R. Korshak." Making it plain, Glaser mandated that "my intent" is that Korshak "shall assist in the administration, management and conduct of this business," meaning ABC.[95] According to one account, Glaser's prime client, Louis Armstrong, unburdened himself of the myriad resentments he had harbored over the years concerning the man he once had praised. "I don't doubt," said Wein, "that his feelings of resentment, which had many years to accrue, were sincere."[96]

Roach, who later in life performed with his daughter, remained, in his words, "a strong advocate of the ERA [Equal Rights Amendment]," changing the U.S. Constitution to guarantee gender equality. "It relates in some ways to black people's struggle here and abroad," he said. Thus, he chose to "support it vigorously." Why hadn't there been more women in the music, he was asked. "They haven't had an opportunity"; thus, "we were going into nightclubs" at "14 and 15 years old," he said of himself and his male colleagues. "It's not customary to let a girl out to do these things."[97] Max—and Maxine—Roach grabbed headlines for their stellar performances with the Uptown String Quartet, which he saw as an antidote of sorts. "The music itself has become so macho," he proclaimed in 1993. "The audiences were male everywhere we went in the world," which USQ helped to change. "When the record company asked for play on the classical stations even though we were dealing with a string quartet, the classical jocks wouldn't play it because if Max Roach's name is connected with it, then it's jazz." With this new quartet "women began to come to the concert hall in droves," as the "face of the audience changed."[98]

Thus, as one door closed, others opened. Such was the perception when Dexter Gordon took time from gigging in Copenhagen to act in a critically acclaimed movie directed by French cineaste Bertrand Tavernier. "Think of the movie as music," was the message to a saxophonist-cum-actor; "some moments have to be fast and loud; some quiet and economical."[99] *Round Midnight*, the story of a gifted musician with a substance abuse problem who leaves Manhattan behind and relocates to Paris, was in many ways not only autobiographical but a synecdoche for generations of musicians past. Chan Parker, widow of Charlie Parker, was moved to write what she called a "fan letter": "Dear Dex . . . I saw the film in [New York] at a private screening and my daughter and I went to see it in Paris the other day. We both cried," confessing, "You have two groupies." The daughter, an offspring of saxophonist Phil Woods, conceded "even though as a child . . . when people would ask me (even in front of my Dad) who my favorite sax player was, I would say Dex. Now you're my favorite movie star."[100]

Across the globe, Willis Conover was still racking up kudos for his broadcasts on Voice of America. By January 1990, Nigeria was far ahead of Poland—by a factor of four—in sending fan mail to him (bringing up the rear were Hungary and the Soviet Union).[101] This had become a consistent pattern.[102] In 1986, for example, the "mail count" showed Nigeria still ahead of second-place Poland.[103] By 1982, Conover had conducted 10,000 programs and showed no indication of slowing down.[104] By March 1991, his career was capped when Nobel Laureate Lech Walesa, the hero of anti-communist Poland, invited him to dinner at the Polish Embassy in Washington, where the chief envoy gushed, "In my country, you are a legend," which was not far wrong.[105] By 2012, Branford Marsalis was lamenting "Cold War foolishness," but at that juncture, this phenomenon, however defined, had accomplished its goals.[106]

Expert practitioners of the music were deemed to be legends in Japan, despite hiccups like Fuller's detention on drug charges. Speaking of the archipelago, Art Blakey asserted that his visit there "was the first time that I experienced real freedom. . . . We' ve played a lot of countries but never has the whole band been in tears when we left. My wife cried all the way to Hawaii."[107] Looking back on an illustrious career, Benny Golson in 2009 continued to rhapsodize about his euphoric reception in the archipelago. "We were their heroes," he said simply. This had a downside in that this hero worship meant they were "illegally recorded" during live performances, with the release of discs driving down the value of their legitimate music in the marketplace. Still, Golson admitted that Japan "was one of my favorite places." But Golson also appreciated Germany, where he resided for a while, not least because his daughter honed her linguistic skills. Already she spoke a "little Japanese," and during their European tenure she wound up speaking German, French, and Spanish. "I love it," he said of Germany, "we love it there."[108] This linguistic skill was an often unrecognized by-product of the life of the peripatetic musician. Eric Gravatt, a drummer born in 1947, who performed alongside McCoy Tyner and with Weather Report, was once espied "reading Chinese letters [and] diaries."[109] Understandably, given his long tenure in Quebec, Oscar Peterson spoke excellent French, while pianist Dwike Mitchell and his partner, Willie Ruff, horn man and bassist, both studied Russian. The source of this information, Leonard Feather, could chat amiably in French and German.[110]

By 1975, trumpeter Don Cherry was residing in Sweden and spent time hitchhiking throughout the continent, not just picking up snatches of lingo along the way but absorbing a different way of living. He noticed that "Common Market" nations, speaking of the western sector of the continent, were "more possessive of their time and things," while due east, "everyone picks you up because they realize that everybody's trying to help each other."[111] By 2012, Branford Marsalis was co-signing the perception, articulated for decades, that the music he helped to popularize received a warmer reception in Europe. He referred to London's BBC and commented, "It's funny, they do stuff on American culture better than us," speaking of his homeland.[112]

By August 1981, Yusef Lateef was teaching in Nigeria. Earlier, he had stopped playing at venues that sold alcohol, which restricted his opportunities tremendously in the United States. Still, he concluded, "I'd rather teach than to work in that type of environment anymore. I pray that I never have to do that again," referring to performing at these "smoke cellars." He remained in West Africa until 1985, and it is evident that his experience there, bracketed by his ordeals at home, proved to be trenchantly inspiring. His sprawling *African American Epic Suite* confronted slavery and the Middle Passage. While in Nigeria, he also "did research into the Fulani tribe," deepening his knowledge and overall awareness of history. His fondness for Africa notwithstanding, Lateef echoed the view that has ricocheted through the decades and continues to push expert artists overseas: "The masses of people," he says, "who appreciate African American music may be in Europe. There are over 300 festivals in Europe every year. I don't think we have that many here," he said of his homeland. There was further reason for Lateef to sour on the land of his birth: "my older son," he lamented, "[is] a disabled veteran from the Vietnam War."[113] Randy Weston, pianist and composer, also moved to Africa, Morocco in his case, with a similar positive experience. [114]

BRANFORD MARSALIS CONTENDS that the "glory days" for the music that made him famous were the "thirties, forties and fifties," with a decline in succeeding decades with the death of Coltrane and Miles Davis moving away from his earlier styles.[115]

Dave Liebman sees "the image of the long-distance runner and the idea of the artist as a long-distance runner" as being coterminous. "The race," he says, "going against the all, breakaway" from the "wall of pain" brought by the indignity of performing at disrespecting venues and exhausting rounds of practice. "The idea of [the] marathon runner" seized his imagination when contemplating the working musician.[116]

The philosopher Theodor Adorno has been cited for the proposition that "no artist is able to overcome, through his own individual resources, the contradiction of enchained art within an enchained society. The most which we can hope to accomplish is the contradiction of such a society through emancipated art, and even in this attempt he might well be the victim of despair." "True art," said the Russian revolutionary, Leon Trotsky, was inherently revolutionary.[117]

Ahmet Ertegun was no revolutionary, but even he was emboldened by the freeing of Nelson Mandela in February 1990. Later that year he signed an anti-apartheid chain letter and instructed a subordinate to find "ten other colleagues" to do the same.[118]

By way of contrast, in 1993 Lionel Hampton served as Honorary Chair of the inauguration of incoming mayor Rudy Giuliani, in New York City, who prevailed in an intense race-baiting campaign against the vanquished David Dinkins, Gotham's first black mayor. Hampton went above and beyond the call of duty by praising the victor lavishly.[119]

Also reflective of forbidding times was the fact that by 1997, music mogul Clive Davis felt compelled to rebuke a trade publication, instructing that he and his colleagues "strongly protest what is clearly a personal crusade . . . against the genre of rap albums . . . the bias is much too blatant."[120] From bebop to hip-hop, musical forms devised by African Americans faced a steeply uphill climb in the land of their birth.

THE LIVELIHOODS OF HOLLYWOOD musicians have long been under siege, as the City of Angels is losing a significant number of scoring jobs to Britain, and since movies provide a more stable source

338   JAZZ AND JUSTICE

of income than television, this is no minor matter.[121] There has also been a decline of jazz clubs in Washington, D.C. The Bohemian Caverns on U Street closed in 2016. The Black Fox Lounge, Café Nema, U-Topia, and HR 57 all have disappeared, as has Capital Bop's DC Jazz Loft. The Howard Theatre near the university of the same name has dropped most of its jazz programming, as has the Atlas Performing Center. On the other hand, now featuring the music are, among others, the basement bar at the Graham Hotel in Georgetown, Alice's Jazz and Cultural Society in Brookland, Blues Alley, Twins Jazz—and the Kennedy Center. There are many others too, including Brixton, Epicure, Milk Boy, Arthouse, and Mr. Henry's Sotto.[122]

Washington had attracted one of the largest populations of Ethiopian descent in the nation, and in 2016 Getachew Mekurya, the Ethiopian saxophonist and jazz performer with global reach, passed away at the age of eighty-one.[123] But not dying with him was the music he popularized.

During the summer of 2018, Quincy Jones's six-decade career as a musician, composer, arranger, conductor, executive, magazine founder, entrepreneur, humanitarian, and producer was celebrated, with special attention accorded his seventy-nine Grammy nominations (winning twenty-seven Grammys). The celebration took place at the Umbria Jazz Festival in Italy, marking its 45th anniversary as one of the most popular events of its type globally. Picturesque Perugia, the heart of Umbria, sits on a hilltop and is festooned with cobblestone streets, and the main activity occurred on the piazza in the midst of a historic museum and churches surrounded by cafés serving delicious food, not to mention gelato shops, stores with local crafts and street musicians, dancers, and puppeteers. Jones's special guests and friends appeared, including Brazilians, Cubans, and Italians like Paolo Fresu, a foremost trumpeter, who performed. The assembled orchestra played some of Jones's compositions from his various TV scores. His reminiscences included revealing that Erroll Garner gave him the composition "Misty" at the airport in Paris in 1958, and he then promptly gave it to vocalist Sarah Vaughan to perform. He also spoke about his involvement with Dr. King and later, Nelson Mandela.[124]

It was not just senior citizens like Jones who were basking in success. By 2019 the saxophonist widely viewed as the brightest star in the music's firmament, Kamasi Washington, born in 1981, was receiving rave reviews after performing in London. He and his band, said a seemingly astonished viewer, did not play in a "subterranean club" but, instead, to "5000 people of both sexes, various races and many ages."[125] Despite claims that the music was dead—or dying—Washington's ascension tended to belie these age-old nostrums.

The music had come a long way since its beginnings in the late nineteenth century. However, the overall climate in the United States in the early twenty-first century—a surging white supremacy, an unleashed capitalist class, a weakened labor movement—indicated that despite victories, the path ahead would continue to be rocky indeed.

Notes

Introduction

1. Buck Clayton, *Buck Clayton's Jazz World* (New York: Oxford University Press, 1987), 71.
2. On the global trends that served to destroy slavery see, for example, Gerald Horne, *Confronting Black Jacobins: The United States, the Haitian Revolution, and the Origins of the Dominican Republic* (New York: Monthly Review Press, 2015); Gerald Horne, *Negro Comrades of the Crown: African Americans and the British Empire Fight the U.S. Before Emancipation* (New York: New York University Press, 2013). On the global trends that served to erode Jim Crow, see, for example, Gerald Horne, *Powell v. Alabama: The Scottsboro Boys and American Justice* (New York: Watts, 1997); and Gerald Horne, *Black Revolutionary: William Patterson and the Globalization of the African American Freedom Struggle* (Urbana: University of Illinois Press, 2013).
3. Al Rose, *Eubie Blake* (New York: Schirmer, 1979), 64.
4. Andy Fry, *Paris Blues: African American Music and French Popular Music, 1920–1960* (Chicago: University of Chicago Press, 2014), 56–57, 93.
5. Anna Hartwell Celenza, *Jazz Italian Style: From its Origins in New Orleans to Fascist Italy and Sinatra* (New York: Cambridge University Press, 2017), 179.
6. Benny Carter, oral history, October 13–14, 1976, Institute of Jazz Studies, Rutgers University, Newark.
7. Vanessa Gezari, "The View from Hollywood," interview with Mark Boal, *Columbia Journalism Review* 55, no. 2 (2016): 42–57, 45. See also John Powell, *Why You Love Music* (Boston: Little, Brown, 2016).
8. Billy Taylor and Teresa L. Reed, *The Jazz Life of Dr. Billy Taylor* (Bloomington: Indiana University Press, 2013), iv. See also Maxine Gordon, *Sophisticated Giant: The Life and Legacy of Dexter Gordon* (Berkeley: University of California Press, 2018), 169: "In jazz history, lots of stories that become accepted as facts are memories that

change over the years. . . ." Unfortunately, this tendency articulated by Ms. Gordon is not unique to histories of this musical form. See, for example, G. Michael Fenner, *The Hearsay Rule* (Durham: Carolina Academic Press, 2013).

9. Note, *Downbeat* 17, no. 2 (1950):13 [aa],Reel 4, Columbia University, New York City.

10. Leonard Feather, "The Logistics of Jazz," n.d., Box 12, Leonard Feather Papers, University of Idaho, Moscow, ID. See also Marshal Royal and Claire Gordon, *Jazz Survivor* (London: Cassell, 1996): Royal's memoir argues that the music flourished in Los Angeles, as it gained altitude in New Orleans.

11. Von Freeman, oral history, May 23–24, 2000, National Museum of American History, Washington, D.C.

12. *New York Herald Tribune*, May 9, 1954, Dave Brubeck Papers, University of the Pacific, Stockton, CA.

13. Eddie Barefield, oral history, February 26 1977, Missouri Historical Society, University of Missouri, Kansas City. See also *Los Angeles Times*, February 3, 2019: The late pianist Donald Shirley—subject of a recent award winning film—asserted that there was no improvisation in the music since musicians agreed beforehand on the harmonies. Cf. Stephen Rush, *Free Jazz, Harmolodics and Ornette Coleman* (New York: Routledge, 2017).

14. Joe Rene, oral history, September 8, 1960, Tulane University.

15. Miranda Kaufmann, *Black Tudors: The Untold Story* (New York: Oneworld, 2017), 10, 11: "Trumpets have been used to mark power, status, military might and even divine power in civilizations across the world. The walls of Jericho tumbled down at the sound of trumpets. The Jewish New Year, Rosh Hashanah, is also known as the Feast of the Trumpets, because the Torah stipulates the day should be marked with trumpet fanfares . . . in some northern Nigeria kingdoms, the capture of the royal trumpeters effectively signaled a coup d'état . . . African musicians had been playing for European monarchs and nobility since at least the twelfth century, in a tradition that owed much to medieval Islamic courts from Spain to Syria. In 1194 turbaned black trumpeters accompanied the Holy Roman Emperor Henry VI on his triumphal entry into Palermo in Sicily. . . . James IV of Scotland employed a Moorish drummer in the early years of the sixteenth century." See also Eric Porter, *What Is This Thing Called Jazz? African American Musicians as Artists, Critics, and Activists* (Berkeley: University of California Press, 2002). I have sought to avoid mimicking the provocative and enlightening theses that are so well represented in this book.

16. Charles Hersch, *Subversive Sounds: Race and the Birth of Jazz in New*

Orleans (Chicago: University of Chicago Press, 2007), 5. James Lincoln Collier avers that "the world of jazz began to integrate racially in 1908," well before the debut of Negro baseball star in 1947, Jackie Robinson, often given credit for being the premier pioneer in desegregation. It was then that "the white violinist Emile Flindt joined the black pianist Fate Marable on a riverboat . . . by 1936 Benny Goodman was offering a racially mixed group to white audiences. . . ." *Times Literary Supplement* [London], November 23, 2018.

17. Pat Griffith, "The Education of Max Roach," *Downbeat* 39, no. 5 (1972): 16–17. See also Kenneth Robert Janken, *Rayford Logan and the Dilemma of the African American Intellectual* (Chapel Hill: University of North Carolina Press, 1993), 16: The pianist and bandleader, Duke Ellington, referred to his music not as "jazz" but as "Negro Music."

18. Philip V. Bohlman and Goffredo Plastino, eds., *Jazz Worlds/World Jazz* (Chicago: University of Chicago Press, 2016), xiii.

19. Artie Shaw, oral history, October 7–8, 1992, National Museum of American History.

20. Interview with Randy Weston, *Be-Bop and Beyond* 2, no. 2 (1984): 16–22, Southern California Library for Social Studies and Research, Los Angeles. .

21. Len Lyons, "Milt Jackson: Dollars and Sense," *Downbeat* 42, no. 9 (1975): 14–15, 14.

22. Maxine Gordon, *Sophisticated Giant: The Life and Legacy of Dexter Gordon* (Berkeley: University of California Press, 2018), 64.

23. Tom Stoddard, *Jazz on the Barbary Coast* (Berkeley: Heyday, 1998), 187. On the global implications of the "candelabra," see, for example, S. Frederick Starr, *Red and Hot: The Fate of Jazz in the Soviet Union* (New York: Limelight, 2004); Mike Zwerin, *Swing Under the Nazis: Jazz as a Metaphor of Freedom* (New York: Cooper Square, 2000); Michael Kater, *Different Drummers: Jazz in the Culture of Nazi Germany* (New York: Oxford University Press, 1992); Jeffrey H. Jackson, *Making Jazz French: Music and Modern Life in Interwar Paris* (Durham, NC: Duke University Press, 2003); George McKay, *Circular Breathing: The Cultural Politics of Jazz in Britain* (Durham, NC: Duke University Press, 2005); Matthew F. Jordan, *Le Jazz: Jazz and French Cultural Identity* (Urbana, IL: University of Illinois Press, 2010); Jeremy Lane, *Jazz and Machine-Age Imperialism: Music, "Race," and Intellectuals in France, 1918–1945* (Ann Arbor: University of Michigan Press, 2014); Everett Taylor Atkins, *Blue Nippon: Authenticating Jazz in Japan* (Durham, NC: Duke University Press, 2001); Andrew Jones, *Yellow Music: Media Culture and Colonial Modernity in the Chinese Jazz Age* (Durham, NC: Duke University Press, 2001); Gwen Ansell, *Soweto Blues: Jazz, Popular Music*

and *Politics in South Africa* (New York: Continuum, 2004); Steven Feld, *Jazz Cosmopolitanism in Accra* (Durham, NC: Duke University Press, 2012); Robin D. G. Kelley, *Africa Speaks, America Answers: Modern Jazz in Revolutionary Times* (Cambridge, MA: Harvard University Press, 2012); Jason Borge, *Tropical Riffs: Latin America and the Politics of Jazz* (Durham, NC: Duke University Press, 2018). The preceding notwithstanding, the book in hand focuses heavily on African American artists and their struggles.

24. Martin Williams, "Zutty," *Downbeat* 30, no. 21 (1963): 18–19, 18. Cf. Marshal Royal and Claire Gordon, *Jazz Survivor* (London: Cassell, 1996), 67: "It's hard for any man in his right mind to put his finger on when jazz began. To start with, nobody knows exactly what jazz is . . . knows what the word jazz stands for, nor who the person was who named that type of music."

25. See Philippe Carles and Jean-Louis Comolli, *Free Jazz/Black Power*, (Jackson, MS: University Press of Mississippi, 2015) Songwriter and entrepreneur W. C. Handy, reportedly heard in Memphis as early as 1905 the kind of music that New Orleans was to claim as its own. The authors point out that the blues, work songs, spirituals, and other precursors of the new music were not the peculiar province of southern Louisiana.

26. Vertical file on Memphis music, January 24, 1985, Memphis Public Library.

27. *Chicago Tribune*, March 26, 1985.

28. Clyde Woods, *Development Arrested: The Blues and Plantation Power in the Mississippi Delta* (New York: Verso, 1998). See also Adam Gussow, *Beyond the Crossroads: The Devil and the Blues Tradition* (Chapel Hill, NC: University of North Carolina Press, 2017).

29. *Press Scimitar*, March 28, 1958.

30. Wayne Dowdy, *Hidden History of Memphis* (Charleston, SC: History Press, 2010), 13. In addition to Faulkner, the author points to the film of King Vidor, *Hallelujah*, made in Memphis, as an example of this Faulknerian trend.

31. Kathy J. Ogren, "Performance Crossroads: The Significance of the Jazz Controversy for Twenties America" (PhD diss., Johns Hopkins University, 1985), 163.

32. Jack V. Buerkle and Danny Barker, *Bourbon Street Black: The New Orleans Black Jazzman* (New York: Oxford University Press, 1973), 14, 18.

33. Stephen Longstreet, *Sportin' House New Orleans and the Jazz Story: A History of the New Orleans Sinners and the Birth of Jazz* (Los Angeles: Sherburne, 1965), 165.

34. George Malcolm Smith, "Cuban Natives . . ." *Downbeat*, 6(Number 3, March 1939): (8. 1939), Columbia University, New York City.

35. Jerome Handler, "The Barbados Slave Conspiracies of 1675 and 1692," *Journal of Barbados Museum and Historical Society*, 36, no. 4 (1982): 312–33, 314.

36. Statute, August 8, 1688, in Richard Hall, ed., *Acts Passed in the Island of Barbados from 1643 to 1762* (London, 1764), Barbados National Archives.

37. Toby Gleason, ed., *Music in the Air: The Selected Writings of Ralph J. Gleason* (New Haven: Yale University Press, 2016), 3. The musician Nick LaRocca said that the first time the word "jazz" was used was at a club in the early First World War era, when a woman shouted the term out as musicians played, declaring "jazz it up boys, give us some more jazz." This term was then added to his band's name: See *Tempo*, October 1936, John Steiner Collection, University of Chicago. The musician known as Chink Martin said that the term "jazz" had negative connotations, use of which could ignite an assault. Chink Martin, oral history, October 19, 1966, Tulane University.

38. Emile Barnes, oral history, January 3, 1962, Tulane University.

39. Celenza, *Jazz Italian Style*, 28.

40. Marva Griffin Carter, *Swing Along: The Musical Life of Will Marion Cook* (New York: Oxford University Press, 2008), 27.

41. Diedre O'Connell, *The Ballad of Blind Tom, Slave Pianist: America's Lost Musical Genius* (New York: Overlook, 2009), 66.

42. See, for example, Gerald Horne, *The Counter-Revolution of 1776: Slave Resistance and the Origins of the United States of America* (New York: New York University Press, 2014); and *The Apocalypse of Settler Colonialism: The Roots of Slavery, White Supremacy and Capitalism in Seventeenth-Century North America and the Caribbean* (New York: Monthly Review Press, 2018).

43. Neil Leonard, *Jazz and the White Americans: The Acceptance of a New Art Form* (Chicago: University of Chicago Press, 1962), 26.See also *Los Angeles Times*, February 14, 2019: The late Negro composer, William Grant Still, declared that the blues, from which the new music sprang, "are the secular music of the American Negro and are more purely Negroid than many spirituals. They show no European influence at all," thus intensifying hostility among some.

44. Celenza, *Jazz Italian Style*, 91.

45. Clark Terry, oral history, June 15 and 22, 1999, National Museum of American History.

46. Ibid. Dolphy, unfortunately, is an exemplar of the music for more reasons than one. Pianist Herbie Hancock is among those who were taken

aback by the murky circumstances surrounding his tragic 1964 death in Germany. He collapsed at a performance, but when he was taken to hospital, the medical staff apparently assumed he was on drugs and "left him to detox. Eric didn't do drugs—he was diabetic" and, consequently, he died when insulin was not administered: Herbie Hancock, *Possibilities* (New York: Viking, 2014), 49. The tragic consequence of being misunderstood is also a trademark of the music.

47. Nat Hentoff, oral history, February 17–18, 2007, National Museum of American History.

48. Whitney Balliett, "Three Tones," *The New Yorker*, September 7, 1981, 39.

49. Milt Hinton, oral history, Institute of Jazz Studies.

50. Milton Hinton and David Borger, *Bass Line: The Stories and Photographs of Milt Hinton* (Philadelphia: Temple University Press, 1988), 7.

51. William Ivy Hair, *Carnival of Fury: Robert Charles and the New Orleans Race Riot of 1900* (Baton Rouge: Louisiana State University Press, 1976), 91.

52. Elliot Meadow, "Make Room for Billy Harper," *Downbeat* 38, no. 13 (1971): 16–17, 17.

53. Interview with Ellis Marsalis, *Vieux Carré Courier*, June 18, 1971, Vertical File: "Racism and Jazz," Tulane University-New Orleans.

54. Lewis Porter, "Some Problems in Jazz Research," *Black Music Research Journal* 8, no. 2 (1988): 195–206, 199.

55. Ingrid Monson, *Freedom Sounds: Civil Rights Call Out to Jazz and Africa* (New York: Oxford University Press, 2007) 18.

56. Jackie McLean, oral history, July 20–21, 2001, National Museum of American History.

57. Clipping, May 17, 1919, Box 2; and Chronology of Europe's life, Box 1, James Reese Europe Papers, Schomburg Center for Research in Black Culture, New York Public Library. See also Reid Badger, *A Life in Ragtime: A Biography of James Reese Europe* (New York: Oxford University Press, 2007). The ironically surnamed Europe was emblematic of the music for other reasons. He helped to invent the dance known as the "foxtrot," organized Negro musicians into a union, and led the first African American symphony orchestra to appear at Carnegie Hall. His music was on the grand scale, boasting scores of musicians on brass and orchestral strings, voices, percussion, and a banjo choir. He played ragtime and vaudeville hits, popular marches, all while recording frequently: *Financial Times* [London], October 27–28, 2018.

58. Stanley Dance, *The World of Count Basie* (New York: Scribner's, 1980), 328. See also Amber R. Clifford, *Queering Kansas City: Gender, Performance and the History of a Scene* (Lincoln, NE: University of Nebraska Press, 2018).

59. Benny Golson and Jim Merod, *Whisper Not: The Autobiography of Benny Golson* (Philadelphia: Temple University Press, 2016), 183.

60. Brian Priestley, *Chasin' the Bird: The Life and Legacy of Charlie Parker* (New York: Oxford University Press, 2006), 41, 42.

61. George Lewis, *A Power Stronger than Itself: The AACM and American Experimental Music* (Chicago: University of Chicago Press, 2008), x.

62. Charles Mingus, *Beneath the Underdog: His World as Composed by Mingus* (New York: Bantam, 1972).

63. Gene Santoro, *Myself When I Am Real: Life and Music of Charles Mingus* (New York: Oxford University Press, 2000), 95, 193.

64. Max Roach, interview, November 22, 1995, Box 51, Max Roach Papers, Library of Congress, Washington, D.C.

65. John W. Sewell to Sue Mingus, February 20, 1955, Box 57, Charles Mingus Papers, Library of Congress.

66. Noal Cohen and Michael Fitzgerald, *Rat Race Blues: The Musical Life of Gigi Gryce* (Berkeley: Berkeley Hill, 2002), 310, 311. See also *Gay City News* [New York City], August 2, 2018: Clubs in Manhattan generally— the epicenter for performance of the music—were controlled generally by organized crime figures, including the now famous Stonewall Inn, viewed widely as the site for an eruption of a new stage in the gay rights movement in 1969. Competitors of these notorious figures were at times murdered, and police officials often were bribed by mobsters. See also Martin Duberman, *Stonewall* (New York: Plume, 1994).

67. Douglas Thompson, *The Dark Heart of Hollywood: Glamour, Guns and Gambling—Inside the Mafia's Global Empire* (Edinburgh: Mainstream, 2013), 165.

68. John Chilton, *Roy Eldridge: Little Jazz Giant* (New York: Continuum), 147.

69. Clark Terry, *Clark: The Autobiography of Clark Terry* (Berkeley: University of California Press, 2011), 140.

70. Frank R. Hayde, *Stan Levey: Jazz Heavyweight, the Authorized Biography* (Solana Beach, CA: Santa Monica Press, 2016), 35, 213, 97.

71. Miles Davis with Quincy Troupe, *Miles, the Autobiography* (New York: Simon & Schuster, 2011).

72. *New York Amsterdam News*, January 3, 2019.

73. Steven L. Isoardi, *The Dark Tree: Jazz and the Community Arts in Los Angeles* (Berkeley: University of California Press, 2006), 25.

74. *Los Angeles Times*, June 22, 2015.

75. Ishmael Reed, "The NOI, the Mob and Sonny Liston," *Black Renaissance* 15 (2015): 12–17, 13. On the conflict between the Nation of Islam and the traditional mob, see, for example, Arnett D. Waters, *Black Mafia* (New York: Vantage, 1973).

76. Sonny Rollins, oral history, February 28, 2011. National Museum of American History.
77. Panama Francis, oral history, September 13, 1978, Institute of Jazz Studies.
78. Ted Vincent, "The Community That Gave Jazz to Chicago," *Black Music Research Journal* 12, no. 1 (1992): 43–55, 47.
79. Paul Barbarin, oral history, January 7, 1959, Tulane University.
80. Celenza, *Jazz Italian Style*, 3, 12, 109. Also see Taylor with Reed, *The Jazz Life of Dr. Billy Taylor*, 22: "In the 1920s white artists took most of the credit for jazz. . . . On May 1, 1912 James Reese Europe gave the first-ever jazz concert at Carnegie Hall. Though rarely cited in history books."
81. Nick LaRocca, *Tempo*, October 1936, John Steiner Collection, University of Chicago. Bassist Eddie Dawson, born in 1884, said the term "jazz" was first used in bands when he was playing around Basin and Iberville in New Orleans: Eddie Dawson, oral history, August 11, 1959, Tulane University.
82. Comment, *Downbeat* 4 (Number 3, March 1937): 1,4,1 (1937).
83. Nick LaRocca, oral history, May 21, 1958, Tulane University.
84. Johnny Lala, oral history, September 24, 1958, Tulane University.
85. *Melody Maker*, March 4, 1961,
86. Jelly Roll Morton to "Mr. Carew," in William Russell, compiler, *"Oh, Mister Jelly": A Jelly Roll Morton Scrapbook* (Copenhagen: Jazz Media, 1999), 247–48. See also Michael Gerber, *Jazz Jews* (Nottingham: Five Leaves, 2009).
87. Al Rose, *I Remember Jazz: Six Decades Among the Great Jazzmen* (Baton Rouge: Louisiana State University Press, 1987), 48. See also Ellie Horne to William Russell, January 10, 1944, Folder 6; and April 16, 1944, Folder 10, William Russell Papers, Williams Research Center, New Orleans.
88. Excerpt from memoir by Vi Redd, Box 12, Leonard Feather Papers, University of Idaho-Moscow. See also Nichole T. Rustin and Sherrie Tucker, eds., *Big Ears: Listening for Gender in Jazz Studies* (Durham, NC: Duke University Press, 2008). On Balliett, see his undated comment in Box 147, John Steiner Collection, University of Chicago. For more on the struggle against sexism in the music, see *New York Times*, April 30, 2018.
89. Touré, *Never Drank the Kool-Aid: Essays* (New York: Picador, 2006), 59.
90. Buddy Collette and Steven Isoardi, *Jazz Generations: A Life in American Music and Society* (New York: Continuum, 2000), 52.
91. Note, *Downbeat* 37, no. 2 (1970): 8.
92. Note, *Downbeat* 37, no. 9 (1970): 11.
93. Note, *Downbeat* 37, no. 14 (1970): 11.

94. Note, *Downbeat* 37, no. 21 (1970): 12.
95. *Kansas City Star*, February 20, 1990 and, *Kansas City Call*, January 26, 1962.
96. *New York Post*, November, 1989.
97. Hampton raising funds for the GOP presidential ticket: *Jet*, November 12, 1984,
98. Daniel Silverman of National Labor Relations Board to Lionel Hampton Orchestra, August 4, 1989, Box 1, Lionel Hampton Papers: Hampton is charged with "unfair labor practices." See also Marshal Royal, *Jazz Survivor*, 71: Hampton "learned early on that it was good politics to name tunes after disk jockeys. The first was 'Jack the Bell Boy' named for a well known late night disc jockey in Los Angeles."
99. Joe Wilder, oral history, August 25–26, 1992, National Museum of American History. Hampton may not have been unique in his aversion to labor organizing. See Marshal Royal, *Jazz Survivor*, 105: Trumpeter Reunald Jones accompanied bandleader Count Basie and was "very adept at keeping up with the union rules, the way that musicians should be treated, their pay, when extra pay was due and so on . . . he'd go down to the Union, Local 802" frequently, which "grated on Basie's feelings" and, thus, the portly pianist "let him go. . . ."
100. Johnny De Droit, oral history, December 4, 1969, Tulane University.
101. Johnny De Droit, oral history, March 16, 1973, Tulane University.
102. Walter White to James Petrillo, November 2, 1943, Box IIA347, NAACP Papers, Library of Congress.
103. Clipping, 1944, Box 8, Leonard Feather Papers.
104. Legal Brief by William Gould and Melvin Wulf, circa 1974, Third Circuit Court of Appeals, Box 4, African American Jazz Preservation Society of Pittsburgh, Oral History Project, University of Pittsburgh: Speaking for the "Black Musicians of Pittsburgh" organized in the wake of the merger of the previously separate unions, the lawyers pointed to the "statistical exclusion of blacks from Executive Board positions" in the merged union, Local 60-471 of the American Federation of Musicians, AFL–CIO. I believe, generally speaking, that the push toward desegregation was justifiable historically; however, the manner in which it was executed, often involving, as in the music business, independent Negro entities being masticated and swallowed by competitor union locals often dominated by Euro-American leaders who were not progressive, was catastrophic on a number of levels. Cf. Gerald Horne, *The Rise and Fall of the Associated Negro Press: Claude Barnett's Pan-African News and the Jim Crow Paradox* (Champaign, IL: University of Illinois Press, 2017).
105. Report, January 7, 1991, Folder 54, William Russell Papers, Williams Research Center-Historic New Orleans Collection. On Bridges,

see Gerald Horne, *Fighting in Paradise: Labor Unions, Racism and Communists in the Making of Modern Hawaii* (Honolulu: University of Hawaii Press, 2011).

106. John Hammond to Larry Harris, September 18, 1973, Box 37, John Hammond Papers, Yale University. According to writer A.B. Spellman, the celebrated musician Ornette Coleman—as of 1966—had made ten albums and "has never received a royalty check large enough to pay his phone bill. In fact, one company informed him in 1965 that he owed *them* money . . . one record of Ornette's was reissued three times and had a gross sale of 25,000 copies," representing a "clear case of fraud. . . ." See A.B. Spellman, *Four Lives in the Bebop Business* (New York: Pantheon, 1966), 111.

107. David Rockefeller to "Dear Mica and Ahmet," July 5, 1989, Box C1, Ahmet Ertegun Papers, Rock and Roll Hall of Fame Library and Archives, Cleveland. Atlantic Records was once known as "The House that Ruth [Brown] Built," in recognition of the profiteering at the expense of the talented vocalist, who had to hire the skillful attorney, Howell Begle, to litigate on her behalf in an attempt to secure adequate compensation: *Washington Post*, January 4, 2019, and *New York Times*, January 11, 2019.

108. J. J. Johnson, oral history, February 26–27, 1994, National Museum of American History: The trombonist recalled a time when the saxophonist was playing in New York City with Miles Davis, "an hour and ten or fifteen minute set. Then they would be offstage for about forty-five minutes. As soon as they came offstage for their break, Coltrane would go into the basement area and practice until time to go back onto their bandstand, which meant he was literally playing all night long without a break."

109. Martin Torgoff, *Bop Apocalypse: Jazz, Race, the Beats and Drugs* (New York: Da Capo, 2016), 90.

110. Ron Carter, oral history, May 16, 2011, National Museum of American History.

111. Walter White to Fiorello La Guardia, March 23, 1943, Box IIA347, NAACP Papers.

112. Walter White to Clarence Cameron White, December 18, 1939, Box IIA619, NAACP Papers.

113. Memorandum from Charles Buchanan, March 29, 1943, Box IIA347, NAACP Papers.

114. George Mulholland of the New York Police Department referencing FBI Report, May 1, 1943, Box IIA347, NAACP Papers. On Davis, see Gerald Horne, *Black Liberation/Red Scare: Ben Davis and the Communist Party* (Newark, DE: University of Delaware Press, 1994).

115. Proposal for JAM: Jazz America Marketing, 1980, Box 163, Billy Taylor Papers, Library of Congress. In the same box, see also an undated "Confidential Memorandum" that says one recording session can produce multiple albums and a "break-even point" for a jazz album is between 4,000 and 8,000 units. Then there is the global market, deemed "extremely important"; thus, if 8,000 units are sold in the United States, this usually meant sales up to 5,000 in Japan, 2,000 in France, 2,000 in Italy, 3,000 in Germany.

116. Clive Davis, *Inside the Record Business* (New York: Morrow, 1975), 133, 145.

117. Ahmet Ertegun to Barbara Ross, April 24, 1990, Box C1, Ahmet Ertegun Papers, Rock and Roll Hall of Fame, Cleveland..

118. Ahmet Ertegun to Stell Pathouli, July 12, 1991, Ahmet Ertegun Papers.

119. Karla Borja and Suzzanne Dieringer, "Streaming or Stealing? The Complementary Features Between Music Streaming and Music Piracy," *Journal of Retailing and Consumer Services* 32 (2016): 86–95.

120. *Business Week*, February 11, 2019.

121. Peter Tschmuck, *The Economics of Music* (Newcastle upon Tyne: Agenda, 2017), 98.

122. Tanner Mirrlees, *Hearts and Mines: The U.S. Empire's Culture Industry* (Vancouver: University of British Columbia Press, 2016).

123. For further context that serves to illuminate this book see, for example, George Fredrickson, *Racism: A Short History* (Princeton, NJ: Princeton University Press, 2002); Victor Perlo, *Economics of Racism U.S.A.: Roots of Black Inequality* (New York: International, 1975); John Eaton, *Political Economy: A Marxist Textbook* (London: Lawrence & Wishart, 1949).

1. Original Jelly Roll Blues

1. Gwen Midlo Hall, *Africans in Colonial Louisiana: The Development of Afro-Creole Culture in the Eighteenth Century* (Baton Rouge: Louisiana State University Press, 1995). See also Arthur La Brew, *Black Music in a Slave State: New Orleans Before Storyville* (Detroit: Michigan Music Research Center, 2000). See also Frank Buchmann-Moller, *Someone to Watch Over Me: The Life and Music of Ben Webster* (Ann Arbor: University of Michigan Press, 2009), 2: In the early nineteenth century, says this biographer of the talented horn man, Webster's great-grandmother was snared and dragged to Kentucky from her homeland, Guinea, in West Africa.

2. Tellingly, a number of the leading musicians professed Native American ancestry, while during Mardi Gras, Euro-Americans often dressed as Negroes and Negroes as Native Americans: Hair, *Carnival of Fury*, 78.

See for example, Chico Hamilton, oral history, January 9–10, 2006, National Museum of American History, Washington, D.C.. This premier drummer said, "My mother was Mexican, Indian, German Jew. My father was Afro-American and Scottish." Percy Heath said his own mother was "part Choctaw." See Percy Heath, oral history, July 23, 2001, National Museum of American History. Presumably this ancestry also applies to his celebrated brothers, also noted musicians, and their offspring, who could be described similarly. See also Jon Hendricks, oral history, August 17–18, 1995, National Museum of American History: This vocalist's mother was part Cherokee and his grandmother was "full blooded [indigene] and married a son of the biggest slave owner in Virginia, James McGaffick, Sr., [who] owned more slaves than anybody in Virginia . . . [Cherokees] were the musicians and the poets of the seven tribes . . . makes me one-eighth Cherokee." See Sheila Jordan, oral history, August 29–30, 2011, National Museum of American History: This vocalist and songwriter had "Native American [ancestry] on my grandfather's side. Also on my father's side . . . they called us half-breeds," disparaging her Cherokee heritage. Born in Detroit, abutting Ontario, she recalled that Canadians "weren't into the same kind of prejudice that they were in the U.S." Russell "Big Chief" Moore was a trombonist, born in 1912, and an indigene—Pima—born in Arizona. See Isiah Morgan, oral history, September 3, 1958, Tulane University. Clark Terry described bassist Oscar Pettiford as being of "Indian descent." Clark Terry, oral history, June 15, 22, 1999, National Museum of American History. In the same interview, he said the same of saxophonist Wardell Gray: "He's from Oklahoma. He was some sort of an Indian. Choctaw or something." Don Cherry, trumpeter, was said to possess a "certain kind of Oklahoma Choctaw logic," derived from his indigenous ancestry. See Peter Occhiogrosso, "Emissary of the Global Music: Don Cherry," *Downbeat* 42, no. 16 (1975): 14, 15, 39, 15. The drummer Jack DeJohnette, was of Seminole and Crow descent: Jack DeJohnette, oral history, November 10–11, 2012, National Museum of American History. The guitarist and vocalist George Benson, said that his grandmother was "full blooded Indian.." See George Benson, oral history, April 17–18, 2011, National Museum of American History. Buck Clayton, *Buck Clayton's Jazz World* (New York: Oxford University Press, 1987), 12: "Being part Cherokee Indian on my Dad's side of the family." Tom Bethel, *George Lewis: A Jazzman from New Orleans* (Berkeley: University of California Press, 1977), 16. Lewis was of Choctaw heritage. The grandfather of pianist Cecil Taylor was, he said, a "'full fledged Indian, a Kiowa,'" and "'my mother also had Indian blood.'" See Whitney Balliett, "Cecil," *The New Yorker*, May 5 1986,

108. See also Harry Edison, oral history, May 1981, Institute of Jazz Studies, Rutgers University, Newark: "My father was a Hopi Indian." In this interview it was also noted of Duke Ellington, "did you know that Duke was part Indian. . . . " "Pettiford was an Indian." His interlocutor, Stanley Dance, responded, "There must be some Indian thing in this music . . . Johnny Hodges' mother was a Mexican . . . Paul Gonsalves was Portuguese." Red Norvo, oral history, May 2, 1977, Institute of Jazz Studies: Johnny Hodges's grandmother "was Indian," according to the questioner, Helen Dance. The same was true, it was said, for the bassist Joe Mondragon and, further, said Norvo, Indian influence is "clearly there in Jack [Teagarden]." See also George "Red" Callender, oral history, August 13, 1981, Institute of Jazz Studies: Born in Virginia with roots in Barbados, his family, he said, "traces back to 1700" to Scotland, with ancestors who "married Indian women, African women and mulatto women . . . I have freckles . . . and red hair." His grandmother was "half Indian . . . with high cheekbones." The mother of the vocalist Mildred Bailey was Native American. See John Szwed, *Billie Holiday: The Musician and the Myth* (New York: Viking, 2015), 91. See also Brian Priestley, *Chasin' the Bird: The Life and Legacy of Charlie Parker* (New York: Oxford University Press, 2006), 8: This musician was said to be of partial Choctaw ancestry. See also A.B. Spellman, *Four Lives in the Bebop Business*, 50–51. Pianist Cecil Taylor asserts, "My mother's maiden name was Ragland. She has Indian blood too . . . my mother's mother was an Indian. . . ." I am aware that during the era of Jim Crow when African ancestry was disparaged, a tendency arose among some Negroes to claim indigenous ancestry. See also *New York Times*, September 18, 2018: The mother of "Big Jay McNeely"—he was a pioneer saxophonist—made "Indian blankets and quilts that his father sold to supplement the family's income."

3. Alice Zeno, oral history, November 14, 1958, Tulane University. See Gene Ramey, oral history, no date, Institute of Jazz Studies: "My grandfather, John Glasco, was half-Comanche." See Art Farmer, oral history, June 29–30, 1995, National Museum of American History: "My grandmother's mother was a member of an Indian tribe and she was so mistreated by the white people that she went with the black people." See also undated clipping, Box 110, John Steiner Collection, University of Chicago. Here Farmer asserts that his grandmother was "part Blackfoot Indian" and her mother was "all Blackfoot." The spouse of vibraphonist Lionel Hampton, who proved essential to his artistic and financial success, was born in Oklahoma on a reservation and, he said, was of indigenous ancestry: Lionel Hampton with James Haskins, *Hamp: An Autobiography* (New York: Amistad, 1993), 33. Howard McGhee,

born in 1918 in Oklahoma, and a trumpeter, was also of partial Native American ancestry: oral history, November 16, 1983, Institute of Jazz Studies. Chanteuse Abbey Lincoln said that her grandmother was "probably an Indian" and other ancestors were "mostly Indian." See Abbey Lincoln, oral history, December 17–18, 1996, National Museum of American History. Saxophonist Charles Lloyd declares that "Sally 'Sunflower' White Cloud was my great grandmother on my [grand] father's side . . . She refused to walk on the 'Trail of Tears' . . . when they took her land," the ignoble expulsion of indigenes from the U.S. Southeast westward in the early nineteenth century. "She was from a larger Cherokee tribe but she was Choctaw." According to composer and arranger Johnny Mandel, Joe Mondragon was "Apache, Mexican Indian really" and a "great bass player besides." He also was an inspiration for Miles Davis's haunting album *Sketches of Spain*. Johnny Mandel, oral history, April 20, 1995, National Museum of American History. "My grandmother was an Indian," said pianist and vocalist Dorothy Donegan, born 1922. "My grandfather . . . was Irish," she added. Dorothy Donegan, oral history, April 5–6, 1998, National Museum of American History. From the musicological viewpoint, there needs to be deeper interrogation of the impact of indigenous influences on U.S. popular music generally.

4. Ira Dworkin, *Congo Love Song: African American Culture and the Crisis of the Colonial State* (Chapel Hill: University of North Carolina Press, 2017), 123. See also Jeroen Dewulf, *From the Kingdom of Kongo to the Congo Square: Kongo Dances and the Origins of the Mardi Gras Indians* (Lafayette: University of Louisiana-Lafayette Press, 2017).

5. Gene Ramey, oral history, no date, Institute of Jazz Studies.

6. George "Red" Callender, oral history, August 13, 1981, Institute of Jazz Studies.

7. John McCusker, *Creole Trombone: Kid Ory and the Early Years of Jazz* (Jackson, MS: University Press of Mississippi, 2012), 80.

8. Henry A. Kamen, *Music in New Orleans: The Formative Years, 1791–1841* (Baton Rouge: Louisiana State University Press, 1966), vii, 233, 234.

9. Stephen Longstreet, *Sportin' House: A History of the New Orleans Sinners and the Birth of Jazz* (Los Angeles: Sherbourne, 1965), 165. See also Emily Epstein Landau, *Spectacular Wickedness: Sex, Race and Memory in Storyville New Orleans* (Baton Rouge: Louisiana State University, 2013).

10. Comment by Creole George Guesnon, June 21, 1958, September 18, 1959, and May 25, 1967, Folder 92, William Russell Papers, Williams Research Center, New Orleans.

11. John Wiggs, oral history, August 26, 1962, Tulane University.
12. Hair, *Carnival of Fury*, 75.
13. Joseph Thomas, oral history, September 29, 1960, Tulane University.
14. Mary Lucy Hamill O'Kelly, oral history, May 4, 1958, Tulane University.
15. Clark Terry, oral history, June 15, 22, 1999, National Museum of American History.
16. Garry Boulard, "Blacks, Italians and the Making of New Orleans Jazz," *Journal of Ethnic Studies* 16, no. 1 (1988): 53–66, 53. By 1890, those of Italian descent were 10 percent of the population of New Orleans and by 1930 they were the largest of sixteen "white ethnic groups in the city"; about 70 percent of this group had arrived from Sicily, whose ties to Mediterranean Africa are well known. Sicilians were perceived as friendlier to Negroes than other Europeans. See Richard Gambino, *Vendetta: A True Story of the Worst Lynching in America, the Mass Murder of Italian Americans in New Orleans in 1891, the Vicious Motivations Behind It and the Tragic Repercussions that Linger to This Day* (Garden City, NY: Doubleday, 1977), 49, 56.
17. Paul Barbarin, oral history, March 27, 1957, Tulane University. The attraction of Negro musicians to Paris—and vice versa—should be viewed in this context. See also Maxine Gordon, *Sophisticated Giant: The Life and Legacy of Dexter Gordon*, 13, 16, 169: The towering saxophonist had roots in both France and Madagascar, a former French colony. His maternal grandfather "learned French from his father, studied Spanish and dabbled in Russian and Chinese. . . . Dexter learned French" and later in life "moved between language with ease—French, Danish, English, Spanish. . . ."
18. Bud Scott, interview, 1939–1940, Folder 4, William Russell Papers. See also Frank Amacker, oral history, July 1, 1960, Tulane University: Here it is claimed that Bolden played the loudest of any trumpeter he ever heard.
19. Charles Elgar, oral history, May 27, 1958, Tulane University. For more on the strength of Bolden's sound, see Emile Barnes, oral history, October 1, 1959, Tulane University.
20. Johnny De Droit, oral history, December 4, 1969, Tulane University. This familiarity with various languages became a hallmark for many of these musicians. Elvin Jones, a drummer and brother of other noted musicians, such as pianist Hank Jones and horn man Thad Jones, recalled that "my uncle used to speak Greek and Armenian. And I was fascinated by the languages." Elvin Jones, oral history, June 10–11, 2003, National Museum of American History.
21. Johnny De Droit, oral history, December 4, 1969, Tulane University. The background of the musician Don Albert was suggestive of the varied roots of the new music. This trumpeter was born in New Orleans

in 1908, and his grandfather's grandfather was from the Dominican Republic and was associated with the notorious pirate Jean Lafitte. His spouse was part Filipino, Chinese, and Turkish. See Don Albert, oral history, May 27, 1972, Tulane University: At the same site, see the September 18, 1972, oral history interview with Albert, where he acknowledges that he speaks French.

22. Albert Burbank, oral history, January 4, 1962, Tulane University.

23. Buddie Burton, oral history, September 7, 1959, Tulane University.

24. George "Pops" Foster, *The Autobiography* (Los Angeles: University of California Press, 1971), 4.

25. Pops Foster, oral history, August 24, 1958, Tulane University.

26. Paul Beaulieu, oral history, June 11, 1960, Tulane University.

27. Bella Cornish, oral history, January 13, 1959, Tulane University.

28. Danny Barker, oral history, July 21–23, 1992, National Museum of American History, .

29. Ferrand Clementin, oral history, August 2, 1873, Tulane University.

30. Don Albert, oral history, September 18, 1972, Tulane University.

31. Israel Gorman, oral history, October 21, 1959, Tulane University.

32. "Fan" Borgeau, September 13, 1972, Tulane University.

33. William I. Horne, "Victor Eugene Macarty: From Art to Activism in Reconstruction-Era New Orleans," *Journal of African-American History*, 103 (Number 4, Fall 2018): 496–525, 523.

34. John F. Nau, *The German People of New Orleans* (Leiden: Brill, 1958), 103, 111, 112.

35. Noah Cook, oral history, September 6, 1960, Tulane University.

36. Bella Cornish, oral history, January 13, 1959, Tulane University.

37. Charles Elgar, oral history, May 27, 1958, Tulane University.

38. Hair, *Carnival of Fury*, 78.

39. Gambino, *Vendetta*, 61.

40. Patti Hagan, "One Hundred," *New Yorker*, February 28, 1983, 84. Blake, says his biographer, "learned an important lesson" then. "Never sit with your back to the door. If trouble walks in, you've got to see it quickly enough to duck. Today, whether in his own home or in a plush hotel restaurant, he still demands to be seated facing the doorway." Al Rose, *Eubie Blake* (New York: Schirmer, 1979), 32.

41. David Gilbert, *The Product of Our Souls: Ragtime, Race and the Birth of the Manhattan Musical Marketplace* (Chapel Hill: University of North Carolina Press, 2015).

42. Foster, *The Autobiography*, 93.

43. Appeal from the Second Recorder's Court for the City of New Orleans, Louis Barthe Recorder, City of New Orleans Plaintiff and Appellee versus Lulu White, Defendant and Appellant, Original Brief on Behalf

of City of New Orleans, March 1918, Williams Research Center, New Orleans. See also Herbert Asbury, *The French Quarter: An Informal History of the New Orleans Underworld* (New York: Knopf, 1936). For more on White, see Emily Clark, *The Strange History of the American Quadroon: Free Women of Color in the Revolutionary Atlantic World* (Chapel Hill: University of North Carolina Press, 2013).

44. See, for example, Danny Barker, *Buddy Bolden and the Last Days of Storyville* (London: Cassell, 1998).

45. Paul Barbarin, interview, December 4, 1968, Folder 18, William Russell Papers, Williams Research Center, New Orleans. See also Alecia P. Long, *The Great Southern Babylon: Sex, Race and Respectability in New Orleans, 1865–1920* (Baton Rouge: Louisiana State University Press, 2004).

46. Joseph "Fan" Borgeau, oral history, September 13, 1972, Tulane University.

47. Joseph "Fan" Borgeau, oral history, September 24, 1959, Tulane University.

48. Gary Krist, *Empire of Sin: A Story of Sex, Jazz, Murder and the Battle for Modern New Orleans* (New York: Crown, 2014), 189.

49. Thomas Brothers, *Louis Armstrong's New Orleans* (New York: Norton, 2006), 256.

50. McCusker, *Creole Trombone*, 93. See also Bud Scott, interview, 1939–40, Folder 4, William Russell Papers. Buddy Bolden, the well-known horn man, "used his hand, a glass or a cup for a mute . . . he could actually make his cornet talk. If he'd see a certain girl in the dance hall he wanted to talk to, he'd use his cornet to call her & you'd swear it really sounded like 'Mary Come Here.'"

51. Manuel Manetta, oral history, March 21, 1957, Tulane University.

52. Johnny Lala, oral history, September 24, 1958, Tulane University.

53. Comment by Barney Bigard, May 25, 1969, Folder 28, William Russell Papers.

54. Comment by Eubie Blake, June 5, 1969, Folder 31, William Russell Papers.

55. Howard Reich and William Gaines, *Jelly's Blues: The Life, Music and Redemption of Jelly Roll Morton* (New York: Da Capo, 2003), 98.

56. Manuel Manetta, oral history, March 21, 1957, Tulane University.

57. Comment by Hayes Alvis, October 21, 1968, Folder 7, William Russell Papers.

58. Frances Mouton Oliver, oral history, May 10, 1969, Tulane University.

59. Whitney Balliett, *American Musicians: 56 Portraits in Jazz* (New York: Oxford University Press, 1986), 17, 19.

60. Comment by Volly de Faut, November 21, 1970, Folder 63, William Russell Papers.

61. Comment by Paul Barbarin, December 4, 1968, Folder 18, William Russell Papers.
62. Comment by Danny Barker, August 28 and December 21, 1968, Folder 20, William Russell Papers.
63. Stanley Dance, "Earl Hines," *Stereo Review* 44, no. 2 (1980): 72.
64. *Downbeat*, October 1940, John Steiner Collection, University of Chicago.
65. Ibid.
66. Gambino, *Vendetta*, 63.
67. Comment by Volly de Faut, November 21, 1970, Folder 60, William Russell Papers.
68. William Russell, oral history, August 31, 1962, Tulane University. See also William Russell, oral history, September 4, 1962, Tulane University. Barney Bigard, a clarinetist who played with Duke Ellington, also "passed" occasionally. In Los Angeles he wanted to join the "white" musicians' local union affiliate since they got better jobs. The brother of musician George Baquet—Achille Baquet—also "passed" and was part of the "white" local when he played with comic Jimmy Durante in New York City.
69. Clark Terry, oral history, June 15 and 22, 1999, National Museum of American History.
70. Hair, *Carnival of Fury*, 77.
71. William Howland Kenney III, "Jazz and the Concert Halls: The Eddie Condon Concerts, 1942–1949," *American Music* 1, no. 2 (1983): 60–72, 61.
72. Clayton, *Buck Clayton's Jazz World*, 12.
73. David A. Varel, *The Lost Black Scholar: Resurrecting Allison Davis in American Social Thought* (Chicago: University of Chicago Press, 2018), 145. The impact of the new music on generations of intellectuals of African descent is worthy of further exploration. See Stuart Hall, *Familiar Stranger: A Life Between Two Islands* (Durham: Duke University Press, 2017), 129: This preeminent thinker with Jamaican and British roots concluded that "Miles Davis had put his finger on my soul."
74. Louis Armstrong, *Satchmo: My Life in New Orleans* (New York: Prentice-Hall, 1954), 34, 36.
75. Danny Barker, *A Life in Jazz* (New York: Oxford University Press, 1986), 71.
76. Gambino, *Vendetta*, ix, 56, 78, 97. See also "Correspondence in Relation to the Killing of Prisoners in New Orleans," March 14, 1891 (Washington, D.C.: Government Printing Office). See also John F. Coxe, "The New Orleans Mafia Incident," *Louisiana Historical Quarterly* 20, no. 4 (1937): 3–46.

77. Lynell Thomas, "Neutral Ground or Battleground? Hidden History, Tourism and Spatial (In) Justice in the New Orleans French Quarter," *Journal of African-American History*, 103(Number 4, Fall 2018): 609–636, 629.

78. Hair, *Carnival of Fury*, 70.

79. Bethel, *George Lewis*, 8. For another account of the 1900 tumult, see Frank Adams, oral history, January 20, 1959, Tulane University.

80. Jeremy F. Lane, *Jazz and Machine Age Imperialism: Music, 'Race' and Intellectuals in France, 1918*–1945 (Ann Arbor: University of Michigan Press, 2013), 5; see also Philippe Carles and Louis Comolli, *Free Jazz/Black Power* (Paris: Gallimard-Folio, 2000).

81. Peter Tschmuck, *The Economics of Music* (Newcastle upon Tyne: Agenda, 2017).

82. Leonard Feather, "The Jazz Renaissance and Where to Find It," *Los Angeles Magazine*, no date, Box 9, John Steiner Collection, University of Chicago. The recording engineer Cosimo Mattasa, born in New Orleans in 1926, saw the "cutterhead," a tool deployed in his craft, as being essential. "Mother Nature invented it and they discovered it," that is, "you had to pay a royalty" to Western Electric "to use it. Including on every record you sold! . . . Record companies paid a royalty . . . little guys didn't have a chance to use it unless they had a lotta money . . . you needed twenty hundred dollars up front to lease the cutterhead." Then, German and British inventors made a cheap duplication, further impacting the economics of recording. Cosimo Mattasa, oral history, July 17, 1993, Tulane University.

83. Brad Tolinski and Alan di Perna, *Play It Loud: An Epic History of the Style, Sound, and Revolution of the Electric Guitar* (Garden City, NY: Doubleday, 2016).

84. J. Krivine, *Jukebox Saturday Night* (Secaucus, NJ: Chartwell, 1977), 19, 23.

85. Krist, *Empire of Sin*, 199, 213, 282, 283.

86. Edmond Souchon, oral history, May 7, 1958, Tulane University.

87. *Downbeat*, June 7, 1973, Box 143, John Steiner Collection, University of Chicago.

88. Clark Terry, oral history, June 15 and 22, 1999, National Museum of American History.

89. Celenza, *Jazz Italian Style*, 16.

90. Jack Laine, oral history, April 25, 1964, Tulane University.

91. Frank Amacker, oral history, July 1, 1960, Tulane University.

92. *Downbeat*, October 1940, Box 131, John Steiner Collection, University of Chicago.

93. Stella Oliver, oral history, April 22, 1959, Tulane University.

94. Freddie Moore, oral history, June 19, 1959, Tulane University. Saxophonist Norman Kellogg Mason, born in the Bahamas in 1895, also had dental problems. Norman Kellogg Mason, oral history, February 6, 1960, Tulane University.

95. George "Big Nick" Nicholas, oral history, March 1980, Institute of Jazz Studies.

96. Norman Brownlee, oral history, May 5, 1961, Tulane University.

97. Don Ewell, oral history, December 1, 1960, Tulane University.

98. Herman Autrey, oral history, April 23, 1975, Institute of Jazz Studies.

99. Len Lyons, "Piano Worship: Oscar Peterson," *Downbeat* 42, no. 21 (1975): 14.

100. Horace Silver, *Let's Get to the Nitty Gritty: The Autobiography* (Berkeley: University of California Press, 2006), 172.

101. Harrison Barnes, oral history, January 29, 1959, *Tulane University.*

102. Joseph Borgeau, oral history, September 24, 1959, *Tulane University.*

103. Herbie Hancock, *Possibilities*, 31.

104. *Houston Chronicle*, August 5, 2018.

105. Freddie Moore, oral history, 19 June 1959, Tulane University. See also Walter C. Allen and Brian A. L. Rush, *King Joe Oliver* (Belleville, NJ: Allen, 1955).

106. Max Roach, interview, April 4, 1996, Box 53, Max Roach Papers, Library of Congress, Washington, D.C. See also Frank R. Hayde and Stan Levey, *Jazz Heavyweight*, 151: Levey, a drummer, had hands that were "drawn up permanently from this thick, disfiguring scarring, occurring deep in his palms." Of course, his earlier career as a boxer may have contributed to this problem.

107. Bill Holman, oral history, February 18–19, 2010, National Museum of American History.

108. Horace Silver, interview, *Be-Bop and Beyond*, 3, no. 2 (1985): 1-3, Southern California Library for Social Studies and Research-Los Angeles. Age discrimination might also be a factor in forcing artists to perform unnecessarily. The drummer Stan Levey observed that employers "wanted younger musicians. I could see the handwriting on the wall. You get used up. You get used up and thrown out." This pressure compelled musicians of a certain age to go beyond the limit of endurance.

109. Frederick J. Spencer, *Jazz and Death: Medical Profiles of Jazz Greats* (Jackson: University Press of Mississippi, 2002), xii, 124.

110. Ronald L. Morris, *Wait Until Dark: Jazz and the Underworld, 1880–1940* (Bowling Green, OH: Bowling Green State University Popular Press, 1980), 2, 4.

2. What Did I Do To Be So Black and Blue?

1. Milt Hinton and David Berger, *Bass Line: The Stories and Photographs of Milt Hinton* (Philadelphia: Temple University Press, 1988), 32.
2. Lionel Hampton, *Hamp: An Autobiography* (New York: Amistad, 1993), 49.
3. Russell Procope, oral history, March 6, 1979, Institute of Jazz Studies, Rutgers University, Newark.
4. Eddie Barefield, oral history, November 20, 1978, Institute of Jazz Studies.
5. Imelda Hunt, "An Oral History of Art Tatum During His Years in Toledo, Ohio, 1909–1932" (PhD diss., Bowling Green State University, 1995), 57, 58, 59, 61. Perhaps it was the venues in which he performed that helped to induce the fabled pianist's prodigious appetite for alcohol. See Marshal Royal, *Jazz Survivor*, 52: Royal and Tatum "would start out drinking Pabst Blue Ribbon [beer], stacking the empty cans on the floor and see if if we could pile them up to the ceiling before the evening was over."
6. W. R. Wilkerson, *Hollywood Godfather: The Life and Times of Billy Wilkerson* (Chicago: Chicago Review Press, 2018), 9: Unfortunately, Wilkerson, a major investor in this illicitness, "incinerated all paperwork housed at the [Hollywood] *Reporter* from its founding in 1930" to about 1952, which could have illuminated the dark corners of this ugly business.
7. Joel Vance, *Fats Waller: His Life and Times* (Chicago: Contemporary, 1977), 72.
8. John Chilton, *Roy Eldridge: Little Jazz Giant* (New York: Continuum, 2002), 65, 147.
9. Charles E. Rose, "The American Federation of Musicians and Its Effect on Black Musicians in St. Louis in the Twentieth Century" (Master's thesis, Southern Illinois University, Edwardsville, 1979), 31. See also Timothy C. Richards, *Crooks Kill, Cops Lie: The True Story of the St. Louis Mobster Wars* (St. Louis: Bluebird, 2012).
10. Bill Lhotka, *St. Louis Crime Chronicles: The First 200 Years, 1764–1964* (St. Louis: Reedy Press, 2009), 139. See also John Cleophus Cotter, "The Negro in Music in Saint Louis" (master's thesis, Washington University in St. Louis, 1959).
11. Daniel Waugh, *Gangs of St. Louis* (Charleston, SC: History Press, 2010), 79. See also Eleanore Berra Marfisi, *The Hill: Its History, Its Recipes* (St. Louis: Bradley, 2003).
12. Daniel Waugh, *Egan's Rats: The Untold Story of the Prohibition Era Gang That Ruled St. Louis* (Nashville: Cumberland House, 2007), 132, 190.
13. Miles Davis with Quincy Troupe, *Miles: The Autobiography* (New York: Touchstone, 1989), 19, 15.

14. Cab Calloway, *Of Minnie the Moocher and Me* (New York: Crowell, 1976), 10, 44, 42, 85–88, 110, 115–16, 128, 141.
15. Milt Hinton, oral history, n.d., Institute of Jazz Studies.
16. Hinton and Berger, *Bass Line*, 115, 122.
17. Barry Singer, *Black and Blue: The Life and Lyrics of Andy Razaf* (New York: Schirmer, 1992), 99.
18. Lena Horne as told to Helen Arnstein and Carlton Moss, *In Person* (New York: Greenberg, 1950), 38.
19. Howard Eugene Johnson with Wendy Johnson, *A Dancer in the Revolution: Stretch Johnson, Harlem Communist at the Cotton Club* (New York: Fordham University Press, 2014), 26.
20. Danny Barker, oral history, July 21–23, 1992, National Museum of American History.
21. Dempsey J. Travis, *Norman Granz: The White Moses of Black Jazz* (Chicago: Urban Research, 2003), xxvii. See also Dempsey J. Travis, *An Autobiography of Black Jazz* (Chicago: Urban Research, 1983).
22. Ada "Bricktop" Smith with James Haskins, *Bricktop* (New York: Athenaeum, 1983), 166, 167, 169.
23. Benny Carter, oral history, October 13–14, 1976, Institute of Jazz Studies.
24. Leonard Feather, *Los Angeles Times*, January 12, 1990.
25. Nick Tosches, *King of the Jews* (New York: HarperCollins, 2005), 235, 252, 258, 290–91.
26. Singer, *Black and Blue*, 188–89.
27. Charles W. Turnbull and Christian J. Lewis, "Casper A. Holstein: Unusual Humanitarian" (Charlotte Amalie, St. Thomas, U.S. Virgin Islands: VI Department of Education, 1974).
28. John Chilton, *Ride, Red, Ride: The Life of Henry "Red" Allen* (London: Cassell, 1999), 50.
29. Shirley Stewart, *The World of Stephanie St. Clair: An Entrepreneur Race Woman and Outlaw in Early Twentieth Century Harlem* (New York: Lang, 2014), 2. See also Catherine Rottenberg, ed., *Black Harlem and the Jewish Lower East Side: Narratives Out of Time* (Albany: State University of New York Press, 2013).
30. Elizabeth Schroeder Sclabach, *Along the Streets of Bronzeville: Black Chicago's Literary Landscape* (Urbana, IL: University of Illinois Press, 2013), 10, 54, 58, 63. See also William Howland Kenney, *Chicago Jazz: A Cultural History, 1904–1930* (New York: Oxford University Press, 1993).
31. Kenney, *Chicago Jazz*, 8, 11.
32. Benjamin Franklin, *Jazz and Blues Musicians of South Carolina: Interviews with Jabbo, Dizzy, Drink and Others* (Columbia, SC: University of South Carolina Press, 2008).

33. Howard Reich and William Gaines, *Jelly's Blues: The Life, Music and Redemption of Jelly Roll Morton* (New York: Da Capo, 2003), 99–100.
34. Hinton and Berger, *Bass Line*, 17.
35. John J. Binder, *The Chicago Outfit* (Chicago: Arcade, 2003), 7, 119.
36. Alyn Shipton, *Hi-De-Ho: The Life of Cab Calloway* (New York: Oxford University Press, 2010), 26, 42, 72.
37. Ron Chepseiuk, *Black Gangsters of Chicago* (Fort Lee, NJ: Barricade, 2007), 33.
38. Stephen Longstreet, *Storyville to Harlem: Fifty Years in the Jazz Scene* (New Brunswick, NJ: Rutgers University, 1986), 59.
39. Clippings, 1926–27, Chicago Crime Scrapbooks, Chicago History Museum. See also Frank R. Hayde, *Jazz Heavyweight, 72*: Bandleader Woody Herman, born in 1913 of German and Polish parents, recalled a time when racketeers shot him in the leg after a night listening to pianist Earl Hines at Al Capone's "Grand Terrace Ballroom."
40. Ron Chepesiuk, *Gangsters of Harlem: The Gritty Underworld of New York's Most Famous Neighborhood* (Fort Lee, NJ: Barricade, 2007), 39. See Also Steven R. Cureton, *Black Vanguards and Black Gangsters: From Seeds of Discontent to a Declaration of War* (Lanham, MD: University Press of America, 2011).
41. Scrapbook, 1920s, Louis Armstrong Archive, Queens College, New York.
42. Laurence Bergreen, *Louis Armstrong: An Extravagant Life* (New York: Broadway, 1997), 481, 270, 278, 279, 374, 376.
43. Terry Teachout, *Pops: A Life of Louis Armstrong* (Boston: Houghton Mifflin, 2009), 207.
44. Milt Hinton, oral history, no date, Institute of Jazz Studies.
45. Joe Glaser to George Hoefer, July 15, 1959, vertical file on Joe Glaser, Institute of Jazz Studies.
46. Ibid.
47. *Downbeat*, 24 July 1969, Institute of Jazz Studies, Rutgers University, Newark.
48. W.R. Wilkerson, *Hollywood Godfather*, 90.
49. *Downbeat*, 24 July 1969, Institute of Jazz Studies, Rutgers University, Newark.
50. Ibid.
51. *Chicago Defender*, February 11, 1928,
52. Ernie Anderson, "Joe Glaser and Louis Armstrong: A Memoir," December 1994, Louis Armstrong Archive.
53. Ricky Riccardi, *What a Wonderful World: The Magic of Louis Armstrong's Later Years* (New York: Pantheon, 2011), 11.
54. Clipping, circa 1920s, scrapbook, Louis Armstrong Archive.

55. Clipping, 1930s, scrapbook, Louis Armstrong Archive.
56. Teachout, *Pops*, 102.
57. Undated article on Glaser, Box 113, John Steiner Collection, University of Chicago.
58. "A Good One-Two," in Whitney Balliett, *American Musicians: 56 Portraits in Jazz* (New York: Oxford University Press, 1986), 114–21, 118.
59. "Sunshine Always Opens Out," in ibid., 80–96, 83, 85.
60. Stanley Dance, "Earl Hines," *Stereo Review* 44, no. 2 (1980): 75.
61. Stanley Dance, "Earl 'Fatha' Hines," *Stereo Review* 32, no. 1 (1974): 81.
62. Al Van Starrex on Earl Hines, July 1970, file on Hines, Institute of Jazz Studies.
63. Dance, "Earl 'Fatha' Hines," 77.
64. Earl Hines, "How Gangsters Ran the Band Business," Box 117, John Steiner Collection.
65. Richard Boyer, "The Hot Bach," in Mark Tucker, ed., *The Duke Ellington Reader* (New York: Oxford University Press, 1993), 224.
66. "Irving Mills Dies at 91; Jazz Music Publisher," *New York Times*, April 23, 1985, and biographical material in vertical file on Mills, Institute of Jazz Studies. See also Michael Gerber, *Jazz Jews* (Nottingham, UK: Five Leaves, 2009).
67. Calloway, *Of Minnie the Moocher and Me*, 110.
68. Terry Teachout, *Duke: The Life of Duke Ellington* (London: Robson, 2013), 58, 180–81.
69. "From Kirkeby," n.d., Box 11, Folder 1, Ed Kirkeby Collection, Institute of Jazz Studies.
70. Ed Kirkeby to Edith Waller, December 16, 1944, Box 11, Folder 1, Ed Kirkeby Papers.
71. Interview with Leonard Feather, June 10, 1990, Box 11, Leonard Feather Papers.
72. Mark Tucker, *Ellington: The Early Years* (Urbana, IL: University of Illinois Press, 1991), 99, 116, 189, 210.
73. Ronald L. Morris, *Wait Until Dark*, 151.
74. *New York Age*, July 9, 1927, and "A Cotton Club Miscellany," compiled and edited by Steven Lasker in vertical file on the Cotton Club, Institute of Jazz Studies.
75. *New York Times*, July 8, 1981.
76. Stuart Nicholson, *Reminiscing in Tempo: A Portrait of Duke Ellington* (Boston: Northeastern University Press, 1991), 68, 82, 98.
77. Virgil W. Peterson, *The Mob: 200 Years of Organized Crime in New York* (Ottawa: Green Hill, 1983), 184.
78. Hampton and Haskins, *Hamp*, 16, 29.

79. *San Francisco Chronicle*, September 1, 1986.
80. Mezz Mezzrow and Bernard Wolfe, *Really the Blues* (repr., New York: Citadel, 1990), 3, 60, 61, 66.
81. Max Kaminsky, *My Life in Jazz* (New York: Harper and Row, 1963), 38.
82. Danny Barker, *A Life in Jazz* (New York: Oxford University Press, 1986), 113, 122, 126–27, 157.
83. Eddie Barefield, oral history, November 20, 1978, Institute of Jazz Studies.
84. Ibid.
85. James Lincoln Collier, "More Jazz Clubs," *West View News*, August 2016, See also Jim Haskins, *The Cotton Club* (New York: Random House, 1977).
86. Patrick Burke, *Come In and Hear the Truth: Jazz and Race on 52nd Street* (Chicago: University of Chicago Press, 2008), 30, 38.
87. Dr. Billy Taylor with Teresa L. Reed, *The Jazz Life of Dr. Billy Taylor* (Bloomington: Indiana University Press, 2013), 22.
88. Paul Chevigny, *Gigs: Jazz and the Cabaret Laws in New York City* (New York: Routledge, 2005), 57.
89. Elizabeth Pepin and Lewis Watts, *Harlem of the West: The San Francisco Fillmore Jazz Era* (San Francisco: Chronicle, 2006). See also *San Francisco Chronicle*, February 8, 1998
90. Marva Griffin Carter, *Swing Along: The Musical Life of Will Marion Cook* (New York: Oxford University Press, 2008), 27, 45, 92, 109.
91. Press release, April 1937, Reel 4, no. 789, Series D, Press Releases, Claude Barnett/Associated Negro Press Papers, Chicago History Museum. See also Gerald Horne, *The Rise and Fall of the Associated Negro Press: Claude Barnett's Pan-African News and the Jim Crow Paradox* (Urbana: University of Illinois Press, 2017); and Horne, *The Color of Fascism: Lawrence Dennis, Racial Passing and the Rise of Right-Wing Extremism in the U.S.* (New York: New York University Press, 2006).
92. Al Rose, *I Remember Jazz: Six Decades Among the Great Jazzmen* (Baton Rouge: Louisiana State University Press, 1987), 63–64.
93. Danny Barker, oral history, July 21–23, 1992, National Museum of American History.

3. One O'Clock Jump

1. Roy Wilkins, *Standing Fast: An Autobiography* (New York: Viking, 1982), 60, 61, 63, 76, 87.
2. Frank R. Hayde, *The Mafia and the Machine: The Story of the Kansas City Mob* (Fort Lee, NJ: Barricade, 2010), 26.
3. *Newsweek*, March 21, 1938.

4. *Time*, February 22, 1937.
5. Monte M. Poen, ed., *Letters Home by Harry Truman* (Columbia, MO: University of Missouri Press, 1984), 86.
6. Lawrence H. Larsen and Nancy J. Hulston, "Criminal Aspects of the Pendergast Machine," *Missouri Historical Review* 91, no. 2 (1997): 168–80, 169, 170, 171, 172, 173, 174, 175, 176, 179.
7. Marc Rice, "The Bennie Moten Orchestra, 1918–1935: A Kansas City Jazz Ensemble and Its African American Audience" (PhD diss., University of Kentucky, 1998).
8. Charles E. Coulter, *"Take Up the Black Man's Burden": Kansas City's African American Communities, 1865–1939* (Columbia: University of Missouri Press, 2006), 114–15, 271–73.
9. Reginald Tyrone Buckner, "A History of Music Education in the Black Community of Kansas City, Kansas, 1905–1954" (PhD diss., University of Minnesota, 1974), 68, 69, 109, 129.
10. Lewis Grout, Chief Probation Officer to Hon. Merrill E. Otis, U.S. District Judge, Criminal Case 14536-14569, July 17, 1940, Criminal Case Files (1879–1972), Record Group 21, Records of the U.S. District Courts, Western District of Missouri, Western Division, Kansas City, Case Files, National Archives and Records Administration, Kansas City.
11. Ibid., memorandum, n.d., *U.S. v. Pendergast*, U.S. District Court.
12. Lawrence H. Larsen and Nancy J. Hulston, *Pendergast!* (Columbia: University of Missouri Press, 1997), 108. See also Gene Powell, *Tom's Boy Harry: The First Complete Authentic Story of Harry Truman's Connection with the Pendergast Machine* (Jefferson City, MO: Hawthorn, 1948).
13. William M. Reddig, *Tom's Town: Kansas City and the Pendergast Legend* (Philadelphia: Lippincott, 1947), 249.
14. William Ousley, *Open City: True Story of the K.C. Crime Family, 1900–1950* (Overland Park, KS: Leathers, 2008), 7, 74, 95, 100.
15. Kathy J. Ogren, "Performance Crossroads: The Significance of the Jazz Controversy for Twenties America" (PhD diss., Johns Hopkins University, 1985), 35.
16. *U.S. v. Lazia*, Box 313 and Box 314, Record Group 21, Records of the U.S. District Court Western District of Missouri, Kansas City, Criminal Case Files 12021-12028, including "Transcript of Evidence," Filed June 6, 1934. At the same site, see also Box 278, Record Group 21, Records of U.S. District Court, Criminal Case Files 10815-10839, National Archives and Records Administration, Kansas City.
17. *Kansas City Times*, March 5, 1934.
18. *St. Louis Globe Democrat*, December 1, 1934.
19. Clipping, July 10, 1934, vertical file, Kansas City Public Library.

20. Ross Russell, *Jazz Style in Kansas City and the Southwest* (Berkeley: University of California Press, 1971), 22.

21. John Daily, "No Non-Irish Need Apply in Boss Pendergast's Kansas City," paper delivered at the American Conference for Irish Studies, Savannah, March 5-9, 2008, Chuck Haddix Files, University of Missouri, Kansas City. Nowadays, it is quite common for some Euro-Americans to argue that their ancestors endured roadblocks not unlike that which derailed Negroes and, thus, if they could overcome, why can't Negroes do the same? This is simply another route to rationalize white supremacy and Negro subjugation.

22. Buddy Tate, oral history, February 17, 1977, Missouri Historical Society.

23. Eddie Durham, oral history, February 22, 1977, Missouri Historical Society.

24. Count Basie, oral history, February 15, 1977, Missouri Historical Society.

25. Frank Driggs and Chuck Haddix, *Kansas City Jazz: From Ragtime to Bebop—A History* (New York: Oxford University Press, 2005), 6-7.

26. Linda Dahl, *Morning Glory: A Biography of Mary Lou Williams* (New York: Pantheon, 1999), 1-5.

27. Durham, oral history, February 22, 1977.

28. Dave Oliphant, *Jazz Mavericks of the Lone Star State* (Austin: University of Texas Press, 2007), 23.

29. Nathan W. Pearson, *Goin' to Kansas City* (Urbana, IL: University of Illinois Press, 1987), 94, 97, 100, 101, 103.

30. Al Rose, *I Remember Jazz: Six Decades Among the Great Jazzmen* (Baton Rouge: Louisiana State University Press, 1987), 104. See also Pops Foster as told to Tom Stoddard, *The Autobiography of a New Orleans Jazzman* (Los Angeles: University of California Press, 1971): "Lulu White herself could handle three men at once—one in every hole. She called that her around the world trip. . . . Lulu herself liked women for sex" (93).

31. Stanley Crouch, *Kansas City Lightning: The Rise and Times of Charlie Parker* (New York: HarperCollins, 2013), 218.

32. Gene Ramey, oral history, January 9, 1977, Missouri Historical Society.

33. Buster Smith, oral history, 1977, Missouri Historical Society.

34. Dave Gelly, *Being Prez: The Life and Music of Lester Young* (New York: Oxford University Press, 2007), 45.

35. Walter C. Allen and Brian Rust, *King Joe Oliver* (Belleville, NJ: WCA, 1955), 33.

36. Barbara Kukla, *Swing City: Newark Nightlife, 1925-1950* (Philadelphia: Temple University Press, 1991), 44.

37. Juan Tizol, oral history, November 15, 1978, Institute of Jazz Studies, Rutgers University, Newark.

38. John Levy with Devra Hall, *Men, Women and Girl Singers: My Life As a Musician Turned Talent Manager* (Silver Spring, MD: Beckham, 2000), 32, 18.

39. Sunnie Wilson and John Cohassey, *Toast of the Town: The Life and Times of Sunnie Wilson* (Detroit: Wayne State University Press, 1998), 50, 65. See also Paul R. Kavieff, *The Violent Years: Prohibition and the Detroit Mobs* (Fort Lee, NJ: Barricade, 2013).

40. Kukla, *Swing City*, 26.

41. Ibid., 113, 156, 158, 179.

42. Steven R. Cureton, *Black Vanguards and Black Gangsters: From Seeds of Discontent to a Declaration of War* (Lanham, MD: University Press of America, 2011).

43. Bob Luke, *The Most Famous Woman in Baseball: Effa Manley and the Negro Leagues* (Washington, D.C.: Potomac, 2011), x, xii, 4, 18, 29, 51.

44. Rebecca T. Alpert, *Out of Left Field: Jews and Black Baseball* (New York: Oxford University Press, 2011), 63. The author contends that behind the idea of Negroes clowning in baseball and basketball were such entrepreneurs as Abe Saperstein, Ed Gottlieb, and Syd Pollock.

45. Sam Wooding, oral history, April 22–25, 28, 1978, Institute of Jazz Studies.

46. Interview with Jabbo Smith, June 1981, Jabbo Smith Papers, University of South Carolina, Columbia

47. Lowell Dwight Dickerson, "Central Avenue Meets Hollywood: The Amalgamation of the Black and White Musicians' Unions in Los Angeles" (PhD diss., University of California, Los Angeles, 1998), 51, 67. See also Peipin and Watts, *Harlem of the West*, and *San Francisco Chronicle*, February 8, 1998.

48. Gerald Horne, *Fire This Time: The Watts Uprising and the 1960s* (Charlottesville, VA: University of Virginia Press, 1995).

49. Betty Hillmon, "American Composer at Home and Abroad," *Black Perspectives in Music* 14, no. 2 (1986): 143–80.

50. File on Bechet, September 15, 1922, HO45/24778, National Archives of United Kingdom-London (hereafter NAUK)

51. Ibid.

52. John Chilton, *Sidney Bechet: The Wizard of Jazz* (New York: Oxford University Press, 1987), 77, 84, 21.

53. Glover Compton, oral history, June 30, 1959, Tulane University.

54. Sidney Bechet, *Treat It Gentle* (New York: Hill and Wang, 1960), 131.

55. Darnell Howard, oral history, April 21, 1957, Tulane University.

56. *Daily Express*, October 14, 1925.

57. Gerald Horne, *Paul Robeson: The Artist As Revolutionary* (London: Pluto, 2016).

58. Memorandum, 1925, LAB2/1188/edar3406/1925, National Archives, London.

59. British Empire Union to Margaret Bonfield, July 1, 1929, LAB2/1188, National Archives, London.

60. Memorandum, 1930, WO32/3907, National Archives, London.

61. Catherine Parsonage, *The Evolution of Jazz in Britain, 1850–1935* (Burlington, VT: Ashgate, 2005), 173.

62. *Financial Times*, February 3-4, 2018.

63. Ken Colyer, oral history, September 21, 1959, Tulane University.

64. Roy Carew, oral history, June 21, 1961, Tulane University.

65. Johnny De Droit, oral history, March 16, 1973, Tulane University.

66. Taylor and Reed, *The Jazz Life of Dr. Billy Taylor*, 71.

67. Wooding, oral history, April 22–25, 28, 1975, Institute of Jazz Studies.

68. Foster, *The Autobiography of a New Orleans Jazzman*, 56, 132.

69. Willie Foster, oral history, January 21, 1959, Tulane University.

70. Lawrence Douglas Harris, oral history, June 6, 1961, Tulane University.

71. Eric Hobsbawm, *The Jazz Scene* (New York: Pantheon, 1993), 30, 330.

72. Release, January 1928, Reel 1, #107, Part I, Press Releases, Barnett/Associated Negro Press Papers, Chicago History Museum.

73. Release, May 1929, Reel 1, #551, Part I, Press Releases, Barnett/Associated Negro Press Papers, Chicago History Museum.

74. Naresh Fernandes, *Taj Mahal Foxtrot: The Story of Bombay's Jazz Age* (Delhi: Roli, 2012), 9, 95.

75. Undated Article, Box 146, John Steiner Collection, University of Chicago.

76. Buck Clayton, oral history, February 15, 1977, Missouri Historical Society.

77. Hinton and Berger, *Bass Line*, 154. See also Gerald Horne, *Race to Revolution: The U.S. and Cuba During Slavery and Jim Crow* (New York: Monthly Review Press, 2014).

78. Benny Carter, oral history, October 13–14, 1976, Institute of Jazz Studies.

79. Interview with Leonard Feather, June 10, 1990, Box 11, Leonard Feather Papers, University of Idaho, Moscow.

80. Buddy Tate, oral history, March 1980, Institute of Jazz Studies. On Pittman in Brazil see Gerald Horne, *The Deepest South: The U.S., Brazil and the African Slave Trade* (New York: New York University Press, 2007), 252.

81. Samir Amin, *A Life Looking Forward: Memoirs of an Independent Marxist* (London: Zed, 2006), 140.

82. Charlie Barnet with Stanley Dance, *Those Swinging Years: The Autobiography* (Baton Rouge: Louisiana State University Press, 1984), 139.

83. Taylor and Reed, *The Jazz Life of Dr. Billy Taylor*, 68.

84. *Downbeat*, June 15, 1942. Reel 1, Stanford University.

85. Release, September 1944, Reel 29, #400, Part I, Press Releases, Claude Barnett/Associated Negro Press Papers, Chicago History Museum. In the same collection see also Release, October 1946, Reel 33, #1066, Part I, Press Releases. Sidney Garner, U.S. Negro, given credit for catapulting Carmen Miranda to fame and fortune, returned to France postwar. He had left New York in 1914, saw four years of service during the war and lived in France where he became a "financial success"—before being interned by German occupation forces. And see Release, April 1947, Reel 34, #538, Part I, Releases. A number of Negro musicians chose to stay in Paris, so alienated from the United States that they chose to stay in Paris even after the German takeover and the appearance of signs in shops reading, "We don't serve Negroes or Jews."

86. *Downbeat*, November 15, 1942. Reel 1, Stanford University.

87. Sam Wooding, oral history, April 22–May 8, 1975, National Museum of American History.

88. *Downbeat*, March 1, 1943. Reel 1, Stanford University.

89. Gerald Horne, *Facing the Rising Sun: African Americans, Japan and the Rise of Afro-Asian Solidarity* (New York: New York University Press, 2018).

90. Clark Halker, "A History of Local 108 and the Struggle for Racial Equality in the American Federation of Musicians," *Black Music Research Journal* 8, no. 2 (1988): 207–22, 215.

91. Travis, *The Autobiography of Black Jazz*, 472.

92. Machito [Frank Grillo], oral history, May 1980, Institute of Jazz Studies. See also Alexandre Abdoulaev, "Savoy: Reassessing the Role of the 'World's Finest Ballroom' in Music and Culture, 1926–1958" (PhD diss., Boston University, 2014).

93. Vertical file on Mario Bauza, undated article, Institute of Jazz Studies.

94. Undated Release from Visual Arts Research and Resource Center, Institute of Jazz Studies; and Peter Watrous, "Mario Bauza, Band Leader, Dies; Champion of Latin Music Was 82," *New York Times*, July 12, 1993.

95. Gelly, *Being Prez*, 97. See also Douglas Henry Daniels, *Lester Leaps In: The Life and Times of Lester "Pres" Young* (Boston: Beacon Press, 2002): This is the fullest exploration of this creative artist.

96. Barnet with Dance, *Those Swinging Years*, 77.

97. Vertical file on Charlie Barnet, obituary, September 6, 1991, Institute of Jazz Studies.

98. "Trummy" Young, oral history, September 17–18, 1976, Institute of Jazz Studies. The critic Leonard Feather concurs in asserting that Benny Carter—not Goodman—had the first multiracial band. Feather, *The Jazz Years: Eyewitness to an Era* (New York: Da Capo, 1987), 35.

99. Barnet with Dance, *Those Swinging Years*, 160.

100. Ben Yagoda, *The B Side: The Death of Tin Pan Alley and the Rebirth of the Great American Song* (New York: Riverhead, 2015), 43.

4. Hothouse

1. Ira Gitler, *Swing to Bop: An Oral History of the Transition in Jazz in the 1940s* (New York: Oxford University Press, 1985). See also Frank Hayde, *Jazz Heavyweight*, 61: "Bebop was characterized by breakneck tempos, disorienting rhythms, hip chord substitutions and dissonant tritons—also called 'flatted fifths'," amounting to a "test of a man's [sic] endurance. . . . " These musicians had to "think fast to play fast," which was a "metaphor for the quickening of postwar life in a more urban and industrial but still segregated" nation. This music "expressed frustration, anger and sarcastic humor," an updating of the epistemology of the blues, in other words. See also Maxine Gordon, *Sophisticated Giant*, 47. "Bebop was created by musicians who refused to fight in World War II," that is, "some musicians like Connie Kay and Sun Ra were conscientious objectors," and founding father of the new musical form, Dizzy Gillespie, refused to serve in the military also. Later the trumpeter wrote a tune, "Blue Bikini," about the "1946 atomic bomb tests on Bikini Atoll. . . ." The language of the "boppers" anticipated, then underscored the new form of music; their argot was a phonic rendering of certain drumming patterns, for example: "'oop bop sh'bam; . . . 'obla dee' . . . 'budeedah' . . ." See Philippe Carles and Jean-Louis Comolli, *Free Jazz/Black Power*, 131.

2. Leonard Feather, "The Jazz Renaissance and Where to Find it," Los Angeles, n.d., ca. 1975, Box 9, Leonard Feather Papers, University of Idaho, Moscow.

3. Porter with Keller, *There and Back*, 68.

4. John Chilton, *The Song of the Hawk: The Life and Recordings of Coleman Hawkins* (Ann Arbor: University of Michigan Press, 1990), 77.

5. Michael Flamm, *In the Heat of the Summer: The New York Riots of 1964 and the War on Crime* (Philadelphia: University of Pennsylvania Press, 2017), 203; *New York Post*, July 23, 1964. Max Roach, interview, December 8, 1978, Box 52, Max Roach Papers, Library of Congress: In the early 1940s as Dizzy Gillespie was playing a tune called "Bebop," a critic asked him what he had been doing and then "misunderstood

what [the trumpeter] was saying," and this is how a single tune came to define an entire genre.

6. Ben Korall, *Drummin' Men: The Heartbeat of Jazz, The Bebop Years* (New York: Oxford University Press, 2002), 61.

7. David Hadju, *Lush Life: A Biography of Billy Strayhorn* (New York: Farrar, Straus and Giroux, 1996), 48, 73, 78, 100, 196, 224, 257. Though much is made of the attraction of certain musicians to heroin and cocaine, alcohol unleashed like damage. As one observer said of piano genius Art Tatum, he "could really put away the beer." Tribute, n.d., Box 73, Series 3, Sub Series 1, Willis Conover Papers, University of North Texas, Denton, Texas. As with harder drugs, the stress of the business could drive an artist to drink. Promoter George Wein said that "Hot Lips" Page got drunk in response to a mild critique of his playing: "I hit where it hurt," Wein said apologetically: "you can't do that to a musician." See George Wein, oral history, May 11, 2011, National Museum of American History. Gene Gammage, a drummer born in 1931, had a similar experience. He played alongside vocalist Bobby Short, but, said fellow drummer Jimmy Cobb, "he didn't like" that kind of music, "so he got a . . . drinking habit and he really got off into it." Jimmy Cobb, oral history, July 26–27, 2010, National Museum of American History.

8. Cedar Walton, oral history, October 2–3, 2010, National Museum of American History. From "Trummy" Young, oral history, September 17–18, 1976, Institute of Jazz Studies: Henry "Rubberlegs" Williams, born in 1907, was a "big sissy, you know, great big guy . . . about 6'4", he weighed about 240, and he loved Johnny Hodges," fellow performer, "so he used to walk up to Johnny and—let me feel it man; he'd grab down there and grab . . . Hodges' penis . . . so, Johnny, he say, . . . I just let him go feel it . . . and then he go on." But then Charlie Parker put the "equivalent to 75 Benzedrine tablets . . . in the coffee to let it soak. . . . Rubberlegs was already half drunk . . . had some bad liquor . . . he didn't drink nothing but cheap liquor" and then "wanted some coffee . . . so he grabbed the coffee up and drank it." and "he really got wild after that . . . he had fists big as hams . . . we all was getting kind of frightened." But all apparently ended well.

9. Ed Kirkeby to Fats Waller, August 25, 1943, Box 6, Folder 22, Ed Kirkeby Papers, Institute of Jazz Studies, Rutgers University-Newark..

10. *Chicago Daily News*, December 15, 1943.

11. Levy with Hall, *Men, Women and Girl Singers*, 43.

12. Cass Sunstein, *The Second Bill of Rights: FDR's Unfinished Revolution and Why We Need It Now More than Ever* (New York: Basic, 2006).

13. Claude McKay, *Harlem: Negro Metropolis* (New York: E. P. Dutton, 1940), 119.

14. Barnet with Dance, *Those Swinging Years*, 50, 58.
15. Randy Weston, *African Rhythms: The Autobiography* (Durham, NC: Duke University Press, 2010), 27.
16. George Wein, oral history, May 11, 2011, National Museum of American History.
17. Buddy DeFranco, oral history, November 8–9, 2008, National Museum of American History.
18. Chico Hamilton, oral history, January 9–10, 2006, National Museum of American History.
19. Robin D. G. Kelley, *Thelonious Monk: The Life and Times of an American Original* (New York: Free Press, 2009), 117–18, 120. See also Frank Hayde, *Jazz Heavyweight*, 131: Here bandleader Benny Goodman is accused of "secretly recording our shows," that is, those involving drummer Stan Levey, with "recording equipment hidden under the stage," presumably to avoid compensating musicians when this stolen music was released on disc.
20. Toby Gleason, ed., *Music in the Air: The Selected Writings of Ralph J. Gleason* (New Haven: Yale University Press, 2016), 29, 12.
21. "No Bop Roots in Jazz: Parker," *Downbeat*, 16, Number 17 (September 9, 1949): 1,
22. Max Roach, interview, January 28, 1981, Box 52, Max Roach Papers.
23. Nat Hentoff, "Race Prejudice in Jazz: It Works Both Ways," *Harper's* 218, no. 1309 (1959): 73, Hogan Jazz Archive, Tulane University.
24. Charles Rossi, "New Orleans," January 24, 1941, vertical file on World War II and Jazz, Hogan Jazz Archive, Tulane University. See also Christopher Wilkinson, *Big Band Jazz in Black West Virginia, 1930–1942* (Jackson: University Press of Mississippi, 2012).
25. Arch Ayres, undated article, Jazz Ltd. Papers, Chicago History Museum.
26. Levy with Hall, *Men, Women and Girl Singers*, 98.
27. Quincy Jones, *Q: The Autobiography* (New York: Doubleday, 2001), 301.
28. *Philadelphia Inquirer*, June 25, 1987.
29. *Philadelphia Inquirer*, November 8, 1988.
30. John Broven, *Record Makers and Breakers: Voices of the Independent Rock 'n' Roll Pioneers* (Urbana, IL: University of Illinois Press, 2010), 243.
31. Josh Alan Friedman, *Tell the Truth Until They Bleed: Coming Clean in the Dirty World of Blues* (New York: Backbeat, 2008), 11, 12.
32. Gene Santoro, *Myself When I Am Real: The Life and Music of Charles Mingus* (New York: Oxford University Press, 2000), 95.
33. Charlie Barnet with Stanley Dance, *Those Swinging Years*, 65. Reportedly, Louis Armstrong knew Luciano and visited him in Naples

in the 1940s: Ernie Anderson, "Joe Glaser & Louis Armstrong," Part II, Storyville, March 1, 1995, Louis Armstrong Archive, Queens College, New York City.

34. Ellie Horne to William Russell, May 26, 1944, MS 517, Folder 11, William Russell Papers, Williams Research Center, New Orleans.

35. Gerald Horne, *Fighting in Paradise: Labor Unions, Racism and Communists in the Making of Modern Hawaii* (Honolulu: University of Hawaii Press, 2011).

36. John Hammond, *John Hammond on Record: An Autobiography* (New York: Summit, 1977), 228.

37. Note on Bridges, in William Russell, compiler, *"Oh, Mister Jelly": A Jelly Roll Morton Scrapbook* (Copenhagen: Jazz Media, 1999), 56671, 566. See also George Seltzer, *Music Matters: The Performer and the American Federation of Musicians* (Metuchen, NJ: Scarecrow Press, 1989).

38. Walter White to James Petrillo, July 1, 1942, Box IIA347, NAACP Papers, Library of Congress.

39. James Petrillo to Walter White, November 9, 1943, Box IIA347, NAACP Papers.

40. Gus Russo, *Supermob: How Sidney Korshak and His Criminal Associates Became America's Hidden Power Brokers* (New York: Bloomsbury, 2006), 45.

41. Gelly, *Being Prez*, 92.

42. Max Gordon, *Live at the Village Vanguard* (New York: St. Martin's, 1980), 67.

43. Walter White to Fiorello La Guardia, March 23, 1943, Box IIA517, NAACP Papers.

44. Crouch, *Kansas City Lightning*, 13.

45. Chilton, *Roy Eldridge*, 65.

46. "Canteen Heads Have Row Over Mixed Dancing," *Downbeat*, 10, Number 8 (April 15, 1943): 1, 5. April 15, 1943.

47. "White Woman" to Walter White, April 28, 1943, Box IIA517.

48. Statement to Savoy, April 28, 1943, Box IIA517, NAACP Papers.

49. AFM Local 802 to Walter White, April 26, 1943, Box IIA517, NAACP Papers

50. Gelly, *Being Prez*, 97. The trombonist "Trummy" Young recalled an instance when the pianist Willie "The Lion" Smith—"he looks white anyway"—was ordered off the bandstand by a policeman who yelled, "You can't be playing with them. He had to carry his birth certificate around with him. That's the only way . . . he could get to play with us." Young, oral history, September 17–18, 1976, Institute of Jazz Studies. In the same interview Young spoke of returning home to Savannah

to bury his recently deceased mother but since the wake was mixed racially the police arrived and ordered dispersal, warning: "'Tell the fellows they have to go home.'"

51. Hentoff, "Race Prejudice in Jazz," 73.

52. Porter with Keller, *There and Back*, 17, 20, 67.

53. Gerald Horne, *Class Struggle in Hollywood: Moguls, Mobsters, Stars, Reds, and Trade Unionists, 1930–1950* (Austin: University of Texas Press, 2001).

54. Benjamin Cawthra, "Duke Ellington's 'Jump for Joy' and the Fight for Equality in Wartime Los Angeles," *Southern California Quarterly* 98, no. 1 (2016): 5–58.

55. "L.A. Columnist Takes Slam at Discrimination," *Downbeat*, 10, Number 5 (March 1, 1943): 6.

56. Halker, "A History of Local 108 and the Struggle for Racial Equality in the American Federation of Musicians," 207–22, 215.

57. Benny Carter, oral history, October 13–14, 1976, Institute of Jazz Studies.

58. Oliphant, *Jazz Mavericks of the Lone Star State*, 23.

59. See Danny Barker, oral history, January 13, 1981, Institute of Jazz Studies. See also Luigi Monge, "Death by Fire: African American Popular Music on the Natchez Rhythm Club Fire," in Robert Springer, ed., *Nobody Knows Where the Blues Come From: Lyrics and History* (Jackson: University Press of Mississippi, 2006), 76–107, 76: On April 23, 1940, a fire at this club killed nine of the twelve members of the band of Walter Barnes—only the drummer and bassist escaped, along with a driver and valet, leading to almost a dozen songs about this tragedy. See also Gene Ramey, oral history, n.d., National Museum of American History: "Somebody set that dance hall on fire and burned up all those musicians."

60. Buster Smith, oral history, January 13, 1981, Institute of Jazz Studies. The frequent plaint by Negro musicians that they felt compelled to play differently before Euro-American audiences raises questions about how and why the music evolved the way it did, particularly since more money—potentially—was to be made before this audience, compared to others. See also diary of Paul Barnes, Tulane University: the same point is made here. See also James Maher to Leonard Feather, August 21, 1994, Box 8, Leonard Feather Papers, University of Idaho-Moscow: "There were about two thousand white people going to Harlem clubs every night by 1928, a figure revealed in the *Daily News* in a week long series."

61. Gregory Davis, *Dark Magus: The Jekyll and Hyde Life of Miles Davis* (San Francisco: Backbeat, 2006), 23.

62. Hentoff, "Race Prejudice in Jazz," 73.
63. *Downbeat*, August 11, 1954.
64. Danny Barker, *A Life in Jazz*, 157, 166.
65. Hentoff, "Race Prejudice in Jazz," 73.
66. Marshall Royal, oral history, October 25, 1977, Institute of Jazz Studies.
67. See Christopher Wilkinson, *Jazz on the Road: Don Albert's Musical Life* (Los Angeles: University of California Press, 2001).
68. "Calloway Aids Solution of Bus Problem," *Downbeat*, 9(Number 14, July 15, 1942): 1.
69. Margaret McKee and Fred Chisenhall, *Beale Black and Blue: Life and Music on Black America's Main Street* (Baton Rouge: Louisiana State University Press, 1981), 68.
70. Mike Levin, "Bus Situation to Eliminate Most Colored Bands," *Downbeat*, 9 (Number 15, August 1, 1942): 23.
71. "L.A. Columnist Takes Slam at Discrimination," *Downbeat*, 10 (Number 5, March 1, 1943): 6.
72. Young, oral history, September 17–18, 1976.
73. Feather, *The Jazz Years*, 120. According to horn man Phil Woods, it was Barnet who "had the first mixed band: six alcoholics, six junkies and six potheads." Phil Woods, oral history, June 22–23, 2010, National Museum of American History.
74. Buster Smith, oral history, January 13, 1981, Institute of Jazz Studies.
75. Herman Autrey, oral history, April 23, 1975, Institute of Jazz Studies. For Callender quote, See Callender and Elaine Cohen, *Unfinished Dream: The Musical World of Red Callender* (New York: Quartet, 1985), 46.
76. Excerpt from *Jazz News*, 1944, MSS 506, Folder 98, William Russell Papers.
77. Rex Stewart, *Jazz Masters of the Thirties* (New York: Macmillan, 1972), 40.
78. Barker, *A Life in Jazz*, 126–27.
79. Art Farmer, oral history, June 29–30, 1995, National Museum of American History.
80. Charles Emge, "'Not a Negro' Says Bigard Seeking Membership in White Musicians' Union," *Downbeat*, 10 (Number 24, December 15, 1943), 3.
81. See for example Gerald Horne, *The Counter-Revolution of 1776: Slave Resistance and the Origins of the United States of America* (New York: New York University Press, 2014).
82. "Bigard Rejected for Membership in White Union," *Downbeat*, 11 (Number 4, February 15, 1944): 1.
83. "Bigard at Oakland Club with Ofay Crew," *Downbeat*, 12 (Number 10, May 15, 1945): 6.

84. Young, oral history, September 17–18, 1976.
85. George "Red" Callender, oral history, August 13, 1981, Institute of Jazz Studies.
86. Marshall Royal, oral history, October 25, 1977, Institute of Jazz Studies.
87. Hamilton, oral history, January 9–10, 2006, Institute of Jazz Studies.
88. Jon Hendricks, oral history, August 17–18, 1995, National Museum of American History.
89. Elvin Jones, oral history, June 10–11, 2003, National Museum of American History.
90. Horne, *Facing the Rising Sun*, 2018.
91. Gerald Horne, *Black Liberation/Red Scare: Ben Davis and the Communist Party* (Newark, DE: University of Delaware Press, 1994).
92. Gerald Horne, *Black Revolutionary: William Patterson and the Globalization of the African American Freedom Struggle* (Urbana: University of Illinois Press, 2013).
93. Hammond, *John Hammond on Record*, 85, 87, 157, 187.
94. Frank Kofsky, *Black Music, White Business: Illuminating the History and Political Economy of Jazz* (New York: Pathfinder, 1998), 12.
95. Barker, *A Life in Jazz*, 158.
96. Danny Barker, oral history, July 21–23, 1992, National Museum of American History.
97. John Chilton, *Billie's Blues: The Billie Holiday Story, 1933–1959* (New York: Da Capo, 1975), 97, 108.
98. Levy with Hall, *Men, Women and Girl Singers*, 70.
99. David Ritz, *Faith in Time: The Life of Jimmy Scott* (New York: Da Capo, 2002), 9. 94.
100. John Broven, *Record Makers and Breakers*, 58.
101. Jimmy Scott, oral history, September 23–24, 2008, National Museum of American History.
102. Porter with Keller, *There and Back*, 80.
103. Young, oral history, September 17–18, 1976.
104. Buster Smith, oral history, January 13, 1981, *Institute of Jazz Studies.*
105. Haddix, *Bird*, 56.
106. Callender, oral history, August 13, 1981.
107. John Hammond to Walter White, May 21, 1942, Box IIA347, NAACP Papers.
108. Walter White to John Royal, October 27, 1939, Box IIA347.
109. Release, January 12, 1940, Box IIA619, NAACP Papers. Press Release, no author
110. Billy Taylor, oral history, November 19–20, 1993, National Museum of American History.

111. Nat Hentoff, oral history, February 17–18, 2007, National Museum of American History.

112. Note, *Downbeat*, 13, Number 16 (July 29, 1946): 1.

113. William Grant Still to Walter White, January 10, 1940, Box IIA619, NAACP Papers.

114. Chilton, *Sidney Bechet*, 143, 154.

115. Tom Bethel, *George Lewis: A Jazzman from New Orleans* (Berkeley: University of California Press, 1977), 115.

116. Terry, *The Autobiography of Clark Terry*, 54, 55, 56.

117. Haddix, *Bird*, 18, 34, 25, 67.

118. Lorraine Gordon, *Alive at the Village Vanguard: My Life In and Out of Jazz Time* (Milwaukee: Leonard, 2006), 53.

119. Weston, *African Rhythms*, 44, 42: He adds, "Working the kind of hours many of these musicians were accustomed to, some felt the need for some kind of boost, some kind of stimulant . . . because when you go on that stage and get involved in that arduous creative process, sometimes you have to somehow remove yourself from what's really going on in everyday life. . . . Some drank beer, some liked bourbon, scotch or some other alcohol, some musicians liked to smoke reefer, some even liked cocaine." He argues that heroin came years after the war ended. See also in Box 102, John Steiner Collection, University of Chicago, William Howland Kenney III, "Jazz and the Concert Halls: The Eddie Condon Concerts 1942–1949," *American Music* 1, no. 2 (1983): 60–72, 61: There was a "long association of jazz with alcohol." Condon "nearly died of pancreatitis in 1936. He and many of his colleagues had become accustomed to running up bar tabs that consumed most of their paychecks," to the pleasure of their employers. "Many musicians suffered from alcoholism" worsened by long hours, sapping energy, leading to seeking even more "liquid energy" on the false premise that this would reenergize the body and the mind. Craftily culpable entrepreneurs had a tendency to compel "some clubs" to be "closed every thirty days, issued a new lease to a dummy lessee and reopened under a new name." Frankie Newton, perhaps the musician who was most advanced ideologically—he "indoctrinated me," said producer George Wein—was also an alcoholic; "the minute [he] got a dollar," said Wein, "he went into a club and bought everybody drinks." Wein, oral history, May 11, 2011.

120. Crouch, *Kansas City Lightning*, 45, 304.

121. Hendricks, oral history, August 17–18, 1995, National Museum of American History.

122. Tribute, ca. 1956, Box 73, Series 3, Sub Series 1, Willis Conover Papers, University of North Texas, Denton, Texas..

123. Hank Jones, oral history, May 16, 2010, National Museum of American History.
124. Ramey, oral history, n.d., National Museum of American History. He adds that once "we on our way to New Orleans . . . gotten just through Baton Rouge and cops caught us and said, 'You Yankee niggers huh?' . . . In Texas they used to do that . . . when we were kids get some guy and lynch and drag him through the black neighborhood or something.'"
125. Priestley, Chasin' the Bird, 34, 41, 55, 5.

5. We Speak African!

1. See, for example, Maxine Gordon, Sophisticated Giant, 96: "At midnight on December 31, 1947 the second recording ban began. All union members were forbidden to record. The inciting issue was the demand from the American Federation of Musicians that record companies pay a percentage of sales into a union fund which would help support unemployed musicians . . . the recording ban lasted for one year, until December 1948. During the period of the ban, the long playing 33 rpm record was introduced, followed by the 45 rpm disc. These formats changed jazz recording completely," allowing more music per disc while the 45 facilitated the jukebox ascendancy. See also Red Callender and Elaine Cohen, Unfinished Dream: The Musical World of Red Callender (London: Quartet, 1985), 73: As of 1947–1948, "companies were making records like they were going out of style," with potential impact on quality.
2. Louis Menand, "The Invention of Rock and Roll," The New Yorker, November 16, 2015.
3. DeFranco, oral history, November 8–9, 2008, National Museum of American History.
4. Louis Armstrong to Leonard Feather, December 21, 1946, Louis Armstrong Archive.
5. Chico Hamilton, oral history, January 9–10, 2006, National Museum of Amerian History.
6. Machito [Frank Grillo], oral history, May 1980, Institute of Jazz Studies.
7. Barnet with Dance, Those Swinging Years, 95.
8. Lena Horne as told to Arnstein and Moss, In Person, 38.
9. "Girl Trumpeter Tastes Southern Chivalry and Color Ousts Mab's Men", Downbeat, 13 (Number 16, July 29, 1946): 1.
10. Lief Bo Petersen and Theo Rehak, The Music and Life of Theodore "Fats" Navarro (Lanham, MD: Scarecrow Press, 2009), 7, 10. Reportedly, Navarro was nicknamed "Fat Girl" "because he was so chubby and liked to mock the gestures of what he called 'screaming fags.'" See Davis, Dark Magus, 40. See also Hank Jones, oral history, May 16, 2010.

Born in 1918, pianist Jones grew up in Michigan and listed to Canadian radio's CKOW. "They used to put a lot of Fats Waller records on later," beginning at 10 p.m.

11. See vertical file on Fats Navarro, Institute of Jazz Studies.
12. *Oakland Tribune*, January 19, 1958
13. *Los Angeles Times*, May 19, 1991. See also Matthew R. Pembleton, *Containing Addiction: The Federal Bureau of Narcotics and the Origins of America's Global Drug War* (Amherst: University of Masssachusetts Press, 2018).
14. Petersen and Rehak, *The Music and Life of Theodore "Fats" Navarro*.
15. Carl Woideck, *Charlie Parker: His Music and His Life* (Ann Arbor: University of Michigan Press, 1996), 138.
16. Martin Torgoff, *Bop Apocalypse: Jazz, Race, the Beats & Drugs* (New York: Da Capo, 2015), 178.
17. *New York Times*, January 20, 2002.
18. *Village Voice*, April 30–May 6, 2003.
19. Mario Bauza, oral history, December 13–14, 1978, Institute of Jazz Studies.
20. *Cubop! The Life and Times of Maestro Mario Bauza* (New York: Caribbean Cultural Center, 1993). Institute of Jazz Studies.
21. *New York Times*, 18 May 1977.
22. Horne, *Race to Revolution*. Max Salazar, "The Fast Life and Death of Chano Pozo," n.d., ca. 1978, in vertical file on Chano Pozo, Institute of Jazz Studies.
23. Ibid.
24. Dizzy Gillespie with Al Fraser, *To Be, or Not . . . to Bop: Memoirs of Dizzy Gillespie* (Garden City, NY: Doubleday, 1979), 320, 319, 115.
25. Donald L. Maggin, *Dizzy: The Life and Times of John Birks Gillespie* (New York: Harper, 2004), 216.
26. Babs Gonzales, *I Paid My Dues: Good Times . . . No Bread* (New York: Lancer, 1967).
27. Gerald Horne, *The Counter-Revolution of 1776*.
28. Jackie McLean, oral history, July 20–21, 2001, National Museum of American History.
29. Torgoff, *Bop Apocalypse*, 16, 25, 55.
30. Sally Howell, *Old Islam in Detroit: Rediscovering the Muslim American Past* (New York: Oxford University Press, 2014), 241.
31. Curtis Fuller, oral history, September 25–26, 2010, National Museum of American History.
32. Richard O. Boyer, "Bop," *The New Yorker*, July 3, 1948. Box 112, John Steiner Collection. Buster Scott, a musician with Lionel Hampton's orchestra, changed his name to Abdul Hameed. See Terry, *Clark*, 92–93.
33. Yusef Lateef, oral history, June 21, 2000, National Museum of American

History. On Ahmadiyya, see Gerald Horne, *The End of Empires: African Americans and India* (Philadelphia: Temple University Press, 2008).

34. Slide Hampton, oral history, April 20-21, 2006, National Museum of American History.

35. DeFranco, oral history, November 8-9, 2008, National Museum of American History..

36. Mike Hennessey, *Klook: The Story of Kenny Clarke* (Pittsburgh: University of Pittsburgh Press, 1990), 57.

37. See for example Sidney Finkelstein, *Jazz, a People's Music* (New York: Citadel Press, 1948).

38. Taylor and Reed, *The Jazz Life of Dr. Billy Taylor*, 24, 119.

39. Maxine Gordon, *Sophisticated Giant*, 195.

40. Red Callender and Elaine Cohen, *Unfinished Dream: The Musical World of Red Callender* (London: Quartet, 1985), 73.

41. Coney Woodman in Clora Bryant et al., eds., *Central Avenue Sounds: Jazz in Los Angeles* (Berkeley: University of California Press, 1998), 98-102, 98.

42. Morroe Berger, Edward Berger, and James S. Patrick, *Benny Carter: A Life in American Music* (Lanham, MD: Scarecrow Press, 2000).

43. George Wein, *Myself Among Others: A Life in Music* (New York: Da Capo, 2003), 45, 217.

44. Chilton, *Billie's Blues*, 1975, 62, 67.

45. Nat Hentoff, oral history, February 17-18, 2007, National Museum of American History.

46. Art Hodes, oral history, February 15-16, 1979, Institute of Jazz Studies.

47. Wilson and Cohassey, *Toast of the Town*, 121, 122, 125.

48. Horne, *Paul Robeson*.

49. Hentoff, oral history, February 17-18, 2007.

50. Travis, *The Autobiography of Black Jazz*, 340.

51. Artie Shaw, oral history, October 7-8, 1992, National Museum of American History.

52. Howard Kimeldorf, *Reds or Rackets? The Making of Radical and Conservative Unions on the Waterfront* (Berkeley: University of California Press, 1988).

53. Lena Horne, as told to Arnstein and Moss, *In Person*, 161.

54. Buddy Collette with Steven Isoardi, *Jazz Generations: A Life in American Music and Society* (New York: Continuum, 2000), 128, 130.

55. Max Roach, "Draft 1996," Box 53, Max Roach Papers.

56. Max Roach, interview, January 28, 1981, Box 52, Max Roach Papers.

57. Bryant et al., eds., *Central Avenue Sounds*, 114-33, 126.

58. Collette with Isoardi, *Jazz Generations*, 52.

59. Frank Foster, oral history, September 24-25 and November 22, 1998, National Museum of American History.

60. McLean, oral history, July 20–21, 2001, National Museum of American History.

61. Press release, February 11, 1947, Box 78, Series VIII, Erroll Garner Papers, University of Pittsburgh.

62. Hammond, *John Hammond on Record*, 294.

63. "Jim Crow Halts Granz Date in New Orleans," *Downbeat*, 16, Number 22 (November 18, 1949): 2.

64. Jones, oral history, May 16, 2010.

65. Clipping, 1946, Box 8, Leonard Feather Papers, University of Idaho-Moscow.

66. "Negro Group Seeks Break for Players," *Downbeat*, 14 (Number 13, June 18, 1947). 14.

67. *Los Angeles Times*, July 15, 2015.

68. Collette with Isoardi, *Jazz Generations*, 123.

69. Hal Holly, "Negro Group Seeks Break for Players," *Downbeat*, 14 (Number 5, April 22, 1947), 10.

70. Interview with Roy Porter, *Be-Bop and Beyond* 3, no. 4 (1985): 3, Southern California Library for Social Studies and Research, Los Angeles.

71. *Kansas City Star*, January 19, 1945.

72. McLean, oral history, July 20–21, 2001.

73. Priestley, *Chasin' the Bird*, 71, 78. See also Ross Rusell to Chan Parker, March 12, 1972, Box 3, Ross Russell Papers, University of Texas-Austin: This critic, producer, and early chronicler of the saxophonist's life asserted, "I can't ignore the many wild aspects of Bird's life . . . I see these aberrations as efforts to insulate himself from the vicious atmosphere of night clubs, bookers, agents, publishers and other types in the commercial music business. . . ."

74. Davis, *Dark Magus*, 40.

75. Levy with Hall, *Men, Women and Girl Singers*, 86.

76. Nesuhi Ertegun to Ahmet Ertegun, September 21, 1949, Box C1, Ahmet Ertegun Papers, Rock and Roll Hall of Fame Archives, Cleveland.

77. Robert Greenfield, *The Last Sultan: The Life and Times of Ahmet Ertegun* (New York: Simon and Schuster, 2011), 162. See also Willie Dixon with Don Snowden, *I Am the Blues: The Willie Dixon Story* (New York: Da Capo, 1989), 185, 186, 192, 193, 195. Dixon castigates the Chess brothers of Chicago and the brother of Benny Goodman— Harry Goodman—whose company exploited Negro artists. Goodman ran a publishing company from New York City. Leonard Chess also owned a Chicago radio station that appealed to a Negro audience, WVON ("Voice of the Negro"), and was a lifetime member of the NAACP. He also recorded pianists Ahmad Jamal and Ramsey Lewis. The Chess family garnered significant wealth from the exploitation of

Negro artists, many of whom were left impoverished. Leonard Chess alone left an estate of $28 million. Naturally, Chess had an entente with racketeers. Chess attained vertical integration by controlling a pressing plant, distribution company, and radio station.

78. Bill Gottlieb, *Downbeat*, 14 (Number 10, May 7, 1947), 1.
79. Kofsky, *Black Music, White Business*, 39.
80. Torgoff, *Bop Apocalypse*, 180.
81. Hentoff, oral history, February 17–18, 2007, National Museum of American History.
82. Stewart, *Jazz Masters of the Thirties*, 31. See also Levy with Hall, *Men, Women and Girl Singers*, 74: Billie Holiday's "pimp and hustler," who also invested in nightclubs, beat her and supplied her with drugs.
83. Shaw, oral history, October 7–8, 1992.
84. Hentoff, oral history, February 17–18, 2007.
85. J. J. Johnson, oral history, February 26–27, 1994, National Museum of American History.
86. Taylor, oral history, November 19–20, 1993.
87. Jimmy Rowles, oral history, 1984, Institute of Jazz Studies.
88. Priestley, *Chasin' the Bird*, 71.
89. Joe Wilder, oral history, August 25–26, 1992, National Museum of American History.
90. Barry Harris, oral history, August 20, 2010, National Museum of American History.
91. DeFranco, oral history, November 8–9, 2008.
92. Terry, *Clark*, 146.
93. Dahl, *Morning Glory*, 206, 207.
94. Diane Wood Middlebrook, *Suits Me: The Double Life of Billy Tipton* (Boston: Houghton Mifflin, 1998); Leslie Gourse, *Madame Jazz: Contemporary Women Instrumentalists* (New York: Oxford University Press, 1995).
95. Von Freeman, oral history, May 23–24, 2000, National Museum of American History.
96. Clora Bryant in Clora Bryant et al., eds., *Central Avenue Sounds*, 342–68, 356.
97. Shaw, oral history, October 7–8, 1992.
98. Taylor, oral history, November 19–20, 1993, National Museum of American History.
99. Interview with Clora Bryant, *Be-bop and Beyond* 3, no. 4 (1985): 9–16.
100. DeFranco, oral history, November 8–9, 2008.
101. Terry, *Clark*, 92–93, 106–07. Emphasis in original.
102. Bryant et al., eds., *Central Avenue Sounds*, 261–81, 277. See also Horace

Tapscott, *Songs of the Unsung: The Musical and Social Journey of Horace Tapscott* (Durham, NC: Duke University Press, 2001).

103. Tony Perchard, *Lee Morgan: His Life, Music and Culture* (London: Equinox, 2006), 136.
104. Shaw, oral history, October 7-8, 1992.
105. Percy Heath, oral history, July 23, 2001, National Museum of American History.
106. "Worrisome Days Along the Street," *Downbeat*, 13 (Number 23, November 4, 1946), 1
107. "Four Spots Left . . ." *Downbeat*, 16 (Number 2, January 15, 1947), 3.
108. "Jazz Booming," *Downbeat*, August 26, 1949. Max Roach says the music moved downtown after the civil unrest in Harlem in 1943, in Interview, April 26, 1992, Box 58, Max Roach Papers, Library of Congress, Washington DC.
109. Bill Moody, *The Jazz Exiles: American Musicians Abroad* (Reno: University of Nevada Press, 1993), 116.
110. Hendricks, oral history, August 7-18, 1995, National Museum of American History.
111. Johnson, oral history, February 26-27, 1994, National Museum of American History.
112. McLean, oral history, July 20-21, 2001, National Museum of American History.
113. Horne as told to Arnstein and Moss, *In Person*, 161.
114. Interview, January 28, 1981, Box 53, Max Roach Papers.
115. Max Roach, "Draft 1996," Box 53, Max Roach Papers.
116. Taylor, oral history, November 19-20, 1993.
117. Ibid.
118. Hentoff, oral history, February 17-18, 2007. Lena Horne agreed with John Levy, while adding how agents were prone to cheat Negro "performers . . . the commission is frequently much higher. . . . They pay whatever the agent asks because they are afraid that if they refuse, the agent will, in turn, refuse to represent them." Thus, an agent "had written a clause into my contract which stated not only that I was to pay them 20 percent of my salary but also that they were to receive 30 percent of everything I earned in theatres, cafés, and other special bookings." Horne as told to Arnstein and Moss, *In Person*, 150, 231. According to drummer Max Roach, saxophonist Stan Getz "made more money than Bird, Prez, Duke and Monk combined! He had an apartment in Paris, a house in Costa del Sol, a mansion upstate. He used to invite us, Basie, and Duke up there a lot. [Dave] Brubeck owns radio stations across the country, they made a lot of money just for

being white. . . . When Duke died he didn't have zip . . . nothing . . . Compare Benny Goodman's estate with Louis's. . . . Bird didn't make any money . . . Getz could buy and sell Duke and [Coleman] Hawkins, [Sonny] Rollins, [Col]Trane together!" See Roach, "Draft 1996" Box 53, Max Roach Papers, Library of Congress-Washington, D.C.

119. Lateef, oral history, June 21, 2000, National Museum of American History. Critics, in turn, could be biting assayers of their peers. Ross Russell, a critic and early chronicler of bebop, is an example. See, for example, Russell to Martin Williams, November 10, 1968, Box 4, Ross Russell Papers, University of Texas-Austin: "I can never forgive the knife job Feather did on me. . . ." Russell also found bias in the journal of record, *Downbeat*, because of critics' malfeasance since "over the years," this publication "has praised the [Stan] Kentons and overlooked the [Lester]Youngs and [Charlie] Parkers and I wonder whether they have really changed. . . ." In the same collection and box, see also Ross Russell to Martin Williams, November 30, 1968: "I find [Dan] Morgenstern's reviews so much school girl puffery . . . not to be taken seriously as actual criticism . . . both [Ralph] Gleason and [Nat] Hentoff," fellow critics, "are suffering from over exposure and over writing. Nat's recent liner notes are really pretty bad. What's worse is that they are not literate."

120. Johnson, oral history, February 26-27, 1994, National Museum of American History.

121. *Melody Maker*, March 20, 1948.

122. *Melody Maker*, February 7, 1948.

123. Louis Armstrong to Leonard Feather, December 21, 1946, Louis Armstrong Archive, Queens College, New York City: The name came from "Mr. Brooks of the 'Melody Maker' magazine," during a 1932 visit to England, adding "I shall never forget the wonderful ovation they gave me on my first trip over there. . . . These memories will carry old 'Satchmo' to his grave."

124. Shaw, oral history, October 7-8, 1992.

125. Taylor, oral history, November 19-20, 1993.

126. Louis Armstrong to Leonard Feather, December 5, 1946, Louis Armstrong Archive.

127. Ellie Horne to William Russell, January 10, 1944, Folder 6, MS 517, William Russell Papers, Williams Research Center, New Orleans. Emphasis in original.

128. Ellie Horne to William Russell, April 16, 1944, Folder 10, William Russell Papers.

129. Ellie Horne to William Russell, May 26, 1944, Folder 11, MS 517, William Russell Papers.

130. Hennessey, *Klook*, 194, 197.
131. Bill Moody, *The Jazz Exiles*, 60.
132. Kelley, *Thelonious Monk*, 53, 57.
133. Buddy Collette in Bryant et al., eds., *Central Avenue Sounds*, 134–63, 153.
134. Benny Golson and Jim Merod, *Whisper Not: The Autobiography of Benny Golson* (Philadelphia: Temple University Press, 2016), 85.
135. "European Exodus Gains Momentum," *Downbeat*, 15 (Number 14, July 14, 1948), 1.
136. Heath, oral history, July 23, 2001, National Museum of American History.
137. Hampton, oral history, April 20–21, 2006.
138. Hennessey, *Klook*, 70, 90, 189, 192. See also September 1944, Reel 29, No. 471, Part I, Press Releases, Claude Barnett/Associated Negro Press Papers, Chicago History Museum: "Negro musicians have made Montmartre famous. . . . Some of them made large fortunes and should have owned at least half of Montmartre." Foremost among these figures was Louis Mitchell, the "first to introduce a cabaret in the Montmartre on the American style. . . . He made several fortunes but lost them all. His wife, Antoinette, from Washington, D.C., was considered one of the most beautiful women in Parisian circles." There was also "Palmer Jones who with his wife, Florence, made famous Chez Florence in Rue Blanche." Also noted were "Opal Cooper, Harvey White, Sammy Jones, Roscoe Burnett, and Louis Vaughan Jones, who is now a violin professor at Howard." In the same collection, see also September 1946, Reel 33, No. 985, Part I, Press Releases: Joseph "Frisco" Bingham, a U.S. Negro, was known as the "Black King" of Paris. Owner of a Rolls-Royce automobile and father of a "mulatto" son, he arrived from San Francisco in 1919 where he performed as a drummer, singer, and dancer. He was there when Palmer and Florence Jones opened one of the first cabarets in Montmartre owned by a U.S. Negro, which quickly became a rendezvous for local elites. Bingham went on to buy his own cabaret and became friendly with Langston Hughes, Josephine Baker, and Ada "Bricktop" Smith. Born ca. 1894, he spoke thirteen languages, including Russian, Greek, Chinese, and Arabic and by the late 1930s had two clubs in London. See also September 1946, Reel 33, No. 890, Part I, Press Releases: Frank "Big Boy" Goody, a forty-five-year-old musician from New Orleans, just arrived from Brazil where he went in November 1939 with his "French wife." This saxophonist and clarinetist had toured Brazil and Argentina with his thirteen-piece band. There he met Louis Coles, a vocalist, and Booker T. Pittman, a descendant of Booker T. Washington and William Grant, who had departed Paris in 1931 for Buenos Aires.

139. Hentoff, oral history, February 17–18, 2007.
140. Hal P. Mills, "Commies Spell Doom to Shanghai Entertainment," *Downbeat*, 16 (Number 23, December 2, 1949), 2.

6. Lullabye of Birdland

1. Howard Johnson with Wendy Johnson, *A Dancer in the Revolution*, 128. See also Contract between Ellington and NAACP, January 21, 1950, Box IIC344, NAACP Papers: The composer would pay for the hall, musicians, ticket printing, advertising, etc. for an extravaganza at the posh Metropolitan Opera House in Manhattan. See in the same box Walter White to "Dear Duke," November 26, 1951: He sought a check for $3000 since "we have almost entirely exhausted the reserves we laid by during the war chiefly from sums sent voluntarily to us" by Negro soldiers; hence, the NAACP must be "sharply reduced" which "would be a tragedy for the Negro. . . ." See also Greenfield, *The Last Sultan*, 30, 90. Likewise, Johnson's account notwithstanding, it was reported around the same time that Ellington felt that Negroes "ain't ready" for desegregation. Cohen, *Duke Ellington's America*, 301. Perhaps jokingly, pianist Cedar Walton referred to himself as a "Democratic Socialist, yeah." See Cedar Walton, oral history, October 2–3, 2010, National Museum of American History. According to horn man Art Pepper, Lee Koenig had been a movie producer but was accused of being a Communist; seeking a new livelihood he began Contemporary Records, "the first to record the legendary Ornette Coleman. . . . His whole operation was very different. . . . An honest man . . . felt very safe with him." Art Pepper, *Straight Life: The Story of Art Pepper* (New York: Schirmer, 1979), 193, 194. Max Margulis, a founder of the leading label that was Blue Note, was a "left-wing activist" according to one analyst and wrote for publications produced by the U.S. Communist Party: Richard Cook, *Blue Note Records: The Biography* (Boston: Justin, Charles, 2003), 235.
2. James Elmer Hutchinson, "Bebop: A Narcotic," *New Foundations* 3, no. 1 (1949): 37–43. Box 22, Marshall Stearns Papers, Institute of Jazz Studies., Rutgers University, Newark.
3. Russell Hope Robbins, "Bop and Society," *Harlem Quarterly* 1, nos. 3–4 (1950): 9–15, 10. "There were musicians working toward the bop idiom as early as the late 1930s," Box 22, Marshall Stearns Papers.
4. Krivine, *Jukebox Saturday Night*, 1977, 43–44.
5. *Chicago Tribune*, March 26, 1950.
6. On the foregoing see, for example, memorandum, January 10, 1946, Box 42, Virgil W. Peterson Papers, Chicago History Museum. See also *Chicago Sun*, December 10, 1945; *Chicago Tribune*, March 9, 1940; *Chicago Daily News*, March 11, 1941; *Chicago Daily News*, June 20, 1941; *Chicago Tribune*,

September 20, 1941; *Chicago Tribune*, September 21, 1941; *Chicago Daily News*, September 27, 1943; *Chicago Sun*, October 28, 1943.

7. *Chicago Daily News*, February 24, 1948.
8. *Chicago Tribune*, March 26, 1950.
9. Memorandum, February 21, 1950, Box 42, Virgil W. Peterson Papers, Chicago History Museum.
10. *Chicago Daily News*, April 22, 1964,
11. *Chicago Reader*, August 18, 1989. Box 2, Frank H. Holzfeind Papers, Chicago History Museum.
12. Joe Segal, oral history, October 6, 2014, National Museum of American History.
13. Clipping, February 6, 1955, Box 2, Frank H. Holzfeind Papers.
14. Virgil Peterson, *The Juke Box Racket* (Chicago: Chicago Crime Commission, 1954), Chicago History Museum. See John L. Williams, *American Mistress: The Life and Times of Eartha Kitt* (London: Quercus, 2013), 183. Moreover, as the jukebox industry and the rise of Las Vegas suggest, there was a confluence of interests between and among Italian and Jewish American mobsters. See, for example, James Kaplan, *Sinatra: The Chairman* (New York: Doubleday, 2015), 186.
15. Laurence Bergreen, *Louis Armstrong: An Extravagant Life* (New York: Broadway, 1997), 482.
16. *Variety*, June 11, 1969.
17. Frank Holzfeind to Joe Glaser, March 30, 1953, Box 2, Frank H. Holzfeind Papers.
18. Memorandum on Charles Gioe, September 16, 1954, Box 30, Virgil Peterson Papers, Chicago History Museum.
19. "Disc Bootleggers Are Waxing Fat on Stolen Goods," *Downbeat*, 17 (Number 2, June 16, 1950): 10
20. Memorandum on Charles Gioe, September 16, 1954, Box 30, Virgil W. Peterson Papers.
21. Red Callender and Elaine Cohen, *Unfinished Dream*, 97.
22. Jamelle Baruck Dolphin, *Recorded in Hollywood: The John Dolphin Story* (North Charleston, SC: CreateSpace, 2011), x, 49, 64, 86, 91, 101, 103. For more on the impact of disproportionate policing generating disproportionate results, see Szwed, *Billie Holiday*, 48: The singer was "followed nightly" by police officers bent on finding drugs, which virtually guaranteed that their mission would be attained. See also "Landry Gets Prison Term," *Downbeat*, 17, Number 22 (November 3, 1950),1. Louis Landry, operator of the New Orleans Swing Club in San Francisco, "found guilty on a narcotics charge," just as Holiday and Armstrong had been slated to perform there. Typically, the union did not help matters when the local in Los Angeles ruled in 1954 that any member convicted on charges of

drug possession would be suspended: "L.A. Union Strikes at Narcotics Violators," *Downbeat*, 21(Number 11, June 2, 1954): 1.

23. Thomson, *The Dark Heart of Hollywood*, 104.

24. "Hazel Scott Collects Damages from Suit," 17 (Number 11, *Downbeat*, June 2, 1950): 11.

25. Ralph J. Gleason, "Swingin' the Golden Gate," *Downbeat*, 17 (Number 13, June 30, 1950): 18.

26. Halker, "A History of Local 108 and the Struggle for Racial Equality in the American Federation of Musicians," 207–23, 214.

27. "B. Carter Loses Local 767 Election. . ." *Downbeat*, 20 (Number 1, January 14, 1953): 1.

28. Gillespie with Fraser, *To Be or Not to Bop*, 131–32.

29. Peter Benjaminson, *The Story of Motown* (Los Angeles: Rare Bird, 2018), 29.

30. Cook, *Blue Note Records*, 98, 100, 118.

31. Max Gordon, *Boston Review*, November 1985, Vertical File, Institute of Jazz Studies.

32. Stephen Petrus and Ronald D. Cohen, *Folk City: New York and the American Folk Music Revival* (New York: Oxford University Press, 2015), 159.

33. Scott M. Deitche, *Cigar City Mafia: A Complete History of the Tampa Underworld* (Fort Lee, NJ: Barricade, 2004), 85, 86.

34. Clark Terry, oral history, June 15 and 22, 1999, National Museum of American History.

35. John Levy, oral history, December 10–11, 2006, National Museum of American History.

36. Jimmy Heath and Joseph McLaren, *I Walked with Giants: The Autobiography of Jimmy Heath* (Philadelphia: Temple University Press, 2010), 76.

37. Joe Wilder, oral history, August 25–26, 1992, National Museum of American History.

38. John Levy, oral history, December 10–11, 2006.

39. Teddy Reig, "Mississippi Rag," February 1991, vertical file on Teddy Reig, Institute of Jazz Studies.

40. Teddy Reig with Edward Berger, *Reminiscing in Tempo: The Life and Times of a Jazz Hustler* (Metuchen, NJ: Scarecrow Press, 1990), 8, 27, 29, 34. Interestingly, both Reig and Lubinsky wed Negro women. Reig, "Mississippi Rag." Joe Segal, a Chicago promoter, said, "My wife was black," in oral history, October 6, 2014, National Museum of American History. The favoritism shown toward those like Allen Eager often soured relations with their Negro counterparts, stultifying solidarity. See Lou Donaldson, oral history, June 20–21, 2012, National Museum

of American History: speaking of the Euro-American horn man Phil Woods, he said, "I like Phil. I like Phil very well, because Phil was one of the few white guys that, when he got famous, he didn't forget the black guys. A lot of the white guys, once they got famous, made a couple of records and ran off with the white bands."

41. Denton and Morris, *The Money and the Power*, 47.

42. Michael J. Ybarra, *Washington Gone Crazy: Senator Pat McCarran and the Great American Communist Hunt* (Hanover, NH: Steerforth, 2004), 660.

43. Ibid., 663, 257, 3. See also Gerald Meyer, *Vito Marcantonio: Radical Politician, 1902–1954* (Albany: State University of New York Press, 1989). The postwar boom also encompassed Miami Beach, which featured Jim Crow in locals of the union, which, in turn, may shed light on why bandleader Tommy Dorsey excoriated bebop and was rebuked in response by Nat Cole, Mel Tormé, and Woody Herman, with the latter terming this newest version of the new music as the "music of the youth." "Battle Jim Crow in Miami Locals," *Downbeat*, 16 (Number 18, September 23, 1949): 1, 2, and Ralph G. Gleason, "T.D. Told to Open Ears to Bop," *Downbeat*, 16(Number 18, September 23, 1949): 1, 12.

44. Transcript of minutes, Gaming Control Board, February 8, 1961, Nevada State Library and Archives, Carson City.

45. Final Report of the Special Crime Study Commission on Organized Crime, November 15, 1950, Box 66, Gaming Board Records, Nevada State Library and Archives.

46. Application of Fred Whelan, n.d., Transcript of Minutes, Gaming Control Board: "Past record of many and various arrests including grand theft (twice), robbery (three times) and forcible sexual assault (many times) . . . bootlegger, gambler, bookmaker. . . . Claims no liking for Mickey Cohen or for any member of the Mafia, he appears to know them well." His specialty was buying cheap liquor and pouring it into empty bottles bearing expensive labels. The "applicant emphatically denied any connection with Murder, Inc." though it was believed that he was "indirectly associated with Murder, Inc. from about 1945 to about 1947" and had ties to "Bugsy" Siegel.

47. James McMillan, oral history, 1997, University of Nevada, Reno.

48. Clarence Ray, oral history, 1991, University of Nevada, Reno.

49. Prentiss Walker, oral history, 1974, University of Nevada, Reno.

50. Ruth Sweet, oral history, June 1978, University of Nevada, Reno.

51. Lee Henry Lisby, oral history, June 1978, University of Nevada, Reno. Cora Williams, a Negro woman, also recalled atomic testing: "In the early 50s we would arise . . . about 4 a.m . . . blast would go off. . . . See the big mushroom come up after the blast and you could actually see

NOTES TO PAGES 161–164

the blast. . . . Hotels would be filled because so many people would come from the various states just to see the atomic blast. . . . Mostly after the blast [there] was always. . .a dust storm."

52. Interestingly, though Jewish Americans across class and ideological lines were supportive of the formation of the state of Israel in 1947–48, Dalitz, said one analyst, was "for the Arabs." Ybarra, *Washington Gone Crazy*, 684.

53. Ronald A. Farrell and Carole Case, *The Black Book and the Mob: The Untold Story of the Control of Nevada's Casinos* (Madison: University of Wisconsin Press, 1995), 26, 36–38, 107. See also William F. Roemer, *The Enforcer: Spilotro—The Chicago Mob's Man Over Las Vegas* (New York: Fine, 1994).

54. *Las Vegas Sun*, March 2, 2014, Vertical File, "African Americans in Las Vegas," Nevada Historical Society, Reno.

55. *Las Vegas Review Journal*, November 26, 1996.

56. Frank Foster, oral history, September 24–25 and November 22, 1998, National Museum of American History.

57. William "Bob" Bailey, oral history, December 1978, University of Nevada, Reno.

58. *Reno Gazette Journal*, February 26, 2001, Vertical File, Nevada Historical Society, Reno.

59. Porter with Keller, *There and Back*, 96.

60. Abbey Lincoln, oral history, December 17–18, 1996, National Museum of American History.

61. William Bailey, oral history, December 1978, University of Nevada, Reno. As for the actual Mississippi, saxophonist Charles Lloyd, born in Memphis in 1938, had a grandfather who controlled 1,600 acres of prime farmland in Holly Springs, Mississippi, and in neighboring Byhalia, south of his place of birth. It was in 1918 when the inevitable happened. A Euro-American man threatened him, and the grandfather responded murderously. Miraculously, he was acquitted. The Ku Klux Klan bayed for his blood. "He was a big inspiration on me," said Lloyd, one of the more financially successful artists among a group routinely exploited. "[William] Faulkner wrote a book called *Intruder in the Dust*" evoking these themes of racism and revenge and "he knew my grandfather . . . he tried to base it somehow off that." Lloyd knew "the game is always rigged" against those of his ancestry in North America but another lesson gleaned was that one could fight back—and win— even in Jim Crow Mississippi.

62. *Nevada State Journal*, March 29, 1930.

63. *Nevada State Journal*, February 8, 1931.

64. *Nevada State Journal*, December 3, 1949.

65. *Reno Gazette Journal*, February 26, 2007. Ben Fruita, a Japanese American, received a gambling license in Reno in 1931: *Reno Gazette Journal*, November 28, 1931. As Fong was setting up shop, the singer and actor Abbey Lincoln was having a shattering experience due east in Salt Lake City. "We went to get something to eat," she said, "and we couldn't get served anywhere," even at a Chinese restaurant where they "hollered at us, 'no service, no service.'" The rebuff contributed to a raucous argument with her pianist subsequently: "He got up off the piano and pushed me to the floor and I sprained my ankle. I couldn't get up off the floor. I worked on crutches for two weeks." Then his spouse "came with me to the hotel and put my foot in a pail of hot water and Epsom salts and cried and told me that she was sorry but that he was—he had been in the Army and he was shell-shocked and that he carried a gun"—and no doubt was unsettled by bigotry. Lincoln, oral history, December 17–18, 1996, National Museum of American History.

66. Minutes of Tax Commission, August 5, 1952, Nevada State Library and Archives.

67. Denton and Morris, *The Money and the Power*, 4, 12, 28, 36, 57.

68. James. B. McMillan, oral history, 1997, University of Nevada, Reno.

69. Woodrow Wilson, oral history, 1989, University of Nevada, Reno. Emphasis in original.

70. James A. Gay, oral history, December 1978, University of Nevada, Reno.

71. Cora Williams, oral history, September 1978, University of Nevada, Reno.

72. Bailey, oral history, December 1978. See also Ernest N. Bracey, *The Moulin Rouge and Black Rights in Las Vegas* (Jefferson, NC: McFarland, 2009); and Helen Townsell-Parker, *A Cry for Help: A Chronological History of a Black Community in Northern Nevada* (North Charleston, SC: CreateSpace, 2010).

73. Louis Armstrong to "Mr. Glaser," August 2, 1955, Louis Armstrong Archive (emphasis in original). See also Ernie Anderson, "Joe Glaser and Louis Armstrong: A Memoir," Part I, *Storyville*, December 1994. Absent convincing evidence, Anderson asks if the tie between the two was "homosexual." Glaser, he says, also had an obsession with younger women. Still, given the shark-like essence of the industry, artists were bereft of multiple options. The author recalls a time when musicians flocked to Glaser's "luxurious" office in Manhattan in the high-rent district of 57th Street and Fifth Avenue; there Negro artists most notably "seemed to sit . . . for days or even weeks" to grab a minute of his high-priced time.

74. Joe Glaser to Louis Armstrong, August 17, 1956, Louis Armstrong Archive.

75. Louis Armstrong to "Mr. Glaser," August 2, 1955.
76. Sarah Ann Knight, oral history, June 1978, University of Nevada, Reno.
77. John Dennis Dombrink, "Outlaw Businessmen: Organized Crime and the Legalization of Casino Gambling" (PhD diss., University of California, Berkeley, 1981), 103, 134.
78. Moe, *Mob City*, 11, 15.
79. Stan Britt, *Long Tall Dexter: A Critical Musical Biography of Dexter Gordon* (New York: Quartet, 1989), 74.
80. See for example, Carole Marks, *Farewell—We're Good and Gone: The Great Black Migration* (Bloomington: Indiana University Press, 1989).
81. Maxine Gordon, *Sophisticated Giant*, 109, 111, 123–124.
82. Frank Hayde, *Stan Levey*, 105.
83. Julilly Kohler-Hausmann, *Getting Tough: Welfare and Imprisonment in 1970s America* (Princeton: Princeton University Press, 2017), 91.
84. Johnny Mandel, oral history, April 20, 1995, National Museum of American History.
85. Bill Quinn, "Lou's Blues: Alto Saxophonist Lou Donaldson's Gloomy View of the Jazz Future," *Downbeat*, 36, Number 3 (February 6, 1969), 15–18, 35, 15.
86. Vertical file on Wardell Gray, Institute of Jazz Studies.
87. *Melody Maker*, June 4, 1955.
88. Ted Gioia, *West Coast Jazz: Modern Jazz in California, 1945–1960* (New York: Oxford University Press, 1992), 58.
89. Roy Porter, interview, *Be-Bop and Beyond* 3, no. 4 (1985): 1, Southern California Library for Social Studies and Research.
90. Clark Terry, oral history, June 15 and 22, 1999, National Museum of American History.
91. Philip Sillman to Ate van Delden, March 2007, Box 14, Folder 4, Adrian Rollini Collection, Institute of Jazz Studies. Stan Levey, a drummer and former accompanist of both Gillespie and Parker, accused fellow musician, Al Haig of murdering his spouse—though he was acquitted: he "strangled his wife. Killed her, And got off! . . . everybody knows he did it." As for trombonist Frank Rosolino he says he shot both of his sons as they slept—one died instantly, the other survived—then committed suicide. See Frank Hayde, *Stan Levey*, 201, 206.
92. Donald L. Maggin, *Stan Getz: A Life in Jazz* (New York: Morrow, 1996).
93. Letter from Jack Tracy, *Downbeat*, 21 (Number 6, March 24, 1954): 6.
94. "Dope Menace Keeps Growing," *Downbeat*, November 17, 1950.
95. Mandel, oral history, April 20–21, 1995.
96. Max Roach, interview, November 29, 1995, Box 51, Max Roach Papers, Library of Congress.

97. Lincoln, oral history, December 17–18, 1996, National Museum of American History.
98. Lou Donaldson, oral history, June 20–21, 2012, National Museum of American History. Apparently, Charlie Parker was also "bad with the money." See Billy Shaw to Frank Holzfeind, September 22, 1950, Box 2, Frank H. Holzfeind Papers: "I would definitely suggest that you do not permit Charlie Parker or his manager to draw much money prior to pay day, since confidentially speaking, Charlie has a great habit of drawing advances and when he has to meet this payroll, he is usually short."
99. Martha Glaser to "Dear Tim," May 14, 1951, Box 68, Erroll Garner Papers, University of Pittsburgh.
100. Letter from Martha Glaser, July 30, 1952, Box 68, Erroll Garner Papers.
101. Martha Glaser to "Mr. Rea," September 12, 1952, Box 78, Erroll Garner Papers. She also thought Garner had another distracting problem: "Erroll's been incorrigible beyond belief. . . . So 'tail crazy' . . . he's running around with a married dame, Peggy Thomas, whose husband is liable to shake up Erroll too." Martha Glaser to "Dear Andrew," November 8, 1952, Box 78, Erroll Garner Papers.
102. Martha Glaser to "Dear Anita," April 12, 1953, Box 78, Erroll Garner Papers.
103. Martha Glaser to "Dear Andy," September 30, 1953, Box 78, Erroll Garner Papers.
104. Martha Glaser to "Dear Andy," September 17, 1953, Box 78, Erroll Garner Papers.
105. Martha Glaser to "Dear Andrew," November 8, 1952, Box 78, Erroll Garner Papers.
106. George Avakian, oral history, September 28, 1993, National Museum of American History.
107. Dave Brubeck to Cliff Aranson, November 15, 1950, Box 1A.1, Dave Brubeck Papers, University of the Pacific, Stockton, CA.
108. George Wein, oral history, May 11, 2011, National Museum of American History.
109. Undated clipping, Box 116, John Steiner Collection, University of Chicago.
110. Contract with Adderley, July 20, 1956, Box 1, Frank H. Holzfeind Papers, Chicago History Museum.
111. Artie Shaw, oral history, October 7–8, 1992, National Museum of American History.
112. *Nevada State Journal*, December 11, 1960. Scrapbook, Alice Smith Papers, University of Nevada, Reno.

113. William Douglass in Bryant et al., eds., *Central Avenue Sounds*, 233–54, 233, 250–51, 252.

114. "Music Men Named in Red Hunt," *Downbeat*, 18, Number 22 (November 2, 1951): 1.

115. "Music is Combating Communism," *Downbeat*, 19, Number 20 (October 8, 1952): 1.

116. Dickerson, "Central Avenue Meets Hollywood," 248.

117. "L.A. Merges Negro, White AFM Locals," *Downbeat*, 20, Number 9 (May 6, 1953): 2.

118. Hector Joe Garino, "Three U.S. Orks Hits in Montevideo Appearances," *Downbeat*, 18, Number 7 (April 6, 1951): 1.

119. Leonard Feather, "No More White Bands for Me says Little Jazz," *Downbeat*,18, Number 10 (May 18, 1951): 1.

120. Leonard Feather, "Jazz in Europe," *Downbeat*, 18, Number 16 (August 10, 1951): 1.

121. Donaldson, oral history, June 20–21, 2012. See also Gerber, *Jazz Jews*.

122. Press release, September 1952, Reel 49, no. 737, Part I, Press Releases, Claude Barnett/Associated Negro Press Papers, University of Chicago.

123. Press release, June 1950, Reel 43, no. 693, Part I, Press Releases, Claude Barnett/Associated Negro Press Papers.

124. Press release, October 1951, Reel 47, Part I, Press Releases, Claude Barnett/Associated Negro Press Papers: "What many American born Negroes discern," said journalist Roi Ottley, is that "being in Europe has much to offer. . . . [The] Negro abroad enjoys a self-respect, dignity and personal worth unknown to his fellows at home." In the same collection, see also December 26, 1951, Reel 47, no. 653: "Negro soldiers would rather serve abroad than at home. . . . Prefer to be in Japan, Korea, Germany" than the United States. "Almost to a man Negro soldiers will tell you they are treated better anywhere in the world than in America. . . . Democracy works better in proportion to the distance you are from the United States . . . 'distance lends enchantment to democracy,'" said Kelly Miller. "His point was that America was more interested in democracy abroad than at home." See September 1951, Reel 46, no. 751: Negro educator Rufus Clement, traveling in Europe, said: "Once an old German doorman sidled up to us and said softly that Negro Americans were better liked than the other Americans." Margaret Burroughs in Mexico spoke similarly: "The Mexican people have very friendly feeling toward Negro people. . . . 'Gringoes' and their attitudes about race are in the minority in Mexico—and thank God they have not been able to bring their anti-Negro practices into this beautiful country," September 1951, Reel 46, no. 838: She also wrote: "I will remember the many, many times when the Mexican people, waiters, waitresses, taxi drivers and plain

people in the streets took us to their hearts and went out of their way for us simply because we were Negroes and therefore more like them and more understanding than some of the white American tourists with their condescending attitudes. I will remember also the consternation of the white Americans who could not understand why and how we received so much service and interest when we had far less money than they had. . . . The feeling of being in a country where the majority of people were brown like me" was similarly overwhelming. October 1951, Reel 46, no. 1101. See also August 1952, Reel 49, no. 591: "American Negroes have come to Paris in a steady and growing stream since World War I. . . . Negro tourists have multiplied every year since the end of the war. . . . More than 2,000 American Negro tourists in Paris last summer by present indications . . . One can sometimes tell how long some [Euro] Americans have been in Paris and from what section of the country they come by the length of time he stares as a Negro walks by, or by the comment he makes."

125. *Downbeat*, 22, Number 10 (February 25, 1953): 11.
126. *Chicago Tribune*, April 17, 1988.
127. *New York Times*, August 25, 1972.
128. *Downbeat*, May 18, 1955.
129. George Avakian to Joe Glaser, May 15, 1956, Louis Armstrong Archive, Queens College, New York City.
130. "King Cole Combo to Play England," *Downbeat*, 17, Number 16 (August, 1950): 1.
131. Hobsbawm, *The Jazz Scene*, 200.
132. Johnny Mandel, oral history, April 20, 1995, National Museum of American History.
133. Nat Hentoff, "Classical Color Line?" *Downbeat*, 19, Number 5 (March 7, 1952): 1.
134. Hannah Altbush, "AFM Report: High Unemmployment, Low Salaries," *Downbeat*, 22, Number 3 (February 9, 1955): 1.
135. Artie Shaw, oral history, October 7–8, 1992, National Museum of American History.
136. "AFM at Santa Barbara–Petrillo Reveals Dim View of Musicians' Earnings," *Downbeat*, 19, Number 13 (July 2, 1952): 1.
137. "A Healthy Outlook for Record Industry," *Downbeat*, 21, Number 8 (April 21, 1954): 20.
138. Hannah Altubush, "Negro TV, Radio Jobs Almost Nil, Survey Finds," *Downbeat*, 22, Number 6 (March 23, 1955): 3.
139. Cohen and Fitzgerald, *Rat Race Blues*, 2, 165–67, 310–12.
140. Nat Hentoff, "A New Jazz Corporation. . . ." *Downbeat*, 22, Number 12 (October 19, 1955): 10-11. *Christian Science Monitor*, January 6, 1983.

141. Benny Golson, oral history, January 8–9, 2009, National Museum of American History.

142. Elizbeth Uihlen McGregor, *Jazz and Postwar French Identity: Improving the Nation* (Lanham, Maryland: Rowman & Littlefield, 2016).

7. Haitian Fight Song

1. William "Monk" Montgomery, oral history, October 30–November 2, 1980, Institute of Jazz Studies, Rutgers University, Newark..

2. "Trummy" Young, oral history, September 17–18, 1976, Institute of Jazz Studies (emphasis in original). Note: Mingus died in 1979.

3. John F. Goodman, ed., *Mingus Speaks* (Berkeley: University of California Press, 2013), 159, 186.

4. Max Roach, interview, August 1, 1996, Box 96, Max Roach Papers, Library of Congress.

5. Richard Atkinson to Charles Mingus, n.d., Box 54, Charles Mingus Papers, Library of Congress.

6. Max Roach, interview, n.d., Box 59, Max Roach Papers.

7. Henry Cater to Debut Records, May 3, 1955, Box 57, Charles Mingus Papers, Library of Congress.

8. Harold Lovette to R. M. Chatton, April 4, 1955, Box 58, Charles Mingus Papers.

9. R. M. Chatton to Harold Lovett, April 19, 1955, Box 58, Charles Mingus Papers.

10. Letter from John Sewell, February 20, 1955, Box 57, Charles Mingus Papers.

11. Goodman, ed., *Mingus Speaks*, 299. See "Prestige," *Downbeat*, 24, Number 12 (June 13, 1957): 17–18. Weinstock was the "youngest label owner in jazz today," running an "offshoot of a record store on 47th Street off Sixth Avenue." He resided in Teaneck, New Jersey, worked closely with engineer Rudy Van Gelder, and had tight control of musicians' "masters" or control over their recordings, which was money in the bank.

12. Celia Mingus to H. F. Longfelder, January 24, 1955, Box 57, Charles Mingus Papers.

13. Charles Mingus to Sherman Records Sales Company, December 9, 1954, Box 59, Charles Mingus Papers.

14. Silver, *Let's Get to the Nitty Gritty*, 56.

15. Gordon, *Live at the Village Vanguard*, 107.

16. Goodman, ed., *Mingus Speaks*, 203, 147.

17. Max Roach, memoir, 1997, Box 54, Max Roach Papers.

18. Jackie McLean, oral history, July 20–21, 2001, National Museum of American History. Reportedly, at a performance in Manhattan, Mingus

"hit . . . Jimmy Knepper in the mouth and broke his tooth—music was all over floor, score paper," undated clipping , Box 123, John Steiner Collection, University of Chicago. Mingus added epithet to injury by terming Knepper a "white faggot." Speaking of Mingus, "Trummy" Young said, "He'd get angry and he might punch a trombone player in the mouth . . . which is ridiculous. Because when your teeth and your lips are sore, you cannot play a brass instrument." Young, oral history, September 17–18, 1976, Institute of Jazz Studies. See also vertical file on Buddy Collette, n.d., Southern California Library for Social Studies and Research, Los Angeles. Juan Tizol, a trombonist born in Puerto Rico in 1900, recalled a time when Mingus lunged at him with a knife, though he conceded, "I used to sometimes carry a knife with me," while in this case the bassist "grabbed this piece of iron" too. See Juan Tizol, oral history, November 15, 1978, Institute of Jazz Studies. It was not just Mingus; arguably the exploitation and racism to which artists were subjected often left them in a foul mood. Producer George Avakian recalled a night when Miles Davis "and Max Roach had an argument out on the sidewalk and actually. . . . [Miles] beat Max pretty badly and injured him." See George Avakian, oral history, September 28, 1993, National Museum of American History. Then there was the time that Mingus and critic LeRoi Jones [Amiri Baraka], were tussling roughly in New York City. Genari, *Blowin' Hot and Cool*, 280. Likewise, Mingus's fellow Angeleno, drummer Chico Hamilton, declared that at one point "I didn't know whether I wanted to be a pimp or a musician. . . . I think all dudes go through that at one time or another." See Chico Hamilton, oral history, January 9–10, 2006, National Museum of American History.

19.   Marian McPartland, oral history, January 3–4, 1997, National Museum of American History.

20.   Proceedings from the 10th and 11th Annual Black Musicians' Conference, University of Massachusetts, Amherst, ca. 1970s, Box 59, Max Roach Papers.

21.   Max Roach, interview, n.d., Box 59, Max Roach Papers.

22.   Clipping, February 1991, vertical file on Teddy Reig, Institute of Jazz Studies.

23.   William R. Bauer, *Open the Door: The Life and Music of Betty Carter* (Ann Arbor: University of Michigan Press, 2002), 136.

24.   Max Roach, interview, "Draft 1996," Box 51, Max Roach Papers. Levy was stabbed fatally.

25.   Sonny Rollins, oral history, February 28, 2011, National Museum of American History. As with many male musicians and unlike many of their female peers, Rollins had an attentive spouse who attended

to many of the non-musical aspects of his life and helped to rescue him from the anomie that ensnared so many artists. See, for example, Lucille Rollins to Michael Contat, January 23, 1978, Box 78, Sonny Rollins Papers, Schomburg Center, New York City: Sonny Rollins, she said, "has more dead or destroyed friends (or some sick ones, some in seclusion) than live ones almost . . . it has taken us literally 20 years to devise some kind of formula so that Sonny can work and live in this business and remain strong, healthy (physically & emotionally) . . ."

26. Hank Jones, oral history, May 16, 2010, National Museum of American History.

27. "Snooky" Young, oral history, February 24–25, 2009, National Museum of American History.

28. Goodman, ed., *Mingus Speaks*, 135.

29. Remarks by Buddy Collette in Bryant et al., *Central Avenue Sounds*, 134–63, 148, 157, 159, 162. For a 1941 picture of Collette conferring with Robeson, see vertical file on Buddy Collette, Southern California Library for Social Studies and Research, Los Angeles: the photo is from the *Los Angeles Times*, October 15, 2000.

30. Collette with Isoardi, *Jazz Generations*, 130.

31. Vertical file on Buddy Collette, no date, Southern California Library for Social Studies and Research.

32. Collette with Isoardi, *Jazz Generations*, 110.

33. Max Roach, interview, May 12, 1988, Box 57, Max Roach Papers.

34. Max Roach, interview, 1995, Box 58, Max Roach Papers.

35. Horne, *The Apocalypse of Settler Colonialism*.

36. Max Roach, interview, November 13 and 15, 1995, Box 51, Max Roach Papers.

37. Max Roach, interview, n.d., Box 59, Max Roach Papers.

38. Max Roach, interview, November 22, 1995, Box 51, Max Roach Papers.

39. Ibid.

40. Max Roach, interview, May 12, 1988, Box 57, Max Roach Papers.

41. Max Roach, interview, 1989, Box 58, Max Roach Papers.

42. Max Roach, interview, April 25, 1990, Box 58, Max Roach Papers. Sonny Rollins agreed with this evaluation. See his Remarks, undated, Box 99, Sonny Rollins Papers: "When Miles used . . . me on his sessions, it was a sort of answer to the West Coast, cool sound that he had helped develop with Gerry Mulligan and Lee Konitz. What we were doing was a sharp turn away from that direction. Some people saw it in a 'white jazz' versus 'black jazz' way. . . . Miles said the reason he changed his style as the years went on is because as he got older, he wasn't able to play as he did in the '40s and '50s . . . [he] didn't want to be a relic; he

always wanted to be moving with the times. I share that trait with him
... I can't recreate something I did in 1950."

43. Max Roach, interview, 1990, Box 58, Max Roach Papers.
44. Elvin Jones, oral history, June 10–11, 2003, National Museum of American History.
45. Quincy Jones, oral history, September 7, 2008, National Museum of American History.
46. Golson and Merod, *Whisper Not*, 232.
47. Percy Heath, interview, in Gleason, *Conversations in Jazz*, 111–29, 117.
48. Jimmy Cobb, oral history, July 26–27, 2010, National Museum of American History.
49. Reig with Berger, *Reminiscing in Tempo*, 102.
50. Interview, December 4, 1995, Box 51, Max Roach Papers.
51. Roach, "Draft 1996." Drummer Jimmy Cobb, born in 1929, also found it noteworthy that "at one time Stan Getz was making more money than Miles [Davis]." Jimmy Cobb, oral history, July 26–27, 2010, National Museum of American History. The prominent writer, Ishmael Reed sent Sonny Rollins a lengthy litany detailing the woeful exploitation of Black musicians. See Letter, December 4, 2013, Box 99, Sonny Rollins Papers: Here he details the alleged theft of the singing style of vocalist Jimmy Scott by Johnny Ray; the misdeeds of Chess Records which signed bogus songwriting contracts with artists, unduly favoring executives; the murderous attacks on King Curtis and Jaki Byard, along with the mysterious death of Albert Ayler: the list of infamy is lengthy.
52. Chico Hamilton, oral history, January 9–10, 2006, National Museum of American History.
53. Gail Lumet to John Hammond, October 23, 1980, Box 19, John Hammond Papers.
54. Goodman, ed., *Mingus Speaks*, 162.
55. Hampton, *Hamp*, 16, 24, 29, 40, 96, 132, 166, 167.
56. Jon Hendricks, oral history, August 17–18, 1995, National Museum of American History.
57. Maurice Jackson, "Jazz, 'Great Black Music' and the Struggle for Racial and Social Equality in Washington, D.C.," in Maurice Jackson et al., eds., *D.C. Jazz: Stories of Jazz Music in Washington, D.C.* (Washington, D.C.: Georgetown University Press, 2018), 1–34, 14.
58. "Mercer Ellington Starts Disc Firm," *Downbeat*, 17, Number 18 (September 22, 1950): 2.
59. Priestley, *Chasin' the Bird*, 92, 97.
60. Wein, *Myself Among Others*, 164.
61. Silver, *Let's Get to the Nitty Gritty*, 142.

62. Horace Silver, interview, *Be-Bop and Beyond* 3, no. 2 (1985): 2, Southern California Library for Social Studies and Research.

63. Hannah Altbush, "AFM Ruling Bars Members from Record Co. Ownership," *Downbeat* 20, Number 23 (November 18, 1953): 1.

64. Silver, *Let's Get to the Nitty Gritty*, 157.

65. Joe Segal, oral history, October 6, 2014, National Museum of American History.

66. "Frankie Newton Dies . . ." *Downbeat* 2, Number 8 (April 21, 1954): 36.

67. Nat Hentoff, "Counterpoint," *Downbeat* 23, Number 17 (August 22, 1956): 31-32.

68. "Louis Denies he was Undisturbed by Racial Barriers," *Downbeat* 23, Number 18 (September 5, 1956): 28.

69. Remarks, n.d., Box 11, Leonard Feather Papers, University of Idaho, Moscow.. For a vivid illustration of the music at a turning point, see the entire issue of *Downbeat*, 22, Number 18 (September 21, 1955).

70. Hilary Holt to Iola and Dave Brubeck, November 26, 1954, Box 1, Series C, Dave Brubeck Papers, University of the Pacific, Stockton, CA.

71. Leonard Feather, interview, June 10, 1990, Box 11, Leonard Feather Papers.

72. Chan Parker to Ross Russell, March 25, 1974, Box 3, Ross Russell Papers, Harry Ransom Center, University of Texas, Austin..

73. Gelly, *Being Prez*, 11, 116, 125, 139. At this point, pianist George Shearing was routinely garnering $5,000 weekly at clubs: See Levy with Hall, *Men, Women and Girl Singers*, 98.

74. Travis, *The Autobiography of Black Jazz*, 196.

75. Max Roach, memoir, 1997, Box 54, Max Roach Papers.

76. Joe Glaser to Mary Lou Williams, May 6, 1954, Box 21, Folder 7, Mary Lou Williams Papers, Institute of Jazz Studies.

77. Wein, *Myself Among Others*, 168.

78. Dorothy Donegan, oral history, April 5-6, 1998, National Museum of American History. The elder McClain owned the "It Club. . .. [the] hippest spot in the city for modern jazz." See Robin D. G. Kelley, *Thelonious Monk*, 367-68.

79. Max Roach, "Draft 1996," Box 53, Max Roach Papers.

80. Bauer, *Open the Door*, 141.

81. Levy with Hall, *Men, Women and Girl Singers*, 112, 122. The socioeconomic structure of the United States as a whole often slotted Jewish Americans in the middle stratum where they often bumped into African Americans seeking to climb the class ladder, inducing abrasions. Cf. Peter Benjaminson, *The Story of Motown* (Los Angeles: Rare Bird, 2018), 102. The affluent African American entrepreneur, Berry Gordy, who founded a major entertainment conglomerate, apparently

was unaware of Nazi genocide in Europe: "Not until the 1960s for instance did [he] learn about the massacres of European Jews during World War Two. ..." "Is this really true?" he asked. "This guy Hitler, did he really kill six million? ..." he asked.

82. Art Farmer, oral history, June 29–30, 1995, National Museum of American History.

83. Tad Hershorn, *Norman Granz: The Man Who Used Jazz for Justice* (Berkeley: University of California Press, 2011), 265, 359–60.

84. Silver, *Let's Get to the Nitty Gritty*, 113.

85. Martha Glaser to Erroll Garner, March 16, 1955, Box 68, Erroll Garner Papers, University of Pittsburgh.

86. *Baltimore Afro-American*, July 22, 1955. See also Chris de Vito, ed., *Coltrane on Coltrane: The John Coltrane Interviews* (Chicago: Chicago Review, 2010).

87. Panama Francis, oral history, September 13, 1978, Institute of Jazz Studies. Interestingly, Euro-American vibraphonist Red Norvo, born in 1908, "always got along with Joe Glaser very well because he never—he'd never give anything but a straight answer if I asked him a question. ... We had a great relationship and he was very fond of Eve," his spouse, and was "fond of the children" too. See Red Norvo, oral history, May 2, 1977, Institute of Jazz Studies. By way of contrast, pianist Horace Silver found that Glaser's agency "did practically nothing for us." See Silver, *Let's Get to the Nitty Gritty*, 172. Mingus's first musical job was with Norvo: at a time when studio musicians in Los Angeles were garnering $600 weekly, the bassist received $130. Besides, Norvo angered Mingus for accommodating Jim Crow when a producer objected to including a Negro musician; instead of resisting, Norvo complied. In those dark days, Negro musicians in Hollywood had to enter studios via back or side doors: Goodman, *Mingus Speaks*, 149, 105.

88. *New York Times*, March 2, 2017.

89. Report, November 21, 1955, FO371/114444, National Archives, London. Bandleader Charlie Barnet was among those who hated the musical trends adumbrated by the "British invasion." Barnet with Dance, *Those Swinging Years*, 193.

90. Bill Holman, oral history, February 18–19, 2010, National Museum of American History.

91. Wein, *Myself Among Others*, 203.

92. Art Farmer, oral history, June 29–30, 1995, National Museum of American History. Of course, there were downsides to being abroad, according to drummer Chico Hamilton: "In Paris they thought I was Martinique and they hate them. In Belgium they thought I was from the Congo, they hate them. In England, they thought I was Indian, they

hate [them]." Thus, "I used to have to wear my passport." This was in the 1950s, and "at first it was funny, but after a while it got to be a drag." Hamilton, oral history, January 9–10, 2006, National Museum of American History. As for Gryce's alleged "paranoia," consider the words of drummer Roy Haynes concerning pianist Bud Powell. The latter "went to that hospital for 18 months . . . when he came out of there, which may have been '50 or '51 they had injected him with a whole bunch of whatever. He was almost like a vegetable at some points." Roy Haynes, oral history, May 15, 1994, National Museum of American History.

93. Max Roach, "Draft 1996," Box 53, Max Roach Papers.

94. Quincy Jones, oral history, September 7, 2008, National Museum of American History.

95. Kansas City Star, April 2, 2000.

96. George "Big Nick" Nicholas, oral history, March 1980, Institute of Jazz Studies.

97. Montgomery, oral history, October 30–November 2, 1980, Institute of Jazz Studies.

98. David Baker, oral history, June 19–21, 2000, National Museum of American History.

99. Interview, January 28, 1981, Box 53, Max Roach Papers.

100. Holman, oral history, February 18–19, 2010. See Melody Maker, January 22, 1949: Kenton "quits! . . . forsakes music to study psychiatry."

101. Horne, The Counter-Revolution of 1776.

102. Porter with Keller, There and Back, 96.

103. Lenoard Feather, "Dear Stan," Downbeat, 23, Number 20 (October 3, 1956): 17.

104. Nat Hentoff, oral history, February 17–18, 2017, National Museum of American History.

105. Letter from Martha Glaser, August 14, 1955, Box 78, Erroll Garner Papers. In the same collection and box, see her letter to "Dear Dean" Jennings, February 22, 1958. She was upset about his reportorial assessment of her client, which focused unduly on his eccentricities and his alleged "lightweight character" and "malapropos"; "your item about $10,000 for compulsive phone calls will bring the Tax Department on [his] head" and "YOU KNOW THIS," she veritably shouted in capital letters; it "DEFINITELY HURTS HIM IN TERRIBLY IMPORTANT AREAS."

106. Glaser to Jennings, February 22, 1958.

107. Bob Thiele and Bob Golden, What a Wonderful World: A Lifetime of Recordings (New York: Oxford University Press, 1995), 75.

108. Max Roach, interview, May 16, 1988, Box 53, Max Roach Papers.

See also LeRoi Jones [Amiri Baraka], "Jazz and the White Critic," in William J. Harris, ed., *The LeRoi Jones/Amiri Baraka Reader* (New York: Thunder's Mouth, 2000), 179–85.

109. Roach, "Draft 1996." See also *New York Times*, July 18, 2018: "There are more than double the number of male film critics than female critics and that, according to a new study, has a demonstrable impact on how films starring and directed by women are reviewed."
110. Shirley Horn, oral history, June 13–14, 1996, National Museum of American History.
111. Yusef Lateef, oral history, June 21, 2000, National Museum of American History.
112. Gene Lees to Iola Brubeck, February 27, 1961, Box 1A5, Dave Brubeck Papers, University of the Pacific, Stockton, CA.
113. Feather, *The Jazz Years*, 115–26.
114. Raymond Herricks to Dave Brubeck, ca. 1958, Box 1, Series C, Dave Brubeck Papers.
115. Kofsky, *Black Music, White Business*, 84.
116. Kenny Burrell, oral history, February 16–17, 2010, National Museum of American History.
117. Silver, *Let's Get to the Nitty Gritty*, 73. The intra-racial contradictions expressed by Silver were not unique to him. Herman Roberts, a Negro club owner in Chicago, once said, "A lot of people thought I was prejudiced. I hired yellow bartenders with pretty [naturally straightened] hair and girls who looked like that too because I thought it was good business." Quite properly, he conceded by 1983, "Today I might get turned out of town for that kind of nonsense." Singer Joe Williams, who accompanied Count Basie frequently, recalled with bitterness, "The truth is that my skin was too shady [dark] for . . . club owners . . . I was about twenty-five or twenty-six years old before I felt comfortable enough with my blackness to remove that cross of inferiority from my shoulders." It was said further that Nat King Cole "opened the doors for darker-hued male entertainers two decades before the 'Black Is Beautiful' crusade of the 1960s." See Travis, *The Autobiography of Black Jazz*, 196, 468.
118. Ron Carter, oral history, May 16, 2011, National Museum of American History. Popularity in Japan was also a savior for Sonny Rollins. His first trip there was for three weeks in 1963; then it was two lucrative weeks in 1983, three gainful weeks in 1985, four well-paid weeks in 1988; etc. See Visa Application Form, circa 1990, Box 78, Sonny Rollins Papers Schomburg Center, New York City.
119. Hank Jones, oral history, May 16, 2010, National Museum of American History.

120. Roach, interview, Box 58, 1995, Max Roach Papers.

121. Wein, *Myself Among Others*, 148.

8. Kind of Blue

1. Battiste, *Unfinished Blues*, 58, 149, 52. As class solidarity came under assault, as in the former Yugoslavia, ethnic tensions and nationalism flowered. Thus, Meyer Lansky, leading mobster, was a firm supporter of Israel. See, for example, Robert Lacey, *Little Man: Meyer Lansky and the Gangster Life* (Boston: Little, Brown, 1991). Morris Levy, one of the major shapers of the music we call jazz, handed out Israeli bonds as gifts. See, for example, Fred Goodman, *Allan Klein: The Man Who Bailed out the Beatles, Made the Stones and Transformed Rock and Roll* (Boston: Houghton Mifflin, 2015), 23–24.

2. *Los Angeles Times*, June 22, 2015.

3. Leonard Feather, interview, June 10, 1990, Box 11, Leonard Feather Papers, University of Idaho, Moscow.

4. See for example *Guardian*, May 3, 2018.

5. Phil Woods, oral history, June 22–23, 2010, National Museum of American History. See also Chan Parker to Ross Russell, October 10, 1974, Box 3, Ross Russell Papers, University of Texas, Austin: Speaking of her betrothal to Woods, the former spouse of Charlie Parker asserted, "I think he did marry me because I was Bird's widow."

6. Press release, July 1956, Reel 60, No. 649, Part I, Press Releases, Claude Barnett/Associated Negro Press Papers.

7. Curtis Fuller, oral history, September 25–26, 2010, National Museum of American History.

8. Hobsbawm, *The Jazz Scene*, xliii.

9. Souvenir program, October 15, 1957, Box 3, Lionel Hampton Papers, University of Idaho, Moscow.

10. "Current Biography," October 1971, Box 3, Lionel Hampton Papers.

11. Clipping, September 15, 1976, Box 3, Lionel Hampton Papers.

12. Jimmy Owens, oral history, August 19–20, 1993, Lionel Hampton Papers.

13. Annie Ross, oral history, January 13–14, 2011, National Museum of American History.

14. Memoir by Marshal Royal, in Bryant et al., *Central Avenue Sounds*, 22–50, 45.

15. "Sinatra Chronology" and Transcript of Meeting, October 22, 1963, Nevada Gaming Commission and State of Nevada Gaming Control Board, Nevada State Library and Archives, Carson City.

16. Memorandum, May 6, 1958, Box 30, Virgil W. Peterson Papers, Chicago History Museum.

17. January 21, 1955, Box 42, Virgil W. Peterson Papers.
18. Greenfield, *The Last Sultan*, 158.
19. Clipping, February 12, 1958, Box 42, Virgil W. Peterson Papers.
20. *Billboard*, March 3, 1958.
21. *Billboard*, January 17, 1958.
22. Virgil Peterson to Robert F. Kennedy, February 20, 1958, Box 42, Virgil W. Peterson Papers.
23. Reig with Berger, *Reminiscing in Tempo*, 39–40.
24. *New York Times*, November 15, 1960.
25. *New York Times*, November 27, 1960.
26. Chevigny, *Gigs*, 64.
27. Mehmet Munir to Headmaster, St. Alban's, April 16, 1935, Box C1, Ahmet Ertegun Papers, Box C1, Ahmet Ertegun Papers, Rock & Roll Hall of Fame-Library & Archives, Cleveland, Ohio. See letter to Ertegun, January 23, 1956, Box C1, Ahmet Ertegun Papers: "Your mother . . . gave me some Christmas presents to smuggle out of Turkey. . . . I was able to smuggle them through Izmir by disguising myself as a Greek Orthodox priest escaping from anti-Cypriot rioters or rather anti-enosis rioters. Those long robes will encompass anything and usually smell so awful that custom officials can't get near you."
28. "Cheat Sheet," n.d., Box C1, Ahmet Ertegun Papers.
29. Greenfield, *The Last Sultan*, 127.
30. John Baxter to "Dear Dave," December 12, 1957, Box 1, Series C, Dave Brubeck Papers, University of the Pacific, Stockton, CA.
31. Robert Larimer to Dave Brubeck, May 10, 1956, Box 1, Series C, Dave Brubeck Papers.
32. Hall Hill to Dave Brubeck, November 26, 1957, Box 1, Series C, Dave Brubeck Papers.
33. Dave Brubeck to Steve Race, June 17, 1955, Box 1 A.1, Dave Brubeck Papers.
34. B. J. Furgerson to Dave Brubeck, October 22, 1957, Box 1, Series C, Dave Brubeck Papers.
35. Bob Bundy of Associated Booking Corporation to "Dear Dave," October 6, 1959, Box 1, A.3, Dave Brubeck Papers.
36. James Bancroft to Dave Brubeck, February 16, 1955, Box 1 A. 1, Dave Brubeck Papers.
37. Don and Peg Logan to "Dear Dave," May 6, 1958, Box 1, Series C, Dave Brubeck Papers.
38. Cyrus King to Max Weiss, ca. 1954, Box 1A, Dave Brubeck Papers.
39. Hugh Hefner to Dave Brubeck, May 17, 1955, Box 1A.1, Dave Brubeck Papers.

40. Interview with Quincy Jones in Gleason, *Conversations in Jazz*, 20–61, 27, 35, 36, 37. See also Greenfield, *The Last Sultan*, 65, 159. Ruth Brown, singer, born in 1928, proclaimed that "with the likes of Morris Levy, you going in to expect statutory rape. With Atlantic [Records], it was a case of date rape." Paul Marshall said of Levy that he "looked like an animal and talked like he was out of the movies."

41. Thiele and Golden, *What a Wonderful World*, 38, 93, 94, 95.

42. Clora Bryant, interview, *Be-Bop and Beyond* 3, no. 5 (1995): 2, Southern California Library for Social Studies and Research Los Angeles,

43. See, for example, Horne, *The Counter-Revolution of 1776*.

44. Don Gold, "Terry Gibbs," *Downbeat* 25, Number 9 (May 1, 1958): 20.

45. Shirley Horn, oral history, June 13–14, 1996, National Museum of American History.

46. See, for example, Horne, *Fire This Time*.

47. Magnificent Montague with Bob Baker, *Burn, Baby! Burn!* (Urbana: University of Illinois Press, 2003), 70, 57, 71, 82, 101, 64. On Montague's role in Los Angeles, see Horne, *Fire This Time*.

48. Dolphin, *Recorded in Hollywood*, 140.

49. Bryant, interview,

50. Shirley Horn, oral history, June 13–14, 1996, National Museum of American History.

51. Greenfield, *The Last Sultan*, 90. Cf. Eric Goldstein and Deborah R. Weiner, *On Middle Ground: A History of the Jews of Baltimore* (Baltimore: Johns Hopkins University Press, 2018) and Hasia R. Diner, *How America Met the Jews* (Providence, RI: Brown Judaic Studies, 2017).

52. Shirley Horn, oral history, June 13–14, 1996.

53. Max Roach, interview, November 7, 1995, Box 51, Max Roach Papers. See Tom McIntosh, oral history, December 9–10, 2011, National Museum of American History: "I did a couple of arrangements for Dinah Washington," said this trombonist and composer, but she was not paid and instead she invited him to visit her. Upon arrival, he noticed she was "getting undressed . . . she says, 'C'mon boy, take your clothes off.' I said, 'Wait, wait.' I had just become one of Jehovah's Witnesses and . . . newly married" and demurred. The vocalist was upset, he says and exhorted, "Take your money," which he presumably did.

54. Marian McPartland, oral history, January 3–4, 1997, National Museum of American History.

55. Leonard Feather, Playboy Jazz Festival Program, 1987, Box 012, Leonard Feather Papers.

56. Nesuhi Ertegun to Leonard Feather, April 9, 1962, Box 9, Leonard Feather Papers. Of course, Feather was far from flawless. The British-born critic

began working for Duke Ellington in 1942 and became a partner with Johnny Mercer in a recording concern. He termed "questionable" the misdeeds of Irving Mills who placed his name on Ellington's compositions: "I don't think he wrote a note of music in his life" (though he had little to say about being a critic and agent and producer, despite the presumed conflicts of interest). Feather said he penned "Mighty Like the Blues" but noticed that Mills put his name on it and had to be forced to remove it. He also dated Helen Oakley before she became Helen Dance, the partner of Stanley Dance, a critic Feather criticized. Leonard Feather, interview, June 10, 1990, Box 11, Leonard Feather Papers. Feather opportunistically "cooked" up an album, says Clark Terry, titled *Cats versus Chicks*. Clark Terry, oral history, June 15 and 22, 1999, National Museum of American History. Marian McPartland also assailed Feather, assaying him to be a walking conflict of interest. "He got mad at me once," she said, "because he said I have never played any of his tunes" when she was hosting a radio program. "He called me up and bawled me out over the phone," though he could have gone a step further: publish a critical essay on her alleged deficits as a musician. It was also Feather who told her coarsely that she had "Three strikes against her. She's English, white and a woman." Interestingly, though residing in the United States for most of her career, she added, "I never have become an American citizen." McPartland, oral history, January 3–4, 1997.

57. Clora Bryant, interview, *Be-Bop and Beyond*.

58. Kofsky, *Black Music, White Business*, 37.

59. See Ross Russell to Chan Parker, March 12, 1972, Box 3, Ross Russell Papers, University of Texas, Austin. "Red Rodney had an unbelievable life . . . .narcotics bust . . . went to law school in San Francisco graduating #2 in his class . . . .sophisticated crime spree that netted $20,000 before the FBI caught up with him. . . ." When the authorities caught up with him, they "broke . . . all of the teeth in his upper jaw. . . ."

60. Roy Porter, interview, *Be-Bop and Beyond* 3, no. 5 (1985): 2

61. Joel Dinnerstein, *The Origins of Cool in Postwar America* (Chicago: University of Chicago Press, 2017).

62. Douglas Henry Daniels, *Lester Leaps In: The Life and Times of Lester 'Pres' Young* (Boston: Beacon Press, 2002). The culture of masculinity was so pronounced within the community of musicians that Davis's accompanist, Herbie Hancock, noticed that his sister, Jean, a budding artist, "just wanted to be one of the boys. One time we even caught her in the bathroom trying to pee standing up." See Herbie Hancock, *Possibilities*, 8.

63. Lee Konitz, oral history, February 14–15, 2011, National Museum of American History.

64. Leonard Feather to Stan Kenton, n.d., Box 8, Leonard Feather Papers.
65. Leonard Feather to *Melody Maker*, May 13, 1950, Box 8, Leonard Feather Papers.
66. Leonard Feather, undated letter to *Village Voice*, Box 8, Leonard Feather Papers. In the same collection, Box 012, see the undated missive from Ralph Gleason to Feather. This critic, after assailing fellow critic Nat Hentoff, added, "I don't agree with you . . . that critics shouldn't write about other critics. . . . I used to credit Nat with being, even when annoying, a man of good will. This is no longer my belief." Feather, who also criticized the critic James Lincoln Collier, argued that he had an advantage over his U.S. peers defined as "white": since British-born he was able to see Negroes as humans and heroes more easily and not just as "menial[s]." Collier's book on Ellington, he said, "has done a lot of harm." See Leonard Feather, remarks, n.d., Box 11, Leonard Feather Papers. Of course, musicians may have been the harshest critics—of critics: See Sonny Rollins, to Michael Contat, January 23, 1978, Box 78, Sonny Rollins Papers, Schomburg Center, New York City: "I have usually found my critics or anyone not directly involved, lacking in understanding of the vicissitudes of the business in which I am involved. I gave my life for music but I do not want to end up with a needle in my arm or dead or destroyed much too early in life . . . because I have seen too many friends and great black (and white) musicians end that way myself . . . I also suspect that many of these critics don't want to see an artist survive . . . I have been open and trusting in our talks—something I would not ordinarily be with a critic . . . what may not be clear is how hard one must fight for such freedom to play and live in a semi-healthy and sane way in this business . . . ."
67. Walter Hofer to Baronet Records, November 30, 1960, Box 78, Erroll Garner Papers.
68. Martha Glaser to Walter Hofer, November 28, 1960, Box 78, Erroll Garner Papers. See also Sonny Rollins to Ralph Kaffel, April 12, 1992, Box 80, Sonny Rollins Papers: The saxophonist asked why his correspondent was "using something like twenty reels of tapes to make one approximate 36-38 minute recording LP. I would not like to see these outtakes transferred to any other company in the event of a sale—while legally that company could be prevented from using them without my consent—it would be awfully tempting . . . we have had 3 instances of this happening—with RCA, Impulse, Blue Note . . . the damage is done in that the recordings are against our will and it has taken approximately two years each to handle this litigation. . . ." In the same collection, see also Lucille Rollins to S. Edward Katz, August 8, 1981,

NOTES TO PAGE 409

Box 80: Rollins' manager was "very angry" since tapes of his post-1961 hiatus in performing were now being sold; "we like Japan Victor very much and they do a very good job there for Sonny's records ... our feeling then was that since everyone seems to have copies sooner or later someone is going to bootleg it anyway. . . ." In the same collection and box, see also the 1982 litigation in New York featuring Rollins versus RCA: The saxophonist's counsel "recently became aware of a record album containing renditions of musical compositions performed by him that was released in France" without the artist's approval, a situation worsened by the reality that the recordings were "imperfect and not artistically satisfactory. . . ." Litigation was expensive and time consuming, and often unavailable to leading artists like Rollins. See, for example, S. Edward Katz to Sonny Rollins, September 1, 1989, Box 78, Rollins Papers: "My usual fee on a pre-litigation collection matter . . . is $200.00/hr. plus disbursements or 25% of the amount actually collected and received, whichever is greater. . . ." Of course, frayed nerves, which many artists had in surplus already, were the result when large sums were involved, as the attorney for the estate of protean composer, lyricist, and arranger, Billy Strayhorn, discovered when contesting claims of the heirs of Duke Ellington: Stuart Prager to Alan Shulman, May 12, 1994, Box 79, Billy Strayhorn Papers, Library of Congress, Washington, D.C.: "I was astounded that you hung up on me during our telephone conversation," as opposing counsel was "trying to bully me and our clients . . . I will not respond to your anger with more anger. . . ." As for tangled estates, perhaps an inexorable result of tortured lives and continuing notoriety, see Ross Russell to Chan Parker, August 12, 1972, Box 3, Ross Russell Papers: There was the "incredible chaos of Bird's [Parker's] life and the scarcely less incredible 'chaos' of the 'estate.'" A signal was sent at the saxophonist's funeral when this "atheist" was given a funeral not in line with his philosophy—there was a "refusal to allow any jazz to be played" and "pall bearers almost drop[ped] the coffin. . . ." See Chan Parker to Ross Russell, March 17, 1972, Box 3, Ross Russell Papers. Innovative horn man, Ornette Coleman, began his career in Texas playing at a "gambling joint—the music was a cover for gambling"—and it appears that this trend did not cease when he migrated and, as in a clip joint, continued to be cheated. See A.B. Spellman, *Four Lives in the Bebop Business*, 111, 89.

69. "Trummy" Young, oral history, September 17–18, 1976, Institute of Jazz Studies.

70. Hammond, *John Hammond on Record*, 328.

71. Lee Konitz, oral history, February 14–15, 2011, National Museum of American History.

72. Leonard Feather, remarks, September 1961, Box 8, Leonard Feather Papers. Cf. Ross Russell to Charles Delaunay, May 10, 1970, Box 3, Ross Russell Papers: "Shelly's Manne-Hole" in "Hollywood" was "now probably breaking even and perhaps losing money. It keeps going because Shelly cares. . . ." See also A.B. Spellman, *Four Lives in the Bebop Business*, x: "Benny Goodman took much of his group's approach from Fletcher Henderson's innovations and Goodman is now one of America's wealthiest musicians. Henderson died . . . broken and frustrated."

73. Mike Amezcua, "On the Outer Rim of Jazz: Mexican-American Jazzmen and the Making of the Modern Pacific Borderlands, 1950–1969," *Journal of Social History* 50, no. 2 (2016): 410–31.

74. Monson, *Freedom Sounds*, 180.

75. Davis, *Dark Magus*, 58.

76. Curtis Fuller, oral history, September 25–26, 2010, National Museum of American History. The musician adds that when he accompanied Quincy Jones, he and his fellow sidemen "had a thing, we called the guy an HNIC [Head N-word in Charge]" and "it's always the light one! No darkies in there now!" He responded in kind: "We didn't date light skinned girls."

77. Minutes of Gaming Control Board, September 17, 1962, Nevada State Library and Archives, Carson City. For more on the tie between Las Vegas and Havana, see the following articles from the *Nevada State Journal*: March 27, 1958; April 24, 1958; April 26, 1958; May 8, 1958; May 27, 1958.

78. Clifford Jones to Gaming Control Board, February 1959, Minutes of Nevada Tax Commission, Nevada State Library and Archives.

79. Minutes of Tax Commission, July 30, 1956, Nevada State Library and Archives.

80. Memorandum from R. E. Cahill, Chair of Gaming Control Board along with GCB members William Simon and William Gallagher, April 25, 1958, 03030601, Gov-0237, GCB, Nevada State Library and Archives.

81. Jimmy Cobb, oral history, July 26–27, 2010, National Museum of American History. Cobb was not unique. Saxophonist Harold Battiste was reportedly paid a skimpy $125 to play saxophone on the huge hit by mega-stars Sonny and Cher, "I've Got You Babe." "That's all," he said: *Los Angeles Times*, June 22, 2015.

82. Williams, *American Mistress*, 183.

83. Jack Colhoun, *Gangsterismo: The United States, Cuba and the Mafia, 1933 to 1966* (New York: OR Books, 2013), 24.

84. Max Roach, interview, February 16, 1989, Box 58, Max Roach Papers.

85. *Las Vegas Review Journal*, April 15, 1957. See also *Nevada State Journal*, February 8, 1931.

86. Minutes of Tax Commission, September 4, 1951, Nevada State Library and Archives.

87. Minutes of Tax Commission, January 21, 1948, Nevada State Library and Archives.

88. Minutes of Tax Commission, December 19, 1948, Nevada State Library and Archives.

89. Eddie Palmieri, oral history, July 8, 2012, National Museum of American History.

90. Clarence Ray, "Black Politics and Gaming in Las Vegas, 1920s–1980s," Oral History Program, University of Nevada, Reno.

91. *Reno Evening Gazette*, April 9, 1959; *California Voice*, February 13, 1959.

92. William H. "Bob" Bailey, oral history, December 1978, University of Nevada, Reno.

93. Note, *Downbeat* 26, Number 3 (February 5, 1959): 9.

94. Cook, *Blue Note Records*, 136, 187. Subsequently, drummer Billy Higgins, born in 1936, argued that "one of the main reasons [Blue Note] became so successful was because of the A&R man," that is, a key executive, "who was between the musician and the producer," who happened to be Quebec. "Alfred Lion and Francis Wolff [the owners of the label] were two Jewish cats from Germany and they really didn't know who to get" but managed to snag Quebec, who was then replaced by another top-notch musician, Duke Pearson, pianist, born in 1932. See Billy Higgins, interview, *Be-Bop and Beyond* 2, no. 3 (1984): 2, Southern California Library for Social Studies and Research Los Angeles, See also A. B. Spellman, *Four Lives in the Bebop Business*, 10, 73, 74: Taylor "has worked variously as a delivery man for a Madison Avenue coffee shop, record salesman, cook and dishwasher." Taylor added: "'Some of the gigs I've had working uptown, Harlem uptown, were gigs for five dollars, and you worked from eight until four in the morning. This was in the early 1950s." Unsurprisingly, after a series of setbacks, the avant-garde keyboardist "went into analysis. It was Sullivan analysis."

95. Philly Joe Jones, interview, *Be-Bop and Beyond* 3, no. 2 (1985): 4.

96. Bryant, interview, *Be-Bop and Beyond*.

97. Johnny Griffin, interview, *Be-Bop and Beyond* 4, no. 2 (1986).

98. Shirley Horn, oral history, June 13–14, 1996.

99. Dom Cerulli, "Tony Scott," *Downbeat*, 25, Number 15 (July 24, 1958): 14. See also Gerald Horne, *White Supremacy Confronted: U.S. Imperialism & Anticommunism vs. the Liberation of Southern Africa, from Rhodes to Mandela* (New York: International, 2019), 273.

100. Clark Terry, oral history, June 15 and 22, 1999.

101. *Village Voice*, April 26, 2017.

102. Babatunde Olatunji, interview, *Be-Bop and Beyond* 5, no. 3 (1987): 3.

103. Stanley Turrentine, oral history, November 23, 1997, Box 3, African American Jazz Preservation Society of Pittsburgh, Oral History Project, University of Pittsburgh.

104. Toshiko Akiyoshi, oral history, June 29, 1998, National Museum of American History. On Wilson, see, for example, Horne, *Black Liberation/Red Scare.*

105. Memoir, n.d., Box 8, Leonard Feather Papers.

106. See for example Horne, *Facing the Rising Sun.*

107. Von Freeman, oral history, May 23–24, 2000, National Museum of American History.

108. Douglas A. Ramsey to Dave Brubeck, January 14, 1956, Box 1, Series 1C, Dave Brubeck Papers.

109. Hank Jones, oral history, May 16, 2010, National Museum of American History.

110. Hobsbawm, *The Jazz Scene*, 146.

111. Moody, *The Jazz Exiles*, 60, 116, 118.

112. Note, *Downbeat*, 25, Number 1 (January 9, 1958): 11.

113. Priestley, *Chasin' the Bird*, 87. See also A. B. Spellman, *Four Lives in the Bebop Business*, 24: Reportedly, it was a "well known fact that many of the bars in New York City" were "Mafia owned. . . . Mafia ownership of some of the city's most prosperous clubs and discoteques" also obtained.

114. Jimmy Cobb, oral history, July 26–27, 2010, National Museum of American History. See also Ashley Kahn, *Kind of Blue* (New York: Da Capo, 2000).

115. Reig with Berger, *Reminiscing in Tempo*, 90.

116. George Coleman, oral history, November 11, 2014, National Museum of American History.

117. "White Local 6 Kills Move to Integrate," *Downbeat* 24, Number 3, (January 23, 1957): 11.

118. Dickerson, "Central Avenue Meets Hollywood," 248.

119. See John Hammond to Roy Wilkins, February 27, 1959, Box IIIA178, NAACP Papers: A "very serious situation" existed in the union, he claimed, since the desire to "integrate the many segregated locals in such cities as Chicago, Kansas City, Philadelphia and Buffalo are being thwarted by the Negro officials and delegates themselves. The leader of the fight to prevent integration is Harry Gray, president of the all-Negro Chicago Local 208 . . . many Negro officials of segregated locals have an economic stake in segregation. Integration among orchestras is almost an impossibility as long as there are Jim Crow locals." Of course, today's orchestras remain largely comprised of musicians of European descent despite decades of "integration." In any case,

NAACP liberals had difficulty in understanding that having predominantly Euro-American locals, not known for their progressivism, not
least on the anti-racism front, swallow Negro locals, may have been a
step forward for "integration" but was disastrous otherwise, complicating the realization of a truer desegregation. Hammond, a long time
NAACP member, may have neglected to include in his calculation the
obdurateness of the union. See E. A. McKinney, Musicians Protective
Association of St. Louis to T. A. Curtis, April 22, 1932, Box C413,
NAACP Papers: "Colored delegates to the international convention"
of the union "will gradually be eliminated." See also Walter White to
William Green of American Federation of Labor, May 3, 1932, Box
C413: The union is "discriminating against Negro musicians through
a provision that these musicians be segregated in subsidiary locals
absolutely dominated and controlled by the white locals. . . ." To many
rank-and-file Negro musicians then being attracted to the Nation of
Islam, it appeared that "integration" was just another ploy to attain
racist domination.
120. *Entertainment Weekly*, August 13, 1993, Box 8, Leonard Feather Papers,
University of Idaho-Moscow.
121. Higgins, interview, 1984.
122. Statement by John Chancellor, n.d., Box 73, Series 3, Sub Series 1,
Willis Conover Papers, University of North Texas, Denton..
123. Leaflet, December 18, 1956, Louis Armstrong Archive.
124. Note, *Downbeat*, 24, Number 1(January 9, 1957): 8.
125. Penny von Eschen, *Satchmo Blows Up the World: Jazz Ambassadors Play
the Cold War* (Cambridge, MA: Harvard University Press, 2006), 260.
126. Article, n.d., Box 17, Series 3, Sub Series 1, Willis Conover Papers.
127. *New York Times*, September 13, 1959.
128. Willis Conover, typescript, June 7, 1959, Box 73, Series 3, Sub Series 1,
Willis Conover Papers.
129. Geoff Atkinson to Willis Conover, December 13, 1957, Box 7, Series 3,
Sub Series 1, Willis Conover Papers.
130. Stan Kenton to "Dear Willis," May 20, 1957, Box 7, Series 3, Sub Series 3.
131. George Wein, oral history, May 11, 2011, National Museum of American
History. See also Willis Conover to Roger Stevens, March 10, 1971, Box
73, Willis Conover Papers: "I thought white racism was all in the past
in the circles I move in, anyway, until I produced a jazz festival in New
Orleans, in 1969. The anti-black, anti-jazz, anti-'outsider' (anyone from
outside New Orleans) pressures and intrigues" were palpable.

9. I Wish I Knew How It Would Feel To Be Free
1.   Cary Ginell, *Walk Tall: The Music and Life of Julian "Cannonball"*

Adderley (Milwaukee: Leonard, 2013), 129, 131. See also Leonard L. Brown, ed., *John Coltrane: and Black America's Quest for Freedom* (New York: Oxford University Press, 2010).

2. Horne, *Fire This Time*.
3. Transcript of minutes, April 5, 1960, State Gaming Control Board, Nevada State Library and Archives, Kansas City.
4. Isoardi, *The Dark Tree*, 62–63, 92.
5. Levy with Hall, *Men, Women and Girl Singers*, 192.
6. Sonny Rollins, oral history, February 28, 2011, National Museum of American History. See also Sonny and Lucille Rollins to "Dear Michael," March 18, 1979, Sonny Rollins Papers, Schomburg Center, New York City: "Japan was very successful but very hectic. We will be in Europe again this year—from about June 28-July 14 . . ." Involved, inter alia, were "3 Scandinavian festivals" and "2 days at Pori, Finland."
7. Annie Ross, oral history, January 12–14, 2011, National Museum of American History. Sonny and Lucille Rollins were not as taken with Baldwin, whose reputation has grown since his untimely death in 1987. Sonny and Lucille Rollins to "Dear Michael," March 18, 1979. The elfin writer had been recruited to write a script that the saxophonist and his manager found wanting. ". . . he is of course a beautiful writer, maybe because he has been out of the country too long," he "seems to be really not in touch with the present way or present realities. . . ."
8. Marion Brown to Willis Conover, August 4, 1968, Box 9, Willis Conover Papers, University of North Texas, Denton..
9. Adam Shatz, "Free at Last: Mal Waldron's Ecstatic Minimalism," *The Nation* 305, no. 4 (2007): 32–36, 34, 35.
10. Krin Gabbard, Review of *Chasing Trane: The John Coltrane Documentary*, *Journal of American History* 105, no. 1, (2018): 240. See also Bob Thiele, Undated Article, Black Fire Music Collection, Emory University-Atlanta: Herein is noted Coltrane's interest in "Eastern Religion as well as Eastern Music . . ."
11. Ira Gitler, "Dexter Drops In," *Downbeat* 36, no. 11 (1969): 15.
12. Leonard Feather, "Riffing from Paris to Pinsk," *Rogue*, January 1964, Box 8, Leonard Feather Papers, University of Idaho, Moscow..
13. James Moody, oral history, August 19–20, 1993, National Museum of American History.
14. Abbey Lincoln, oral history, December 17–18, 1996, National Museum of American History. According to Annie Ross, her performing partner, Jon Hendricks, "had a very annoying habit of telling any woman that he wanted to be with, 'I'll make you a singer.' It was awful. I'd have these hostile women saying, 'I can sing. Jon Hendricks told me . . . I was told that I could sing and I will . . . replace you'." It was "pretty lousy. It

was usually when alcohol had been prevalent." See Ross, oral history, January 13–14, 2011, National Museum of American History.
15. Charles Lloyd, oral history, October 20, 2014, National Museum of American History.
16. Yusef Lateef, oral history, June 21, 2000, National Museum of American History.
17. Jackie McLean, oral history, July 20–21, 2001, National Museum of American History.
18. Maya Angelou to "Dear Abbey and Max," January 6, 1961, Box 76, Max Roach Papers, Library of Congress. She added acidulously about London: "The men are like faggots and probably are."
19. Weston, *African Rhythms*, 100.
20. Cohodas, *Spinning Blues into Gold*, 154, 171.
21. Levy with Hall, *Men, Women and Girl Singers*, 142.
22. Collette with Isoardi, *Jazz Generations*, 146.
23. Leonard Feather, "On the Racial Front," Box 8, Leonard Feather Papers.
24. John Dankworth, *Jazz in Revolution* (London: Constable, 1998), 134–35.
25. Ralph Gleason to Leonard Feather, September 10, 1963, Box 8, Leonard Feather Papers. Cf. Max Roach to Dee Dee Daniels, September 6, 1961, Box IIIA139, NAACP Papers: He wanted to organize a tour to raise funds for the NAACP and added, "We not only are in full sympathy with what the association is working toward, but we also realize the need and the urgency involved in our common struggle for advancement." Herbert Wright to Dr. Morsel, August 1, 1961, Box IIIA139: He wished to "discuss the possibilities for presenting [Roach's] 'Freedom Now Suite' on a national tour of [NACCP] branches, youth councils and college chapters. . . ."
26. Denise Sullivan, *Keep on Pushing: Black Power Music from Blues to Hip-Hop* (Chicago: Lawrence Hill, 2011), 25.
27. Nat Cole to Roy Wilkins, June 26, 1963, Box IIIA44, NAACP Papers.
28. Leaflet, August 16, 1963, Box IIIA44. Also involved were Jack Benny, architect Paul Williams, and movement leader, James Forman and James Farmer. As often happened with such events, controversy ensued as to the amounts allocated to each beneficiary. See Roy Wilkins to Chris Taylor, September 3, 1963, Box III44 and in the same box, Leo Branton to Chris Taylor, September 30, 1961: The beneficiaries received about $4,000 each with Cole donating an additional $1,000 to the NAACP.
29. Leaflet, October 1959, Box IIIA44.
30. Laplois Ashford to Miriam Bachner, March 6, 1964, Box IIIE35, NAACP Papers.
31. Dave Brubeck to Congressman William St. Onge, June 3, 1965, Series

1C, Box 2, Dave Brubeck Papers, University of the Pacific, Stockton, CA.

32. Aretha Franklin to Clive Davis, May 14, 1982, Clive Davis Papers, Rock and Roll Hall of Fame, Cleveland.
33. Aretha Franklin and David Ritz, *Respect: The Life of Aretha Franklin* (New York: Little, Brown, 2014), 42.
34. Leonard Feather, Article, 1961, Box 8, Leonard Feather Papers.
35. William Gavin to John Garland, February 12, 1971, Box 73, Willis Conover Papers.
36. Frank Shakespeare to Willis Conover, July 28, 1969, Box 9, Willis Conover Papers.
37. Willis Conover to "Mrs. Winchester," n.d., Box 21, Series 1, Sub Series 3, Willis Conover Papers.
38. Gerald Horne, *Mau Mau in Harlem? The U.S. and the Liberation of Kenya* (New York; Palgrave, 2009).
39. Willis Conover, 1961, Box 73, Willis Conover Papers.
40. Annie Ross, oral history, January 13–14, 2011.
41. Frank Foster, oral history, September 24–25 and November 22, 1998, National Museum of American History. At the same site, see also Dan Morgenstern, oral history, March 28–29, 2007: The "Jazz and Peoples Movement, which addressed itself to getting more representation for jazz on television. The tactics they used was to do sit-ins at the tapings," involving the steadfast "Charles Mingus . . . Archie Shepp . . . Rahsaan." There was this "wonderful discussion on the [Dick] Cavett [show] which consisted of Andy Cyrille, Cecil Taylor and Freddie Hubbard" that featured "some idiotic statements." For a pointed rebuke of Morgenstern, see Andrew Cyrille, "Jazz, Cavett and the JPM: An Exchange," *Downbeat* 38, no. 2 (1971): 13.
42. A. B. Spellman, *Four Lives in the Bebop Business*, 26-27.
43. Philippe Carles and Jean-Louis Comolli, *Free Jazz/Black Power* (Jackson: University Press of Mississippi, 2015), 156.
44. Collette with Isoardi, *Jazz Generations*, 174.
45. Max Roach, memoir, December 11, 1995, Box 51, Max Roach Papers.
46. Max Roach, interview, November 7, 1995, Box 51, Max Roach Papers.
47. Max Roach, interview [in Detroit], no date, Box 59, Max Roach Papers.
48. Roy Wilkins to Branches, October 3, 1961, Box IIIA139, NAACP Papers.
49. Abbey Lincoln, oral history, December 17–18, 1996.
50. Max Stanford to "Dearest Roaches," April 2, 1964, Box 70, Max Roach Papers.
51. Abbey Lincoln, oral history, December 17–18, 1996.
52. Randy Weston, interview, *Be-Bop and Beyond* 2, no. 2 (1984): 2.

53. Porter with Keller, *There and Back*, 103.
54. Jimmy Owens, oral history, September 10–11, 2011, National Museum of American History.
55. Leonard Feather to John Hammond, October 25, 1965, Box 11, John Hammond Papers, Yale University, New Haven..
56. Gleason, *Music in the Air*, 16.
57. John Hammond to Leonard Feather, August 22, 1961, Box 11, John Hammond Papers.
58. Hammond, *John Hammond on Record*, 365.
59. Branford Marsalis, oral history, May 24–25, 2012, National Museum of American History.
60. Whitney Balliett, "Ellington Slips By," *The New Yorker*, December 28, 1987, 90–91. Box 8, Leonard Feather Papers.
61. Alan Heineman, "Is LeRoi Jones a Racist?" *Downbeat* 36, no. 11 (1969): 19, 28.
62. Dan Morgenstern, oral history, March 28–29, 2007, National Museum of American History.
63. Elaine Mokhtefi, *Algiers, Third World Capital: Freedom Fighters, Revolutionaries, Black Panthers* (London: Verso, 2018), 92, 94.
64. Maxine Gordon, *Sophisticated Giant*, 157, 160.
65. Leonard Feather, Article, 1961, Box 8, Leonard Feather Papers.
66. Letter from U.S. Embassy, March 10, 1966, Box 9, Series 3, Sub Series 1, Willis Conover Papers. Conover also was in touch with Max Gordon of the Village Vanguard. See his letter to Max Gordon, June 13, 1961, Box 9A, Series 3, Sub Series 1, Willis Conover Papers.
67. Willis Conover, review of book by Frank Kofsky, n.d., Box 17A, Series 3, Sub Series 1, Willis Conover Papers.
68. Iola Brubeck to Willis Conover, April 8, 1958, Box 1, Series 1C, Dave Brubeck Papers.
69. Frances Church to Iola Brubeck, June 6, 1960, Box 1A4, Dave Brubeck Papers.
70. Victor Lownes III (Executive Producer) to Dave Brubeck, August 17, 1959, Box 1 A3, Dave Brubeck Papers.
71. Hugh Hefner to Dave Brubeck, October 5, 1960, Box 1A4, Dave Brubeck Papers.
72. Hugh Hefner to Dave Brubeck, February 11, 1960, Box 1A4, Dave Brubeck Papers.
73. "Mike" to "Dear Dave and Oli," April 21, 1960, Box 1A4, Dave Brubeck Papers.
74. Michael Maloney to Alfred Lorber, April 27, 1960, Box 1A4, Dave Brubeck Papers.
75. Michael Maloney to Walter Dean, February 15, 1961, Box 1A4, Dave Brubeck Papers.

76. Michael Maloney to Walter Dean, December 29, 1961, Box 1A5, Dave Brubeck Papers.

77. Iola Brubeck to "Dear Jim," March 8, 1959, Box 1A3, Dave Brubeck Papers.

78. Dave Brubeck to Harold Davison, May 27, 1959, Box 1A3, Dave Brubeck Papers.

79. Lyman B. Stookey (Grosse Pointe Memorial Church, Michigan) to Joe Glaser, March 29, 1960, Box 1A4, Dave Brubeck Papers.

80. Iola Brubeck to Joe Glaser, April 26, 1960, Box 1A4, Dave Brubeck Papers.

81. Dave Brubeck to Michael Maloney, September 12, 1963, Box 1A7, Dave Brubeck Papers.

82. Joe Wilder, oral history, August 25–26, 1992, National Museum of American History. Goodman played alongside bandleader and trombonist Tommy Dorsey, born in 1905, and according to Marian McPartland, they shared more than a bandstand. "We used to hear all these stories about how terrible Tommy was. He had a quarrel with Charlie Shavers," trumpeter, born in 1920, and "he put [him] out of the car and left him on the road and drove away." Cf. Walter White to Benny Goodman, May 6, 1954, Box IIA273, NAACP Papers: He heard from "our mutual friend, Lionel Hampton, that you are not only willing but enthusiastic about helping us," meaning the NAACP.

83. Tom McIntosh, oral history, December 9–10, 2011, National Museum of American History.

84. Iola Brubeck to Roiman Waschko [Warsaw], May 18, 1960, Box 2, Dave Brubeck Papers. See also Lucille Rollins to Michael Contat, June 15, 1976, Box 78, Sonny Rollins Papers: "When you're 'on the road,' people don't understand the utter exhaustion and time involved," including "backstage hassles" and resultant "physical exhaustion. . . ."

85. Gene Lees to Iola Brubeck, February 27, 1961, Box 1A5, Dave Brubeck Papers. In the same collection, Box 2, see Dr. Richard Wang to Dave Brubeck, April 23, 1963: Note reference to C. Glenn Cambor, Gerald M. Lisowitz, and Miles D. Miller, "Creative Jazz Musicians: A Clinical Study," Psychiatry 25, no. 1 (1962): 1–15.

86. Barbara Bruff to Dave Brubeck, January 14, 1960, Box 2, Dave Brubeck Papers.

87. Tarea Hall Pittman et al. to Dave Brubeck, January 13, 1960, Box 2, Dave Brubeck Papers.

88. Lorraine Hansberry and Robert Nemiroff to "Dear Dave," May 6, 1963, Box 1A7, Dave Brubeck Papers.

89. A. Philip Randolph to Dave Brubeck, July 11, 1963, Box 1A7, Dave Brubeck Papers.

90. Taylor and Reed, *The Jazz Life of Dr. Billy Taylor*, 148.
91. Ginger Kuhle to Dave Brubeck, no date, Box 2, Dave Brubeck Papers.
92. J. M. Haynes to Dave Brubeck, January 14, 1960, Box 2, Dave Brubeck Papers.
93. Jack Archer to Dave Brubeck, November 8, 1960, Box 1A4, Dave Brubeck Papers.
94. Hannah Campbell to Ralph Gleason, February 10, 1960, Box 1A4, Dave Brubeck Papers.
95. Chico Hamilton to "Whom It May Concern," April 25, 1963, Box 2, Dave Brubeck Papers. Interesting, the justly reviled Joe Glaser found Brubeck to be "one of my favorite clients and I have enjoyed a wonderful relationship with him throughout the years." Joe Glaser to Mort Lewis, March 10, 1960, Box 1A4, Dave Brubeck Papers.
96. Milt Hinton to Willis Conover, July 11, 1973, Box 73, Willis Conover Papers.
97. Weston, *African Rhythms*, 117.
98. Joe Glaser to Dominick Mones [Jazz Workshop], May 7, 1962, Box 54, Charles Mingus Papers.
99. "Paul" to Mingus, November 30, 1961, Box 54, Charles Mingus Papers.
100. Sinatra File and State Gaming Control Board, *Complainant vs. Park Lane Enterprises and Frank Sinatra*, 1963, Complaint, Nevada State Library and Archives.
101. Transcript of Meeting, October 22, 1963, Nevada State Gaming Commission and State of Nevada Gaming Control Board, Nevada State Library and Archives.
102. Memorandum by Edward A. Olsen, 1963, date occluded, State Gaming Control Board, Nevada State Library and Archives.
103. Virgil W. Peterson, "A Report on Chicago Crime for 1967," Nevada State Library and Archives.
104. Virgil W. Peterson, memorandum, June 6, 1962, Box 30, Virgil Peterson Papers.
105. David Solomon, memorandum, November 11, 1964, Box 54, Charles Mingus Papers.
106. Clark Halker, "A History of Local 108 and the Struggle for Racial Equality in the American Federation of Musicians," 207–22, 207, 208, 213.
107. *Chicago Sun-Times*, June 18, 1960.
108. Ramsey Lewis, oral history, September 28–29, 2011, National Museum of American History.
109. Moses Avalon, *Confessions of a Record Producer: How to Survive the Scams and Shams of the Music Business* (San Francisco: Backbeat, 2002), 3.
110. Abbey Lincoln, oral history, December 17–18, 1996.

111. Yusef Lateef, oral history, June 21, 2000.
112. Thomas Tolnay, "Lee Konitz: Creative Communicator," *Downbeat* 38, no. 4 (1971): 12–13.
113. Charles Lloyd, oral history, October 20, 2014, National Museum of American History.
114. McLean, oral history, July 20–21, 2001. For the Preceding paragraph see Owens, oral history, September 10–11, 2011.
115. Gabbard, review of *Chasing Trane*, 238–40, 238.
116. Branford Marsalis, oral history, May 24–25, 2012. Cf. Lucille Rollins to Michael Contat, December 29, 1979, Box 78, Sonny Rollins Papers, Schomburg Center, New York City.: "Sonny is spending about 8 hours a day in his studio practicing and writing music."
117. Jackie McLean, oral history, July 20–21, 2001.
118. Goodman, *Allan Klein*. See also *Wall Street Journal*, July 11–12, 2015.
119. John Levy, oral history, December 10–11, 2006, National Museum of American History. See also Leonard Feather, "Jazz and Race," February 1963, Box 8, Leonard Feather Papers. Staton filed suit, stating that she was being conflated unfairly with the Nation of Islam and thus her music was being boycotted and clubs refused to hire her. In heavily Black Clarksdale, Mississippi, it was reported that the tune by the NOI's Louis Farrakhan, "White Man's Heaven Is Black Man's Hell," received more jukebox play than Ray Charles's hits.
120. Max Roach, interview, November 7, 1995, Box 51, Max Roach Papers.
121. Marian McPartland, oral history, January 3–4, 1997, National Museum of American History.
122. Hubert Laws, oral history, March 4–5, 2011, National Museum of American History. Though pianist Cedar Walton said that Jim Crow was more intense in Dallas than Fort Worth, it is unclear if he ever spent much time in Houston. Cedar Walton, oral history, October 2–3, 2010, National Museum of American History. Tom McIntosh remembered an occasion at Harlem's Apollo when the father of dancers Gregory and Maurice Hines started yelling, "Hey everybody! You know what I think about the Bible?" He then approached the startled trombonist, "picks up my Bible and throws it in the trash . . . he was upset over the fact that Jehovah's Witnesses," a religious group to which he belonged, "had the reputation of not taking part in the Civil Rights Movement." Tom McIntosh, oral history, December 9–10, 2011, National Museum of American History.
123. Clark Terry, oral history, June 15 and 22, 1999, National Museum of American History.
124. Jimmy Owens, oral history, September 10–11, 2011.
125. Weston, *African Rhythms*, 83, 87, 89, 114. Interestingly, Weston

objected to both "free" jazz, associated with Coleman, and "cool" jazz, associated with certain Euro-American musicians.

126. Gleason, ed., *Music in the Air*, 64.

127. Weston, *African Rhythms*, 224–25.

10. Song for Che

1. Note, *Downbeat* 39, no. 1 (1972): 9.

2. Max Roach, interview, September 2, 1979, Box 57, Max Roach Papers, Library of Congress.

3. Interview, ca. 1993, Box 59, Max Roach Papers.

4. Lee Konitz, oral history, February 14–15, 2011, National Museum of American History.

5. Bregman, letter, *Downbeat* 42, no. 1 (1975): 8.

6. Denise Sullivan, *Keep on Pushing*, 132.

7. Max Roach, handwritten lecture notes, 1976, Box 59, Max Roach Papers.

8. Pat Griffith, "The Education of Max Roach," *Downbeat* 39, no. 5 (1972): 16–17.

9. Leonard Feather, "TV Soundings," *Downbeat* 38, no. 7 (1971): 13. Perversely, on this same program comic actor Godfrey Cambridge handed Sullivan an "Afro wig" and proclaimed him to be an "honorary Negro."

10. Note, *Downbeat* 38, no. 13 (1971): 8.

11. Max Stanford (also known as Muhammad Ahmad) to "Brother Max," January 2, 1972, Box 70, Max Roach Papers.

12. Note,, *Downbeat* 38, no. 9 (1971): 10–11, 10.

13. *The Hilltop* [Howard University], April 24, 1970.

14. *The Hilltop*, October 9. 1970.

15. Note, *Downbeat* 39, no. 6 (1972): 11.

16. "Lee Morgan: The Last Interview," *Downbeat* 39, no. 8 (1972): 11.

17. Note, *Downbeat* 37, no. 2 (1970): 7.

18. Note, *Downbeat* 37, no. 1 (1970): 7. On the fascinating dual union experiment, see Daniel Rosenberg, *New Orleans Dockworkers: Race, Labor, and Unionism, 1892–1923* (Albany: State University of New York Press, 1988).

19. Undated information sheet, Box 4, African American Jazz Preservation Society of Pittsburgh, University of Pittsburgh.

20. Brief by William Gould and Melvin Wulf, BMOP v. Local 60-471, American Federation of Musicians, AFL–CIO, African American Jazz Preservation Society of Pittsburgh.

21. William Gould to Thomas Miller and De Ruyter Camp, March 8, 1977, African American Jazz Preservation Society of Pittsburgh.

22. Shakura A. Sabur, "The Roots of the African American Musicians' Local No. 471 of the American Federation of Musicians in the City of Pittsburgh, 1920-1966 and Beyond," 1996, Box 4, Oral History Project, African American Jazz Preservation Society of Pittsburgh.

23. John Hughes, oral history, April 14, 1996, Box 2, Oral History Project, African American Jazz Preservation Society of Pittsburgh.

24. Joe Harris, oral history, August 7, 1998, Box 2, Oral History Project, African American Jazz Preservation Society of Pittsburgh.

25. Herman Hill, oral history, September 23, 1997, Box 2, Oral History Project, African American Jazz Preservation Society of Pittsburgh.

26. *Muhammad Speaks*, February 13, 1970.

27. James E. McConnell to Richard Smith, December 10, 1971, Box 33, K0431, Kansas City Federation of Musicians Papers, Missouri Historical Society, Kansas City.[emphasis-original]

28. Ralph Gleason to Leonard Feather, September 10, 1963, Box 8, Leonard Feather Papers.

29. *Kansas City Times*, March 3, 1977.

30. *Kansas City Star*, February 25, 1979.

31. Ibid.

32. *Kansas City Star*, February 26, 1979.

33. *Kansas City Star*, February 27, 1979.

34. *Kansas City Star*, March 1, 1979.

35. *Kansas City Star*, May 23, 1979.

36. Jack Newfield, *Only in America: The Life and Crimes of Don King* (New York: Morrow, 1995), 1, 2.

37. Gleason, ed., *Music in the Air*, 121.

38. *Denver Post*, August 20, 1972.

39. Transcript of minutes, June 1, 1967, State Gaming Control Board, Nevada State Library and Archives, Carson City. On Roselli and Smiley, see Horne, *Class Struggle in Hollywood*, 22-23, 105, 121, 102.

40. Transcript of minutes, April 19, 1966, State Gaming Control Board.

41. Transcript of minutes, March 30, 1967, State Gaming Control Board.

42. Leonard Feather, "The New Breed—Tycoons Who Dominate Las Vegas," n.d., Box 8, Leonard Feather Papers, University of Idaho, Moscow.

43. Preston Love to Leonard Feather, June 11, 1968, Box 10, Leonard Feather Papers.

44. Report by Howard Klein, January 1969, Projects, RG 1.2 (FA 387), Series 200, Sub Series 200, R: United States—Humanities and Arts, Box 287, Rockefeller Foundation Records, Rockefeller Archive Center, Sleepy Hollow, New York.

45. Walter Anderson to Norman Lloyd, March 30, 1969, Projects, RG 1.2 (FA 387), Series 200, Sub Series 200, R: United States—Humanities and

Arts, Box 287, Rockefeller Foundation Records, Rockefeller Archive Center.

46. Note, *Downbeat* 38, no. 7 (1971): 13.

47. Kwasi Konadu, *A View from the East: Black Cultural Nationalism and Education in New York* (Syracuse, NY: Syracuse University Press), 28. For Guyana, see Gerald Horne, *Cold War in a Hot Zone: The United States Confronts Labor and Independence Struggles in the British West Indies* (Philadelphia: Temple University Press, 2007).

48. *West View News* [New York], August 7, 2016.

49. Note *Downbeat* 42, no. 1 (1975): 44.

50. Bob Palmer, "Sam Rivers: An Artist on an Empty Stage," *Downbeat* 42, no. 3 (1975): 12–13, 33, 12.

51. Note, *Downbeat* 39, no. 13 (1972): 21.

52. Stanley Dance to "Dear Mercer [Ellington]," November 26, 1962, Box 27, Stanley Dance Papers, Yale University.

53. Note, *Downbeat* 39, no. 6 (1972): 12.

54. Tom Tolnay, "Double Take: Ron Carter and Richard Davis," *Downbeat* 39, no. 9 (1972): 14–15, 35.

55. Iola Brubeck to D. Stuart Hemingway, Jr., March 4, 1965, Series 1 C, Box 2, Dave Brubeck Papers, University of the Pacific, Stockton, CA.

56. Note, *Downbeat* 37, no. 5 (1970): 30.

57. Scott Saul, *Freedom Is, Freedom Ain't: Jazz and the Making of the Sixties* (Cambridge, MA: Harvard University Press, 2003), 305.

58. John Hammond to Nat Shapiro, February 10, 1970, Box 19, John Hammond Papers, Yale University.

59. Herbie Hancock, *Possibilities*, 137.

60. Denis Sullivan, *Keep in Pushing*, 80, 116, 118.

61. Harold Battiste, *Unfinished Blues: Memories of a New Orleans Music Man* (New Orleans: Historic New Orleans Collection, 2010), 117, 58, 149, 52.

62. Gerald Wilson, oral history, February 15, 2010, National Museum of American History.

63. Press release, ca.1973, Box 13, Ivan Black Papers, New York Public Library: Also performing were Ted Curson, Kenny Burrell, Billy Taylor, and Bill Evans, among others. In the same collection and box, see also press release, February 12, 1973: Also performing were Jaki Byard, Paul Desmond, Roland Hanna, Illinois Jacquet, Thad Jones, Howard McGhee, Charles McPherson, Jimmy Owens, Buddy Tate, Tony Williams, Larry Ridley, et al.

64. Nancy Wilson, oral history, December 6, 2010, National Museum of American History.

65. McCoy Tyner, oral history, December 7–8, 2011, National Museum of American History.

66. Michael Bourne, "McCoy Tyner," *Downbeat* 40, no. 20 (1973): 14–15.
67. Ashley Kahn, *The House that Trane Built: The Story of Impulse Records* (New York: Norton, 2006).
68. *Washington Post*, March 24, 2017.
69. Dave Liebman, oral history, January 4–5, 2011, National Museum of American History.
70. "Monk" Montgomery, oral history, October 30–November 2, 1980, Institute of Jazz Studies.
71. Note, *Downbeat* 40, no. 1 (1973): 14.
72. Note, *Downbeat* 40, no. 4 (1973): 20.
73. Herbie Hancock, *Possibilities* (New York: Viking, 2014). According to his spouse and manager, Sonny Rollins's "five [favorite] records included Hancock's "Headhunters," along with Coltrane's "A Love Supreme," Lester Young's "Savoy Jump," Ben Webster's "I Surrender Dear," and Coleman Hawkins's, "Body and Soul." Lucille Rollins to Gretchen Horton, June 5, 1976, Box, Sonny Rollins Papers.
74. Ronald Pawley to John Hammond, September 12, 1971, Box 19, John Hammond Papers.
75. Michael Bourne, "Ornette's Interview," *Downbeat* 40, no. 19 (1973): 16–17, 17.
76. Porter with Keller, *There and Back*, 127, 117, 136.
77. Don Ellis to John Hammond, October 17, 1966, Box 10, John Hammond Papers.
78. Juan Tizol, oral history, November 15, 1978, Institute of Jazz Studies.
79. John B. Litweiler, "There's a Mingus Among Us," *Downbeat* 42, no. 4 (1975): 12–13, 32.
80. Griffith, "The Education of Max Roach," 16–17.
81. Kelley, *Thelonious Monk*, 413.
82. Maxine Gregg to Gail Roberts, June 13, 1977, Box 5, Dexter Gordon Papers, Library of Congress.
83. Konitz, oral history, February 14–15, 2011.
84. Liebman, oral history, January 4–5, 2011.
85. Frank Harding to Paul Kurzenberger, March 16, 1978, Box 5, Dexter Gordon Papers.
86. Lou De Caro to Dexter Gordon, December 5, 1981, Box 5, Dexter Gordon Papers.
87. Press release, May 9, 1973, Box 15, Leonard Feather Papers.
88. *Los Angeles Times*, May 7, 1969.
89. Norman Granz to Leonard Feather, November 11, 1970, Box 8, Leonard Feather Papers.
90. John Hammond to Walter Dean, November 9, 1965, Box 10, John Hammond Papers.

91. Report, July 20, 1964, Box 27, Stanley Dance Papers.
92. Manfred Lehman to Stanley Dance, April 7, 1967, Box 27, Stanley Dance Papers.
93. Iola Brubeck to "Mr. West," March 21, 1969, Series 1C, Box 3, Dave Brubeck Papers.
94. George Avakian, oral history, September 28, 1993, National Museum of American History. Avakian had a unique fondness for Ellington; he "saw" him "standing stark naked in a dressing room" and noticed that he was "well endowed by the powers."
95. John Hammond to Bruce Lundvall, October 25, 1972, Box 10, John Hammond Papers.
96. Ibid.
97. Abbey Lincoln, oral history, December 17–18, 1996, National Museum of American History.
98. Kelley, *Thelonious Monk*, 426.
99. Jimmy Cobb, oral history, July 26–27, 2010, National Museum of American History.
100. *New York Times*, October 10, 1969, *Teo Macero Collection*, New York Public Library.
101. John Hammond to Leonard Feather, April 1, 1970, Box 11, John Hammond Papers.
102. "Trummy" Young, oral history, September 17–18, 1976, Institute of Jazz Studies.
103. Terry, *Clark*, 182.
104. John Hammond to Lawrence Gellert, November 16, 1966, Box 11, John Hammond Papers.
105. Joe Glaser to Leonard Feather, April 19, 1966, Box 9, Leonard Feather Papers.
106. Brubeck to "Mr. West," March 21, 1969.
107. Roach, handwritten lecture, 1976. Box 59, Max Roach Papers.
108. Panama Francis, oral history, September 13, 1978, Institute of Jazz Studies.
109. "Big Nick" Nicholas, oral history, March 1980, Institute of Jazz Studies.
110. Undated clipping, Box 123, John Steiner Collection, University of Chicago..
111. Wilbur Rowand to Dave Brubeck, February 27, 1967, Series 1 C, Box 2, Dave Brubeck Papers.
112. Iola Brubeck to William Smith, June 30, 1964, Series 1C, Box 2, Dave Brubeck Papers.
113. Iola Brubeck to David Van Kriedt, February 20, 1964, Series 1 C, Box 2, Dave Brubeck Papers.
114. *Downbeat* 37, no. 15 (1970): 8.

115. *St. Petersburg Times*, June 8, 1991.
116. Joachim Berendt to "Dear Dave," January 24, 1967, Series 1C, Box 2, Dave Brubeck Papers.
117. Undated clipping, Box 94, John Steiner Collection.
118. Dave Liebman, oral history, January 4–5, 2011, National Museum of American History.
119. Levy with Hall, *Men, Women and Girl Singers*, 241.
120. John Gennari, *Blowin' Hot and Cool: Jazz and Its Critics* (Chicago: University of Chicago Press, 2006), 9.
121. Nadine Cohodas, *Spinning Blues into Gold: The Chess Brothers and the Legendary Chess Records* (New York: St. Martin's, 2000), 294.
122. Betty Carter, interview with Acklyn Lynch, circa 1977, Box 66, Max Roach Papers.
123. Jimmy Cobb, oral history, July 26–27, 2010., National Museum of American History.
124. Panama Francis, oral history, September 13, 1978, Institute of Jazz Studies..
125. Herb Nolan, "Donald Byrd: 'Infinite Variations,'" *Downbeat* 40, no. 13 (1973): 18–19, 36, 19.
126. N. D. Marvin to Dexter Gordon, no date, Box 5, Dexter Gordon Papers.
127. Undated clipping, Box 122, John Steiner Collection.
128. *New York Times*, October 2, 1967.
129. Niranjan Jhaveri to Maxine Gregg, March 23, 1977, Box 5, Dexter Gordon Papers.
130. Ibid.
131. Taylor and Reed, *The Jazz Life of Dr. Billy Taylor*, 190.
132. Gerald Horne, *White Supremacy Confronted: U.S. Imperialism and Anticommunism vs. the Liberation of Southern Africa, from Rhodes to Mandela* (New York: International Publishers, 2019).
133. Willis Conover, remarks, October 12, 1976, Series 3, Sub Series 1, Box 17, Willis Conover Papers, University of North Texas, Denton..
134. *New York Times*, August 5, 2018.
135. "Blindfold," *Downbeat* 42, no. 3 (1975): 27.
136. Thomas Byrne to John Reinhardt, September 23, 1977, Box 12, Series 3, Sub Series 1, Willis Conover Papers.
137. Interview with Willis Conover, *Editorial Research Reports*, September 11, 1981, Box 4, Series 1, Sub Series 3, Willis Conover Papers.
138. William Safire to Willis Conover, April 20, 1973, Series 3, Sub Series 1, Box 17, Willis Conover Papers.
139. *Washington Post*, September 19, 1971.
140. Note, *Downbeat* 38, no. 21 (1971): 10.
141. *New York Times*, November 21, 1977.

142. *New York Times*, November 28, 2015.
143. See, for example, Horne, *The Counter-Revolution of 1776.*
144. Kenny Clarke to "Dear Max," September 3, 1970, Box 70, Max Roach Papers.
145. Letter from Leonard Feather in *Jazz Forum*, May–June 1992, Box 8, Leonard Feather Papers.
146. Leo Walker, letter to editor, June 19, 1980, Box 8, Leonard Feather Papers.
147. "Slam" Stewart, oral history, January 16, 1979, Institute of Jazz Studies.
148. Undated clipping, Box 114, John Steiner Collection.
149. *St. Petersburg Times*, April 3, 1987.
150. Undated clipping, Box 110, John Steiner Collection.
151. Clipping, November 1989, Box 123, John Steiner Collection.
152. *Chicago Daily News*, July 5, 1969.
153. Howard McGhee, oral history, November 16, 1983, Institute of Jazz Studies (emphasis in original).

11. The Blues and the Abstract Truth

1. Henry Kissinger to "Dear Ahmet," July 6, 1983, Box C1, Ahmet Ertegun Papers, Rock and Roll Hall of Fame, Cleveland.
2. Advertisement, *Downbeat* 39, no. 1 (1972): 21.
3. Steve Ross to Ahmet Ertegun, May 23, 1990, Ahmet Ertegun Papers.
4. A. F. McNaughton to John Hammond, May 30, 1975, Box 16, John Hammond Papers, Yale University (emphasis in original).
5. *Wall Street Journal*, August 15, 2018.
6. Ahmet Ertegun to Ilhan Mimaroglu and Diane Zabawski, August 23, 1990, Ahmet Ertegun Papers. Revealingly, by the 1990s the estates of Ellington and his bandmate, Billy Strayhorn, were squabbling over the riches generated by their music. See *Wall Street Journal*, December 20, 1993, Box 77, Billy Strayhorn Papers, Library of Congress: "Trial between the heirs of two of the U.S.'s best known jazz composers . . ." In the same box, see *New York Law Journal*, December 20, 1993: The court was "deciding for the first time that a song's harmony can be copyrighted," referring to *Satin Doll*. See also Gregory Morris to Stuart Prager, August 8, 1991, Box 79, Billy Strayhorn Papers: "The recovery of royalty and interest monies from Ruth Ellington and Tempo Music has been no easy task." See also Stuart Prager to Gregory Morris, April 10, 1995, Box 79: As for Lena Horne, "can we now assert a claim against her for the Strayhorn songs on her last album." Cf. Neil Diamond, described biographically as "among the top 25 best-selling artists in the world" and "widely recognized as a leading songwriter, recording artist and performer" by the *Los Angeles Times*, September

NOTES TO PAGES 317-319

14, 2018, complained that "federal copyright law does not protect recorded music before 1972. Instead "pre-'72" recordings are subject to a patchwork of state laws that amount to a legal obstacle course, both for artists like me and for digital radio services . . . when my music is played on digital and satellite radio services, I receive a small amount of songwriting royalties but no royalties as the recording artist . . . sound recordings didn't receive federal copyright protections until 1972, recordings made before 1972 are covered only under state law." Those who are optimistic about the prospect of those like Diamond to change the law were heartened when in late 2018—in a kind of Pearl Harbor for union incumbency—the press reported that the "leadership team of the New York local of the musicians' union, the union's largest local in the nation, was voted out of office on Tuesday when in a stunning upset, amid concerns over the underfunded musicians' pension plan and the broader changes facing music, the original gig economy . . . [the] first contested election in nine years at Local 802." *New York Times*, December 7, 2018.

7. Memo from Helen Oakley Dance, July 22, 1986, John Steiner Collection, University of Chicago.
8. John Hammond to Gerard Durking [Vice President for A&R, CBS], October 29, 1981, Box 16, John Hammond Papers.
9. Kelley, *Thelonious Monk*, 403.
10. "Many Sided Harold Mabern," *Downbeat* 38, no. 18 (1971): 15, 36.
11. Note, *Downbeat* 38, no. 9 (1971): 9.
12. Dave Liebman, oral history, January 4–5, 2011, National Museum of American History.
13. Kenny G to Clive Davis, May 6, 1992, Clive Davis Papers, Rock and Roll Hall of Fame, Cleveland.
14. Kenny G to Clive Davis, March 11, 1999, Clive Davis Papers: The saxophonist was a tireless letter writer and promoter of his work, this at a time when many of his peers were busily practicing or scrambling to get paid.
15. Ahmet Ertegun to John Spencer, August 27, 1990, Ahmet Ertegun Papers.
16. "DeJohnette on DeJohnette," *Downbeat* 42, no. 3 (1975): 16, 32–33, 33.
17. Reig with Berger, *Reminiscing in Tempo*, 119.
18. James Maher to Leonard Feather, August 21, 1994, Box 8, Leonard Feather Papers, University of Idaho, Moscow.
19. Arnold Jay Smith, "Newport Sketch: George Wein Looks at the '75 Festival," *Downbeat* 42, no. 13 (1975): 10.
20. Branford Marsalis, oral history, May 24–25, 2012, National Museum of American History.

21. Charles Suber, "The First Chorus," *Downbeat* 40, no. 1 (1973): 4.
22. Ibid., 6.
23. Taylor and Reed, *The Jazz Life of Dr. Billy Taylor*, 191.
24. Terry, *Clark*, 203.
25. *Quarter Notes*, June 1982, Box 89, John Steiner Collection. *Milwaukee Journal Sentinel*, September 11, 1986.
26. *New York Times*, May 12, 1989. *San Antonio Light*, May 13, 1989.
27. Eddie Palmieri, oral history, July 8, 2012, National Museum of American History.
28. *Wall Street Journal*, June 6, 1988, Box 2, Gene and Janie Harris Letter Collection, Boise State University, Idaho.
29. Howie Mandel, "Grover Washington, Jr.: No Tricks to Mister Magic's Music," *Downbeat* 42, no. 13 (1975): 14–16, 14.
30. Lee Underwood, "McCoy Tyner: Savant of the Astral Latitudes," *Downbeat* 42, no. 13 (1975): 12–14, 13.
31. Herb Nolan, "Dues on Top of Dues: Stanley Turrentine," *Downbeat* 42, no. 18 (1975): 12–13, 39, 12.
32. Paul Mills to "Dear Earl," August 5, 1971, Box 1, Earl Hines Papers, University of California, Berkeley.
33. Stanley Dance to Earl Hines, March 4, 1978, Box 1, Earl Hines Papers.
34. President Johnson to Mr. and Mrs. Hines, October 10, 1967, Box 1, Earl Hines Papers. Cf. Sonny Rollins to Michael Contat, January 23, 1978, ibid.
35. President Ford to "Dear Earl," June 11, 1976, Box 1, Earl Hines Papers.
36. Ray Schoenke to Earl Hines, January 15, 1980, Box 1, Earl Hines Papers.
37. Larry Bennett to Stanley Dance, February 11, 1976, Box 1, Earl Hines Papers.
38. Frankie R. Nemko, "Monk Montgomery: Pioneer's Dues," *Downbeat* 42, no. 8 (1975): 16–17.
39. Letter to Attorney Edward Hearn, May 31, 1979, Box 1, Earl Hines Papers.
40. Murray Petersen to Attorney Albert Kessler, June 10, 1976, Box 1, Earl Hines Papers.
41. Ellis Marsalis, oral history, November 8–9, 2010, National Museum of American History.
42. Branford Marsalis, oral history, May 24–25, 2012, National Museum of American History.
43. Delfeayo Marsalis, oral history, January 13, 2011, National Museum of American History.
44. Note, *Downbeat* 38, no. 21 (1971): 9.
45. Carol Thompson to Bruce Lundvall, August 8, 1980, Box 19, John Hammond Papers.
46. "Jazz Roster," July 31, 1980, Box 19, John Hammond Papers.
47. "Jazz Artists . . ." 1980–81, Box 19, John Hammond Papers.

48. CBS Memo, July 23, 1980, Box 19, John Hammond Papers.
49. George Russell, oral history, May 3–5, 2004, National Museum of American History.
50. *Memphis Commercial Appeal*, August 23, 1973.
51. *Memphis Commercial Appeal*, February 3, 1974.
52. *Memphis Commercial Appeal*, November 14, 1974.
53. *Memphis Press Scimitar*, May 30, 1974.
54. *Memphis Press Scimitar*, December 27, 1975.
55. *Memphis Press Scimitar*, January 13, 1976.
56. *Memphis Commercial Appeal*, February 8, 1976.
57. *Memphis Commercial Appeal*, February 10, 1976.
58. *Memphis Commercial Appeal*, July 22, 1976.
59. Rob Bowman, *Soulsville: The Story of Stax Records* (New York: Schirmer, 1997).
60. Gerald Posner, *Motown: Music, Money, Sex and Power* (New York: Random House, 2002), 199.
61. Barry Manilow to Clive Davis, January 20, 1986, Clive Davis Papers.
62. *Los Angeles Times*, March 8, 1992.
63. Gerald Horne, *White Supremacy Confronted.*
64. Interview with Billy Moore, 1984, Box 8, Leonard Feather Papers. See also Barry Kernfeld, ed., *The New Grove Dictionary of Jazz* (New York: Grove, 2004).
65. *New York Times*, July 29, 2009.
66. George Russell, oral history, May 3–5, 2004, National Museum of American History.
67. Jack Lind to Dexter Gordon, April 7, 1989, Box 6, Dexter Gordon Papers.
68. *Asahi Evening News*, no date, Box 8, Leonard Feather Papers.
69. Sue Graham Mingus to Mario de Jesus, Editorial Musical Latino Americana, March 8, 1986, Box 6, Dexter Gordon Papers..
70. *Memphis Press Scimitar*, June 2, 1972.
71. Report to the Council on Membership Relations, October 19, 1971, Box 156, Billy Taylor Papers, Library of Congress.
72. *ASCAP v. CBS*, October 1977, Box 158, Billy Taylor Papers.
73. Gunther Schuller, oral history, June 3–4, 2008, National Museum of American History.
74. Benny Golson, oral history, January 8–9, 2009, National Museum of American History.
75. Daniel Silverman of NLRB to Lionel Hampton, August 4, 1989, Box 11, Lionel Hampton Papers.
76. Undated Leaflet, Box 1, Lionel Hampton Papers.
77. Press Release from Local 802, Box 11, Lionel Hampton Papers.

78. *New York Metro News*, February 11, 1972, Box 11, Lionel Hampton Papers.
79. *Detroit Free Press*, June 7, 1985; *New York Post*, June 4, 1985.
80. Clipping, September 15, 1976, Box 11, Lionel Hampton Papers.
81. *Jet*, November 12, 1984.
82. *San Francisco Chronicle*, September 1, 1986.
83. Undated clipping, Box 89, John Steiner Collection.
84. *Milwaukee Journal Sentinel*, June 29, 1998.
85. *Wall Street Journal*, July 12, 1989; *Newark Star-Ledger*, July 13, 1989.
86. Lucille Rollins to S. Edward Katz, March 22, 1992, Box 80, Sonny Rollins Papers, Schomburg Center, New ork City..
87. Lucille Rollins to Gretchen Horton, January 24, 1977, Box 80, Sonny Rollins Papers.
88. Newspaper clipping, 1977, Box 80, Sonny Rollins Papers.
89. George Benson, oral history, April 17–18, 2011, National Museum of American History.
90. Clive Davis to Aretha Franklin, December 12, 1988, Clive Davis Papers.
91. Max Roach, interview, December 11, 1995, Box 51, Max Roach Papers.
92. *Los Angeles Times*, October 29, 1988.
93. *New York Times*, January 16, 2006.
94. Russo, *Supermob*, 353.
95. Last Will and Testament of Joseph Glaser, June 27, 1969, Louis Armstrong Archive, Queens College, New York City.
96. Wein, *Myself Among Others*, 300.
97. Max Roach, interview, January 28, 1981, Box 51, Max Roach Papers.
98. Max Roach, interview, February 5, 1993, Box 58, Max Roach Papers.
99. Bertrand Tavernier to Dexter Gordon, n.d., Box 6, Dexter Gordon Papers. See also Ross Russell to Chan Parker, January 3, 1979, Box 3, Ross Russell Papers, Harry Ransom Center, University of Texas, Austin: "Hollywood has always crapped up 'jazz films'."
100. Chan Parker to "Dear Dex," October 8, 1986, Box 6, Dexter Gordon Papers. Cf. Ross Russell to Chan Parker, September 8. 1972, Box 3, Ross Russell Papers. See also Krin Gabbard, *Jammin' at the Margins: Jazz and the American Cinema* (Chicago: University of Chicago Press, 1996). Cf. *New York Times*, November 4, 2018, containing an early report on the award-winning film, *Green Book*.
101. Monthly Mail Report, ca. 1990, Box 16, Series I, Sub Series 3, Willis Conover Papers.
102. Ibid.
103. "Mail Count," September 29, 1986, Box 19, Series I, Sub Series 3, Willis Conover Papers.
104. *New York Times*, May 20, 1982.

105. VOA Release, March 21, 1991, Box 5, Series 1, Sub Series 3, Willis Conover Papers.
106. Branford Marsalis, oral history, May 24–25, 2012.
107. Article, 1967, Box 8, Leonard Feather Papers.
108. Benny Golson, oral history, January 8–9, 2009, National Museum of American History.
109. Bob Protzman, "Profile," Downbeat 42, no. 13 (1975): 14.
110. Article, 1962, Box 8, Leonard Feather Papers.
111. Peter Occhiogrosso, "Emissary of the Global Music: Don Cherry," Downbeat 42, no. 16 (1975): 14–15.
112. Branford Marsalis, oral history, May 24–25, 2012.
113. Yusef Lateef, oral history, June 21, 2000, National Museum of American History.
114. Randy Weston, African Rhythms: The Autobiography (Durham: Duke University Press, 2010).
115. Branford Marsalis, oral history, May 24–25, 2012.
116. Dave Liebman, oral history, January 4–5, 2011, National Museum of American History.
117. Isoardi, The Dark Tree, 290. See also Nate Chinen, Playing Changes: Jazz for the New Century (New York: Pantheon, 2018).
118. Ahmet Ertegun to March Schulman, November 11, 1990, Box 1C, Ahmet Ertegun Papers.
119. Press release, November 22, 1993, Box 15, Leonard Feather Papers.
120. Clive Davis to Timothy White, Billboard, August 12, 1997.
121. Los Angeles Times, August 19, 2017.
122. Washington Post, February 2, 2018.
123. New York Times, April 11, 2016.
124. New York Amsterdam News, July 26–August 1, 2018.
125. Financial Times [London], March 9-10, 2019.

Index

Battiste, Harold: NOI and, 213;
  record label of, 18, 212
Bauza, Mario, 92, 122; Cuban music
  and, 124; Local 802 and, 124–25
the Beatles, 202, 275
Beaulieu, Paul, 33
bebop, 122, 370n1; criticism for, 150;
  Cuban artists and, 125; dancing
  and, 95; dissatisfaction and, 109–
  10; external strains on musicians
  of, 149–50; Hopkins and, 109; Jim
  Crow and, 101–2; Levy, M., and
  Midtown, 141; Parker and, 101; at
  soda fountain, 100; World War II
  and, 96; youth culture and, 121,
  352n2
bebop revolt, 127–28, 149
Bechet, Sidney, 43, 45; abroad,
  83–84
Beiderbecke, Bix, 136
Bell, Al, 326–27
Benjamin, Playthell, 184
Benson, George: background of,
  331–32; profits of, 27; success of,
  332–33
Berendt, Joachim, 308
Berlin, Irving, 94, 142
Bernie, Ben, 87
Bernstein, Leonard, 277
big band era, 89
Bigard, Barney, 36, 111, 115, 357n68
Bilbo, Theodore, 256
Binga, Eudora Johnson, 57
Birdland, 231; Levy, M., and, 17,
  100, 140, 212; as mob front, 157
Birger, Shachna Itzak, 51
Bishop, Walter, 127
Black Musicians Association, 22
Black Musicians of Pittsburgh
  (BMOP), 285–86

Black Nationalism, 126; musical
  turn and, 261; Rockefeller grant
  and, 292–93
Black Panther Party (BPP), 295; Shepp
  and, 262; Thornton and, 283
Black Power, 22; Giancana and,
  17–18
Blackwell, Otis, 306
Blake, Eubie, 7, 15; prostitution and,
  35; women and, 77–78, 303, 317,
  355n40
Blakey, Art, 127, 137, 139, 147, 169,
  190, 237, 253, 274, 335
Blanchard, Terrence, 324
Bley, Paul and Carla, 257
Blue Note, 274–75
blues, 11
Blume, August, 200
Blythe, Arthur, 325
BMI (Broadcast Music Inc.), 89–90
Bolden, Buddy, 32, 33, 39, 41, 42,
  354, 356n50
bolita, 157
Boone, Pat, 225
Boone, Richard, 168
bordello culture, 21–22
Borgeau, Joseph "Fan," 33, 36, 46
Bott, Fenton T., 43
Brand, Dollar "Abdullah Ibrahim,"
  237–38
Braxton, Anthony, 295
Bridges, Harry, 25, 101–2
Briggs, Arthur, 90
Briggs, Jimmy, 132
Brinson, Ted, 226
British invasion, 202, 305;
  Magnificent Montague and, 225–
  26; Negro music and, 225
Bronze Records, 18
Brown, Clifford, 190